CHINA'S STRUGGLE FOR THE RULE OF LAW

Also by Ronald C. Keith

COMPARATIVE POLITICAL PHILOSOPHY
(*editor with Anthony Parel*)
THE DIPLOMACY OF ZHOU ENLAI
ENERGY, SECURITY AND ECONOMIC DEVELOPMENT IN EAST ASIA (*editor*)

China's Struggle for the Rule of Law

Ronald C. Keith
Professor of Political Science
University of Calgary, Alberta

M
St. Martin's Press

First published in Great Britain 1994 by
THE MACMILLAN PRESS LTD
Houndmills, Basingstoke, Hampshire RG21 2XS
and London
Companies and representatives
throughout the world

A catalogue record for this book is available
from the British Library.

ISBN 0-333-58673-5

Printed in Great Britain by
Ipswich Book Co Ltd
Ipswich, Suffolk

First published in the United States of America 1994 by
Scholarly and Reference Division,
ST. MARTIN'S PRESS, INC.,
175 Fifth Avenue,
New York, N.Y. 10010

ISBN 0-312-10669-6

Library of Congress Cataloging-in-Publication Data
Keith, Ronald C.
China's struggle for the rule of law / Ronald C. Keith.
p. cm.
Includes bibliographical references and index.
ISBN 0-312-10669-6
1. Rule of law—China. 2. Law reform—China. I. Title.
KNQ2020.K45 1994
340'.11—dc20 93-23256
CIP

For Amy and Leia

Contents

List of Tables

Acknowledgements

The research and writing of this book would not have been possible without the continuous and generous support of the Social Sciences and Humanities Research Council of Canada. I am also indebted to the Chinese Academy of Social Sciences and the law faculties of Beijing and People's Universities for their assistance in organising interviewing with some of China's most influential legal scholars. With the academic hospitality of the Centre of Asian Studies, University of Hong Kong, the author was also able to organise a similar series of interviews in Hong Kong. In the harvesting of materials, I would gratefully acknowledge the assistance of Professor Tao-tai Hsia, Chief, Far Eastern Law Division of the Library of Congress, and Constance Johnson, also of the Library of Congress. Hu Zhenjiang, formerly director of the Materials Centre, People's University, Beijing provided invaluable assistance in the acquisition of Chinese law journal material.

Special thanks are also due to Lin Zhiqiu for his helpful suggestions and his co-operation in allowing the use of a jointly authored article. With the editor's permission, parts of two articles have been updated, revised and incorporated into this book. I wish to thank *China Quarterly* for permission relating to the research note, Ronald C. Keith, 'Chinese Politics and the New Theory of the "Rule of Law"', *The China Quarterly*, no. 125, March 1991, pp. 109–19; and *China Information* for permission relating to Ronald C. Keith and Lin Zhiqiu, 'To Revise, or Not to Revise China's Law on Counterrevolution', *China Information*, vol. 5, no. 4, Spring 1991, pp. 24–42. *China Information* is a quarterly published by The Documentation and Research Center of the Sinological Institute, Leiden University, The Netherlands.

I would also gratefully acknowledge the very able full-time research assistance of Lin Sen as well as the occasional assistance of Wang Renzhong. Lin Sen prepared the appendix listing NPC/NPCSC laws, and his calligraphy is used in the Select Glossary of Chinese Political/Legal Terms. Ding Yijiang prepared the index.

Please note that the *pinyin* system of romanisation is herein considered to be authoritative. Also, a great many Chinese legal authorities have been cited in this volume. Unfortunately, the Chinese journals often fail to cite the affiliation of these authors; however, every effort has been made to provide such affiliation in this text.

RONALD C. KEITH

List of Abbreviations

BR	*Beijing Review*
BL	Basic Law of the Hong Kong Special Administrative Region
BLDC	Basic Law Drafting Committee
CCBL	Consultative Committee of the Basic Law
CCP	Chinese Communist Party
CD	*China Daily*
CQ	*China Quarterly*
FBIS	Foreign Broadcast Information Service
FCA	Final Court of Appeal
HKSAR	Hong Kong Special Administrative Region
ICCPR	International Covenant of Civil and Political Rights
ICESCR	International Covenant of Social, Economic and Cultural Rights
JLG	(Sino–British) Joint Liaison Group
JPRS	Joint Publication Research Service
NPC	National People's Congress
NPCSC	Standing Committee of the National People's Congress
OMELCO	Office of the Members of the Executive and Legislative Councils
OPLC	*Official Proceedings of the Legislative Council, Hong Kong*
PRC	People's Republic of China
RMRB	*Renmin ribao*
SCMP	*South China Morning Post*

1 China's Struggle for the Rule of Law

Up until the late 1970s Chinese political and academic commentary routinely dismissed the 'rule of law' concept as 'bourgeois' propaganda, designed to discredit Chinese socialism and the Chinese justice system, and, even during the Chinese legal reform of the 1980s, Western commentary just as routinely presumed that any Chinese reference to '*fazhi*' connoted 'rule by law' as opposed to the 'rule of law'.[1] In the Western perspective, 'rule by law' merely invoked the existence of law within the state's governing process, while 'rule of law' implied more progressively the supremacy of law and the curtailment of arbitrary government by law.

Since the early 1980s Chinese political and legal circles have significantly focused on a socialist variant of the 'rule of law', as distinguished from 'rule by law'. Although the contemporary struggle to establish the 'rule of law' is related to Deng Xiaoping's 'open door policy' (*kaifang zhengce*), and an internal comparative study of, and response to, Western political and legal experience, it was not inspired by a consciously comprehensive strategy to replicate Western legal development within contemporary Chinese society. The struggle for the 'socialist rule of law' largely originated with an internal political dynamic, which has formally correlated the 'rule of law' and 'socialism with Chinese characteristics'. This dynamic, however, did subsequently allow for a greater degree of borrowing from Western legal experience.

Despite very great Western interest in the related legal protection of human rights in the PRC, there has only been a very modest Western scholarly coverage of internal Chinese debate as to the position of law in China's society and politics. This may be due to a persisting popular assumption that Communist ideology and Marxist–Leninist principles of political organisation axiomatically foreclose any genuine development towards a 'rule of law'.

In the 1980s Deng Xiaoping's leadership focused on the relation between the 'four modernisations' and integrated 'socialist democracy' and 'socialist legality'. While refusing to concede the relevance of the Western 'separation of powers', (*sanquan fenli*), Deng nevertheless argued that the 'rule of law' would be consolidated in China during the 'primary stage of socialism'.

Deng's reflections might well be dismissed as casuistry in light of his personal leadership role in the events of May–June 1989. Certainly,

Western media coverage, at the time, did not take seriously the following October 1989 statement of the President of China's Supreme Court, Ren Jianxin: 'Our country is turning from one which is ruled mainly by government and Party policies to one chiefly administered by laws.'[2]

To a certain extent, Tiananmen Square did influence the progress of domestic legal reform; for example, the already-announced deletion of law on the counterrevolution from the criminal law was postponed. And the 1989 law on demonstration, the drafting of which had precipitated extensive study of both relevant Chinese law and European and American law, ultimately imposed internationally criticised requirements on the right of demonstration.

Before 4 June 1989 socialist legality and socialist democracy were entwined in a practical agenda emphasising the importance of 'political restructuring' (*zhengzhi tizhi gaige).* In his pre-June 4 analysis of the latter, Liu Han of the Institute of Legal Studies, Chinese Academy of Social Sciences (CASS), noted that such restructuring would include the separation of Party and state, the progressive devolution of power, and the reform of government structures, and cadre systems within state structures, as well as the consolidation of the legal system and wider emphasis on the improvement of systems of consultation and democracy throughout society as a whole.

Liu reiterated the distinction between 'rule of law' and 'rule of man' to draw a historical line between autocracy and modern republicanism:

> Thirdly, a great many states in the contemporary world have republican governmental form and democratic politics. Although there is great variation in the class circumstances, content and forms of these states, they can be basically distinguished from states with autocratic governmental form and oligarchical politics which lack constitutional law and the materialisation of 'rule of law' and [instead] practice 'rule of man'. Generally speaking, before the victory of the capitalist revolution, many states in the world...practiced 'rule of man'. Although each state had some form of law, the power of individuals superseded that of the law and hence there was rule of man, not rule of law and there was no legal system in the modern sense.[3]

Liu scarcely departed from prevailing Chinese Marxist analysis when he noted that the 'supremacy of law' was originally inspired in the context of bourgeois revolution. Indeed, since 4 June 1989 there has been less practical focus on 'political restructuring'; however, the 'rule of law' debate has continued in the light of the escalating emphasis on economic reform and a developing legislative response to newly emerging social interests.

The effect of Tiananmen Square should be correctly understood. Pre-June 4 reform and codification of substantive and procedural law was already too sweeping to be substantially rolled back. The US State Department's 1991 conclusion that the post-1989 tightening of political and ideological controls 'seriously undermined' the legal reforms of the 1980s and 'closed off the debate on the relative merits of "rule by man" and "rule by law"' is simply at odds with a serious consideration of the facts.[4]

The debate has continued. Writing in the influential *Zhongguo faxue* (China Legal Studies), Professor Li Long of Wuhan Law School surveyed 'rule of law' models in ancient Greek theory and in modern Soviet, British and French theory. While indicating that the 'separation of three powers' would be inappropriate to China's conditions, he still emphasised the possibility of borrowing concrete forms and methods from other state experiences. Li opined on the critical relation between the rule of law and democracy, and he personally focused on three aspects of the 'rule of law', namely, the emphases on legal order, the legal delimitation of state power and the further development of the relation between law and science.[5]

To cite yet another example of post-June 4 response, Zhang Guicheng, writing in the equally authoritative *Zhengfa luntan* (Tribune of Politics and Law), readily acknowledged that since 1949 a negative attitude had prevailed with regard to the 'rule of law' as a 'bourgeois' concept. However, since the chaos of the Cultural Revolution, the concept had been accorded universal significance for its fourfold contribution to the practice of socialist democracy, to the checks and balances system against the over-concentration of state power – and herein the author carefully picks his way between Montesquieu's 'separation of powers' and the contemporary Deng Xiaoping strategy of 'mutual cooperation and restriction' (*xianghu hexuo xianghu zhiyue)* between state organs – and to the development of productive forces in society and finally to political stability in so far as the rule of law acts to contain the uncertainties accompanying leadership change.[6]

Obviously, there has been a continuous adverse Party reaction against the 'bourgeois' notion of 'separation of powers', and in November 1991 Justice Minister Cai Cheng darkly warned that domestic advocacy of the 'supremacy of law' must not contribute to the hoary Western stratagem of 'peaceful evolution' which deliberately seeks to erode the ideological integrity of China's socialism.[7]

In the same month, however, China issued its first 'white paper' on human rights and this subject has since been regularly featured in the national press and symposia. Despite Cai's remarks, senior political leaders such as Jiang Zemin, Peng Zhen and Wan Li, as well as academic authorities, continue to support the active delimitation of state authority by law. In fact there was in 1992 a much greater political emphasis on the importance of Party and state officials providing a good public example in 'acting according to law'.

The continuing emphases on economic reform and the 'open door' and the emphatic rejection of the 'leftist theses' of the Cultural Revolution has left the Party's most hidebound 'conservatives' (or the 'leftists' who are dogmatically committed to universal class struggle) without a real argument for a return to the old days of 'policy is the soul of law' (*zhengce shi faludi linghun*). Politically, they have not dared to resurrect the universally unpopular line, 'class struggle as the key link'.

In the Tiananmen Square aftermath, the Party reiterated the 1987 'the one centre, two basic points' strategy of the Thirteenth National Party Congress, bringing together competing emphases of economic reform, the 'open door' and the 'four cardinal principles'. Although class struggle received renewed attention in the compelling circumstances of post-Tiananmen Square reaction it was not reinstated as the primary contradiction in a society still considered as in the 'primary stage of socialism'. Tianamen did not change the fact that the Party 'conservatives' had, themselves, suffered terribly under the 'leftist' extremes of class struggle. They could not bring themselves to endorse 'class struggle as the key link' even in the face of the disastrous collapse of socialism in Eastern Europe and the Soviet Union.

In the light of the declining status of class struggle and the ongoing emphasis on economic reform, standard Western historical interpretation of the Chinese legal system as periodically oscillating between what Shao-chuan Leng and Hungdah Chiu once authoritatively described as the formal 'jural' and informal 'societal' models would now seem to deserve some qualification.[8]

There is continuing emphasis on social control and the political fostering of socially approved norms, but there is also a vigorous emphasis on the codification of the law and the subordination of state administration to law. While the mass line, as a problem-solving mechanism in the dialectical investigation and resolution of contradictions in society, has been retained, the mass campaign is no longer a legitimate vehicle in Chinese life, and the 'societal model's' denigration of legal practice and the pervasive mass process of political socialisation are no longer so pre-eminent in the conduct of contemporary Chinese politics.

The changing political conception of society will have far reaching implications for the materialisation of a Chinese 'rule of law'. Furthermore, much of the available Western literature on the subject of human rights in China has drawn on the centrality of class struggle as a factor negating progress towards the development of 'rights' in Chinese society, but this view now deserves careful qualification in the Post-Cold War era as it ignores the very real political limitations, faced by CCP conservatives, and the development of new national debate on the form and materialisation of human rights in post-June 4 politics.[9]

The 'rule of law' is yet to be established in China and will not be won in a day even if the regime 'changes colour' and formally becomes 'capitalist' and 'liberal democratic'. Certainly, the wish for such change should not obscure the underlying pattern of substantive political and legal change. For more than a decade China has become more deeply involved in a qualitative process of legal change rooted in the domestic necessities of changing society and politics. This change warrants in-depth comprehensive study of the comparative Western and Chinese discussions of the 'rule of law'.

WESTERN PERSPECTIVE ON THE 'RULE OF LAW'

In contemporary Western academic argument there is debate as to whether the 'rule of law' has procedural and/or substantive implications, distinguishing rule by due process and rule by right reason.[10] The notion often implies more than the mere existence of, or application of, law in the regulation of the relations between the subjects of a state, and it has acquired a positive connotation of restraining the arbitrary actions of power-holders.

But the 'rule of law' often moves beyond the question of restraint to encompass the expression of the moral consensus of a particular community. Ann Van Wynen Thomas and A.J. Thomas, for example, cite Jennings, the British Constitutionalist, to the effect that the 'rule of law' is 'an attitude, an expression of liberal and democratic principles'. In their view, it is not merely a question of prudential action to preempt anarchy. They extrapolate the following view from Jennings' argument: 'Those who governed by a true rule of law are so governed because in a very real sense they govern themselves.'[11] Thus the 'rule of law' can become a fundamental matter of moral choice as '...it embodies the community sense of right and wrong'.

In the West, the 'rule of law' has, at least up until very recently, enjoyed an unblemished reputation as the very staff of democratic life. For a long time it has invoked both the notion of a check against tyranny – 'a government of laws, not men' and a noble principle, such as that incised on the top façade of the US Supreme Court building: 'Equal Justice for All Under the Law'.

The theoretical roots of such argument are well known not only in Western scholarship, but also in recent Chinese historical and theoretical debate. Aristotle described law as 'intelligence without appetition' and argued that rational principle rather than man should rule. In *The Nicomachean Ethics*, he required that the magistrate act both as the guardian of justice and the proponent of citizen equality before the law.

In the second of his *Two Treatises of Government*, Locke argued that, for the sake of freedom, executive and legislative powers should never be combined in the same hands. Locke advised the subordination of government to law in the following well known statement: 'Whoever has the legislative or supreme power in a common-wealth, is bound to govern by established standing laws, promulgated and known to the people, and not by extemporary decrees.'[12] Also, Montesquieu greatly feared government in which the law was identical with the sovereign's will. In his famous eleventh book of the *Esprit des lois*, he ascribed liberty in England to the separation and deliberate balancing of the legislative, executive and judicial powers. This later became a cardinal principle of American constitution-making as a means of averting any tendency towards 'oriental despotism'.

In addition, and more recently, the Weberian sociology of law distinguished between the procedural and substantive dimensions of the law and underscored the relation between the authority of law and the desired predictability which it lends to economic transactions. Weber's related modernisation theory emphasising the seminal requirement of rational legal authority in modern organisation may not have implied a singular historiography of modern development, but the 'rule of law' has since been popularised as contemporaneous with the development of modern capitalism and the centrality of private property ownership.

Prominent Western defenders of liberal democratic values have travelled to the outposts of beleaguered socialism with the 'rule of law' in their baggage. In 1987, during his leadership of a large US trade and investment delegation to Beijing, Edwin Meese III, then Attorney General of the US, discussed the Chinese and American legal systems. Meese was inspired by Chinese reform. He favourably commented to his host, State Councillor Zhang Jifu: 'Over the course of the last eight years...China has engaged in an exciting process of inquiry aimed at shaping a modern legal order'. As a lawyer, Meese lectured the Chinese on the centrality of the ownership, and the use and conveyance of property in the American legal system and culture saying: 'For Americans, therefore, property rights are fundamental human rights'.[13]

Former US Attorney General Richard Thornburgh, during his 1989 visit to Moscow, recommended that the moribund Soviet Union transform itself into a 'law-abiding state' wherein the legal system is not subordinate to the state '...but rather offers equal justice under the law to everyone, thus fulfilling the law's traditional role as a mediator among conflicting societal interests'. Thornburgh subscribed to a classical liberal view of due process when he described the 'rule of law' as a 'predicate' designed to facilitate the impartial mediation of interests:

> As a predicate to accomplishing these objectives [i.e., judicial independence and mediation based on equality] a 'rule of law' must be established in the Soviet Union. By rule of law I mean not just normative rules but a systemic process that inculcates the principles of limited government, due process and a 'legal culture'.[14]

If it is presumed that this notion is exclusively dependent upon a liberal definition of democracy, the sanctity of the individual in the enjoyment of liberty and property, and the development of a market exchange economy, then it would appear that the PRC still has a long way to go. This does not mean that law cannot be developed in different societies, but at least for some observers in the West it seems to imply that a 'government of laws, not men' is not possible under Chinese socialism – even if such socialism significantly experiments with individual economy and market relations.

This central issue was featured in Richard Baum's distinction between 'rule by law' and 'rule of law', the former connoting 'statist instrumentalism' and the latter, a 'pluralistic law' reflecting 'a delicate balance of social forces, acting as a shield to protect various socio-economic classes and strata against "the arbitrary tutelage of government"'. The former invokes both the doctrines of traditional Chinese legalism and the 'bureaucratic ethos of Soviet socialist legality, as elaborated under Stalin and subsequently transferred to the PRC in the 1950s. The latter evolved out of a flowering pluralism which challenged the political monopolies of the European feudal estates.[15]

The extent to which China's political and legal traditions predisposed modern China to accept either Stalinism or liberal democracy is still quite controversial, and Franz Michael, while emphasising the irreconcilable clash between Chinese Marxism–Leninism and the Western 'rule of law', has argued that the humane dimensions of China's legal tradition might be used as a future foundation for a modern Chinese 'rule of law'. In fact, within contemporary PRC legal history there is a similar argument which attempts to combine the positive elements of China's traditional moral imperium, or 'rule of man', with the modern notion of the 'rule of law'. Some contemporary Chinese reformers, however, are not at all convinced of such a possibility, and one might add that Weberian analysis is likely to find lurking in the self-consciously moral, but ascriptive, dimensions of Chinese 'feelings' (*ganqing*) an obstacle to the development of modern 'rational legal authority'.

Michael's definition of the 'rule of law' is, nevertheless, restated here. In so far as it highlights government by law, equality before the law and the fair mediation of human relations within the community, it provides a useful Western benchmark for comparison with the Chinese definition of the 'rule of law':

> Rule of law is the very foundation of human rights. In the Western legal tradition, law is applied equally to all; it is binding on the lawgiver and is meant to prevent arbitrary action by the ruler. Law guarantees a realm of freedom for the members of a political community that is essential to the protection of life and human dignity against tyrannical oppression and to the regulation of human relations within the community.[16]

THE CHINESE 'RULE OF LAW' DEBATE

Chinese analysis now concedes that Western criticism of China's lack of a 'rule of law' was historically met with Marxist–Leninist counterattacks on 'bourgeois' propaganda. Initially in the early 1980s, the West's focus on 'human rights' in China was treated in the same light. Chinese politics and its related legal theory still routinely counters with reference to the intimate constitutional relation between democracy and law in socialist society. Montesquieu's separation of powers, and its corollary of 'judicial independence' have been widely and openly discussed and even commended within some Chinese intellectual circles, but senior Party leaders, even while subscribing to the virtues of a 'socialist market', will maintain that such concepts constitute a clever, but malicious ingenuity designed to hide the underlying inequities of private ownership.

Li Buyun's authoritative treatment of law, democracy and freedom repeated Marxist historiographical interpretation of Locke and Montesquieu. The 'rule of law' of the European and British bourgeoisie was still the historically progressive outcome of their struggle against the 'rule of man', interpreted in terms of undermining the autocracy of the feudal lords (that is, *fengjian zhuanzhizhuyidi renzhi*), but Li predictably added that theory and practice were skewed under capitalism. Due to the dominance of private property, the principle of equality before the law was not genuinely extended in practice to the people as a whole.[17]

The current Chinese debate over the 'rule of law' originates in the far-reaching political reaction against the Cultural Revolution. The resulting

Party line to create a 'rule-of-law state' (*fazhi guo*) started to take shape as early as December 1978 at the Third Session of the Eleventh National Party Congress. The Congress discussed the 'legal system' (*fazhi*) and 'legalisation' (*faluhua*) without explicit reference to '*fazhi*', 'rule of law'. The Congress determined that the way to avoid any future 'cultural revolutionary' politics was through the entwining of 'democratisation' (*minzhuzhiduhua*) and 'legalisation' (*faluhua*).[18]

The 22 December Congress Communique spotlighted the marriage of legal and democratic principle so as to defend against the arbitrary politics of the late 1960s and early 1970s, which had flagrantly violated the constitutional rights of citizens, including those of some of the most powerful members of the Party leadership:

> In order to safeguard people's democracy, it is imperative to strengthen the socialist legal system so that democracy is systematized and written into law in such a way as to ensure the stability, continuity and full authority of this democratic system and laws; there must be laws for people to follow, these laws must be observed, their enforcement must be strict and lawbreakers must be dealt with.[19]

The same communique called upon judicial and procuratorial personnel to 'maintain their independence' and to 'guarantee the equality of all people before the people's laws and deny any one the privilege of being above the law'.[20]

Deng Xiaoping's earlier speech of 13 December helps interpret the December 22 reference to 'legalisation'. Essentially, Deng subscribed to his own variation of 'government of law, not men':

> Democracy has to be institutionalized and written into law, so as to make sure that institutions and laws do not change whenever the leadership changes or whenever the leaders change their views.... The trouble now is that our legal system is incomplete.... Very often what leaders say is taken as law and anyone who disagrees is called a lawbreaker. That kind of law changes whenever a leader's views change. So we must concentrate on enacting criminal and civil codes, procedural laws and other necessary laws.... These laws should be discussed and adopted through democratic procedures.[21]

Four particular dimensions to the political thought of a state governed by law emerged in Congress debate, namely, 'to perfect the law' (that is, to ensure complete codes of the different categories of law), 'to observe the law, and to act according to law', 'to insure equality before the law' and to strengthen the 'supreme authority of the law' in the life of the state.[22]

The emphasis on perfecting the law, or to create law where there was none, drew on an important new political historiography. In the early 1950s, direct mass action had superseded the force of law just as Party 'policy' was construed as both anterior and superior to 'law'. This was viewed as historically necessary to the making of a revolutionary society, but such supercession became increasingly anachronistic as Deng's political leadership in the 1980s alternatively stressed the need to 'liberate' and to protect legally society's productive forces.

Dong Biwu was often cited for his statements of 1956–7 to the effect that the laws were inadequate and generally unobserved. Dong believed: 'A state without a legal system is not a state in the full sense of the term.'[23] The related Party reaction to the Cultural Revolution produced a thunderous critique of the 'leftist' thesis of 'taking class struggle as the key link'. The theory of class entered into the debate for legal reform in terms of the greater theoretical need to give more weight to the contemporary 'social' as distinguished from the 'class' nature of the law.

Exclusive focus on the 'class' nature of law became a political liability. The Party itself gave the legal circles a green light to work with the 'social nature' of the law in lieu of a growing relative significance of non-antagonistic contradictions among the people in the developing context of socialist commodity production. A leading Beida authority on the history of Chinese legal thought stressed the expansive aspect of the law's 'social nature' in what in the past might have been politically castigated as evidence of an erroneous subscription to the 'theory of no class struggle':

> From the point of general historical trends the law's social nature or the social nature of the law is becoming more and more manifest and the suppressive nature of law is becoming less and less manifest. The laws of social nature are increasingly sharing the common nature of the different classes and thus these laws are increasingly amenable to mutual borrowing, inheritance and reference. In sum not only then are law's social nature and class nature to be distinguished but the two natures are also becoming interrelated.[24]

Scholars, who had dared not publish on the law's 'social' or 'public' nature since the late 1950s denunciation of Professor Yang Feilong quickly returned to the academic lists. In the 1980 issues of one of the nation's leading law journals, *Faxue yanjiu*, (Studies in Law), Wu Daying, who would later succeed Yan Jiaji as head of the CASS Academy of Political Science, and Liu Han clashed with Zhou Fengju over the relative significance of the 'social' and 'class' nature of law.

Jousting legal scholars were, however, always careful to subscribe to one variation or another of 'unification theory', stressing the dual nature of the law. The issue was never more than one of relative weight. Zhou warned that if too much weight was assigned to the law's class nature this would help resurrect 'class struggle as the key link' and negate the revived emphasis on 'equality before the law' (*falu mianqian renren pingdeng*).

Remarkably, for the first time, 'Conservatives' found themselves on the defensive, having to fend off a serious 'liberal' demand for the renovation of legal theory (*faxue lilun gengxin*).[25] This debate was no arid digression into the fields of Marxist–Leninist philosophical speculation. It had far-reaching implications for the development and orientation of law for example, the reduction of law's class nature in the context of socialist commodity production seemingly allowed for the elaboration of the distinction between 'public' and 'private law' and for the corresponding expansion of civil law.[26]

Neither the masses nor the intellectuals initiated the 1980s 'rule of man' versus 'rule of law' debate. Rather than discussing the class origins of Cultural Revolution conflict, the Party elevated law's status as an institutional buffer against 'feudalism' and the 'rule of man' (*renzhi*). The Party wanted to use the law in a new institutional strategy of checks and balances to prevent arbitrary government based upon extremist class politics. Principles such as 'judicial independence', 'equality before the law' and 'open trial' were, therefore, asserted at the spectacular trial of the Gang of Four. Then 'socialist legality' was construed as a check against 'patriarchalism' and personality cult.[27]

The Cultural Revolution became the historical outcome of persisting 'feudalism'. It was no longer the final battlefield upon which the forces of the bourgeoisie and proletariat met to determine the fate of socialism. The legal nihilism (*falu xuwuzhuyi*) of the late 1960s was traced to 'feudal' phenomena such as 'rule of man-ism' (*renzhizhuyi*), 'substituting [the leader's] words for law' (*yi yan dai fa*), and 'follow only what I say', (*yi yan dang*). As discussed in Chapter 2, the issue was treated within a developing historiography which equated the Chinese tradition of Legalism with the 'rule-by-law' as opposed to the modern 'rule-of-law state'.

Whereas, in the past, the Party had urged state judicial and procuratorial personnel to act according to the law, it now conceded that the same emphasis must also apply to itself. In the Party constitution, passed at the Twelfth Congress in September 1982, a new provision required that the Party conducts its activities within the limits prescribed by the State Constitution and the laws of the state. Article 5 of the new state constitution of December 1982 required that all political parties – including the

CCP – would have to abide by the law, and it explicitly noted: 'No organization or individual may enjoy the privilege of being above the Constitution and the law'. The same perspective was reiterated in the revival of the formal subscription to 'equality before the law' in Article 4 of the Law on Criminal Procedure, which stipulated: 'The law is equally applicable to all citizens, and no special privilege whatsoever is permissible before the law.'[28] Similarly, 'substituting party discipline for state law' (*yi dangji daiti guo fa*) was formally, if not consistently in practice, rejected. Party members were warned that acts of corruption would result in criminal prosecution rather than Party discipline.

In its extraordinary resolution of 21 June 1981, the Party ignored its own dialectical strictures requiring the identification of both the negative and positive elements of historical development and rejected the 'leftist theses' as totally incorrect. The Red Guards were criticised for resurrecting 'policy is the soul of law' and for the 'three negations' (*sange fouding*), which had called for the destruction of public security, procuratorial and court organs and the establishment of kangaroo courts to mete out rough 'class' justice to 'capitalist roaders' who had allegedly cowered behind the state's legal apron-strings to escape the righteous fury of the revolutionary masses.

The November 1980–January 1981 trial of the Gang of Four was widely dismissed in the West as a show trial, particularly in its disregard of the rules of evidence and cross-examination; however, its political significance lies in a new insight on the need to deal with factional criminal behaviour 'according to law'. One of the trial judges, Fei Xiaotong, declared that the trial would provide the Chinese people 'with a lesson, vivid and profound, on the rule of law'.[29] 'Legalisation', which was highlighted at the Third Session of the Eleventh Congress, provided the political framework for the trial. Unlike Mao, who had made an error of political judgement, the 'Gang of Four' had committed violent 'crimes', hence *Hongqi* editorialised on the 'two cases' (that is, the 'trial of the Lin Biao counterrevolutionary clique and the Jiang Qing counterrevolutionary clique'):

> In the past, during the movement to suppress counterrevolutionaries, ...we used to act initially according to the policies, since we did not have enough time to formulate the laws.... But the situation was different during the trial of the 'two cases'.... We acted strictly according to the law...from the very beginning we made it clear that we were not interested in the rights and wrongs of any political line but only the distinction between guilt and innocence.[30]

Party endorsement of Article 5 of the state constitution resulted in a stronger distinction between 'policy' and 'law'.[31] Peng Zhen, who had been charged with building the new legal system, argued that if it is to be consistent with its own political theory, the Party, itself, would have to respect the law as the mature outcome of its own policy response to the will of the masses. In directly answering the question as to whether the state or Party constitution had precedence, he opined:

> In my view, the party guides the people in formulating the national Constitution and the law, it leads the people in observing and enforcing them, and it must act within the framework of the national Constitution and the law. Otherwise, there will be no socialist democracy or law to speak of in China.[32]

Emphasising Deng's rejection of the patriarchal practice of 'substituting words for laws', Peng explained that, while the confused early 1940s exigencies of military and political struggle may have warranted the permissive use of 'policy' in the absence of 'law', current resort to the same would negate economic reform in an irrational march back to the revolutionary base areas.[33]

Seizing their opportunity, the legal circles immediately argued that 'law' has more 'stability' than 'policy'. Law offered 'predictability', and it could not be subjected to the arbitrary whims of individual leaders. The law, therefore, could not be changed by the Party without first going through a process of legislative amendment. A leading expert, Zhang Yongming, incisively identified the related need for law to combat the disruptive swings in Chinese politics from 'left' to 'right' and the underlying 'feudal' problem of 'spirit':

> In the past our work was often guided by our leader's spirit which might show inclination toward one orientation one day but the opposite...the next. Very often, some kind of intrinsically good 'spirit' could be freely interpreted by some people according to their own likes and dislikes.... In contrast, laws have the advantage of stability and cannot be changed at will.[34]

One of China's most distinguished legal academicians, Li Buyun, explained the distinction between 'law' and 'policy': '...the policies of the Party usually are regulations and calls which to a certain extent are only principles. The law is different; it is rigorously standardized. It explicitly and concretely stipulates what the people should, can or cannot do.'[35]

The Chinese notion of 'government by law, and not by men', was aired in all the major law journals, including *Zhongguo faxue* (Law of China), *Faxue* (Law Science, Shanghai), *Faxue yanjiu* (Studies in Law) and *Zhengfa luntan* (Tribune of Political Science and Law). According to the author's interviews with law professors at Beida and Renda (People's and Beijing Universities), the academic community responded to the political discussion of the Cultural Revolution law and leadership question by formulating three distinct positions on the relation between the 'rule of law' (*fazhi*), and the 'rule of man' (*renzhi*).[36]

Initially, 'Conservatives' hesitated to endorse the 'rule-of-law state', suggesting that the notion implied a greater emphasis on the law than on the larger context of public morality, popular consciousness and the Party interaction with society. Fan Mingxin, for example, attempted to argue that the distinction between 'rule of law' and 'rule of man' amounted to a specious verbiage which could be dispensed with in favour of the self-evident notions of 'socialist democracy' and 'socialist legality'. The Legalists of ancient China had made much of *fazhi*, rule of law, but their outlook was more autocratic than democratic. Good governance, according to Fan, need not rely on empty talk about 'rule of law'. Good people, on the other hand, were needed to sustain the rule of law, and he emphasised the importance of the human factors relating to the scientific and cultural level of the people.[37] His argument came close to Mao's in its implicit preference for the 'rule of man'.[38]

On the other hand, the political condemnation of 'feudalism' became so compelling that it demanded an unequivocal emphasis on 'rule of law'. Conversely, 'rule of man' had little or no political support. Law professor Zhang Guicheng has provided one of the most incisive critiques of the concept's deficiencies. Not only is it inconsistent with Marx's emphasis on the will of the ruling class, but it encourages personality cults, violent leadership change, official corruption, dogmatic thinking and dependent officialdom.[39]

Ironically, the issue came to a head just before the momentous events of Tiananmen Square. At that time several senior Party leaders were in the midst of an attack on 'new authoritarianism' (*xin quanweizhuyi*) as an anti-democratic and anti-rule-of-law position. Proponents of new authority had characterised the 'spirit' of new authority as soaring above the ideological fray of the past – much like a Platonic philosopher king with shiny wings – but its opponents worried that this would mean that the building of a modern legal system would then become dependent upon the 'rule of man'. Some theorists even lumped together Plato, Thomas Aquinas and Hitler as proponents of *renzhi*, rule of man.[40]

A newspaper report responded to a symposium on new authoritarianism by asking a 'knotty' question:

> The market still relies on the government in its construction. The legal system still relies on rule by men in its construction. Now it is upgrading

> a doctrine-free government and downgrading the doctrine of freedom from government. How to solve this knotty problem?[41]

The related theory of 'elite politics' (*jing ying zhengzhi*) required the elevation of a leader as an upstanding moral, but presumably non-ideological, authority capable of pragmatically pushing though accelerated economic development along the lines of Asia's 'four little dragons', but Party loyalists as well as 'radical' proponents of rational choice and legal procedure saw in the advocacy of 'new authority' a step back into 'feudal' times.[42]

The main controversy was between those who proposed an exclusive focus on the rule of law and those seeking a positive middle position which co-opted coexisting elements of the 'rule of law' and the 'rule of man'. In his reading of the contemporary relevance of Chinese legal history, the President of the Chinese Legal History Association, Zhang Guohua, counted among the latter. Unlike many of his critical colleagues, Zhang favourably cited Xunzi's classical 'combining of fa and li' (*lifa jiehe*) in terms of the contemporary need for a human element in the administration of justice.[43]

Professor Zhang Xin in his book on the legal system and reform added an interesting qualification as to the relevance of the legalist past by distinguishing between ancient Legalist and contemporary understandings of the 'rule of law':

> In sum, the true direction of the present-day Chinese system of government is towards the 'rule of law' and not the 'rule of man.' But this...is not quite the same as the ancient Legalist 'rule of law' which pursued a unified autocracy serving lords and aristocrats; it is a 'rule of law' whereby organisations and individuals strictly observe and act according to law.... In that we have good men and good laws then we have good rule.[44]

There is some parallel here with the Western philosophical controversy as to where to place the greater emphasis – on 'good laws' or on 'good men'.

Critics, such as Li Buyun, were anxious to maximise the 'rule of law' in order to combat 'feudalism' and replied that, given the recent history of the Cultural Revolution, the dangers of feudalism could never be stressed enough and that it was extremely important that *renzhi* not be interpreted in relation to the generality of men, but in terms of the oppression by an all-powerful supreme leader whose words substituted for the law.[45]

In reviewing the question posed by the contemporaneous occurrence of 'rule of law' and 'rule of man' in history, Li drew attention to distinctions between 'law' (*fa*), the 'functions of law' (*fadi zuoyong*), and *fazhi*, the 'rule of law', itself. Neither the existence of law, nor the applied function of the law, guaranteed the evolution of the 'rule of law'. Chinese Legalist 'rule by law' constituted less progress than the European bourgeois attempt to restrain feudalism's 'rule by man' through the 'bourgeois rule of law'.

The latter emphasised man in terms of representative democracy and the separation of powers, but this is apparently a matter of the 'function of man' (*rendi zuoyong*), as distinguished from the systemic dimensions of the 'rule of man' (*renzhi*) under feudalism.[46]

Wang Liming joined the fray, distinguishing between the Legalist notion of 'ruling the state by law', or taking the law to rule the state (*yifa zhi guo*) and the contemporary notion of 'rule of law' (*fazhi*).[47] His distinction flowed from the contrast of modern socialist democracy with the Chinese imperial 'rule-by-law state' which assumed 'the sovereign is the living law'. Wang focused on the difference between rule by the virtuous example of the ruler, namely, 'good person politics' (*xianren zhengzhi*), connoting traditional notions of rulership such as 'rule by virtue' (*dizhi*) and 'find what is right in man' (*wei zheng zai ren*) and the modern democratic notion of the 'rule of law'.[48]

These debates called for a clear definition of the term, 'rule of law'. A senior legal theorist and favourite of senior Party leadership, Sun Guohua, focused on the widespread confusion in the Chinese language usage of two similar sounding compounds, *fazhi*. He argued that the first compound should denote the legal system, in terms of its institutions and codes, while the second conveyed the 'rule of law'. Politicians and academicians alike had been indiscriminately using *fazhi*.[49] China's political leadership explicitly adopted this distinction at a national conference in June 1985 which endorsed a programme to popularise the 'rule of law' as against continuing ignorance and the erroneous tendency to pit the 'rule of law' against the leadership of the Party. Beginning in early July 1985, Hu Yaobang, Li Peng, Qiao Shi Tian Jiyun, Hu Qili, Yao Yilin and Fang Yi started to attend a series of talks on law introduced by Associate Professor Sun Guohua of Renda's law faculty.[50]

In the course of debate the 'rule of law' acquired routine connotations highlighting the 'lofty dignity of law', 'the supreme authority of the law' and the need for universal respect for and observance of the law in society. These emphases owed something to the earlier formulations of the Third Session of the Eleventh Party Congress, and also to long-established implications of Party political vocabulary and epistemology stressing the significance of praxis and the relation between social consciousness and action.

Respect for legal institutions relates to the underlying norms of 'legal culture' (*fa wenhua*): 'Legal consciousness' (*falu yishi*) formally includes both legal psychology (*falu xinli*), or just knowing the law, and 'legal consciousness' (*falu sixiang*), legal thought, implying an understanding of the conceptual roots of law in society.[51] Reference to 'respect for law' (*zunzhong fa*) entails developing a conscious appreciation of the law, whereas 'act according to law' (*yifa banshi*) stresses following through with such consciousness in appropriate social behaviour. The two dimensions are synthesised in the fashioning of a 'rule of law'.

However, the 'rule of law' and the legitimacy of the legal system in terms of public acceptance ties into the politically vital issue of 'social control'. The following argument linked 'new authoritarianism's' self professed 'pragmatism' and its underlying lack of genuine interest in establishing a modern moral authority to its disregard for the 'rule of law':

> Whether it is the government which exercises the power over people, or the people who supervise the government, a certain set of social norms is needed to restrain the behavior of both the people and the government. This calls for a good social control system, that is a social control system with the control by law as the main body, which will include advocating occupational and public morals, supervising public opinion on the basis of freedom of the press and speech...but never will there be control on thought and administrative control which goes beyond the law and the constitution.[52]

China's legal scholars charted a course between Scylla and Charybdis, warning of the dangers of both 'legalism' (*faluzhuyi*) and 'rule of man-ism', (*renzhizhuyi*). The former invoked the anti-democratic features of both traditional legalism and the 'bourgeois' use of law to preserve private ownership, while the latter implied yet another variation of the 'rule of man'.

The spectre of a future leader manipulating the law to impose his arbitrary will upon the people was publicly exorcised. Ni Zhengmao, for example, criticised the confusion of 'the whole people grasping the law' (*quan min zhi fa*) with 'ruling the people by law' (*yi fa zhi ren*).[53] The issue was supposedly settled at a January 1985 Party-sponsored conference which distinguished between the unacceptable features of 'rule by law' and the positive democratic features of a 'rule of law' state.[54] The terms of this debate suggest an interesting parallel with Richard Baum's distinction between 'rule by law' and 'rule of law'.

What Thornburgh had in mind by 'mediation of interests' also seems to have some loose parallel in recent Chinese legal debate. The new General Principles of Civil Law, for example, were intended to take into account the proliferation of new contractual relations within and between more than ten million households involved in commodity and handicraft production in the countryside and to clarify the internal and external responsibilities of individual partnerships.[55]

However, 'interests' in the PRC may not necessarily follow along the anticipated lines of Western interest theory, particularly as there is a much greater focus on the interests of state-sponsored mass organisations, and functional groups in society. This focus has been politically apparent in the Party's historical interest in the state constitutional idea of 'functional representation', which currently dominates in the Chinese People's Political Consultative Conference.

The notion is acquiring new relevance within the domain of law. Groups, national minorities, state and mass associations have become increasingly sensitised to legal status in the general competition for a favourable position within the legislative and budgetary agendas of the central government.

The principles of 'equality before the law' and 'judicial independence' have received very great political attention in the light of public reaction against arbitrary exploitation of the privileges of political leadership. However, the Chinese and Western connotations of 'judicial independence' diverge in a vital way. Chinese socialist 'judicial independence' (*shenpan duli*), for example, refers to the elimination of the Party's political influence in actual judicial decisions rather than the elimination of the Party's influence over the general policy direction of the judicial process; it is not Montesquieu's 'judicial independence' (translated as *sifa duli*) which originates with the 'separation of powers'.

Li Buyun and Wang Hanqin, for example, condemned Party secretaries who either become involved in the personal 'measurement of penalty for certain criminal cases' or refuse to carry out court rulings in economic law cases. But Li and Wang also subscribed to Party leadership over judicial organs. They defined 'leadership' as 'leadership by means of policy and principle and political and ideological leadership, rather than interference in the judicial organs' exercise of their powers'.[56] Deng Xiaoping personally instructed: 'It is not appropriate for the Party to concern itself with matters that fall within the scope of the law. If the Party intervenes in everything, the people will never acquire a sense of the rule of law.'[57] However, the Party has vetted 'legal ideology' as a vital aspect of both 'socialist spiritual civilisation' (*shehuizhuyi jingshen wenming*) and social control, or 'comprehensive management of public order' (*shehui zhi an zonghe zhili*). Party discipline and the enforcement of the law are two parts of the same self-proclaimed strategy for political stability in the context of fast-paced reform. The Party retained its 'guiding role' both to ensure that indeed the law is upheld and that the legal system responds to the necessities of social and economic change.

THE RULE OF LAW AND THE CONTRADICTIONS OF CHINESE LAW-MAKING

While there has been an exponential development of legislation in all the categories of law, the Chinese themselves are aware that fast-track legislation has, at times, moved ahead of society's 'legal consciousness', and that legal norms are not yet firmly anchored in universal social action and society-wide perception. As the charted identification of new law in the Appendix indicates, there has been a bewildering, exponential legislation and codification of law for more than ten years, and it remains to be seen whether the Party's current education programmes can effectively cope with 'legal blindness' (*famang*). After Tiananmen Square, there is still emphasis on the superiority of law over policy, but there is also frequent acknowledgement that laws are not always enforced.[58]

The November 1985 NPC resolution on the dissemination of legal knowledge called for public education with specific focus on the contents of the Constitutional, Civil and Criminal Laws, the Criminal and Civil Laws of Procedure, the Marriage Law, the Inheritance Law, Economic Contract Law, the Military Service Law and the Regulations for Penalising Those Who Disrupt Public Security. Subsequently, 94 and 95 per cent respectively of prefectural and county cadres participated in basic law classes, but such attendance figures, if correct, give little indication of the qualitative acquisition of legal knowledge in terms of knowing both the content of the law and the original intent and reasoning behind the law.[59]

As China enters its second five-year-plan period for the popularisation of legal knowledge, there are no reliable statistics as to the extent of 'legal illiteracy' in society. China's legal circles, however, have been uncompromisingly frank about the complex difficulties of current legal development; for example, a national conference of law experts, which met between 28–31 May 1988 in Zhuhai, highlighted the confusing features of the legal system in the 'first stage of socialist development'. They recognised that the difficulties of 'pluralism' originating with 'one country, two systems'. Indeed, as Hong Kong, Macao and possibly Taiwan integrate with the mainland there will be a perplexing plurality of legal systems operating within the same country.

Many Conference participants regarded the legal system as essentially incomplete, imperfect and transitional. The issue of 'rule of law' versus 'rule of man' had really not been settled, and it was noted that in many areas of social activity there were still no laws. The delegates revealed problems of formally subscribing to 'acting according to law' and the continuing failure to comply with the law, of 'rights' actually interfering with the 'law' and of the 'words [of leaders] substituting for the law'. While subscribing to the

Party's 'four cardinal principles', they also endorsed the principle of 'inheritability' so as to take advantage of the pre-Liberation experience of constructing law and democracy under capitalism.

The Conference described the legal system as in a transitional state, reflecting China's backward 'productive forces' and relatively undeveloped socialist commodity exchange. The complicated 'dualism' in the legal system was also apparent in the ongoing contradiction between 'feudalism' and the modern socialist desire for democracy and rule of law. Within this socio-economic complexity some of the delegates explored how the law might deal with the different 'interest groups' (*liyi qunti*) emerging within the complications of contemporary Chinese socialist society.[60]

Such complex contradictions did not deter China's political leaders from pressing ahead with exponential legislation and economic reform at one and the same time. Very early on Deng Xiaoping settled the debate over the speed of legislation at the Third Plenary Session of the Eleventh Party Congress when he instructed: '...law is better than no law, faster [law-making] is better than slower [law-making] (*you bi mei you hao, gao kuai bi gao man hao*).'[61] Citing the great legislative task ahead and China's lack of trained people, Deng Xiaoping elaborated on his strategy of law-making:

> Therefore, legal provisions will have to be less than perfect to start with, then be gradually improved upon. Some laws and statutes can be tried out in particular localities and later enacted nationally after the experience has been evaluated and improvements have been made. Individual legal provisions can be revised or supplemented one at a time, as necessary; there is no need to wait for a comprehensive revision of an entire body of law. In short, it is better to have some laws than none, and better to have them sooner than later.[62]

To enhance the position of law in society and to prevent any future recurrence of Cultural Revolution, Party leaders endorsed law as superior to policy. Party members were no longer exempt from the principle of 'acting according to law', and the notion of 'equality before the law' was emphasised in self-conscious response to growing cynicism as to Party and state corruption. Li Buyun and Wang Hanqing later wrote in 1986 that the legal system is 'an important symbol of civilised society' and 'equality before the law' should be more manifest under socialism than capitalism:

> In capitalist society, although it is stipulated by law that all men are equal, which is great progress in history, in a society in which 'money makes the mare go', the feudal hierarchy and privileges are actually replaced by the 'privilege of money'. In our socialist society, the system of public own-

ership and distribution according to work is implemented....equality in the economic field naturally requires equality in the political and legal fields.[63]

The struggle for the 'rule of law' originated in the politically inspired correlation of domestic stability and economic reform. The 'predictability' of law was to provide a stable framework within which to mediate the emerging social conflicts of a modernising economy, and yet the new legal structures had to be installed extremely quickly – even at the risk of exacerbating 'legal illiteracy'.

Speed raised the question of the relation of law to society. 'Predictability' and 'unity' whereby the law is known, understood and evenly applied in the same way throughout society were welcomed as necessary to the development of a public respect for law, but the fast-track approach to law-making seemed self-contradictory. Despite commitment to perfecting the law and explicit reservations that the new laws were being improperly observed due to 'legal illiteracy', legal and political leadership circles merrily pressed on with law which was incomplete and experimental.

Commenting in 1982 on the necessary tension between the law's 'stability' (*guidingxing*) and 'flexibility' (*linghuoxing*), Zhang Youyu suggested that as the socialist economic base is established it requires law which offers 'stability', but the latter is not absolute in light of changing socio-economic and political conditions, and legislative principle has to be applied with ongoing sensitivity to reality. While the emphasis on the completeness of the law was justified, it too was not to be considered absolute. Too much law and too much detail was likely to generate mass confusion and to negate the creative adaptation of law to complex reality.[64]

The Party's commitment to the fast-track was predictable in so far as it was compatible with the Party's mass line organisational and theoretical perspectives stressing the combination of principle and 'flexibility' in politics and the corresponding need in law continuously to adjust to underlying social and economic change. The Party had made a clear distinction between 'law' and 'policy', but Party thinking as to how to go about making law still reflected the Party's own formative experience in generating policy through praxis.

The CCP leadership was predisposed to what we might call law-making by praxis. There is in contemporary China little theoretical basis for a conservative strategy of slow evolution of law in relation to social change. On the other one, revolutionary optimism required the law to respond promptly and objectively to such change, hence Deng's reiteration of *yishou zhua jianshe, yishou zhua fazhi* ('grasping production in one hand while grasping the legal system in the other'). On the other hand, incomplete and step-by-step legislation was not only tolerated as an inevitable aspect of praxis; it was viewed positively as the rational outcome of the Party's mass line organisational theory and utilitarian political dialectics.

Legislation and economic reform had to move in tandem as China made the momentous transition away from the political structures of the revolutionary mass campaign to a more complex, modern structure entwining 'socialist democracy and legality'. Zhao Ziyang, in his 1987 report to the Thirteenth National Party Congress, synthesised the various dimensions of this remarkable transition in his remarks on the 'strengthening of the socialist legal system' and the need to define, through law, new society-wide standards of conduct:

> We must attend to legislation and to economic development and reform at the same time. ...on the one hand, we should improve legislation and the procedures for law enforcement, enable the judicial organs to exercise independent authority, as prescribed by law, and enhance citizens' awareness of law; on the other, we should see to it that legislation guarantees good order in economic development.... We should try to define, in terms of laws or rules, what should be encouraged and what should be rejected. Only in this way can we bring about a new standard for political, economic, and social activities. And only in this way can we institutionalize various aspects of the society: the relations between Party and government departments on the one hand and public organizations on the other; the activities within government departments; the relations among the central authorities, local authorities and grass-roots units; the training, selection, employment and replacement of personnel; democracy at the grass-roots level; and consultation between leadership and rank and file. In short, through reform we should gradually establish a legal framework for our socialist democracy and institutionalize it. This is a fundamental guarantee against a recurrence of the 'cultural revolution' and for lasting political stability in our country.[65]

The fast-track strategy included at least two distinctive *modus operandi* for law-making by praxis. These include legislating new codes of National People's Congress law (*falu*), as summations of general principle which are to be applied as practical circumstances warrant, and extending the process of trial and error through the promulgation of temporary laws or regulations (*fagui*) by the State Council and later legislating fully fledged law based on the practical experience of such temporary law.[66]

Deng Xiaoping abandoned the large-scale mass campaign, but he continued to subscribe to the mass line 'style of work' (*gongzuo zuofeng*).

The key feature of this 'work-style' was the practical solution of problems through the direct experience of and related dialectical explanation of the contradictions of reality, hence the central ideological theme of his regime was 'to seek the truth from the facts'.[67]

Deng's strategies for law-making drew from the historical reference points of mass line organisational theory which required the fashioning of policy through the traditional techniques of Party praxis, or practical scientific investigation including 'combining leading and learning', 'going down', 'squatting at key points' and 'combining points with surface'. Without 'investigation and study' among the masses in social reality, the leaders had 'no right to speak' (*meiyou tiaocha yanjiu jiu meiyou fayanquan*). Sound and 'objective' leadership required that leaders go down to learn about actual conditions from the masses and thereupon to adjust policy to reality.[68]

Politically, policy-making had always required a middle course between 'rightist' and 'leftist deviations'. 'Rightist' inertia was caricatured for its unending empirical study and a caution bordering on inaction. 'Rightists' would keep repeating 'chicken feathers cannot fly up to heaven'.[69] But if the 'rightists' negated the importance of political momentum, 'leftist' 'rash advance' simply crashed headlong through the concrete barriers of objective reality. In Mao's own paternalistic metaphor of political timing, the 'leftist' would, over the objections of the mother, push a baby out before nine months, while the 'rightist' would pusillanimously delay until well after nine months.[70]

Sun Yaming's defence of the 10 April 1985 'Decision on Authorising the State Council to Formulate Interim Regulations and Rules on Reform of the Economic Structure and Opening to the Outside World' invoked this same distinctive political vocabulary. Flexible procedure was justified for it would be better to have an immediate step-by-step response to the fluid economic situation rather than waiting for a stable economy and a 'perfect' set of related economic laws.[71]

Deferring to concerns over speed, the legal circles had, themselves, suggested that in fast-developing economic policy areas, the State Council pass legal regulation (*fagui*) as preliminary to the NPC legislation of established law (*falu*). This format would presumably do less damage to the legitimacy of basic or fundamental law (*falu*) as mature policy, for *falu* would only be promulgated after *fagui* had been tested and adjusted within social reality.

The format of the General Principles of Civil Law was justified in terms of the need to rationalise selective practice over time. Citing the complexity of civil law, the lack of related legal experience and the unevenness of development in such a large state as China, Zhang Youyu, Vice-Chairman of the NPC Legal System Work Committee, explained an approach suggestive of mass line emphases on 'combining a general call with specific guidance' and acting in accordance with the appropriate specifics of time and locality (*yin shi zhiyi* and *yindi zhiyi*):

> We lacked experience when economic restructuring had just begun, we could only go on drafting the civil code while promulgating and enforcing some parts as separate laws, parts which were urgently needed and comparatively better prepared.... However, these separate laws make no stipulation about a number of common problems and norms, and...these laws overlap and contradict each other.... To solve these problems, it is good to first formulate the General Principles of the civil codes to set out the basic regulations to be followed in the implementation of separate laws in lieu of promulgation of the civil code.[72]

Richard Baum describes the innovative brevity and generality of the 1982 civil law principles in terms of a 'pyramidal principle of ascending generality in legislation' which conflicts with the traditional Chinese propensity for 'extreme statutory specificity' (or what Bodde and Morris called 'the principle of minute differentiation') which sought to detail every foreseeable circumstance under which the law would apply. While Baum may have been justified in his view of this 'innovation' as a qualification to Communist adoption of the traditional principle of analogy, he treats it as a general departure from Communist legal practice rather than as an extension of the Party's mass-line organisational theory.[73]

Zhang was disinclined to create a complete code without the benefit of experience, but he claimed the law reflected 'intrinsic Chinese characteristics' in its bringing together of selected general principles on common problems and in its legislative detail originating in separate laws.

On yet another front, Wang Hanbin, Chairman of the Legislative Affairs Commission of the NPC, candidly discussed the trial-by-error nature of the new Administrative Procedure Law and the limited scope of legal experience in this field. He seemed to recommend controlled law-making at 'key points' in social reality:

> Third, considering our country's current situation, in which the administrative procedure law is not complete, the administrative divisions of the people's courts are insufficiently sound, and there are problems in conceptual upgrading, habit, adaptability and capacity to withstand strains in regard to the provision in the Law on Administrative Procedure that 'the people are entitled to indict officials,' the scope of cases to be

> accepted for prosecution should not be too large, and instead it should be gradually enlarged so as to promote the smooth implementation of the system of administrative procedure.[74]

Law-making was placed on a deliberate continuum of adjustment and readjustment. The inconsistency in the law which was bound to result was merely an acceptable cost of law-making by praxis. Yao Keming, Director of Research at the Beijing High People's Court, indicated to the author that there had been a remarkable, but somewhat awkward growth of compensation suits relating to administrative malfeasance under the civil law and that this required the immediate promulgation of a separate administrative law; however, he conceded that good laws would not overnight make good citizens. Due to widespread 'legal illiteracy' the leading cadres would, themselves, have to lead the way in filing complaints under the new law.[75] This approach to illiteracy, however, raises the negative dimension of past mass-line experience, marked by deviation such as 'the teacher taking along the student', and the improper substitution of leadership for genuine mass consciousness, as implied in *renzhizhuyi*.

In mass-line terms, legislation must be objectively discovered in practice; it must be rooted in conscious social action. On the other hand, the excesses of 'experientialism' or 'experimentalism', whereby guiding principles and central objectives are obscured in a never ending resort to empirical data, were traditionally excoriated. In the course of reform argument to strengthen the legitimate authority of law, or to promote 'lawful society' (*fazhi shehui*), law was distinguished as more mature than everyday policy, and yet incomplete law was allowed so that law could be introduced in tandem with economic reform. Presumably the superiority of law had still to be upheld even in cases where the law was slow to respond to the necessities of social change.

What if 'law' is announced with great fanfare and then abjectly fails to establish clear guidelines in the mediation of social conflict? The great banner bearing the 'lofty dignity of the law' might then unceremoniously plummet to earth. Scholars debated the merits and demerits of 'preceding legislation' (*chaojian lifa*), or legislating before the completion of a reform campaign, and 'overdue legislation' (*lifa zhihou*), or legislation which falls behind the compelling needs of society and the economy. The 'lofty dignity of the law' is at risk in either case of 'legal but not legitimate' (*hefa bu heli*), or 'legitimate but not legal'. If law does not properly keep up with reform and is miscast, it can act as an illegitimate brake on economic development, but, if reform goes forward without the benefit of law, the law then loses its social relevance, and hence its legitimacy.[76]

As mentioned earlier, there is also the possibility that contemporary legal reform could be swept away in a great nauseous wave of 'neo-authoritarianism' which selectively draws on a Confucian cultural penchant for moral absolutes so as to take political advantage of the popular demand for a rapid rise in the material standards of living. Hypothetical appeals by future leaders for mass compliance with their own idiosyncratic versions of the law so as to exemplify the higher purpose of reform outwardly constituted *fazhizhuyi* (rule of lawism), but the hidden essence was castigated as *renzhizhuyi* (rule-of-manism).

The advocates of 'new authority' argued that, due to the overwhelming backwardness of rural China, the leader's moral tutelage would have to have priority in lieu of the lack of universal 'legal consciousness' in the great hinterland. Indeed, more than 80 per cent of the population still resides in the vast rural areas, and the struggle for the 'rule of law' may well be won or lost there. After 4 June, Wu Daying attacked his predecessor, Yan Jiaqi, at the CASS Academy of Political Science for propagating the notion that China was a *diguo* or imperial state with an 'autocratic system' (*zhuanzhi zhidu*) and that the revolution had never achieved fruition due to rural backwardness.[77]

Not only the Party, but philosophy and political science scholars protested. Fan Zhongxin of the Taiwan Research Institute (CASS) rebutted the notion that no progress had been made:

> The respect for 'heaven, earth, monarch, parent, and teacher' can easily be felt in Chinese peasants' homes. This is really disheartening. But, after all, much progress has been made today. Sometimes there is news about a peasant accusing a county government or an ordinary citizen filing a lawsuit against a mayor. Since the popularization of the knowledge of the law, it is no longer easy for corrupt officials to extort money from the people.[78]

Corruption is, nevertheless, universal and rampant. Also 'disheartening' is the 1991 government survey which found that 60 per cent of the rural population still believes in the Shan Han (God-man), Wu Bo (the woman sorcerer) and the exorcising of evil spirits. During 1991 the Party focused on the countryside in a campaign against the 'six feudal evils', namely, gambling, prostitution, drugs, pornography, superstition and slavery.[79]

The social dimensions of revived feudal superstition and Western materialism have greatly troubled China's political leaders, who are prone to seeking pseudo-Legalist solutions in the punitive dimensions of the criminal justice system. The December 1990 NPC laws on drugs and pornography, for example, stipulated the death penalty or life imprisonment for serious cases of smuggling, producing, selling or distributing pornographic materials.[80]

The Party's slogan, 'four cardinal principles', is now seldom seen on the villagers' walls, whereas one increasingly finds scrawled on these walls, 'act according to law'. Law became urgently necessary to the mediation of the conflicting interests which emerged with the new rural responsibility systems. As of the end of 1986, 20 000 law offices had been opened in the rural counties to assist rural enterprises and to help handle civil disputes.[81] The state has also promoted the implementation of the Organic Law of Villagers' Committees in the hope that 'villagers manage their own affairs, as provided by law'.[82]

The complexity of household-to-household relations has placed an unprecedented premium on the law as a mediating device to solve a multiplicity of competing claims for water and land-rights usage. Law has been called upon to solve issues relating to community, environmental planning, and household production rights. Theoretically, it can resist the rapid reduction of tree cover. Farmers are urged, 'regulate water usage according to law'.

In the 1980s the old command economy was rolled back so far that it is almost inconceivable, even in the post-June 4 conservative political backlash, that the new rural responsibility systems will be dismantled, and as the administrative dimensions of central planning have declined so have the indirect economic and legal dimensions of central policy guidance been reinforced. Furthermore, the importance of legally binding contract has been politically stressed as the role of money and commodity exchange has been expanded.

THE COMPARATIVE DIMENSIONS OF CHINA'S STRUGGLE FOR THE RULE OF LAW

The organisation of this volume's discussion of China's struggle for the 'rule of law' consciously strives to achieve a comparative analysis. This discussion of the 'rule of law' is not limited to procedural matters although, in light of the 'legal nihilism' of the Cultural Revolution, these have certainly been accorded new theoretical significance. The 'rule of law' is related to 'socialist democracy', but even in the post-June 4 political reaction, there has been progressive development of the legal system and legal consciousness as the law has become incrementally materialised in the daily aspects of social and economic life.

The following discussion, therefore, adopts a wide scope of inquiry reviewing Chinese debates regarding both the substantive and procedural dimensions of law and taking the reader across the various categories of law, including constitutional, civil, criminal, economic and administrative law, so as to achieve a general impression of the developing legal response to fast-paced social, economic and political change.

When the author was invited to give a lecture in 1980 to an assembly of CASS social scientists, there was little recognition of the importance of Weberian legal sociology; however, during the the 1980s Weber's discussion of modernisation and law has received increasing attention, as has Western law and legal theory in general. Furthermore, it would be fair to say that foreign legal experience has had a significant influence on the drafting of new Chinese law.

Chapter 2, The Rule of Law within Comparative Legal Cultures, selectively extends the first chapter's discussion of the 'rule of law' versus the 'rule of man' to encompass analysis of Western and Chinese interpretation of traditional and modern Chinese 'legal culture' and the Chinese view of comparative law and the relation of law to traditional and modern society. Special attention will be given to developing the Chinese political and legal perspective on the central issue of 'equality before the law' and the apparent convergence of Western and Chinese sinologies.

Chapter 3, The Conceptualisation and Materialisation of Human Rights, provides an opportunity to review the relation between the 'rule of law' and 'human rights'. China's poor human rights performance has been the subject of widespread international criticism, but the new national debates on the subject have resulted in a clearer Chinese conceptualisation of 'human rights' (*renquan*). Just as the Chinese moved from a static position emphasising the 'rule of law' as 'bourgeois' propaganda to the position that China must have a 'socialist rule of law', the Chinese have now gone beyond the repetition of the argument that Western criticism amounts to a specious 'human rights diplomacy' (*renquan waijiao*), to accept that China should work out its own understanding of 'human rights' and participate as an equal in international debate on the subject.

There has been renewed debate on the comparative relation of Confucianism to the West European natural law tradition. Internal debate reveals new and sharp disagreement over the relation between 'rights' and 'obligations' and the 'universal' as opposed to 'class' nature of 'human rights', but this debate has resulted in progressive expansion of the category of 'rights' so that it is larger than and supersedes the past determinations of positive law regarding 'citizens' rights' (*gongmin jiben quanli*). The debate has also taken up the issue of how the materialisation of such 'rights' in society should come about. There is in the West an established tradition of sinological study. At the same time there is an escalating 'human rights' interest in China, but very few Western scholars have seriously researched the contemporary internal Chinese political and legal debate on the subject.

Chapter 4, Civil Law and 'Civil Society' under a 'Socialist Rule of Law'?, will tentatively assess the current Chinese perspective on the law's impact on society and society's impact on law. Western political and legal theory has also grappled with the fundamental relation of law and society. In China, it is in this area that the issue of 'wholesale westernisation' versus 'socialism with Chinese characteristics' is most controversial. On the one hand, the discussion of individual rights and group interests presages a new focus on what in the West would be called 'civil society', but, on the other, legal reform has often been emphasised from within the political strategy for the development of 'comprehensive management of public order' and the ideological–cultural dimensions of 'socialist spiritual civilisation'.

Will legal reform be subordinate to the larger strategy of social control? Is there greater emphasis on non-judicial state-imposed discipline and informal mass-line community strategies of education and mediation as opposed to increasing the emphasis on the autonomous development of legal procedure? Western critics have often focused on 'education through labour' as a non-legal form of administrative punishment as distinguished from 'reform through labour', authorised under the Criminal Law and applied in court proceedings. Moreover new domestic controversy has focused on whether 'people's mediation' should, as a form of mass organisational democracy, be accorded the right to make legally binding decisions in the absence of any related resort to formal court proceedings.

Currently Article 24 of the State Constitution indicates the following multidimensional strategy of social control:

> The state strengthens the building of socialist spiritual civilization through spreading education in high ideals and morality, general education and education in discipline and the legal system, and through promoting the formulation and observance of rules of conduct and common pledges by different sections of the people in urban and rural areas.[83]

Since Tiananmen Square the Party leadership has placed even greater emphasis on 'comprehensive social control'. Conceptually, 'law' has often been placed on the same level as informal, non-judicial processes of community mediation and administrative regimes of discipline, and one might argue this depreciates the autonomy of the legal system in face of the CCP politics and ideology. The following pre-June 4 CASS definition of this terminology not only raises the relation between education and the necessary coercive dimensions of state authority, but also the relation between the 'rule of law' and 'judicial independence':

> The comprehensive control of social order takes education as its first step. This centers mainly on politics and ideology, the legal system and

> morals, which are related to one another, with mutual overlapping and support. Secondly, it requires a down-to-earth approach to the solution of [society's] practical problems. Lastly, it requires the necessary coercive measures, including the execution of administrative disciplines and legal sanctions. ...there are always some people who violate laws and disciplines, regardless of education and prevention. It will not do to put emphasis only on education and solving practical problems to the loss of the distinction between right and wrong, between guilt and innocence or at the sacrifice of necessary coercive measures.[84]

This CASS definition failed to distinguish between sanction through the judicial process and administrative discipline by state agencies; both forms of sanction were equally legitimate as 'necessary coercive measures' in the achievement of comprehensive social control. Furthermore, the specific inclusion of observing and acting according to the law within the larger organisational framework of comprehensive social control demonstrates that the mass line is still a major reference point in the development of the state and its judicial processes.

The interdiction of mass campaigns has not precluded the application of mass-line organisational strategies in promoting 'legal consciousness' and in coordinating urban residents' committees and villagers' committees and their public security and mediation organisations to stress ideological education in the prevention of crime. Western analysis has often treated communal mediation as possibly a salutary supplement to the judicial process, and administrative discipline, as definitely subversive of the law's authority. However, in dealing with the social changes precipitated by reform and in particular in dealing with problems of juvenile delinquency, the Chinese have renewed their stress on the organisational links between the court system and community organisation.

In the Party's official theory, the 'rule of law' is a subset of 'socialist spiritual civilisation'. This formulation has encompassed the current interdiction against 'class struggle as the key link', and it has endorsed the notion of lawful behaviour in society and the economy, but some legal reformers aspired to elevate the status and autonomy of the law as a precondition of, rather than a subset to, 'socialist spiritual civilisation'.[85]

If Party politics have impacted on the 'rule of law' the social change precipitated in the Party's economic and social policies may also impact on the 'rule of law' in politically unpredictable ways. Chinese political authority has acknowledged the patterns of increasing violence, murder and suicide which have accompanied the social transition generated under economic reform, and this may reinforce a Party law-and-order perspective calling for a tougher, more punitive Criminal Law; however, economic reform has precipitated significant legal change in yet another direction. Legal circles are also struggling to keep up with the changing patterns of property ownership and expanded legal notions of inheritance.

Furthermore, the Party itself is in no position to deal with the new complexities of economic contract, and economic reform cannot take place without political change. Economic reform has created a political space for the development of 'private law'. The civil law has been greatly expanded to accommodate complex social change, and the Chinese have moved away from the traditional viewpoint of 'strongly emphasising criminal law, and lightly emphasising civil law' (*zhongxing, qingmin*).

Indeed China's legal circles are struggling to keep up with rapid changes in society precipitated by economic reform and the 'open door policy'; for example, there is now debate on the failed enforcement of the 1980 Marriage Law in relation to the one-child family policy and an escalating pattern of 'illegal cohabitation', implying cohabitation with a partner who is already married, and 'illegal marriage', including marriage under the ages specified in the current Marriage Law.[86]

Presently, women are more inclined to file for divorce than men, and the climb in cases involving adultery and sexual incompatibility and the recent inclusion of 'third party' reference in divorce cases all suggest the way society may be heading and the way law is responding.[87] The Marriage Law was originally separated out from the Civil Law in response to Soviet precedent and so as to accord it special political significance, but more recently it was incorporated into the Civil Law so as to emphasise the Civil Law content relating to property rights in the new era of economic reform.

The disposition to bring suits and the relative reliance on informal mediation will be important in society's resolution of likely turmoil resulting from the transitions in the economy. In endorsing the fast track, Deng conceded that China lacked a tradition of observing law. In the imperial past the resort to law brought into question the efficacy of moral example as the essence of traditional government, and the law's application proved costly to all of those who chose to become entangled in legal action. The expression, 'good people do not bring suits, and those who bring suits are not good people' (*haoren bu da guansi da guansi bu shi haoren*) summed up the traditional animosity towards the law's application. The supremacy of Confucian principles concerning the moral autonomy of the family had interfered with the development of the civil dimension of the law as suggested in the saying: 'Even an upright official finds it hard to settle a family quarrel' (*qing guan nanduan jia wushi*).

At least formally the law is beginning to intrude into areas where in the past it was forbidden; for example, a man who now beats his wife may be told that he is in violation of the Criminal Law which treats physical abuse within the family separately from general provisions relating to assault. Theoretically, this case might involve the Civil Law, Marriage Law and, in especially serious cases, the Criminal Law. Whereas in the past anyone who neglected his aged parents was liable to stern social censure, now it is also becoming a question of the failure to live up to legal responsibilities under the Criminal Law.[88]

Chapter 5, Law as the Contractual Predicate of Ownership Rights, will focus on the development of Civil Law as it relates to questions of contract, ownership and the 'mediation of interests' as this might be understood in China's specific circumstances. The enhanced distinction between private individual rights and collective and state rights comes with controversy as to the respective spheres of departmental competence between the civil and economic laws. Veering from Soviet example, the Chinese have tended to favour a 'great' as opposed to 'small' civil law tradition. Chinese civil law has laid claim to some of the territory which orthodox socialism might reserve exclusively to economic law in the context of a centrally planned economy.[89] While under socialist theory one may expect that state ownership implies a legally superior position *vis-à-vis* other types of ownership, according to Wang Hanbin, the General Principles of the Civil Law of the PRC, expanded the civil law so that it would more effectively regulate the property relations of equal 'subjects' (*zhuti*). Reformers took the opportunity to stress the application of the general principles in suits involving foreigners on the basis of the 'conflict principle' (*chongtu yuanzi*), and this implied resort to 'private law' as is the case in the 'capitalist' legal context.[90]

Chapter 5 affords an opportunity to review developing issues concerning *liangquan fenkai*, or the 'separation of ownership and operation', and the 'balancing of interests' (*liyi pingheng*) between 'equal subjects' under the Civil Law.[91] 'Respecting the law and abiding by contracts' deals with the legitimacy of new contractual norms governing legal liabilities and the use of state-owned domestic resources. The expanding notion of 'legal person' and the proliferation of independent subjects of civil law relations have spotlighted problems in defining state ownership in the context of reform. Conservative ideology has resisted argument that state ownership is *pro forma* and abstract as 'pure ownership' and has wrestled with qualifications to state ownership which are developing as economic reform permits the 'contracting out' and 'renting out' of state owned property.[92] On the other hand, reformers who support the extension of the commodity economy have argued that the 1986 General Principles of Civil Law is insufficiently clear on the 'subject system' and the rights ownership and operation.[93] The notion of 'separation of ownership and management' has increasingly come under fierce attack within China's legal circles.

In a period of transition marked by mounting social frustration relating to opportune official corruption and the widening economic differentials which flow from a qualified allowance of 'some people will prosper first and others later', this is a substantive and politically controversial area of legal development which straddles the dimensions of economic, administrative and criminal law. It includes increasingly complicated contractual relations within and between state and collective forms of ownership. 'Respecting the law and abiding by contracts' also relates to the implications of the 'open door policy' and the international problem of confidence in China's legal system to guarantee fair protection of patents, assets and resources.

Economic reform has offered tremendous opportunities for economic crime to flourish, and China's political leaders candidly recognise the problem of moving from the past situation whereby state cadres acted on the basis of administrative fiat into a new era whereby law would govern the conduct of the state officials. Zhao Ziyang took particular interest in this problem as early as 1981 when he called upon leading cadres to 'acquire a better mastery of legal measures to maintain economic order':

> A good many laws and regulations pertaining to the economy are being drafted. Economic courts have been established at most levels. Our efforts in this area still need to be greatly reinforced. Some units are unwilling to submit criminal cases in the economic field to the judicial organs, because they think that it is against their interest to do so. This is not only harmful to normal economic activities and hinders an effective crackdown on criminals but also goes directly against socialist legality.[94]

The problem of failing compliance with economic law has recently been highlighted in the political campaign against *sanjiaozhai*, or the proliferation of inter-enterprise debt despite the provisions of the new bankruptcy laws.

Chapter 6, Politics and Criminal Law Change Under Reform, encompasses two central and related thematic concerns. Western 'human rights' advocacy has spotlighted the category of 'political crime' (*zhengzhi fan*), the death penalty and administrative punishment in China. China's lack of Western style 'judicial independence' apparently negates the emergence of any genuine 'rule of law' in China. On this score, Cooper, Michael and Wu noted in 1985: '...it is questionable whether the People's Republic of China has made any permanent progress in rule by law through the adoption of a new criminal code in 1979'.[95] However, the Chinese side continues to deny the existence of such 'crime', and contemporary Western analysis has yet to take fully into account pre- and post-June 1989 internal debate on the anachronistic dimensions of the Criminal Law sections relating to 'counterrevolutionary crime'.

This debate castigated such law as incompatible with the development of modern Chinese society and political life, and on 1 April 1989 it was announced that Article 28 of the State Constitution, which sanctions the notion of 'counterrevolution' in the Criminal Law, was to be amended in April 1990 at the Third Session of the Seventh NPC.[96]

Secondly, Chinese legal circles have focused on the connection between crime and the social changes wrought by economic reform, and this too relates back to the issue of 'unification theory' and how the Criminal Law should respond to 'antagonistic' and 'non-antagonistic contradictions among the people' and the need to reinforce the 'rule of law' as opposed to 'policy' in the regime's political response to changing social and economic environment. It also relates to conflicting perception of the relation between criminal law norms and non-criminal law. Advocates of a 'mild' criminal law responded to the eclipse of revolutionary struggle, the discrediting of 'class struggle as the key link', and the advent of economic modernisation by stressing 'socialist humanism' and the reduction of the categories of 'crime' carrying the death penalty. More 'Conservative' reformers, on the other hand, have successfully expanded such categories to deal with the alarming growth of 'serious economic crime'.

Argument for revision of the 1979 criminal law highlighted the lingering influence of 'taking the class struggle as a key link'; for example, the 1979 law, in its evaluation of the the harm to society caused by criminal behaviour, had focused on political rather than economic consequences. Recently, the economic consequences of the 'criminal' acts of 'legal persons' (*faren*), such as state enterprises and business organisations, have been emphasised in debate concerning comparative American and Chinese law relating to enterprise. The hitherto exclusive focus on the criminal acts of natural persons (*ziran ren*) is under challenge despite the political desire to emphasise Chinese enterprise as *faren* in the context of socialist, as opposed to capitalist economy.[97]

The new Criminal Law and Criminal Law of Procedure were adopted by the NPC on 1 July 1979 and went into effect on 1 January 1980. The emphasis on codification represented a step forward, but it would be inaccurate to suggest there was no previous criminal law. In fact, for purposes of analysis it is especially important to note that the 1979 laws represented an aggregation of existing legislation and draft codes. The 'new' law retained past procedural emphasis on 'flexibility' and 'analogy'. Through the 1980s the persistent application of 'analogy' continued to invite controversy in light of the principle of 'no crime without a law' (*fa wumingwen buwei zui*).

China had a long historical tradition of criminal law, and this area was more developed than the civil law area. Contemporary Chinese explanation has, itself, criticised traditional phenomena of *zhong xing qing min* ('emphasise criminal law, de-emphasise civil law') and *faxing heyi* ('law and punishment are one and the same thing'). Related debate has already highlighted the overlapping of new civil and economic law by criminal law, and the introduction of the 'norms' of Criminal Law into non-criminal law areas.

The making of the new laws of 1979 was informed by political reaction to the Cultural Revolution, a greater regard for legal procedure and a politically necessary subscription to a new ethos rather negatively characterised in the 'three don'ts', namely, 'don't pick on others for their faults, don't put labels on people, and don't use a big stick'. Law was called upon to protect citizens against 'kangaroo courts', religious persecution, the arbitrary invasion of privacy, unlawful imprisonment, illegal search, malicious slander and the confiscation of property. This reaction facilitated debate over the law's limiting of the freedom of citizens in relation to the needs of society and the need to protect rights of citizens as against arbitrary violence associated with personality cult, leadership instability and political persecution.

The progress in 1979 should not be minimised; nevertheless, during the 1980s legal experts increasingly noted that the new code was dated in its response to the unfolding aspects of an increasingly important new area of 'crime', namely, economic crime. If the reaction to the Cultural Revolution gave rise to a new focus on protecting the individual citizen under the Constitution, Criminal Law and Criminal Law of Procedure, growing political concern over the dramatic increases in economic crime argued for a utilitarian legal response to 'crime' which significantly harms society.

The debate included some suggestion that private economy has to be incorporated into the 'objects', protected by Criminal Law. And in the field of 'punishment theory', some experts argued that the criminal law system balance the 'deprivation of freedom' with the 'deprivation of property', i.e., through fines and state confiscation. Under this scheme, fines were to acquire status as a 'main punishment' (*zhuxing*).[98]

This raises the question as to whether 'the rule of law' intrinsically requires a particular weighting of individual and social interests. Chinese legal thinking embraces contradictory extremes in that it not only emphasises the humane features of community mediation, but also the harsh punitive dimensions of capital punishment. In the Chinese legal mind both punishment and leniency in the judicial process is an immediate political matter of organised public education and the assuaging of public sentiment as well as of the specific dispensation of justice to the individual accused.

Does 'the rule of law' require Chinese subscription to the sanctity of the individual in terms of 'presumption of innocence'? Chinese theory alternatively subscribes to 'scientific' principle which rejects both *yuzui tuiding* ('presumption of guilt') and *wuzui tuiding* ('presumption of innocence'). In theory, this is to insure the application of 'seeking the truth from the facts' in the balancing of the individual's right to legal defence and the protection of society's interests.

Chapter 7, Hong Kong and the Rule of Law across 'Two Systems', offers a comparative discussion of the 'rule of law' within Deng Xiaoping's complicated and unprecedented formula of 'one country, two systems'. In terms of explicit legal argument, we can trace the variance in the interpretations of Hong Kong's Basic Law as offered by leading experts and political leaders in both Hong Kong and the PRC.

The issue is extraordinarily complex in its relation of law to sovereignty. Also, the two different social and economic systems partake of different traditions of law, and there are very real questions of interpretation which must be worked out. To what extent, for example, can Hong Kong's final court of appeal be restrained by the 'act of state doctrine'? Can the Hong Kong authorities independently establish such a court? Under what circumstances is the PRC entitled to intervene in Hong Kong affairs so as to head off an 'emergency' situation. The legal issues relating to 'subversion' and the death penalty became especially contentious in the light of the Hong Kong reaction to Tiananmen Square. The PRC is a unitary state, and yet Hong Kong is a special region with powers that range beyond those granted to provinces, or states under some Western federal constitutions.[99]

Hong Kong description of the Basic Law as a 'mini-constitution' (*xiao xianfa*) was meant to enhance Hong Kong's constitutional position *vis-à-vis* the PRC state constitution, but this formulation was not enthusiastically received by all of the PRC members of the Basic Law Committee. In theory, basic law is inferior to constitutional law.

PRC legal debate did raise the issue of the relation between the three legal systems of Hong Kong, Macao and the PRC under the slogan, 'one country, two systems and three laws' (*yi guo liang zhi, san fa*). In the event of conflicting jurisdictions over the criminal law disposition of a case, for example, some experts adopted the principle of trial 'according to place', meaning the place where the consequences of the crime occur.[100]

While the underlying premise of 'two systems' presumes that Hong Kong will enjoy a great degree of legal autonomy so as to protect existing civil rights and law relating to the city's economic prosperity and historical property relations, the 'two systems' have already begun to interact politically at the 'inter-system' level even before the transition has been consummated.

The new administrative law and the proposed amendment to the Criminal Law on 'counterrevolution', for example, were touted in Beijing as examples of China's growing commitment to the 'rule of law'. The issue was tied to PRC reformers' interpretation of the implications of the 'open door'. Hong Kong's prosperity and the related success of the PRC's 'coastal strategy' were politically coopted in argument for PRC legal reform which would help reduce inter-system stress.

Hong Kong lobbyists, for their part, insisted on the need to maintain 'judicial independence' and complained of the lack of the 'rule of law' in the PRC and Beijing's inherrent tendency to support the 'rule of man'.[101] Before 4 June 1989, this pressure resulted in specific responses. Cao Zidan of the NPC's Committee of Legislative Affairs, for example, declared that China's law on counterrevolution was incompatible with the 'coexistence of the "two systems"'.[102] A Hong Kong deputy to the NPC, Liu Yiu-chu warmly responded to the new right of filing suit against administrative organs, saying: 'This will play an active role in safeguarding human rights and stepping up rule by law.'[103] After June 4 the Beijing view was increasingly informed by the fear of Hong Kong-based democracy and human rights agitation spreading to the mainland, and, in Hong Kong, the Legislative Council moved quickly to eliminate locally the death penalty so as to preempt any future adaptation to Mainland law requiring the death penalty in Hong Kong.

'One country, two systems' is unprecedented in that it lies at the interstices of the Soviet, Chinese, Continental, and British legal influences. It is also seminal to the discussion of the Chinese struggle for the 'rule of law' in that it brings together conflicting perspectives on the issues relating to 'government of laws, not men'. Chapter 7's discussion will provide an opportunity to examine both the comparative and dissimilar points of law across the PRC State Constitution, the Basic Law and the June 1991 Hong Kong Bill of Rights Ordinance which incorporated into the law of Hong Kong the provisions of the International Covenant on Civil and Political Rights. While for example, the PRC's law does not enshrine the principle of 'presumption of innocence', the Basic Law and the Human Rights Ordinance both subscribe to such a principle.

The foregoing discussion points to the national and international policy significance of legal reform in China, and it underscores the complexity and difficulty of comparative analysis relating to the content of, and struggle for, the 'rule of law'. There is some folk wisdom in the old Chinese saying that 'crows are black all over the world' (*tianxia wuya yi ban hui*) and there can be no doubt that the Chinese struggle for the 'rule of law' is ultimately a question of domestic ideology and politics; however, this analysis has to hew a path between over-generalisation which too often accompanies assumption concerning the universality of particular values, and cultural relativism negating cross-cultural comparison of national political and legal culture.

Taking into account legal theory and legislative development across substantive and procedural law and the several main 'categories' of law including criminal, civil, economic, administrative and constitutional law, sinology needs to address several large issues, and the above analysis certainly suggests some interesting points of comparison with the Western notion of 'rule of law' implying the limiting of arbitrary government by law and the mediation of conflicting interests through legal means.

What, if any, are the common dimensions by which we might ascertain a basic political commitment to the 'rule of law' in either China or the West? What are the possible minimal political and economic conditions needed to establish the 'rule of law' in China? Are the issues of 'government of laws, and not men' and the 'mediation of interests', or 'balancing of interests' exclusively tied to the specific history of particular forms of capitalist development? Must the 'rule of law' imply a singular conception of checks and balances such as the 'separation of powers' by which to delimit arbitrary government? Is it possible in contemporary China to generate a new social perspective on the law without resort to the pitfalls of 'wholesale Westernisation'? Can CCP mass-line theory make a positive contribution to the development of checks and balances under a Chinese 'socialist rule of law'? Even given the slow down in 'political restructuring', has the economic reform already precipitated a qualitatively new pattern of legal development which contributes to the establishment of the 'rule of law'?

The contemporary Chinese discussion of the 'rule of law' and the related controversies over the content of 'human rights' are still little known in the West. Despite the promise of sinology always to start up an analysis with an explanation of China in Chinese terms, Western literature on China's legal situation presently lacks a comprehensive coverage of relevant Chinese debates affecting legal reform in the various categories of law. This coverage is crucial if we are going to acquire a more contextually accurate and broad-ranging view of the changes in Chinese legal thinking which are likely to have a substantive effect on the contemporary struggle to achieve the 'rule of law' in China.

2 The Rule of Law within Comparative Legal Cultures

The contemporary Chinese 'rule of law' versus 'rule of man' debate constitutes an extremely important, if somewhat convoluted, political and historiographical discussion of the transition of Chinese legal culture from tradition to modernity. The reform advocates of 'rule of law' have compellingly argued for 'modern legal culture', as against the 'rule of man' and the manifestation of 'feudalism' in contemporary politics and society.

Incidental terminological confusion seems inherent in the puzzling Chinese usage of 'feudalism' as the basis for understanding this opposition of rule of law to rule of man. This feudalism, while it may loosely reference the Marxist relationship between economic base and political superstructure, sharply focuses on specific aspects of China's dynastic history which were hardly primary to Marx's rather uninformed discussion of Chinese history.

The European connotations of enfeoffment, military obligation, political fragmentation and property ownership are certainly not implied in the Chinese focus on feudalism as it relates to imperial absolutism and the rule of man. Derk Bodde has argued that feudalism, in its European political implications of fragmentation, may only have occurred in China in 1122–256 BC and in AD 221–589.[1] Western historiography has generally assumed the supercession of feudalism in the making of Chinese empire whereas official Chinese historiography often applies feudalism to the entire period from the Warring States Period (484–221 BC) up to the establishment of the People's Republic in 1949.

The latter historiography was probably inspired by a Chinese Marxist–Leninist political desire to bring the history of the Chinese revolution within the mainstream of a progressive historical movement from feudalism to capitalism to socialism, but it has generated difficulties for comparative analysis of legal development. Professor Wang Shiming, in his comparison of early Chinese and Western European feudalism, for example, refers to European 'feudalism', as distinguished from China's 'autocratic, centralised feudal political system' (*quanzhi jiquandi fengjian zhengzhi*).[2] The latter entailed rule by imperial household, centralised bureaucracy and the centripetal power and cultural homogeneity of the Han population.

Regardless of the idiosyncratic usage of feudalism, what is really important is that it is part of a self-conscious political move to escape the traditional cultural predicament which cast political authority in absolute moral terms as above the law, and this, in turn, has fillipped contemporary examination of the underlying social forces which shaped traditional legal culture.[3] Despite its peculiar appropriation of the term feudalism, contemporary Chinese comparative legal analysis has often produced an informed and constructive debate on the origins and nature of 'rights' and the surviving aspects of past Chinese legal culture which are antithetical to China's newly developing rule of law.

The contemporary Chinese analysis of feudalism moves well beyond traditional heroic moralism versus the depraved villainy of the *danibudao* (i.e. those who defile the 'way') towards the examination of state's underlying political and legal structures, and the related explication of the cultural and social context of changing patterns of authority. While this new historiography still needs to construct the relationship between the protection of state interests as implied in the security system of *baojia* and the contemporary focus on the 'comprehensive management of public order', it has demonstrated intense interest in the use of law to protect the rights of individual citizens. In this regard, there is a new, if somewhat selective, convergence of domestic historiographical explanation with Western political cultural explanation of China's weak legal tradition.

In the mid-1960s, Harvard's prominent authority on Chinese law, Jerome Cohen, noted the Chinese tendency to dismiss Western discussion of the rule of law as merely a propaganda ploy. Indeed, at that time, Cohen's Weberian parallel between Communist and traditional systems of legal sanction which derived from the same 'type of patriarchal obliteration of the line between justice and administration' elicited very little serious comment in Chinese legal circles.[4] Now, however, there is routine reference to the contemporary significance of 'patriarchal ways' and 'autocratic', 'feudal' tendencies which continue to blur distinctions between judiciary and administration, and law and ethics.

Yu Ronggen, for example, offers the following inventory of traditional legal notions of China's agrarian society which still continue to influence contemporary society: 'follow heaven's course' (*shun tian zeshi*); 'combine decorum and law' (*lifa jiehe*); 'law respects rank and status' (*fa you dengcha*); 'supremacy of imperial authority' (*huangquan zhi shang*); 'law comes from the sovereign' (*fa zi jun chu*); 'take the clan as the basis' (*jiazu benwei*); 'ethics and law are inseparable' (*daofa yu falu*); 'judiciary and administration are inseparable' (*sifa yu xingzheng bufen*); 'civil and criminal law are inseparable' (*minxing bufen*); 'combining all types of law into one' (*zhufa heti*); 'use virtue and law together' (*dexing bing yong*); 'value virtue, devalue law' (*gui de jian xing*); 'arbitrary conviction and punishment' (*zuixing shanduan*).[5]

Yu's emphasis on the 'patriarchial' nature of law in Chinese agrarian society has also been explored in the writings of Zhang Jinfan, one of China's most well-known legal historians. Zhang utilises the notion of *eryuan*, or loosely 'dual unity' in his explanation of the close interrelationship of state and clan law in China's agrarian society:

> From before Qin Shihuang's burning of the books up to the Song Dynasty, clan law increasingly gained currency throughout society. By the Ming and Qing [Dynasties] clan law had become an independent, state acknowledged system to the point where some regarded China's ancient law as constituting a dual unity [of state and clan law].[6]

Zhang stressed that legal culture under the spreading power of the patriarchal system rolled law, politics, ethics and philosophy into one, and he ascribed the lack of a strong civil law tradition to the intimate relation of state and clan law.

Apparently, dual unity was very early on explicit in the Han legal treatment of criminal behaviour within the family; for example, there was no penalty for not revealing violent crime in the family, but the physical or verbal assault of parents, or a wife's adultery could bring on the death penalty. Whereas failure to observe the obligatory three years of mourning at the death of a parent could actually incur legal penalties, filial killing to avenge the death of parent was given a comparatively light penalty.[7]

Yu Ronggen argues that, in the late Qing dynasty, agrarian-based sociological phenomena which freely mixed law and ethics was increasingly challenged by Western legal culture and came into contradiction with the modern requirements of industrialisation. This has become conventional wisdom. Yu, nevertheless, subscribes to the current political emphasis on creating a rule of law which specifically responds to 'socialism with Chinese characteristics'. Moreover, he asserts that present Western notion of the rule of law is, itself, in decline, and that the newly developing Chinese rule of law in China should not repeat the West's mistakes. Hence China's particular rule of law must have independent prestige and authority; it must reflect the enduring relevance of a traditional legal cultural perspective which treats man's relations with nature and human relations within society as an organic whole.

Some of Yu's colleagues, however, are more keen to stress feudalism's opposition to the modern attempt to restrain arbitrary state behaviour by law. They emphasise the absolute patriarchal authority of the Son of Heaven as the central predicament of Chinese feudalism. Contemporary manifestation of this predicatment correspondingly requires a strong equality before the law to overcome the 'spirit' of supreme leaders and related Party tendencies such as 'taking policy as a substitute for law' (*yi zhengce daiti falu*), and 'taking policy as the negation of law' (*yi zhengce fouding falu*).

The CCP Central Committee formally defined 'feudal ideology' as 'patriarchal clannishness, autocratic ways, the tendency to seek privileges and to form factions for selfish purpose…'.[8] While Weber might have had difficulty recognising this usage of feudalism, his discussion of rationality in modern organisation as a reaction to personality-based authority and the failure to separate out political personality from office in the impersonal use of state resources and the impersonal judgement of competing claims in law has a clear parallel in the current Chinese debate surrounding the rule of law.

Rule of law supporters have often stressed the predictable, stable character of law as it contributes to the process of rationalisation in the modern Chinese economy. While Party veterans attempted to draw on Marxism–Leninism to highlight the need for greater rationalisation and authority of the law, some dissident intellectuals in the spring of 1989 suggested that China was moving from an 'era of heroes to the era of the common people', and that in the light of the waning charisma of state leaders it was necessary to consolidate law and, in essence, to accelerate the 'routinisation of charisma'.[9]

The contemporary Chinese debate over *fazhi* versus *renzhi* invokes generations of controversy over the respective merits of Confucianism and Legalism and the relative impact of these philosophical schools on the development of the traditional legal system. The contemporary nationalism of official China requires the development of a new legal system which responds to the Chinese characteristics of Chinese socialist society, but its economic, if not its political, agenda for socialist democracy also requires significant criticism of China's legal history. Whereas pre-Cultural Revolution Party historiography required that the 'past serve the present', the post-Cultural Revolution reaction suggested the extent to which the past still lives in the present and conflicts with the creation of a modern legal culture.

There is awareness that the question is not limited to the development of codified law and legal structure, but it also includes the generation of an appropriate social and political consciousness within the leadership and general public. The top party leaders seemed to concede as much when, in 1986, they themselves agreed to 'go back to school' for lessons on the rule of law.[10]

Zhong Zonghu, editorial page editor of the prestigious *Fazhi ribao*, argued in *China Culture Journal* that law under feudalism was '...designed basically to subdue people. People's rights were rarely stipulated. Emperors were exempt from any legal bounds.'[11] Confucianism backed patriarchal moral authority within the family and state and propagated the three cardinal guides (ruler guides subject, father guides son and husband guides wife) and the five constant virtues (benevolence, righteousness, propriety, wisdom and fidelity). Confucianism saw law as only a secondary instrument of rulership, and it gave primary emphasis to the application of *li* or decorum in the governance of social and political relationships. Law was reluctantly used to reinforce the content of *li*, and the five classics often served as the basis for legal judgement.

On the front lines of the legal system, the imperial *xian* magistrates were moulded in an examination process which laboriously exalted Confucian moral teachings and the preeminence of moral example as the basis of good government. Even before the advent of Han Feizi's Legalism, the rule of law versus rule of man issue was already explicit in the writings of Xunzi, who bridged Confucian and later Legalist political philosophy.[12] The Confucian argument for *renzhi* glossed over any inherent contradictions by insisting: 'Law is the basis of good government, but the superior man [*junzi*] is the origin of the law.'[13]

The imperial Confucian view of the relation between Legalist *fazhi*, or rule *by* law and Confucian rule by virtuous example, however, was more a question of dialectical synthesis rather than absolute negation. This is suggested in Mencius' oft-quoted instruction: 'Goodness alone is not sufficient for the exercise of government; laws alone cannot carry themselves into practice'.[14]

The aforementioned unity of *fa* and *li*, law and decorum, (or ritual or rites or propriety) implied *a priori* emphasis on *li* as the substantive basis for the development of *fa*. Renda law professor Liang Zhiping points out that 'all standards lie in *li*' was the principal characteristic of China's ancient law since the Han dynasty and that the process of 'ritual entering law' (*li ru yu fa*) not only incorporated ethics into law, but also turned law into ethics.[15]

Confucianism gave precedence to *li* to emphasise that 'good government relies on man' (*weizheng cai ren*), and *li* became the 'way of ruling men' (*zhi renzhi dao*).[16] Generations of scholars studied the following related gloss taken from the Analects:

> The Master said, 'If the people be led by laws, and uniformity sought to be given them by punishments, they will try to avoid the punishment, but have no sense of shame.' 'If they be led by virtue, and uniformity

> sought to be given them by the rules of propriety [*li*], they will have the sense of shame, and moreover will become good.'[17]

Also, according to Confucius, benevolence would have to precede the authority of the state or the '...people will not obey'.[18] There was nothing in Confucianism to lend real support to the development of law as an open-ended and positive process of political socialisation. The emphasis rather was on finding ways whereby the people avoid morally dubious and contentious litigation. The official's nurturing of the morality within man was supposed to make law redundant. Confucians feared the contentiousness of litigation. The Legalists, however, feared that lack of clarity in the law would jeopardise the political stability of the state.

The Confucian position on law was frontally challenged in the advent of Legalism which sought the state's autonomy from society, gave law a central place in the political life, and challenged the superiority of ethics in Confucian teaching. Some contemporary analysts have argued that Legalism promoted equality before the law within Han Feizi's dictum 'handle all the affairs of state according to law' (*yi ben yu fa*). In combining *fa* and *li*, Confucianism was most interested in ensuring the ascriptive character of the five relationships (*wulun*) between ruler and subject, father and son, husband and wife, elder and younger brother and friend and friend. The Legalists, however, required that the prince make sure his ministers faithfully executed the laws, that law was to be applied equally to everyone despite differences of social status and finally and very importantly that the prince underwrite the law by abiding by it, himself. On this last point, the Legalists intended to challenge the emperor's ability to make law (i.e., the aforementioned *fazi junzhu*), but the emperor, once he had willed law into existence, was advised that it would be politically expedient to abide by his own law.

Professor Wang Liming has taken a leading position in the contemporary rule of law debate, and he has challenged the interpretation of the famous early-twentieth-century liberal reformer, Liang Qichao. According to Wang, Liang incorrectly believed that the Legalists had discovered the rule of law; and he failed to distinguish between the Legalist notion 'ruling the state by law', and the contemporary democratic concept of rule of law. Liang did, however, object to the Legalist notion of 'legislation without discussion' and to the legalism of militarists who, in the 1920s, attempted to use law as an absolute standard at the expense of democracy. In any case, the Legalist emphasis on law was designed to subordinate the people and to reinforce the ruler's absolute political position. The ruler's position was only restricted in terms of self-restraint and self-rectification.[19]

Herrlee Creel's well-known Western historiography also suggests that Legalism was not really interested in using law as a 'safeguard' against unlimited exactions by the state.[20]

The Confucians and Legalists did share a similar penchant for the hierarchical ordering of society. Both schools emphasised the preservation of extant hierarchical social ranking in the 'rectification of names'. The Legalists wished to protect their own particular hierarchy, and their focus on the Confucian recommendation of *li* as an instance of social inequality was politically self-serving. Establishing their own elite in the course of building a new centralised state, they sought to expose the hypocrisy of Confucian ethics and to raise high the importance of 'taking law as education' (*yifa wei jiao*).[21] This educational experience, however, was top-down. It was designed to shape people's behavior and to check deviance from the standards necessary to the exclusive purposes of the state.

Law was to fill the vacuum left by the allegedly fatuous Confucian demonstration of moral example, hence Han Feizi observed: 'The sage in governing a state, does not trust men to do good themselves; he makes it impossible for them to do wrong'.[22] Han simply discounted the efficacy of the moral teachings and example of 'superior men' (*junzi*) when he observed: 'By common observation, the virtuous are few and the worthless many'. He believed that the populace would have difficulties in comprehending the niceties of virtue, but that it would intuitively relate to the necessity of law as a matter of deterrence, hence he reasoned: '...prohibition of evil is a universal standard.'[23]

Legalism did not intend to reflect popular moral and social convention; it promoted cultural autocracy. The CCP's contemporary mass line, at least in formal terms, offered a modern alternative to such autocracy, but ironically the mass line, in its attack on the inequities of Chinese traditional society, formally derived from Sinified foreign experience and ideas.

China's famous intellectual historian, Feng Yulan, described Legalism as an *ex post facto* rationalisation of prevailing trends to centralise the state in the context of the moral degeneracy of the Warring States Period. Legalism called Confucianism to account for the disorder of the times. Confucian protestations of virtue had only aggravated a situation requiring strong government through the consistent application of fixed legal standards. These standards were utilitarian in the context of increasing population and scarcity. The personal bonds of morality which Confucius had sponsored could not meet the new challenge of imperial centralisation. Feng reflected on the transition from feudal to imperial government and relates this transition to the elevation of law as the new basis of state power:

> The sphere and organization of the state and society of that time were very small and simple, and therefore the relationship between rulers and subject, overlord and serf, was a personal one, hence for the feudal lords to maintain the necessary relations between each other, all that was required was a code of social etiquette (*li*).... When the feudal system began to crumble, however the power of the state rulers became, on the one hand, greater and more centralized, while on the other hand the common people gained more independence from their immediate overlords. Thus as the sphere of the state expanded, and its organization became more and more complex, the former close man-to-man relationships became wider and looser. As a consequence, difficulties automatically arose to hinder the attempt to continue government upon a personal basis, so that one after another various states ... promulgated law codes.[24]

Legalism attacked Confucianism by alleging a morally bankrupt rationalisation of inequality. Contemporary Chinese Marxist analysis has often endorsed the Legalist allegations against Confucian sponsored privilege, citing notions such as '*li* affirms rank and status' and 'ritual does not apply to the commoner and law does not apply to the nobleman' (*li buxia shuren, xing bushang daifu*) as reactionary rationalisation sustaining the existing hierarchy of 'slave society'.

Legalism's much vaunted equality before the law derived from an exclusive interest in efficient government. Why did Legalism endorse the notion: 'Law is not honoured when those above violate it'? Hyung Kim's discussion of comparative legal concepts draws our attention to Legalism's real social agenda:

> Legalists neither denied nor objected to the distinction between the noble, the humble, the high and the low, old and young. But all are impartially treated by the law...[and] all should conform to a single law. Impartiality means due process, not equal punishments.[25]

Social equality was not then at issue, the central question was that of an efficient political response to reality of state building. The famous Legalist, Han Feizi, argued that law had to be written and consistent with the needs of the real world. He conceded that law would have to be changed in changing times, but he added a rather interesting caveat concerning the importance of the law's stability: 'If there are great changes to the law's standards in the ruling of a great kingdom then the people will suffer'.[26]

Notwithstanding suspicion of Legalism's self-interested, statist motivation, Legalist criticism of Confucian inequality in law has been highlighted in contemporary assessment of China's traditional legal culture. The Tang code is historiographically treated as the culminating 'convergence of Confucianism and Legalist schools' (*rufa heliu*), whereby Confucianist content and attitude dominated legal thinking such that *li* was taken as primary and punishment, *xing*, as secondary. By the Tang dynasty, AD 618–905, Confucianism had brought about 'combining every type of law into one', hence the ongoing failure to dissociate civil and criminal laws.

Confucianism had also helped nurture a thorny thicket of ascriptive distinctions (*bianyi*) by which the law systematically treats different subjects differently according to their social status and political position. The influence of rank was, for example, explicit in the common saying, 'when one is promoted even his pets go to heaven'. The 'feelings' (*ganqing*) which are conceptually explicit in the particular variations of the five relationships were legitimised in law. Punishment was mitigated in relation to the eight distinctions of Tang feudal law. Legal statutes carefully honoured the ascriptive requirements of noble status, friendship, imperial lineage, reputation, special talent, outstanding service, employment in the imperial household, and respect for foreign guests.

Under the *qing* system, relatives of the imperial family and officials of the fifth rank, who faced the death penalty, were automatically entitled to personal appeal to the Emperor for leniency. The system of *guandang* allowed officials to barter their official positions for leniency.[27] Whereas, under the *shu* system, there was a wide range of buy-out provisions whereby criminal law penalties could be reduced or eliminated for monetary considerations. *Shu* applied in qualified circumstances of graduated severity relating to doubtful conviction, the punishment of minority leaders, the handicapped, and women, as well as to negligent acts relating to death and injury.[28]

The 1980s political focus on the persistence of feudalism in contemporary Chinese society allowed for lively academic debate as to the nature of legal culture in the context of modernisation. Few actually advocated wholesale Westernisation and a great many heartily subscribed to the official line of socialism with Chinese characteristics, but the discussion of feudalism has generated an implicit conceptual convergence with the modern Weberian critique of China's traditional legal system as irrational and ascriptive in nature. The emerging Chinese historiography of China's legal development now widely interprets legal culture in broadly defined terms which touch not only on codification, legal systems and institutionalisation of procedure, but also on underlying questions of public consciousness, moral social order and state power.

Professor He Xiaorong, for example, cites Feng Yulan's historiography to argue that China's traditional legal culture originated in the necessities of the agrarian economy, and that several interlocking perspectives on law strongly reinforced the clan system of patriarchal authority. He details the traditional dimensions of law in terms of its ethical, hierarchical, obligational, static and one-dimensional attributes.[29]

Despite the efforts of Legalism, the social order was not sustained by law, but by ethics dictated by patriarchal authority requiring absolute obedience of the inferior to the superior. Human relations were essentially clan relations, hence there was no real subscription to a principle of universality. Law became an extension of hierarchical norms which formed the ethical basis of social convention encompassed in the Confucian concept of *li*. The harsh social realities of agrarian life generated an exclusive reliance of the individual on the family for survival as well as a oppressive psychology of humility and resignation in the face of natural adversity.

Within this compelling context, law reinforced hierarchy and obligation rather than a notion of rights as separate from obligations. Confucian advocacy of 'cultivating oneself in order to obey heaven' (*xiuji suntian*) reinforced social values such as modesty, reverence, and resignation. Correspondingly, the law was static as individuals were resigned to act as objects rather than as principals or equal subjects in law. This argument of course corresponds well with Western legal historiography; for example, William Jones study of the Qing legal code concluded that there was no civil law in the late imperial context. Law was designed to protect the interests of the imperial state; and it could not conceive of legal relations between citizens. Jones wrote:

> Law was, in terms, an aspect of government designed to protect government. The essential elements of our law had no 'legal' significance whatever in China. There were no 'persons' who, as beings with legal capacity to be bearers of rights (*Rechtssubjekte*), might make declarations of intention (*Willenserklrugnen*), and engage in juristic arts (*Rechtsgeschafte*).[30]

Similarly in He Xiaorong's historiography the law becomes one-dimensional in its exclusive concern with the state's requirements and the regulatory function of law in society. Within the prevailing hegemony of Confucian idealism, pursuit of profit was socially despicable, and hence society lacked utilitarian motivation. There was no social reinforcement to encourage individuals to pursue rights. Involvement in lawsuits was inconsistent with social mores stressing the importance of harmony while a psychological fear of punishment prompted people to avoid lawsuits and to seek communal mediation outside the law. In these circumstances civil law languished, and 'law' was perceived as essentially punitive, or criminal in nature.

According to He, these several interlocking perspectives militated against modern legal culture predicated in industrialisation and commodity economy. Such modern culture alternatively requires the synchronised advance of the legal system, inclusive of the corpus of law and the institutions of law, together with new legal theory and a general understanding of law in society. According to He, this theory and understanding are distinguished by new perspectives on the constitutional idea of law, equality before the law, positive participation in lawsuits, multidimensional development of the law's various specialised departments, the positive development of lawful rights and a dynamic rather than static conception of legal activity.

Legal culture bridges the gap between the formal and institutional dimensions inclusive of the codes, the norms of law, legal institutions and what He calls the idea of law. His colleague, Liu Zuoxiang, similarly refers to the the deep structures of legal psychology, legal consciousness and legal ideology.[31]

To take yet another example of such correlation of form and substance, Jiang Xun in his study of the modernisation of China's legal culture distinguishes the three aspects of the important vertical dimension of legal culture as the external, coordinative and inner aspects. While he subsumes the legal system, norms and operations under external form, he relegates legal psychology, orientation and behaviour to the innermost aspects of culture. The coordinative aspect then includes legal ideas, education and communication. The three aspects correlate in modern legal culture in terms of the comprehensive materialisation of the supremacy of law, independence of law, the unity of law, interposition of law and participation in law.[32]

'Supremacy of the law' invokes a reinforcing correlation of legal psychology and behaviour in the maintenance of the law's supreme authority as well as respect for the authority of the legislature and judiciary within the state system. 'Independence' invokes independence on a number of institutional levels including the independence of legal theory, legislative and judicial independence and the pro-active restriction of undue influence on law enforcement personnel.

'Unity of law' (*falu tongyi*) entails a growing emphasis on consistent harmonisation of law and regulation between different administrative levels and departments of law. 'Interposition', on the other hand, endorses the law's involvement in the control of state activity, and 'participation' infers active citizen involvement in society's legal life, including citizen participation in legislative and judicial processes and an enthusiasm and willingness to refer and defer to the law in the routine solution of disputes.

Jiang discusses the related tensions between policy and law and *fazhi* and *renzhi* in terms of the difficult, shifting alignment between the formal legal system and the norms within legal psychology, orientation and behaviour.

The latter, he argues, constitute the greatest difficulty in the continuous rationalisation of legal life; however, Jiang hopes to set the agenda for research into modern legal culture. His priorities include changing the traditional political overemphasis on the law's class as distinguished from its social nature and a shift from one-sided understandings of the law's function as punishment, prohibition and dictatorship towards a currently more relevant focus on the lawful protection, encouragement and equal adjustment of rights in relation to obligations. Legal communication, he argued, should include the raising of citizens' consciousness as distinct from indoctrination.

Chinese academics have, from a number of new and exciting angles, explored the modernisation of China's legal culture and the theoretical frontiers between legal rationalisation and modern economic development. Jiang Xun, for example, typically observed that the contemporary Chinese legal culture was a composite of four cultural sources including Soviet, traditional Chinese, Western and China's 1940s border-region culture, but then without expressly invoking Max Weber, he stressed 'the continuous rationalisation of legal life'. Legal norms and institutions can be formally declared, but he cautioned that the underlying legal psychology which responds to traditional ethics contemporaneously exists within the modern forms of contemporary legal culture.

Ding Xueliang, on the other hand, boldly cited Weber as well as Tönnies and Durkheim. While this Harvard doctoral research fellow advances a caveat that the equation of modernisation with Westernisation has to be resisted, his discussion of modernisation significantly overlaps Western discussion of the elimination of ascription and particularism and the development of integrative mechanisms which are supposed to respond to the rational requirements of modern economy in its emphases on a high degree of functional differentiation. Ding's mechanisms included not only 'a sound legal system which is guided by the principle of equality and regulates the various activities of members of society' but also maximum citizen participation in national politics and the elevation of a complete set of citizen's rights in opposition to traditional ascription and the related inequitable differentiation between classes or strata.[33]

The study of comparative legal culture has developed within a set of well-known political parameters which, while allowing for critical borrowing from Western legal experience, stipulates that China's legal development must respond to the distinctive character of Chinese socialism. Very few legal academics dared argue for 'complete opening' (*quan fangwei*), as did the leading dissident physicist, Fang Lizhi. Fang bitterly rejected China's backward past *in toto*, and Deng Xiaoping's open door is, by comparison, a selective strategy which allows qualified, rather than unlimited, borrowing of foreign experience.

The correlation of China's rule of law with socialism with Chinese characteristics relates back to the theoretical issue as to how to treat China's past legal development within the international comparative study of law. Shen Zongling as one of China's leading comparativists cites the Chinese legal tradition, or *Zhonghua faxi*, as one of four international traditions, including the Common Law, Civil Law and Soviet legal traditions. He acknowledges that indeed there was in the late Qing dynasty a Westernisation of China's law under the impact of capitalism and its reaction to feudalism, and a later concerted response to the requirements of Soviet law, but he stresses the distinctive Chinese focus on family values.[34]

Actually, contemporary Chinese legal theory offers only a limited and highly selective inventory of the positive aspects of China's legal tradition. While there is a lot of reference to Legalism's equality before the law, there is continuing disagreement over the implications and intent of the Legalist formulation. To cite another example, Zhang Jinfan notes the deep historical roots of Chinese law. Zhang recalls the unearthing in 1975 of the bamboo laws of the Qin and eulogises the concreteness, logic and precision of Qin law.[35]

In a September 1989 Beida interview with the author, Zhang Guohua proudly cited the appearance of *mens rea* in China several hundred years before its first appearance in Europe, but then, in response to the question as to what he would include within the negative attributes of the tradition, he listed a rather devastating series of infrastructural defects including the notion of *yiyandang*, referring to the emperor's exclusive monopoly of the truth, emphasis on agriculture to the neglect of commerce, emphasis on Confucian righteousness to the neglect of profit, gender inequality and hierarchical relations within the family and state as sanctioned in both decorum and law, or *li* and *fa*.

Yu Ronggen highlights the positive relevance of the Chinese traditional attempt to place law within an organic conception of human society and the natural world, and this type of argument often cites the positive features of Chinese mediation which have received significant research attention in Western comparative legal research.

Zhou Weijia, in his comparison of Chinese and American judicial thought, makes the familiar argument that the Chinese tradition places greater emphasis on communal mediation, or 'helping and teaching' (*bangjiao*), which is offered through the work place, the resident committees and village committees. Although Zhou acknowledges that some degree of self-containment is also possible within various American organisations, such *bangjiao* is still too sharply circumscribed in the American context which is unable to resist the strong philosophical undertow of individualism.[36]

The concrete issue of mediation is sometimes tied into more general discussion of the comparative basis of a legal tradition which responds to 'organic naturalism' (*you ji ziranzhuyi*), or the flowing cosmological continuum of man, society, nature and the universe. As Yu Ronggen indicated, the Chinese rule of law should respond to a distinctive philosophical view of the organic whole, but this provides very little fertile soil for the planting of the notion of law as a continuous and autonomous rational authority. Reason in the Chinese legal philosophical context is found inside of nature; it does not independently work on nature.[37] The implications of this for the development of a notion of rights will be more fully explored in Chapter 4's discussion of Chinese perspective on the rule of law and human rights.

The contemporary emphasis on rationality receives only incidental support from the Chinese tradition, and for the most part it has relied upon the leadership's contemporary extrapolations of the mass line requiring scientific investigation and seeking the truth from the facts, and only secondarily on the implicit inferences of legal theory drawn from Western experience and the study of comparative law and modernisation.

While accepting the Chinese emphasis on the rational relation between form and substance so that the Chinese rule of law is firmly rooted in the soil of Chinese society, the prevailing comparative tendency to make the past serve socialism with Chinese characteristics may, at times, seem rather forced in its highly selective focus on discrete characteristics of the Chinese traditional legal culture such as the tentative Legalist notion of equality before the law, and the unique dimensions of the Chinese approach to mediation. The Chinese usage of feudalism as a basis for the explanation of China's weak legal tradition is, in and of itself, idiosyncratic in its terminology and historiography, but it is clear that contemporary political and scholarly opinion has identified and is mobilising against persisting attitudes and orientations which work against the new formal subscription to a Chinese socialist rule of law.

There is developing agreement between Western modernisation theory and political cultural assessment of the Chinese tradition, on the one hand, and the contemporary Chinese historiography of feudalism, on the other. The weight of this comparative critical analysis might suggest that there are more liabilities than assets in China's legal tradition; however, the feudalism debate is politically designed to accentuate the liabilities so as to fully consolidate the rule of law. Authorities like Li Buyun point out, the obstacles of feudalism are so significant that it is necessary to focus exclusively on the rule of law; however, Chinese political culture over the centuries attempted a formal synthesis of Legalist and Confucian philosophical assumptions within imperial bureaucratic organisation. Those in the rule of law debate, who have attempted to see a positive relation between rule of law and rule of man are not necessarily opposed to the entwining of socialist legality and socialist democracy, but they are certainly more in tune with this tradition.

The negative attributes of the rule of man were revealed for all to see in the Cultural Revolution, but the correlation of the rule of law with a Chinese humanistic politics which stresses the importance of moral example in public office and law's immediate relation to moral principle in society should not be dismissed out of hand. Within this context, there is likely to be considerable resistance to a strict bifurcation of the substantive and procedural dimensions of the legal system and culture. It is not merely a matter of cultural relativism to suggest that the rule of law in China must repond to Chinese conditions and that it has to be anchored in Chinese society.

3 The Conceptualisation and Materialisation of Human Rights

Whereas in the early 1980s, Deng Xiaoping linked the call for human rights with opposition to the four cardinal principles, in the early 1990s human rights received official endorsement. Just as in the rule of law debate where China's political leaders and leading scholars staked a claim to an emerging socialist rule of law, now they are attempting to lay claim to a Chinese socialist conception of human rights. Arguably there is, in the latter case, a more deliberate response to international pressure and comparative experience, but the Chinese human rights debate is entwined with the ongoing internal discussion of the rule of law. The domestic issue of the conceptualisation and materialisation of human rights has been centrally located within the contradiction between the rule of law and rule of man, and, in this debate, feudalism has often been castigated for confounding the true relation between rights and obligations.

The study of Chinese human rights discussion and its related legislative consequences has been complicated by the international political perspective on human rights. While foreign observation as to the wholesale violation of human rights in China is regarded by Chinese scholars as an intrusive and non-reciprocal 'human rights diplomacy' (*renquan waijiao*), and there is a corresponding reluctance to permit comprehensive international scrutiny of their domestic human rights performance, the Chinese have, nonetheless, taken the really important step of recognising the validity of human rights terminology. They now emphasise the importance of new domestic and international dialogue on the subject. One of China's most senior law journals, *Zhongguo faxue* (Chinese Legal Studies), for example, invoked the 'two one hundreds' policy and editorially pleaded for a more thoughtful and comparative research on human rights:

> In developing theoretical research on human rights and the legal system we must resist two tendencies; we should neither favour bourgeois liberalism's view of human rights problems nor [foster] a rigid idea of human rights theory. ...we have to emancipate our thinking and to overcome past one-sided understanding which considered human rights as having an exclusively bourgeois patent and which considered our

> own human rights theory and practice as taboo. ...as for bourgeois human rights theories we have to make a concrete historical analysis. This means we will want to criticise bourgeois human rights theory for its idealism...and we will also want to make a 'seeking-the-truth from the facts' assessment and borrow human rights theories from historically progressive thinkers.[1]

CHINA'S 'HUMAN RIGHTS' AND 'CULTURAL RELATIVISM' IN INTERNATIONAL PERSPECTIVE

Western liberal democratic thought often correlates the rule of law qualification of executive discretion with the fundamental rights of the individual. A.V. Dicey exemplified this concern in his definition of the rule of law which interrelated three concepts, namely the supremacy of regular law, legal equality (or what is now more commonly equality before the law), and the development of judge-made constitutional law as 'the consequence of the rights of individuals, as defined and enforced by the courts'.[2]

Chinese theory continues to highlight the importance of group or collective rights and differs substantively on the relation of the individual to state and society, but the debate, which began in 1990, has broken new ground with respect to the legislative and social materialisation of human rights. One of China's brightest Marxist legal theorists, Li Buyun, seemingly veered towards Western liberal democratic argument when he stated: 'Human rights are rights which ought to be enjoyed by virtue of human essence'. And he also stated: 'The comprehensive and effective guarantee of human rights is not only the fundamental goal of modern rule-of-law society, it is also the measure of such a society.'[3]

Western human rights monitoring agencies often become impatient with Chinese explanations of domestic performance which are automatically construed as specious exercises in cultural relativism. While Amnesty International and Human Rights Watch concentrate on documenting selective individual cases of human rights violations, they have not attempted to assess human rights performance on a society-wide basis. They have not researched internal debate and the origins of relevant Chinese legislation. They can neither confirm nor negate China's often undifferentiated statistics – a problem of measurement which has often been frankly acknowledged in US Department of State reporting.

The difficulty in achieving balanced, global perspective on the overall development of China's society and policy, as measured by fair and commonly accepted indicators of human rights performance, may be partly illustrated in the failure of Western governments to reply in depth to Chinese argument to the effect that human-rights dialogue must take into account the history of development and collective rights.

The Chinese are well aware of the growing Western offensive which is designed to modify their behaviour with respect to their human rights performance. They have responded emphasising reciprocity in the development of international definitions and standards. They have fallen back on their own historical diplomatic formulations relating to national self-determination and the mid-1950s principle of *qiutong cunyi*, 'seek common ground while reserving differences', which was originally featured in Zhou Enlai's response to the Cold War.

They have also responded by initiating unprecedented internal debates on the subject of human rights. Western media speculation has suggested a direct relationship between Beijing's publication of the November 1990, 'White Paper on Human Rights', and American Congressional scrutiny of China's most-favoured-nation trading status. In light of such pressure, which is deliberately designed to influence the Chinese, the confused terms of reference and the lack of significant research in Western reporting on China's internal debate on the subject of human rights is truly puzzling.

The *Human Rights Watch: World Report 1992*, for example, reported that the Chinese were less willing in 1991 than in 1990 'to ease up on the relentless repression that they have pursued since...June 4, 1989'.[4] China's 'White Paper' was neither identified nor analysed. Asia Watch, despite its strong commitment to the monitoring of human rights developments, provided no assessment of the emerging terms of national debate and its relation to NPC legislation.

The US State Department's 1991 annual reading of Chinese human rights practices in 1990 incorrectly reported the cessation of debate over the rule of law versus rule of man, but it did cite 'conflicting developments' including a new and positive readiness to engage in 'substantive dialog' on human rights questions. The Department's 1992 reading of Chinese 1991 practices again acknowledged China's 'limited dialog on human rights with its foreign critics'.[5] It differed from Asia Watch in its identification of 'some loosening of repression during the first half of 1991'. China's 'comprehensive white paper' on the subject of human rights was in fact briefly cited. In reply to the Chinese claim that the US was attempting to foist its particular civil rights definition of human rights on to China, the State Department report accused the Chinese of creating 'a dichotomy between economic development and personal and political liberties'.[6]

The US State Department reviews of post-Tiananmen human rights performance in 1990 and 1991 contended that China '...denies that human rights are universal' and '...rejects the concept of universal human rights despite its adherence to the United Nations charter...'.[7] This point, however, stands in need of further explanation, if not correction, particularly as the PRC does not object to the building up of international standards through treaty law provided that it is strictly premised in national self-determination and reciprocity. While continuously subscribing to their own notions of non-interference and self-reliance, the Chinese have traditionally sought to enhance UN commitment to national self-determination and, on this basis, they have often positively cited the principles of the UN Charter and UN Universal Declaration of Human Rights.

However, First World human rights advocacy of Western human rights standards which supersede Third World positive law is viewed with suspicion. The Chinese position emphasises cultural and national differences and is reluctant to impose international standards on domestic rights performance, but it does not willy-nilly endorse an exclusive cultural relevatism which completely negates international society's attempt to develop new categories of universally recognised rights.

China's long recorded opposition to apartheid and consistent support of international sanctions against South Africa demonstrated a more complex approach which provided some albeit heavily qualified space for the development of international standards through the extension of the international obligations of states. Neither PRC nor the US has actually signed the International Covenant on Civil and Political Rights and International Covenant on Social, Economic and Cultural Rights; however, the State Council White Paper cites Chinese UN statements characterising these covenants as important steps in the progressive internationalisation of human rights.[8]

Stung by US Congressional criticism, the Chinese responded with the exaggeration that Americans are only interested in civil rights. In their passion for individualism the US apparently ignores 'collective rights' (*jiti quanli*), or 'group rights' (*qunti quanli*), and the rights of people to development in light of the history of colonialism and neo-colonialism. Chinese observers sometimes fail to acknowledge extant categories of group or collective rights within Western constitutional settings. At times it is as if they have forgotten that the language of national self-determination has its original roots in European diplomatic history, which antedates the modern history of the Third World struggle against colonialism. However, the Chinese are generally correct in their assertion that the PRC has signed more international conventions on human rights than has the US, and they are entitled to their somewhat inconsistent criticism of the American claim that the US federal government cannot sign these conventions for fear of violating the constitutional rights of state governments.[9]

Emphases within American discussion of human rights have varied within and between administrations, and the Chinese might acknowledge that the US State Department reporting does take into limited account social and economic rights relating to gender equality, labour law, religious and minority freedoms in its annual monitoring process. However, the State Department reporting process is not geared towards a comprehensive assessment of human rights performance in relation to a broadly defined focus on development, and its terms of reference do not effectively encompass the countryside where most of China's human beings live.

The Chinese government was predictably pointed in its response to the formal expression of concern of the UN Sub-Commission on Prevention of Discrimination and Protection of Minorities as to serious violations of human rights in the August 1989 resolution, 'Situation on China'. China protested great power violation of the principle of national self-determination and the related manipulation of normal voting procedure as a 'complete violation of the purposes of the United Nations Charter'.[10] Moreover, the Western theory, 'human rights are without state boundaries' (*renquan wu guojie*), allegedly reveals a hidden hegemonic agenda to reduce the principle of non-interference in the Third World, and the Western 'human rights offensive' (*renquan gongshi*) is merely a component of an ongoing strategy to erode the foundations of Chinese socialist society in the latest Cold War instalment of John Foster Dulles' 'peaceful evolution' (*heping yanbian*).[11]

The Chinese deplored the interpretation of the UN Charter and Universal Declaration of Rights in the US statement supporting the 40th anniversary of the 'Universal Declaration of Human Rights' in 1988.[12] Their rejoinders predictably challenged the US recognise the 'third generation' rights of peoples to national self-determination and development.[13]

In his UN Security Council speech of 31 January 1992, Premier Li Peng recapitulated these differences:

> Human rights and fundamental freedoms of the entire mankind should be universally respected. Human rights covers many aspects. They include not only civil and political rights, but also economic, social and cultural rights. As far as the large numbers of developing countries are concerned, the rights to independence, subsistence and development are of paramount importance.[14]

Dutifully repeating the logic of Deng Xiaoping's familiar exegeses on 'seeking the truth from the facts', Li Peng underscored the practical understanding of each country's human rights situation in relation to particular historical and national conditions. His insistence that human rights fall primarily within the sovereignty of each country is a point with which many traditional Western introductory international relations texts would not disagree.

While emphasising national differences Li, nevertheless, announced China's willingness to talk about universal definitions of specific human rights on the basis of the equality between sovereign states:

> It is neither appropriate not workable to demand that all countries measure up to the human rights criteria or models of one or a small number of countries. China values human rights and stands ready to engage in discussion and cooperation with other countries on an equal footing on the question of human rights.[15]

Li Peng's participation in this summit on the configuration of Security Council responsibilities was, in itself, an exercise in human rights international politics. In return for his participation, the PRC was assured that the Security Council would not explicitly assume responsibility for punitive active against Chinese human rights performance. The summit communique mentioned only a watered down commitment to human rights verification as integral to 'a wider effort to maintain international peace and security'.[16]

Whether or not the November 1991 paper represented a genuinely domestic timetable, or as Western observers have claimed, an opportunistic response to the concerns of the US Congress,[17] it was part of a continuing debate on human rights which had been raging in academic and political circles since the spring of 1990. Even in the less than auspicious circumstances of deep political anxiety over June 4th and the subsequent collapse of socialism in Eastern Europe and the former Soviet Union, the debate grew beyond the inconclusive ruminations of the 1980s. This debate formally cited the allegedly specious nature of Western human rights diplomacy but, at the same time, the Chinese government was urged to participate in international debate over the definition of internationally valid human rights. And while no one questioned the point that domestic human rights constituted a greater and more significant category of human rights than international human rights, there was still disagreement over the relative proportions of these categories, the correlation of domestic and international human rights contents and the extent of each country's international obligations in the protection of human rights in other countries.

Professor Xu Xianming, in a journal article on the international comparison of constitutionally endorsed basic rights to life, health and property, noted the steady emergence of world standards:

> Regardless of the many great differences between state systems, there is a common point in that [each] society is constituted in the same humanity. All these same human societies can generally seek common standards in the treatment of human beings. The inheritance and mutual absorption of [different] legal cultures is conceptually located in the same compassionate standard of common human need.[18]

Wuhan social scientist, Xu Goujin, more specifically cited six compulsory areas of direct or indirect international obligation whereby states may justifiably intervene within domestic jurisdiction to protect human rights as against the consequences of invasion, colonialism, international terrorism, genocide, racial segregation and slavery.[19]

In their approach to the distinctive ideological standards regarding human rights in particular states and external international development of common human rights standards, three members of the Jilin University Law School cited the relevance of 'seeking common ground while reserving differences' as the basis for creating international standards. These authors agreed that common standards relating to racial segregation and the treatment of prisoners of war had already emerged, but they also contended that requirements of democracy, which limit this international process of standardisation, are self-evidently progressive:

> each specific ideological standard has its own specially designated sphere of application. Outside this limited scope these standards would lose legitimacy. The substantive feature of the modern democratic spirit is to recognise and conform to the reality of cultural pluralism [*wenhuaduoyuan*].[20]

INTERNAL THEORETICAL HUMAN RIGHTS DEBATE

The Chinese historiography of Western human rights theory has always recognised the centrality and distinctiveness of the natural law tradition's contribution to the Western theory of human rights. While Chinese discussion has not always displayed an awareness of the different Western theories of natural law, it has highlighted the common political assumption that the natural law tradition transcended positive law to protect the rights of individuals. Particularly in the post-World War II era, such assumption has reinforced the notion of the individual not only as an object of international law but also as a legitimate subject with rights *vis-à-vis* states which are no longer the exclusive subjects of international law. Western historical interpretation has in turn emphasised the lack of a tradition of rights in China, as well as the gratuitous nature of rights as granted through the modern Marxist–Leninist state on the basis of an unreserved notion of positive law.

There is controversy in both Chinese and Western sinological study as to the extent to which there was in China's legal tradition any substantive equivalent to the natural law tradition. As discussed in Chapter 2, Chinese Marxist–Leninist scholars have highlighted the authoritarian dimensions of feudal society which stymied any notion of rights. Within Chinese academic and political circles there is also significant agreement that in European history, natural, or human rights (variously *xiran quan* and *tianfu renquan*, as distinguished from contemporary *ren quanli* under Chinese socialism) were progressively promoted by the bourgeoisie in national revolutions against the prevailing feudal social order of Europe.

Chinese analysis has also expressed well-known reservations alleging that the European human rights notion celebrated equality before the law in form only, and its real agenda presumed the protection of existing property rights and inequitable structures of political dominance by capital. More recent historiography has, with qualification, accepted an expansion of rights in bourgeois society's response to fascism, capitalism's expansion of material and technical forces, and its postwar response to socialism as manifest in the social welfare strategy to coopt the working class so as to insure social and economic stability.[21] While capitalist property rights in contrast to subsistence rights are still pivotal human rights in bourgeois society, Chinese Marxist–Leninists occasionally concede the possibility of expanding real workers' rights in the legislation of capitalist countries.

Western interpretation which does claim some degree of parallel anticipation of natural law within Chinese traditional society has focused on the seminal Confucian principle of *li* (decorum or rites), which presupposed a system of ethical norms as *a priori* to the law.

The eminent Sinologist, Joseph Needham recognised an element of natural law in the Chinese intellectual focus on *li* as it implied the ritual manifestation of what is right in society, and he notes that '...*li* was much more important for society than natural law was in Europe'.[22] Western sinology has stressed the relationship between the manifestation of *li* in human society and the cosmological immanence of virtue; however, as discussed in Chapter 2, *li*, in its focus on hierarchical familial relations, provided no support for the universal enjoyment of rights. On the contrary, as ritual entered law it reinforced a complexity of distinctions in the law's ascriptive response to rank and status.

A leading PRC expert on Chinese legal history, Liang Zhiping, has challenged the comparison of *li* with natural law. Conceding that rulership combined *li* and *fa* in an attempted resonance with a morally appropriate natural order of society and the cosmos, he objected to a conceptually loose comparison of the transcendence of Western natural law over positive law with the superiority of *li* in its convergence with *fa*:

> Natural law is a theory of justice. *Li* is a system of rules that were deduced from familial ethical relations. Natural law is a universal and abstract system. *Li* prescribes concrete rules; and it is part of existing law.[23]

For a long time, Western scholarship has exploited the political implications of the moral continuum of man, earth and heaven in the Chinese philosophical tradition. H.G. Creel identified the nature–man continuum as 'sinism'.[24] In discussing Chinese 'organic naturalism', Needham distinguished Chinese 'naturalists', whose investigations into the natural world resulted in 'proto-science', and 'phenomenalists', who projected the harmony and disorder of the natural world into human affairs.[25] Bodde and Morris used this same 'correlative cosmology' to explain the strong penal, and weak civil, nature of China's imperial law:

> The law was only secondarily interested in defending the rights – especially the economic rights – of one individual or group against another individual or group and not at all in defending such rights against the state. What really concerned the law...were all acts of moral or ritual impropriety or of criminal violence which seemed in Chinese eyes to be violations or disruptions of the total social order. ...a disturbance of the social order really meant, in Chinese thinking, a violation of the total cosmic order.[26]

Liang Zhiping associated the notion '*li* is natural law' with the writings of Needham and accepts the manifestation of 'organic naturalism' (*youji ziranzhuyi*) in traditional Chinese legal theory and practice as central to China's legal development; however, he claims to uncover paradoxical notions of nature in the comparison of European and Chinese philosophy. While in Europe, 'natural' really conveyed connotations of the divine and or reason, in China, the notion of *li* invoked the 'natural' feelings associated with familial bonds which were in resonance with the immanent virtue of the cosmos. Reason, in this scheme, was a part of nature within a meaningful cosmos, and behaviour which violated reason was, therefore, unnatural.[27]

Modern Chinese Marxist–Leninist scholarship, especially in its preoccupation with the dangers of feudalism, accepts that there was little basis in the Chinese legal tradition for the development of a modern notion of human rights, but it also interprets the modern socialist development of human rights in terms of a critical interaction with, and a transcendence over an imperfect, but historically progressive bourgeois theory predicated in European assumptions regarding natural law.

This international interaction provides some theoretical basis for the contemporary discovery of an historiographical continuum between Western and Chinese experience. Rao Fang, for example, discusses three generations of human rights, inclusive of the first generation, namely, the European human rights movement of the eighteenth century, the second generation represented in Marx's nineteenth century theory and practice and the third generation drawing on the post-World War II movement for national liberation and independence. Like many other reformers, Rao focuses on the contemporary relevance of China's strategy for economic reform. He links the development of human rights to new emphases on commodity economy and the related requirement of equality – both primary elements of modern development which were threatened by resurgent feudalism during the Cultural Revolution.

Recently, Li Buyun argued that the failure to acknowledge the existence of 'human entitlements' (*yingyou quanli*) would confound legal rights, which would become as 'water without a source' or a 'tree without roots'.[28] He agreed that, at least in form, human entitlements are similar to the natural rights sponsored in Western theory. Although he did not explicitly reference Kant, Li very much liked the European distinction between 'what is' and 'what ought to be'.

His Marxist analysis made a threefold distinction between human entitlements, which ought to be enjoyed, rights which are actualised in social transactions (*shiyou quanli*), and rights which are formalised in law (*fading quanli*). These distinctions purportedly flow from a professed Marxist inclination to distinguish materialism from idealism. While disassociating himself from bourgeois idealism which had so conveniently forgotten to materialise real rights in society, Li, nevertheless, highlighted the positive significance of ideals in society and the continuous correlation of such ideals with the law. In an extended research note in 1992, Li argued for a judicious balancing of the subjective and objective dimensions of law. His explanation of the dual nature of law recognises that law is both autonomous from, and yet reflects and reacts on, the material reality of society. In his view modern contemporary law had to a certain extent to be self-standing, but it was not to replace the norms of human behaviour. On the other hand, if it was only considered to be a reflection of extant human consciousness, it would be no more than a figure made of dough which could be remodelled at will.[29]

In his human rights theory, the modern state has to strive continuously to close the gap between human entitlements and actual rights which must not only achieve legal form through legislation but which must also be materialised in society. Li swiftly moved beyond a singular reliance on positive law to look at the correlation of law with the materialisation of rights in relation to an ethical conception of justice within both Chinese and foreign society:

> Law is a manifestation of justice. The nature of law requires equality before the law. Though this cannot be materialised in a society full of class confrontation, this particular ethical value of the law has played a great part in safeguarding human basic values and dignity over a thousand years of Chinese and foreign history....[30]

Noting that formal legislation of human rights is much easier than the actual naturalisation of rights, Li emphasised that the creation of actual rights, as legal rights, has to correlate with several decisive factors relating to a country's level of political democratisation, including the extent to which commodity production has been developed, the general level of socio-economic and cultural development, and the degree to which the idea of legality and consciousness of human rights has taken hold in society and politics. On this last point, Li underlined the importance of the attitude of national leaders.

Li's ideas were featured at the Chinese Academy of Social Sciences' human rights symposium in June 1991. Quite a few of the participants readily agreed that human entitlements reflect human society's pursuit of ideals, but others predictably argued that human rights should only be identified with actual rights, or those rights which people actually enjoy.[31]

Symposium participants were divided as to whether the emphasis should be on the continuous legislative attempt to recognise human rights ideals or whether human rights can only come from existing law. It is rather extraordinary that even in the context of the official condemnation of the dissident physicist, Fang Lizhi, for his advocacy of 'universally applicable human rights', some participants continued to emphasise the universality, as distinct from the class nature, of human rights.[32] Indeed, during the Cultural Revolution, intellectuals had suffered intense persecution for alledgedly subscribing to the 'theory of human nature'. The latter had erroneously presupposed that at least some human qualities could transcend class distinctions.

Not surprisingly, those who preferred to narrow the scope of human rights to existing law identified with the classical Marxist–Leninist argument against *tianfu renquan*, natural rights, which assumed the superiority of human rights over positive law. Chinese critics of natural law continued to stress that natural law neglects the class nature of human rights, and over-emphasises the rights of the individual.[33] Symposium participants significantly disagreed over the relative importance of the universal and class natures of human rights, but they endorsed the creation of a special research institute for the Marxist study of human rights theory.

Chinese Communist historiography does not waste any time in recognising that the concept of rights was imported into revolutionary China. Western liberal ideas on individual freedom acquired some currency during the May Fourth era of the early 1920s, but the imported Soviet discussion of democracy, rights and obligations apparently had a much greater political impact in the Chinese revolutionary context.

The 1931 constitutional outline of the Chinese Soviet Republic distinguished political, economic, educational, women's and minority nationality rights, and 'political rights' included the right to participate in revolutionary struggle along with democratic freedoms of speech, assembly, publication, association and religious belief.[34] Referring to neither people nor citizens, it embraced the class language of the international struggle struggle against capitalism, and spoke of the universality of the political rights of the labouring masses who, under Article 16, included foreigners working in China.[35]

The early 1940s Chinese human rights regulations of the North China Communist base areas bridged what Professor Rao Fang and many others have referred to as the 'second' and 'third generations'. Professors Zhang Guangxin and Shi Peixing cite the 'Shandong Provincial Regulations concerning Human Rights Protection' (1940), the 'Temporary Regulations of the Jinjiluyu Border Region concerning the Guarantee of People's Rights' (1941), and the 'Shanganning Border Region Regulations for the Guarantee of Human and Property Rights' (1942) as the antecedents of a more impressive development which occurred with the post-1949 creation of socialist public ownership.[36]

Zhang and Shi noted that legislative development of domestic ideas of human rights within each national sphere is connected with a larger process of development at the international level, but they persisted in the typical assumption that a wider domestic materialisation of rights is more likely under socialism rather than capitalism. While in the US money is still 'the breast milk of politics', China is self-consciously attempting to transform 'human entitlements' (*yingran quanli*) into actual and legal citizens' rights.

While Chinese Marxist–Leninist theory presumes a wider materialisation of human rights under socialism, human rights, *per se*, are not described in any of China's post-1949 constitutions. The 1954 state constitution dropped the dated republican constitutional reference to *guomin*, 'national or citizen', to use *gongmin*, 'citizen', and it featured a new reference to 'citizen's basic rights' (*gongmindi jiben quanli*). It was the latter formulation which was incorporated into all subsequent constitutional documents.[37]

Xu Zhongde, a well-known constitutional expert and member of the Hong Kong Basic Law Drafting Committee, resorted to conventional Chinese Marxist theoretical assumptions to explain away the lack of formal constitutional reference to human rights:

> China's constitutions and laws do not use the expression, 'human rights', but 'citizens rights' is used. This 'human rights' requires some precision. Because in class society, 'human' is generally divisible into classes, it is not abstract and it does not supersede classes. In reality, since the 19th Century, excluding the Declaration of the Rights of Man and other political declarations, few capitalist countries used the expression 'human rights' in their constitutions, and in constitutional law they determined the rights of citizens. During early capitalism's struggle with feudal autocracy 'human rights' took on the form of citizen's rights. As this was everywhere the case under capitalist constitutional law, it is no surprise that the expression, human rights, is not used in China's constitution and citizen's basic rights which is used in China's constitution is a scientific concept.[38]

In the pre-1989 discussion of human rights there was only a very circumspect application of the term to China. If it was used at all, it often explicitly connotated citizen rights as these were specifically explained in the Constitution. The *Beijing Review* repeated a *Guangming ribao* commentary which simply regurgitated traditional perspective:

> But compared with those in capitalist countries, these rights in a socialist country with a different social system have at least two fundamental characteristics. One is that, in capitalist countries, the sacredness and inviolability of private property are the most basic rights of the citizen, while the Chinese Constitution stipulates that 'socialist public property shall be inviolable' and 'citizens must take care of and protect public

property.' The other is that citizen's rights in China are actual and not nominal.[39]

The new 1990s focus on human rights has often been rationalised in a more rigorous theoretical emphasis on commodity economy, and the emphasis on public ownership, while still explicit, has become comparatively less pronounced. Furthermore, whereas, in the past, it was enough to suggest that any positive content of human rights was rolled into citizens' rights, even this equivalence can no longer be taken for granted. Human rights gained recognition and in some cases were acknowledged to supersede the category of citizens' rights. Li Buyun, for example, disassociated himself from the 'popular view' that 'human rights are citizens' rights'. In his opinion, this formulation excludes refugees, foreign nationals and persons without nationality from enjoying human rights in China.[40]

'Citizens' rights' (*gongmin quanli*), or 'citizens' fundamental rights' (*gongmin jiben quanli*), usually include groupings of political, economic, cultural and personal rights. Political rights include the rights to elect and be elected and freedoms of speech, assembly, publication, demonstration, procession and association. The Chinese literature is not always clear, but freedom of religious belief and practice as well as the right to education presumably come under 'cultural rights'.

Chinese analysis emphasises the Western distinction between 'substantive' and 'procedural rights', both of which come under citizens' rights, and up until very recently has been extremely hostile to 'rights over things'. Allegedly, such preoccupation seriously jeopardised the bourgeois, as distinct from the socialist, attempt to achieve real equality before the law. 'Personal rights' (*renshen quanli*), in the Western context, popularly come under 'political' or 'civil rights'.

In China, this subcategory had always received constitutional attention, but it received special attention in light of the Cultural Revolutionary experience wherein many people's personal rights to privacy of home and correspondence were grossly violated, and there were illegal detentions, unlawful searches and personal attacks or libellous denigration of the personal dignity of individuals. The importance of legal procedure in the protection of the inviolable person was stressed by a CCP leadership which had first-hand experience of 'great democracy' and the kangeroo justice of uncontrolled mass organisations. Peng Zhen, in his reaffirmation of entwined socialist legality and socialist democracy reminded the entire leadership:

> Many comrades present must have tasted what it was like to be in the hands of Lin Biao and the 'gang of four'. In those days, Lin Biao could freely have a chairman of the state arrested. He could hurt party

> committee vice-chairman, secretaries-general, and so forth..... He could freely punish anyone, search anyone's house, detain anyone, arrest anyone, imprison anyone, frame anyone, slander anyone, torture anyone and kill anyone.... Everything culminated in an attempt on Chairman Mao's life. It may be asked: Without a legal system, how could democracy exist? This is what Lin Biao and the 'gang of four', our teachers by negative example, taught us.[41]

The rights associated in the 1975 and 1978 constitutions with the Cultural Revolutionary *sida*, 'speaking out freely, airing views fully, holding great debates and writing big-character posters', were initially construed as useful democratic means for countering Cultural Revolution 'great democracy',[42] but, in Deng Xiaoping's amendment dropping the *sida* from the constitution, they were inversely associated with the violation of 'personal rights', particularly the person's right to reputation.

Similarly, the inclusion of the following new and apparently imprecise wording of Article 38 in the 1982 State Constitution was the result of an evolving reaction to the violation of person in the Cultural Revolution: 'The personal dignity of citizens of the People's Republic of China is inviolable. Insult, libel, false charge or frame-up directed against citizens by any means is prohibited.'[43] This article together with Article 37 prohibiting unlawful detention and unlawful search of person and Article 39, prohibiting unlawful search of a citizen's home, reflected a more determined political attempt to entrench personal rights, as against the arbitrary interference of misguided positive law which arises with 'personality cult'.[44] This emphasis may conflict with the more customary focus on rights as exclusively granted by the state, for 'personal rights' had to be made to survive the vagaries of particular leadership regimes.

Article 41 of the 1982 Constitution similarly featured the issues of 'libel', 'frame-up' and the 'infringement of the citizen's civic rights by any state organ or functionary' in its emphasis on people's 'supervision' of state administration. Citizens were to enjoy the right to criticise, to make suggestions and formally to charge any state organ or functionary with 'violation of the law' or 'dereliction of duty', but this article contained a double warning. Citizens were warned against the malicious 'frame-up' of cadres, and the latter were warned not to retaliate against complaining citizens.

The promulgation of the general principles of civil law in 1986 generated new political interest in resolving the contradictory tension between the mass media's role of 'supervision by public opinion' which is to serve as a check on arbitrary and illegal state administrative acts and infringement of the citizen's right to reputation. Article 130 of the new civil law allowed for the naming of newspaper and magazine publishers in libel suits. Reporting on the approximately 200 lawsuits in 1988 against the media the Director of the General Office of the Supreme People's Court, Zhou Daoluan, spoke of the need for judicial work to respond to 'unprecedented social phenomena [which] have occurred in the new historical period', and Huang Jie, Chief Judge of the Administrative Division of the Supreme Court called for the acceleration of legislation on journalism.[45]

While the personal rights of the *gongmin*, or 'citizen' had presumably acquired a distinctively socialist connotation in light of the transition to socialism and the supercession of both the traditional notion of 'subject', *chenmin*, and the nationalist or republican revolutionary constitutional idea of *guomin*, or citizen/national, it is a category of rights which was made available even to the 'class enemy'. PRC constitutional law has always provided for the deprivation of the political rights of the class enemy, but it never has stipulated the deprivation of 'personal rights' as part of sentencing. However, 'personal rights' as a subset of 'citizen's rights' are possibly liable to derogation in light of constitutional requirement, as stipulated in Article 51 of the current state constitution underwriting the state's ability to suspend certain individual's 'rights' in order to protect 'interests of state', collective welfare and the exercise of rights by other citizens.

Indeed, it is widely suspected in the West that the PRC's constitutional rhetoric has only granted rights so as to reinforce the individual's service or contribution to the state and society and that, in reality, the emphasis is overwhelmingly on the 'obligations' of citizenship towards the ideological goals set by the Party.

The 1982 constitution, however, signaled a new and qualitative political concern with 'rights' by bringing forward rights and obligations content, shifting it from Chapter Three to Chapter Two of the Constitution. If the 1982 Constitution is compared with the radical 'leftist' constitution of 1975 'obligation' received more priority in 1975 as compared to 1982. The evolving political reaction to the Cultural Revolution led to a stronger theoretical emphasis on 'rights' within the 'unity of rights and obligations' as well as corresponding legislative initiative.

THE EARLY 1990s THEORY OF THE 'UNITY OF RIGHTS AND OBLIGATIONS'

The notion of the unity of rights and obligations was at bottom a European conceptual import, and it was enshrined in the 1923 and 1946 Republican state constitutions; however, the imported concept has always had a Chinese spin in its interpretation. In the dialectics of the CCP, constitutional rights and obligations inevitably come in pairs such as the right and obligation to work and to receive education. 'Rights' are conceived within the 'unity of rights and obligations' (*quanli yiwu yizhixing*, or *quanli yiwu xiang tongyi*). This dialectical relation, although always justified in Marxist terms revealed a certain logic which sometimes roughly parallels Western social contract theory's view of legitimacy and political obligation. Li Buyun, for example, wrote in 1981 that freedom was guaranteed in a protective obligation and that legally restrictive limits on freedom would guarantee citizens a more real and extensive enjoyment of freedom:

> Only through the realisation of the unity between right and obligation can we establish, consolidate, and develop public ethics, public order and public interests and it is only on this basis that we can protect each citizen in the full enjoyment of the individual's political freedoms. Social order is a basic condition of the citizen's enjoyment and realisation of political rights and freedoms. In a case where there is absolute democracy and freedom and non-observance of law there is the appearance but not the substance of freedom.[46]

Not surprisingly, this central perspective on the unity of rights and obligations was reiterated in the regime's formal reaction to the allegedly violent student demonstrations in Tiananmen Square. Hence the advocacy of absolute democracy in the Square allegedly resulted in the unthinking neglect of the citizen's legal obligations, the infringement of rights to personal security and destruction of state property and the violation of state interests in the disruption of a critically important state visit by President Gorbachev.

The Chinese dialectical notion of the unity of rights and obligations originated in a reading of Soviet Marxist–Leninist theory. This unity or dialectical synthesis theoretically represented a more genuine relationship between the individual and state as distinct from the destructive antithesis of the individual and state under capitalism which allegedly negates the true social interests of the individual. The Chinese, in the past, closely followed Marx's argument in 'On the Jewish Question' which attacked the 'rights of man' as distinct from the 'rights of the citizen'. The 'rights of man', according to Marx, were actually the 'rights of egoistic man, of man separated from other men and from the community'.[47]

Unlike in bourgeois society, where individual interests and state interest are dissociated and mutually contradictory, given the supremacy of capital and the resulting inequality before the law, under socialism, rights are to be actually materialised, and the labouring masses supposedly will freely perform obligations to their own state, which sustains their actual enjoyment of rights. In contrast to the alleged inherent inequalities of capitalist ownership, workers under socialism would genuinely enjoy both the right and obligation to work.

On this inseparability of rights and obligations the frequently cited Soviet theorist and defender of Stalin's state constitution, Andrei Vyshinsky, for example, had focused attention on Engels' editing of the draft of the Erfurt programme. Engels changed 'for the equal right of all' to 'for the equal rights and equal obligations of all', for, as he stated: '"*Equal obligations*" are for us a particularly important addendum to bourgeois–democratic *equal rights*, an addendum removing the specifically bourgeois meaning of the latter.'[48]

A contemporary interpretation of such theory by researchers at the NPC's Legal Work Committee predictably argued that human rights under capitalism have to be understood from the point of view of the total sum of productive relations, and that under capitalist theory citizen's rights, inclusive of the freedoms of speech, press, assembly and voting, were brought together with private rights, particularly the private ownership of property, to constitute human rights. In so doing capitalism had sundered the proper relation between civil society and the state, and it then became incumbent upon socialism to create an authentic unity of 'civil man' (*shimin*) and the citizen of socialist society. Rather surprisingly, the authors neglected to insist upon the superiority of the state, and they seemed to place the state and the autonomous development of contemporary society on an equal footing within their own particular unity.[49]

The State Council formally turned, in November 1991, to the unity of rights and obligations in its white paper on human rights. This document clearly stated: 'Legally citizens are the subjects of both rights and duties'.[50] Whereas in the pre-1989 period there was official hesitancy to endorse human rights, the 1991 white paper was disingenuous in its proclamation: 'Since the very day of its founding, the Communist Party of China has been holding high the banner of democracy and human rights'.[51] The white paper also confirmed that the 'right of subsistence' (*shengcun quan*) is the most important human right.[52]

This statement was a watershed in that it represented the first formal adaptation to the terminology of human rights, but much of the underlying argument merely coopted the past logic of citizen's rights. The white paper claimed that Chinese human rights have 'three salient features', namely 'extensiveness' – both in terms of the wider popular enjoyment of rights and in the wider scope in the contents of rights which range across subsistence, personal and political, economic, cultural and social and individual and collective rights – 'equality', by which citizens enjoy 'all civic rights equally irrespective of money and property status as well as of nationality, race, sex, occupation, family background, religion, level of education and duration of residence', and 'authenticity' in that the state '...provides guarantees in terms of system, laws and material means for the realization of human rights'.[53]

Even given the official endorsement of continuity in the rationale for rights, the early 1990s' debate on the relation between rights and obligations was clearly contentious. An Hangzhou University law professor, Sun Xiaoxia, in an important *Zhongguo faxue* article, for example, subscribed to the conventional dialectical proposition that rights and obligations are mutually dependent conceptual categories but he also warned against two extremes, namely 'obligations only as fundamental' (*yiwuzhongxin shuo*), which he believed originated in feudalism's continuing attempt to negate modern democracy, and 'rights only as fundamental' (*quanli zhongxin shuo*). Sun stressed the greater dangers of 'obligation fundamentalism' and gave greater legislative priority to rights as a necessary correction to past fundamentalism.[54]

Professor Wei Shaoying also emphasised the generation of rights as appropriate to the modern development of Chinese socialist democracy, but he clearly rejected the textbook interpretation of 'no obligations without rights and no rights without obligations':

> Since there has been law in our country there has been the practice of obligation fundamentalism [*yiwubenweizhuyi*]. Even unto the present day this autocracy still exists. And we must, in striving for democratic politics, raise the people's rights awareness. If in theory we still consider rights as obligations then undoubtedly obligation fundamentalism will run all the more rampant, and in reality this is certainly not conducive to the establishing of our socialist democracy.[55]

In contemporary theory, obligation fundamentalism has been increasingly associated with the hierarchical features of pre-capitalist society. Zhang Wenxian, a Jilin university law professor, made the following astute observation:

> Generally speaking in pre-capitalist society the relative emphasis on obligation and right was handled on the basis of obligation as fundamental. Obviously, in terms of the politics, economics and thought of slave and feudal class society its primary, even its only value lies in the establishment of the dominant class order. Law in modern society is a

> mechanism which is full of vitality. ...it takes right as fundamental; it vests in the people various political, economic, cultural and social rights and it gives them a full range of ever expanding opportunities of choice and a freedom of action. At the same time so as to insure the materialisation of rights, [modern law] establishes a series of relevant obligations. Obviously the value of modern law, particularly socialist law is not limited to order.[56]

Typically, Chinese debate refuses to place rights and obligations in exclusive opposition. The two sides remain in familiar dialectical tension; however there is continuing controversy since June 4 as to which side of this dialectic should receive the primary emphasis. The trend, particularly in light of continuing official focus on economic reform and growing public and Party concern over the pervasiveness of official corruption, has given relatively new emphasis on rights so as to compensate for a past imbalance.

Party debate on 'rights' and four proposed laws including the press law, the publication law, the association law, and the assembly and procession law, reflected competing assessment of the relative weight and requirements of State Constitutional Articles 35 and 51, detailing personal and political freedoms and the State's powers of derogation, and of the counterpoint between advocates focusing on the past abuse of rights and those who asked how the people might exercise their legitimate rights under Article 41 of the State Constitution so as to administer the state as the 'masters of the country'.[57]

A *Renmin ribao* editorial comment identified and critiqued three distinct positions on control and public order, empowerment of the people, the dominance of rights over obligation and the simultaneous and equal emphasis on guaranteeing rights and improving administration. Those who supported rights to the neglect of obligation were faulted for ignoring the importance of improving state administration so as to safeguard rights in practice and for their preference for declaration as distinct from well-thought-out law: 'It is well known that declarations are different from laws. The basic contents of laws refer to the rights and duties of interested parties, while declarations refers to rights'.

Referring to a groundswell of opinion favouring 'guaranteeing the basic rights', the *Renmin ribao* commentator preferred to emphasise the clear definition of both rights and obligations and within the synthesis of guaranteeing the basic rights and improving administration the former was sanctioned as primary:

> If we work out articles of the laws taking [guaranteeing the basic rights] as the guiding ideology, the laws are also likely to turn into empty

> declarations, if we fail to deal with the relevant problems properly. ...it is necessary to take 'guaranteeing the basic rights' and 'improving administration' into account, but the latter should serve the purpose of the former. In essence all these laws deal with constitutional rights for the people and specific articles regarding the protection of citizen's rights in these respects should be enacted according to Article 35 of the Constitution. It is likewise necessary to hammer out articles to restrain citizens from violating the duties [i.e., the obligations] stipulated in Article 51 of the Constitution. But it should be clearly understood that the articles to 'improve management' are drawn out for effecting the overall objective of 'safeguarding the basic rights'. We should not separate 'improving management' from 'safeguarding the basic rights.'[58]

The emphasis on rights declarations offended some Party leaders, who reacted against any parallel with Western human rights declarations, whereas the synthesis of rights and management embraced a familiar dialectical approach as well as mass-line perspective on the importance of improving management. Certainly, moderate reformers attempted to negotiate the concerns of Conservative opponents by coopting the middle ground between democracy and rights, and efficient state administration.

As for the State Constitution's Chapter Two fundamental rights relating to the freedoms of press, publication, assembly, process and demonstration, there have been significant internal debates, but legislative progress has, in some areas, been delayed largely due to the vicissitudes of politics. A press law was first proposed in 1980, and the pre-June 4 debate on the draft press law precipitated unprecedented consideration of the Party's orthodox theory of the press as well as debates over how to guarantee freedom of the press and whether or not to include a press law and publication law within an omnibus legislative package.[59]

Reformers extended the notion of the mass line and people's supervision in light of growing emphases on democracy and corruption. Some pushed for the independent commercialisation of the press. Others, ignoring orthodox emphasis on obligations and the need for the press to protect and enhance the interests of the state and society, argued for a more arms-length relation between press and government which would allow for authentic supervision of government by the people through more critically objective investigative reporting and critical editorialising.

Advocates of press freedom such as Hu Jiwei, Renda authority on journalism and member of the NPC Standing Committee, put an interesting twist on Conservative concern for stability and order by arguing that the democracy which results from greater press freedom and the mutual understanding between people and government could forestall 'any abrupt explosion of extreme feelings'.[60] There were at least three drafts of a press law circulating before the 'explosion' of June 4, and the subsequent timing of the press law was influenced by post-Tiananmen Square politics.[61] Unlike in the case of the law on assembly, procession and demonstration, where there was a decision to go ahead regardless of expected criticism of the law as a knee-jerk reaction to the Tiananmen 'turmoil', there has been a delay in the legislation of press law. There is a growing post-1989 interest in publication law, but the right of creative freedom has received less political attention than illegal books and obscenity and pornography, which allegedly threaten to corrupt the moral values of youth and undermine the integrity of 'socialist spiritual civilisation'.

The right of association was tentatively addressed in October 1989 State Council regulations regarding the registration of social organisations, which, according to Fan Baojun, Deputy Minister of Civil Affairs, were designed to 'define the legal rights of social groups as well as involving them in China's socialist construction'. Formally, these regulations were supposedly to bridge the citizen's right of association and the state's responsibility for the legal administration of public organisation.[62] Given the imperial history of *baojia* and the contemporary mass-line organisational preference for a party-controlled united front, one may well suspect an ongoing trend which is conceptually rooted in a deep need for harmony in society. The current regulations await more specific administrative regulations to detail the rights and obligations of social organisations and the lawful relation between them and the state.

The regulations focused on the legal recognition through the registration and review of the qualifications of national and an estimated 100 000 local-level social organisations. This was the first major step in checking improper organisational dependence upon state funding, the revival of secret society organisation and the spontaneous development of illegal organisations such as the Autonomous Student Union of Beijing Universities which, in Tiananmen Square, defied the Party's unified leadership over mass organisation and allegedly caused 'severe damage to the State and the party'.[63]

The new 36-article Law on Assembly, Procession and Demonstration, after drafting and re-drafting since the path-breaking third session of the CCP's Eleventh Plenum in December 1978, was actually promulgated on 31 October 1989. An early draft of 24 articles was initially circulated for solicitation of public opinion in accordance with a NPC Standing Committee decision in July 1989. It was circulated despite reformer opposition which worried lest the draft law's emphasis on citizen's rights suffer in the immediate political reaction to Tiananmen Square.[64] There was heated debate within legal circles as to how best to strike the right balance in its provisions between guaranteeing and restricting, or guaranteeing citizen's rights while maintaining the interests of the state and society as stipulated in the principles of the Constitution which still include legally controversial reference to the 'four cardinal principles'.

Song Rufen, Vice-Chairman of the NPC Law Committee, claimed that the original draft wording of Article One was strengthened so as to place mention of the protection of citizen's rights to rally and demonstrate before mention of the maintenance of public order.[65] The new law conforms with a strict reading of the derogatory powers of the state as outlined in Article 50 of the State Constitution, and this is the main substantive concern of the US State Department's rather cursory reporting on this law.[66] The law included ten restrictive provisions regarding the aim, mode, sponsor, time and place of conduct. Chinese analysis once again presumed: 'Only by restricting the illegitimate is it possible better to safeguard the legitimate because they complement each other'.[67] And this position certainly reflects the past tendency to give priority to obligation in the unity of rights and obligations.

The revised final draft included in Article 15 of its second chapter a clear interdiction of citizen participation in demonstrations in localities where they are not resident, and probably emerged out of specific consideration of the politics of Tiananmen Square.[68] Out-of-town student organisers had, despite Beijing student reluctance, taken a hard line in protracting the anti-government demonstrations in the Square. Similarly, the declaration of specific sites such as Great Hall of the People, Zhongnanhai, State Council, Diaoyutai guest quarters for visiting dignitaries, Party headquarters and national airport as off-limits to would-be demonstrators likely emerged from the immediate consideration of the June 4 exigencies. The supplementary Beijing municipal regulations of 28 December 1989, which replaced the 1986 interim provisions on demonstrations, required approvals of both the Beijing municipal government and the State Council for future demonstrations in Tiananmen Square.[69] This special attention reflected the Square's extraordinary symbolic status in the history of the revolution.

Furthermore, new revised reference in Article 32 to legal liability for the payment of damages to public or private property caused during excessively violent demonstrations probably reflected official exasperation with the allegedly wanton destruction of public property during the Tiananmen Square 'turmoil'.[70]

The theoretical issue of disturbances, as in the case of strikes or public demonstration, has always posed an uncomfortable issue as to the proper response of a revolutionary and socialist regime to explicit and public disagreement with the government. Originally, Mao's theory had underlined the continuing relevance of contradictions among the people and between the people and the class enemy under socialism. Theoretically, there is greater possibility of healthy public disagreement with the government under socialism as opposed to capitalism. On the other hand, the need for vigilance against counterrevolution in a hostile international environment had for a long time conflicted with this focus on socialist democracy.

While, in theory, a Marxist regime should fearlessly accept the expression of democracy which comes with non-antagonistic contradictions among the people, such phenomena was often treated within Chinese praxis as if it constituted a fundamental challenge to law and order and to the regime itself. Politically, the Cultural Revolution generated a lasting concern over the need to protect rights as against rule of man. The Party leaders' own personal loss of reputation in the Cultural Revolution had become an extremely important motivating factor in legal reform. Rights had, therefore, to be put out of the reach of individual leaders. Ye Jianying had emphasised this very point in his report on the constitution of 1978:

> The people must have the right to manage the superstructure; we must not interpret the question of the people's rights to mean that only under the administration of certain people can the masses enjoy the right to work, the right to education, the right to social insurance, etc. [Mao] also taught us that, under the socialist system, the right of the working people to manage affairs of state, ...is their supreme and fundamental right, without which they can enjoy neither the right to work, nor the right to education and rest, nor any other right.[71]

Even in the context of post-Tiananmen Square reaction, the politics of the Cultural Revolution played a role in controversies over how the new law would dialectically synthesise protection and restriction, rights and obligations and democracy and the legal system. In trying to push back the parameters of reform, agile reformers politically tapped official mass-line perspective on work style and claimed that democracy could promote order.

Tan Hongkai's reporting of the official rationale regarding the law on assembly, procession and demonstration is especially revealing in its sensitive perception of socio-psychological dimensions of democracy and order. The new law reportedly could fill a democratic need when other channels fail to bring the people's complaints to the attention of government, and hence demonstrations can 'function as "safety valves" of society, letting out resentment and preventing negative moods'.[72]

Tan's assessment frankly acknowledged that out of 500 applications to demonstrate between 1986 and spring 1989 only eight were sanctioned by the Ministry of Public Security; however, he argued that this was not axiomatically the suppression of the right to demonstrate. In his view, the low rate of actual demonstration indicated a positive preference for preemptive mediation. Tan believed that the involved state agencies came under a salutary pressure to assuage the offended parties once they were informed of an application to the Ministry of Public Security to demonstrate, and this explains Chapter Two, Article 10 of the new law requiring initial public-security-vetted consultations between applicants and government departments. Mediation is integral to Chinese political culture and, typically, it is preferred to explicit confrontation involving overt legal challenge; however, external critics are more likely to regard any instance of administrative reconsideration as an anti-democratic stratagem designed to curtail public scrutiny of state administration and the freedom of expression.

The extent to which any discrete issue becomes a matter of public order is the measure of its related political sensitivity. Even apparently modest issues of social welfare can be interpreted in terms of direct confrontation with a regime which has a low threshold of tolerance for disturbances. According to Tan's citation of public security statistics, most of the applications related to individual issues relating to housing, employment conditions, wages, professional titles and household registration but the implications of these applications are sometimes construed in dramatic correlation with the legitimacy of state administration and the socialist state which currently has so much riding on the material improvement of living standards.

While there was formal subscription to the unity of rights and obligations, the new legal provisions on the nature and content of demonstration insured the priorities of public security, the prevention of counterrevolution and the centrality of obligation. Public Security authorities would have sweeping powers of interpretation under Article 12, Chapter Two, which precluded the authorisation of any assemblies, processions or demonstrations which violate basic constitutional principles, endanger national unification, sovereignty or territorial integrity, instigate national separation or undermine public order. And, under Article 8, same chapter, 'sponsors' would have to, in writing five days prior to a planned activity, indicate the placards and slogans which they intended to use.

Citizens, were, however, formally accorded the right of appeal against an unfavourable decision to the local municipal government.

One important area of legislative initiative which has been quite neglected in Western human-rights monitoring and assessment of pre- and post-June 4 development is the new Administrative Litigation Law (also translated as Law of Administrative Procedure) which was allowed to come into effect even in the wake of the 'turmoil'. China's reformers were well aware of the conflicting requirements of order and democracy in this law's treatment of rights and obligations. As well, they were aware of the new law's tenuous relation to long-established principles of state organisation. While there was in Chinese imperial and contemporary history a time-honoured precedent for appealing to political leaders to redress wrongs done to aggrieved individuals and families – and some Western observation has stressed that this negated the development of legal recourse – there was almost no precedent for redress through the suing of government officials.

Professor Pitman Potter has, in his edited translation of the new Administrative Litigation Law, described the political significance of its enactment just after June 4 as 'a major effort to use judicial institutions to control bureaucratic conduct'. While Potter demonstrates a keen awareness of the loopholes in this law and cites progressive internal criticism of those regulations still requiring 'administrative reconsideration' (*xingzheng fuyi*) before the filing of suit, he is fairily impressed with the new direction of the law, noting that for the first time it has brought 'virtually all administrative agencies of government within the jurisdiction of the courts as administrative defendants'.[73]

RIGHTS AND OBLIGATIONS UNDER ADMINISTRATIVE LAW

The mainland authorities began to institute a system of administrative law in 1982 in light of the new constitution's requirements for the people's supervision of state administration. In December 1986 the Ministry of Supervision, which had been disbanded in 1959, was re-established as the Party focused on the pervasive problem of official corruption and the need to improve state administration. In the same year the process of researching and drafting a new administrative procedural law was initiated. The authorities followed the Continental tradition of creating separate courts of administrative law.

In early 1987 administrative law tribunals were established in the intermediate courts of several major cities including Nanjing, Shenzhen,

Shanghai and Wuhan. In the jointly authored study of the new administrative division, Gong Xiangrui underscored the importance of using administrative law in the restricting of power; and he seemingly paraphrased Lord Acton's famous dictum: 'Power without restriction absolutely leads to corruption. This is a law of political science'.[74] Gong's report on the initial stages in five of the eight cities emphasised what were to become constant thematic reservations, namely, the lack of qualified personnel and the vexatious refusal of many government departments to appear in court.

The Administrative Litigation Law, promulgated on 4 April 1989, was, together with the Law on Criminal Procedure and the Civil Procedural Law, hailed as one of the three most important pillars of China's procedural law. The administrative, as distinct from the civil, lawsuit was welcomed as it provided for a broader categorisation of official violation of rights and a new remedy through compensation. Politically, it was rationalised as part of a legal reform strategy to combat corruption and the 'will of the individual', as connotated in 'rule of man', (*renzhi*), and to break through the wall of traditional thinking which presumed that legal punishment does not apply to high-ranking officials. Theoretically, all state agencies were brought under the jurisdiction of the courts.

In a dramatic break from tradition as well as contemporary organisational experience, the new law formally provided new legal recourse in light of official failure to act lawfully to protect citizen's personal and property rights. The deliberately restricted scope of the law still exposed administrative action to legal challenge permitting cases relating to legally improper administrative detainment and confinement, or education through labour, and improper administrative punishments resulting in property losses due to the imposition of fines, cancellation of licences, halting of production, and confiscation or freezing of assets.[75]

The new law was to be a great contribution to both 'the safeguarding of human rights and stepping up rule by law', but it was accompanied with a caution that 'commoners can sue officials' should not be liberally interpreted as 'citizens may file lawsuits against anything'.[76] Indeed, Article 12 expressly excluded lawsuits in four areas relating to 'acts of state' concerning national defence and diplomacy, abstract administrative deeds enforced through regulations, decisions concerning the punishment, appointment and dismissal of personnel and ultimate verdicts made by administrative organs as specified by law, such as decisions by the Copyright Reexamination Commission.

On 9 January 1990, the Supreme People's Procuratorate issued regulations clarifying the criteria for placing on file for investigation and prosecution cases of administrative infringement of citizen's democratic and personal rights and cases of dereliction of duty. Zhang Siqing, Deputy Procurator General, reported that over the preceding ten years procuratorial investigation had heard a total of 283 000 cases of infringement of rights and dereliction of duty, which had resulted in 80 000 cases placed on file for prosecution. The criteria were published to promote awareness as to the legality or criminality of administrative acts. Citizens were to have a better idea of when they could 'use the law as a weapon to protect their legitimate interests', and state functionaries would have a clearer idea of the line between legitimate and illegal administrative actions.[77]

Even during the Conservative backlash following Tiananmen Square the Party and legal reformers were still able to focus on a new status for administrative law. This law was now expected to rise above the mundane level of planned relations between state agencies to consider improving the democratic operation of state administration so that it could then truly serve the people and challenge the 'theory of law as a tool of administration' (*gongju lun*). Reform with its vigorous focus on rights consistently sought to disaggregate Administrative Law from Great Economic Law.

Wang Jiacheng and Zhao Aihua, for example, attacked anachronistic Soviet theory which emphasised that the consent of all parties involved in administrative law relations is not a precondition to administrative action. They challenged the assumption that the necessary nature of administration requires 'inequality', interpreting this viewpoint as a throwback to the 'highly centralised and rule-by-man administrative system' of the Stalinist planned economy.

Alternatively, they argued that all parties involved in new administrative relations must honour the law and that there should be no question of 'will subordination relations' (*yizhi fucong guanxi*) among different subjects engaged in administrative relations. State organs, mass organisations, social associations and individual citizens were all subjects with both rights and obligations under the principle of equality before the law.[78] Article Seven of the 1990 Administrative Litigation Law stipulated that the parties involved have equal legal status, but there is continuing academic argument over 'equal subjects' and the implications for the property rights of the state and state enterprise.

The civil law of the mid-1980s had already advanced a notion of legal person, and state organs could become *jiguan faren*, official legal persons, in cases involving the violation of the lawful rights and interests of citizens, but the civil concept of legal person had yet to be imported into administrative law. In light of the promulgation of administrative procedural law, administrative legal studies have focused on the substantive issue of the 'system of legal relations' (*falu guanxi tixi*) so as to ensure future precision in the definition of subjects engaged in administrative relations and their exact rights and obligations.[79]

The issue of how to perceive the liabilities of state administration came to the fore in light of discussion over whether state organs could be perceived as 'administrative legal person' (*xingzheng faren*) – a somewhat dubious status as they could then be sued by other subjects. Specific state organs would then acquire legally meaningful rights and obligations. They would no longer be exempt from lawsuits just because they happen to be a part of an abstract whole known as the state. Some scholars sought to create a Chinese equivalent to *gongfa ren*, public corporation in British administrative law, or *gongwu faren, les établissements publics* in French administrative law.[80] Under the new 1990 law, administrative organs, after having paid out compensation, were required to instruct the erring functionaries involved to meet some, if not all, of the damages.

The profound political and ideological implications of the 1990s debate on the development of administrative law is likely to effect the status of state administration. The development of judicial recourse may modify customary administrative dependence upon the Procurator General and Ministry of Supervision for a solution to rights infringement.

Under a notion of separation and combination of powers, as formalised in the principle of *fengong hezuo*, sharing of work and cooperation, state administration has hitherto been able to make law in regulatory exercises which are formally supplementary to the law-making of the NPC and its Standing Committee. Once the idea of making state organs administrative legal persons was broached, some scholars even argued that state administrative regulations could no longer serve as a supplementary legitimate basis for judicial review in administrative lawsuits. In his report on the new administrative law's promulgation, Wang Hanbin cautiously addressed instances of conflicting administrative regulation and legal statute by invoking the familiar Party principle of flexibility so as to insure the spirit of the law:

> In hearing cases, the courts may refer to regulations in conformity with law and administrative statutes. As for the regulations not or not completely in conformity with the spirit of the law, the courts may deal with them in a flexible way.[81]

Theoretically, the lawful and rational nature of administrative law was manifest in the conscious synthesis of the competing dialectical concerns explicit in the various principles of 'separation of functions and [mutual] restriction' (*fenquan yu zhiyue*), 'democracy and efficient coordination' *minzhu yu jiaolu xietiao* [for improving state management]' and 'unity of the delegation of responsibility, [public] supervision and review' (*shouquan weituo yu jiandushencha tongyi*).[82]

Early 1990s' arguments related the development of administrative law to democratic reform emphases requiring both the separation of the Party and state and the separation of state enterprise from state administration. During NPC debate on the Administrative Procedural Law it was, for example, argued that, as the government is both owner and administrator of the means of the production, government could not carry out the law's provisions on property rights unless enterprises were freed from state management.[83] As discussed in Chapter 5, this question continued to attract controversy, but certainly the new law assigned new weight to property rights. Furthermore, the emphasis on the equality in court of foreigners and stateless persons was designed to attract foreign investment which seeks a secure domestic legal environment.

Argument over the political and legal position of state administration raised questions concerning the very foundations of the political system. It predictably touched off conservative anxiety over the apparent importation into China of the bourgeois theory of the 'separation of powers' (*sanquan fenli*) as distinct from Chinese theory of the 'unity of legislature and administration' (*huixing heyi*). Within the latter, 'the unity of rights and obligations' was supposedly guaranteed in a Chinese version of separation or differentiation of powers which provided intra-state administrative and judicial checks and balances. Orthodox theory defensively reiterated that, in the Chinese system of separating and combining legislative, administrative and judicial power, there is both a functional differentiation among legislative, administrative and judicial powers and a cooperative unity which insures the dominance of legislative power over administrative and judicial powers and the related materialisation of citizen's rights.[84]

In this theory too exclusive emphasis on administrative law as a democratic exercise deliberately circumscribing state administrative action neglects the central point that, in China, administrative power already belongs to the people, and that an ill-advised focus on limiting government may constitute an unwanted infringement on the people's rights. This discussion included highly suggestive comment on the inapplicability to China of so-called Western 'power control' (*kongquan*) theory. The latter allegedly obscured the degree of executive control over the legislature and judiciary, and the related rule of law notion which formally animates Western judicial independence and administrative law procedure was faulted for the undue weight given to the practical interests of the bourgeoisie.

The new administrative procedural law was not at all self-consciously revolutionary in approach, but its implications were far reaching. On the other hand, the people's courts were under stern interdiction not to interfere in administrative actions taken within the limits of the law.[85] While the courts could pronounce on changes to unfair administrative penalties, they were not empowered to determine changes to such penalties.[86] As for the request for damages or compensation, Wang Hanbin explained that these would be in the first instance handled by the administrative organs and only after would the wronged party have the right to lodge legal proceedings.

At the time of the law's promulgation there were clear indications of widespread concern over the historical tendency of state administration not to comply with the determinations of the people's courts. Wang Hanbin replied to reporters concerns over the potential enforcement of the law arguing that the political realities of legal illiteracy and consciousness required a gradual process of legal reform:

> We need to go through a gradual process to build the Chinese legal system. That some established laws are not strictly complied with is one of the major problems that we face. There is a historical reason for this, namely, China being a country which lacks democratic and legal traditions. Therefore, it takes time for the people to get accustomed to doing things according to law. ...It also takes time for people to get used to using the law to protect their legal rights and interests. That is why currently some people do not do things according to the law, and, as mentioned earlier why some administrative departments interfere in the enforcement of law.[87]

Also, in his view, the new law was not to be construed as a negative restriction on administrative departments; it was rather to improve state management according to law.

China's political leaders have always been aware of the problem of officials protecting officials. The popular rectification of cadres had always been a closely structured and selective process directed under the Party's own proper leadership. Now Wang believed that a lot depended upon the motivation of citizens, and he opined: 'In allowing common citizens to sue..., we must first change our traditional way of thinking, and consider how far we can go and the old traditions we have'.[88] Huang Jie of the Administrative Division of the Supreme Court added that some administrative organs were accustomed to seeing themselves as representatives of the State and viewed their appearance in court as a matter of public disgrace.[89]

This attitude paralleled imperial Confucian concern over the frequent resort to law resulting in a loss of shame and a challenge to the legitimacy of government which was supposed to be based upon the exemplary moral behaviour of officials. The related status-based exemption of imperial officials from criminal law punishment received considerable contemporary attention in light of growing public concern over corruption as the number one concern of contemporary politics. The new law reflected a growing political pressure to take officials to court.

Newspaper commentary on the new law elaborated on the continuing problem of the will of individuals, or in effect the rule of man. Feudal habits of mind, unquestioning deference to authority, the lack of a tradition of democratic involvement in politics, weak notions of rights and institutional ignorance of, and even deliberate and frequent circumvention of the law were all seen as working against the development of procedural law and the rule of law itself.[90] NPC debate reflected the classical dilemma as to whether to wait for the maturation of underlying social forces and related legal culture, or to assist in the aggressive creation of such culture by creating new law which would induce new social practice. Conservative opinion did not hesitate to cite China's backwardness and the lack of rational unity, or harmonisation with existing regulation. Such opinion, in fact, attempted to coopt concern over the lack of legal consciousness and culture to delay the new legislation.

Advocates of administrative law reform, on the other hand, successfully argued that the procedural law had first to be legislatively established so that there would be an opportunity for routine practice and a more meaningful and extensive public educational process, and so that the existing 130 laws and regulations allowing for suits against the government could be more significantly activated in substantive legal proceedings.[91] In short, citizens needed to witness the successful prosecution of state officials. Those who, in the subsequent debates of the early 1990s, subscribed to power control responded vigorously to suggestions that such a theory was necessarily inspired by Western bourgeois theory. The well-published scholar Yang Haikun pointed out the prevailing conditions of corruption within contemporary Chinese administration and counter-argued that Marxism itself had included emphasis on the people's management and supervision of state affairs.[92] Those in the middle wanted both the NPC delegation of power to state administration as well as power control or checks and balances so as to ensure democracy and rights, hence the position: 'There is no delegation of power without power control'.[93]

Although the new law has been recognised as one of the three pillars of procedural law it is of very recent vintage; it lacks an extensive institutional base; and its implications are politically volatile. Liu Fuzhi, in his 3 April 1991 report as Procurator General to the NPC, revealed a few precious, but typically undifferentiated statistics as to the practical operation of the Administrative Division of the People's Courts. By the end of 1990 all 30 of the high-level people's courts had established administrative law tribunals, and over 90 per cent of the middle-level and basic-level people's courts had likewise set up such tribunals. In 1990, 65 per cent of the 10 306 cases concerned public security administration and land administration. This 1990 case-load compared to 1 851 897 first-trial civil cases, 588 143 first-trial economic law cases, and 459 656 first-trial criminal law cases.[94]

CONCLUSION

'Marxism–Leninism Mao Zedong Thought' has, in theory, always allowed for critical borrowing from both China's past experience and foreign experience. In the post-Tiananmen Square period, the dangers of bourgeois liberalism and attendant Westernisation were constantly vilified in the Party press. There was also a strong ongoing focus on feudalism, and, even given the continuing Party's increasing emphasis on Chinese nationalism, China's imperial legal traditions have yet to serve as a significant source of inspiration for contemporary legal reform. Within the shifting lines of domestic political perspective there is substantive argument as to what is Westernisation and what is legitimate critical borrowing. The debate over the correlation of control theory with the separation of powers is a significant case in point.

While the concept of human rights has always been recognised as an import, and for a long time the Chinese simply refused to accept the term's validity in China's specific national and cultural context, the political decision was taken in 1990 to coopt and to sinify this terminology. Chinese human rights have been extensively adumbrated in a major white paper, and formal debate has reconsidered the relation between human rights and citizen's rights. This consideration may entail some adjustment to the latter as a closed 'scientific' category of rights. Even given the curious usage of feudalism in contemporary Chinese argument, the underlying substantive critique of China's political culture which animates concern for contemporary legal culture is wide-ranging and encouraging. Furthermore, rights, as distinguished from obligations, have received more legislative attention than at any other time since 1954, and there is growing legal and political awareness of the shortcomings of rights development and a perceived need to materialise rights in social, as well as formal legal, settings.

However, international recognition of, and external assessment of, the ramifications of the Chinese debate on human rights and the related legislative timetable has been painfully slow. Perhaps this is, in itself, a testimonial to the continuing strength of Cold War polemical analysis which is unreserved in its immutable assumption that socialist regimes are inevitably totalitarian, implacably hostile to any real notion of democratic opposition and, therefore, hopelessly incapable of advancing any notion of human rights at all. Such a baseline for comparative, or non-comparative, research ignores the complexity and the dynamic nature of the modern Chinese states as well as the extent to which economic reform has generated substantive political and legal change.

Obviously, there has been much less internal enthusiasm in post-1989 China for a systematic programme of political reform, or political re-structuring. There has been uneven progress in terms of national human rights policy and legislation, but in the Western media the Tiananmen Square event achieved the distorted proportions of an all encompassing historiographical interpretation which obscures substantive legal reform and the real underlying dimensions of change within contemporary Chinese society and politics.

The post-1989 emphasis on economic reform and the continuous development of new law relating to rights is likely to have deeper and more substantive political implications than what is commonly perceived in the Western human rights' monitoring. Even China's own Party leaders are hard-pressed to understand all of the implications of legal reform which is progressively challenging not only traditional ways of thinking but also orthodox understanding of the unity of rights and obligations and the relation of the state administration to the judicial process in the legislative and social guaranteeing of actual rights.

4 Civil Law and 'Civil Society' under a 'Socialist Rule of Law'?

Prior to the Tiananmen Square event, there was increasing speculation in the Western media as to emerging 'civil society' in the PRC. On the other hand, within China itself, there was a growing awareness of society's changing structure of interests (*liyi jie gou*), as well as related emphases on the rule of law and the civil law's response to the unfolding dimensions of commodity production in the new era of the primary stage of socialism.

There is continuing controversy as to what are the basic requirements of civil society in Western political theory. The late eminent historian, John K. Fairbank, traced the historical origins of such society to the rise of independent towns in the West European reaction to feudalism. Such a society, he suggests, is both democratic and pluralist. It reflects the separation of church and state and the legal development of civil liberties under the supremacy of law.[1]

Drawing from Weber and Habermas, a well-known sociologist, Martin Whyte, more elaborately set out the preconditions which gave rise to European civil society including the rule of law itself, as well as the creation of private property, 'a national market, an open stratification system, urban autonomy, mass education, competing bases for power among elites, and a large middle class'.[2] Fairbank often drew upon Chinese culture to interpret China for Americans, but he did not comment significantly on the CCP's notion of feudalism to explain the dilemma of the contemporary body politic.

In the following observation he was, however, explicit as to 'plainly recognizable continuities': 'The totalitarian claims of Leninism perpetuated the claims of the imperial autocracy. The Neo-Confucian doctrines as absolute truth were substituted by Marxism–Leninism, which was equally all-embracing and absolute.'[3] As a Sinologist, Fairbank always warned outsiders first to evaluate their own prejudicial assumptions as to the Chinese scene. His own conclusion, however, as to the post-Tiananmen 'Chinese movement toward civil society', was somewhat puzzling. The following suggests just how elastic this terminology is, even with respect to its essential core meaning:

> We may justifiably see the Chinese movement toward civil society as a historic trend without jumping to the conclusion that it must lead in China to the Western type of democracy with free elections, representative government and human rights guaranteed by law. On the contrary, a Chinese type of democracy might have, for example, elections within status groups, representation by consensus and within a peer group, with the individual's rights specified more narrowly than in the West.[4]

There appears to be some theoretical confusion as to whether or not civil society can exist within the bosom of modern Chinese totalitarianism. Thomas Gold's analysis argues that civil society existed even in early 1979, on the eve of reform. It was then still functioning 'despite totalitarian structure and practices that the CCP had been trying to implement for three decades'. Moreover, China now has a 'more complex social structure', and even after the dénouement of June 4 there is still 'an increased ability of citizens to deal with each other outside Party control of economic, cultural, social and, sometimes political ends'. This insistence on an elementary continuity of autonomous factors through modern Chinese history has become a *cause célèbre* among Qing and Republican historians, and its implications were strongly stated in a recent *Pacific Affairs* article by Barrett McCormick, Su Shaozhi and Xiao Xiaoming. The latter contend that the Tiananmen Democracy Movement is part of a continuous process favouring the emergence of civil society in China defined in terms of the advent of autonomous political, social and cultural organisations and development of autonomous entrepreneurial economic organisations.[5]

Contemporary Western analysis has yet to establish in convincing detail how civil society has emerged within an allegedly totalitarian context. Gold suggests that such totalitarianism was never complete, but he appears to take Western democracy as an almost exclusive indicator of the presence of civil society. This might suggest that reform within 'socialism with Chinese characteristics' is a superfluous undertaking, and that civil society is ultimately dependent upon Westernisation. While he sees resurgent civil society 'flourishing in the fertile soil of autonomous economic activity', the protest in Tiananmen Square serves as his primary measure of 'nascent civil society' while the leadership's post-June 4 suppression demonstrated the fragility of such society.[6]

In the Western context, the concept of human rights, particularly as it relates to the freedoms of the individual *vis-à-vis* the state, is often related to the notion of civil society which above all else connotes a sphere of activity autonomous from the interventions of the state. Whyte, for example, suggests that the essence of the term connotes 'the existence of institutionalized autonomy for social relationships and associational life, autonomy *vis-à-vis* the state'.[7]

The Chinese have officially adopted the term, 'human rights', but they have yet to endorse 'civil society'. In fact, civil society has no generally accepted Chinese translation even among intellectuals who casually refer to *gongmin shehui,* citizen society, as distinct from mass society, and/or *shimin shehui*, municipal residents' society.[8] Marx's original critique of civil society as an illegitimate rationalisation of private ownership fostering crass materialism and the socially destructive selfishness of atomistic individuals is still very much alive within nationalistic Party circles threatened by the 'spiritual pollution' which comes through China's open door, along with trade and investment. Nevertheless, the notion of rights and interests is slowly gaining ground on the notion of obligations, and the necessity of new legal response to changes brought about by economic reform in society has received increasing priority in contemporary Chinese political and legal thinking.

The post-June 4 Party backlash partly did involve re-statement of Chinese socialist opposition to the separation of powers and the notion of pluralism, but Chinese discussion of the legal resolution of conflicts of interest has continued in the context of urgent adaptation to the consequences of economic reform and the open door. More specifically, legal reform has continuously witnessed significant controversies relating to the division of public and private law and the content and direction of civil law. For a long time after 1949 there was a tendency to focus on the hierarchical interaction of interest relations between the individual producer, the unit of production and the state, or the individual, collective and state interests, but contemporary analysis currently stresses the need to re-think this hierarchy of interests which gave precedence to the requirements of the state plan.

For example, the Director of Civil Law Research and Teaching at Guangxi University, Meng Qinguo, has written of the necessity of diversified contents within the civil law's response to the contemporaneous existence of the natural, primitive commodity and modern commodity economies. He argued in 1988 that a cautious law-making approach was necessary in light of such complicated diversification, but through the early 1990s the controversy as to whether China should have a comprehensive civil code has continued to build, and the Chinese now appear ready to initiate a process to complete the civil code.

Meng's analysis stressed that since 1978 China's 'interest structure' has undergone qualitative change. The pre-1978 structure which presumed the superiority of state administration in the handling of interest conflicts within and between the three levels is, in his view, inappropriate to the changing context of contemporary economic reform. Meng wrote of a new age of property relations, predicated in the emergence of 'equal subjects' before the law:

> Since the start of economic reform, the structure of economic interests in our country has experienced great changes. First of all, the state, collective and individual interests have increasingly become more abstract in classification. Various kinds of concrete economic interest have evolved out of the division of these [original] forms of classification, and they have regrouped in important new ways. These concrete economic interests have become manifest in social factors such as occupation, personal status, culture level, residential area, etc. Different interest groups [*liyi qunti*] such as the individual industrial/commercial household, the peasantry and the intellectuals have naturally formed and developed. Each interest group has its own own economic interest inclination. And, at the same time, the original structure of interests crumbles like an old pagoda.[9]

Meng suggested that the civil law absorb, where appropriate to China's own conditions, the experience of bourgeois civilisation so that law can help achieve a progressive 'balancing of interests' (*liyi pingheng*).[10] Such balancing was, in its far-reaching political and ideological implications, very controversial. It precipitated heated debate across a range of subjects such as the contemporaneous protection of both state and private property, the 'right to goods' (*wuquan*) and the 'equality of legal subjects'. Some nervous members of the legal circles even feared that post-Tiananmen political reaction might entail a concerted effort to eliminate the 1986 General Principles of Civil Law, but, in the early 1990s, there was growing support for the completed codification of civil law; and the NPC finally adopted the Law of Civil Procedure of the People's Republic of China on 9 April 1991, thus consolidating and extending the tentative provisions of the March 1982 trial procedural law.

CIVIL LAW AND THE RULE OF LAW IN CHANGING SOCIETY

Chinese legal reform has expanded, rather than narrowed – as Fairbank suggested – citizen's personal and political rights. While the extremes of Western individualism are still ideologically outlined in routine critiques of capitalist destruction of the individual's links with society, Chinese legal reform has formally, if not always practically, given some limited attention to the individual within the changing interest structure. Mao's hierarchy of interests is undergoing revision in its conceptualisation and definition. Interestingly, some observers have even referred to the 'pluralism' of Mao's three original interests at the individual, collective and state levels.[11]

While there is within legal circles a tendency to avoid explicit identification with related Western notions of judicial independence and separation of powers, Chinese legal reform is, nonetheless, breaking new ground. Within the evolving and specifically Chinese terms of the existing political regime it has attempted to act as Richard Thornburgh's 'predicate', so as to facilitate the impartial 'mediation of interests' under the principle of equality before the law.

The development of civil law has been described as if it were absolutely central to the task of mediation, and this centrality has predictably been featured in the wider condemnation of feudalism. As discussed earlier in Chapter 2, feudal society had generated notions such as that civil and criminal law are inseparable and combining all types of law into one. According to the historical research of Zhang Jinfan, feudalism neglected industry and commerce 'to take agriculture as the foundation'; and it also rejected the legitimacy of private interests, and generated relations of personal dependency. Zhang observed: 'These relations could not produce equality between individuals which reflected the legal relations of right and obligation.'[12]

Again, it was feudalism which, in modern post-1949 society, created the situation whereby policy was substituted for law, civil courts received low priority and civil cases were widely arbitrated by Party and government organisations. In a self-professedly Marxist description of the key role of civil law in China's social and economic reforms, a journal article in *Science of Law* noted the traditional propensity to 'esteem duties and politics' and to negate 'rights and law':

> In the eyes of Marxists, laws, while serving politics, have two characteristics of their own. One is that laws institutionalise the standards of human conduct in the form of written provisions. This is the special function which distinguishes laws from politics and other parts of the

> superstructure. The other characteristic lies in the special effect laws produce on the economic base. Practice has proved that when the strengthening of the economic base and the growth of the productive forces bring about changes in social relations, further advance calls for their adjustment by law.[13]

Press commentary on the urgent need for civil law stressed that, in the 1950s, China had only very tentatively attempted to create such law within a prevailing bias favouring criminal law, and without the benefit of significant experience of capitalist society. Isolated legislation such as the 1950 provisional regulations governing the contractual relations between state administration, state-owned enterprise and cooperatives were passed, but between 1957 and 1978, due to the prevailing leftist condemnation of capitalist restoration and related 'theory of productive forces' and 'theory of dying out of class struggle', laws which responded to the commodity economy were axiomatically capitalistic in nature.[14] The third session of the 11th CCP Central Committee meeting marked an important political watershed separating the previous misguided policy era of class struggle and the new era of the 'four modernisations'. As we have already seen in the world of legal theory, there was growing discussion of the social nature of law.

On 31 March 1986, for example, the *Renmin ribao* featured a public academic disagreement between veteran jurist Zhang Youyu and Zhang Zonghou of the *Fazhi ribao* (China Legal Daily) on the question of whether law is necessarily peculiar to class society. Zhang Zonghou not only doubted the Marxist expectation of the withering of the state and its laws, but he suggested two interpretations of the concept of law, the first relating to a historically narrow view of law in class society and a second, wider interpretation which treated law in the non-class context of primitive and communist society. The current definition of law, in his view, inadequately reflected contemporary circumstances in its focus on laws as the reflection of the will of the ruling class. Zhang argued that the definition of law should be applicable to all social formations. Therefore, he urged the deletion of the following definition from the law texts:

> Law refers to all the rules that govern people's conduct. Such rules reflect the will of the ruling class. They are worked out or approved by the State and are carried out with coercive force.

He wanted to replace the above with the following:

> Law refers to all the rules that regulate interrelationships of society and people. Such rules are worked out or approved by the State or social-managing institutions and are implemented with coercive force.[15]

Coincidentally, there was growing Party emphasis on Mao's famous 1957 treatise, 'Correctly Handle Contradictions Among the People'. Mao's 1957 distinction between antagonistic and non-antagonistic contradictions was exploited to raise the policy and legal significance of non-antagonistic contradictions among the people, and this accorded with new theoretical emphasis on the law's social nature. It was in this political context that the drafting of the general principles of civil law was re-activated; and, in March 1982, the NPC Standing Committee adopted a law on civil procedure for trial implementation.

Civil law reformers sought to appropriate Mao's 1957 theoretical thinking which emphasised the continuance of, and changing nature of contradictions in China's socialist society and the future development of new group as distinct from class, interests. Depending on locale, 60 to 80 per cent of contemporary criminal cases had their origins in civil disputes relating to marriage, family and property. The civil, as distinguished from the criminal law, caseload was much greater, and the importance of the civil law to social stability in the heady times of modernisation, the open door and developing economic exchange with the outside world was no longer in serious dispute.[16]

There was, in the re-evaluation of the contemporary nature of society, greater stress on the need to cope with the modern needs of contract in law. The concept of contract was self-consciously advanced as against entrenched attitudes within the state and enterprise which customarily presumed that contractual rights were conditional upon the political authority of state leaders and departments and the changing requirements of state administration. Contracts now were not to be so easily broken by officials who presumed their political power reached beyond legal requirements.[17]

The tensions wrought by the newly introduced responsibility system in the countryside also required the further development of civil law. The new trial procedural law laid particular stress on the need to maintain the Chinese tradition of mediation as the basis for creating harmony in society. 80 to 90 per cent of civil cases had been solved through mediation and the new emphasis on the formal development of law coopted rather than challenged this emphasis. Advocates of mediation highlighted the simplicity and convenience of a process which supposedly served to engage as well as educate the masses in the solution of community conflict. The new law confirmed the people's mediation committee as a 'mass organisation for mediating civil disputes under the guidance of the grass roots people's government and court'. The *Renmin ribao* gave the following rationale for mediation:

> Problems can be handled through mediation more conveniently and in good time. Large numbers of contradictions among the people are resolved on the first line and are eliminated in the embyronic state. This is greatly conducive to avoiding intensifying contradictions, reducing litigations and safeguarding and strengthening social stability and unity and is well received by the masses. Therefore, it is entirely necessary to define the due legal status of the people's mediation committees in the 'civil procedure law (for trial implementation)'.[18]

Drawing on distinctively Chinese mass-line themes of flexibility and acting according to local expediency, as well as on the importance of China's rural dimensions, the *Renmin ribao* extolled the mass-line provisions for on-the-spot mobile court sessions and for holding appeal cases at the site of the first trial:

> These stipulations provide great convenience for the masses and in particular for the peasants. They are also conducive to the people's court making thorough investigations and trying cases better and faster. Our country is a big country with a large peasant population. No matter what we do, we must take the peasants into consideration'.[19]

Rural attitudes towards the establishment of the rule of law, have been a source of continuing controversy. In one of the few surveys of rural legal consciousness, Zheng Yongliu attempted to extrapolate a number of important generalisations on the basis of the opinions of 831 respondents from 16 Hubei villages. Zheng saw, in an ostensibly negative set of figures, an encouraging shift in rural attitude away from 'personal ties' (*renqing*) and towards the legal resolution of disputes in daily life. There was, for example, a three-way split in reaction to the question: 'What is your opinion of phenomenon which assign greater importance to personal ties than the laws of the state in your daily life?' 20.6 per cent approved of such phenomenon, 44.28 per cent labelled such phenomenon as 'incorrect', and 34.7 per cent opted for 'not entirely correct'. While a majority did not clearly disapprove of the attributes of *renqing shehui* (society of personal relations) or *lisu shehui* (customary society), Zheng was, nonetheless, heartened by the results.

Zheng also reported an interesting breakdown of rural opinion on a three-part question regarding the settlement of economic disputes. Respondents were asked to prioritise three types of dispute resolution, namely, resort to lawsuit, cadre mediation and private settlement with specific reference to three comparative points of relative efficacy, namely, speed of resolution, cost, and level of satisfactory outcome.

On the question of speed there was no contest, as only 10.39 per cent opted for the lawsuit as the speediest means of resolution. Zheng also interjects here that the focus on private settlement reflected the continuing traditional focus on the importance of harmony in rural society. As for costs, only 9.34 per cent viewed the lawsuit as the least expensive dispute mechanism, and herein Zheng notes concern over losing face and hurt feelings. Somewhat incongrously, given the negative sentiment towards the speed and cost of lawsuits, an incredulous 47.29 per cent still regarded the legal-suit mechanism as providing the most satisfactory results. Zheng interprets this positive response in light of sentiment that the law fairly protects peasant interests whereas cadres often require concessions. Private settlement seemed to generate most dissatisfaction.[20]

Given the strong historical orientation of China's criminal-law-based system, the introduction of civil law general principles was widely perceived as a seminal and also very arduous political exercise. The fourth draft of the general principles of civil law was compiled as early as 1982, but these principles were not actually promulgated until 1986. And even then there was emphatic reference to the fact that conditions were not yet ripe for the complete codification of the civil law.

On the other hand, by 1986 the political force of reform was sufficiently powerful as to undermine any lingering prestige of the Soviet model of legal development and to support a major breakthrough in the distinction between civil and economic law. The *Renmin ribao* proclaimed that henceforth economic law would regulate 'the vertical economic relations and administrative management relations between state organs and enterprises and institutions', whereas the civil law would regulate 'the lateral property relations and personal relations between citizens, between legal persons, or between citizens and legal persons.'[21]

The newly promulgated principles reinforced 'equal subjects in law' as between citizens, 'legal' or 'juristic persons' and between citizens and 'legal persons'. Emphasis on the civil law's requirement of voluntary relations between equal parties in law was again deliberately construed as the negation of surviving emphasis on traditional administrative superior-subordinate relationships. As discussed in Chapter 6, reformers established a new formal, but still controversial, emphasis on the separation of the property rights of management and utilisation from ownership, but many details still had to be worked out concerning land management and contractual rights and obligations relating to township enterprise, collective small state enterprise and the individual economy.

In the final stages of revision the NPC's Law Committee tackled some outstanding issues. The draft wording of Article 28, 'Liabilities of a rural household engaged in contracted management would be assumed by members of the household with their property', was changed so as to draw out a parallel between rural household and industrial–commercial liabilities, hence the newly supplemented wording read:

> liabilities of individuals engaged in industrial and commercial undertakings and rural households engaged in contracted management should be assumed by the individual with his own property if the undertaking is run by an individual, and by the household with its own property if the undertaking is run by the household.[22]

Also, in the area of citizen's property and personal rights, the Law Committee enhanced the citizen's opportunity to sue. The originally drafted wording of Article 120 only incorporated reference to suits against government institutions for damage to the legitimate rights and interests of citizens and legal persons, but the revised wording included wider reference to 'government institutions and functionaries'.[23]

The leading civil-law experts and drafters of the new law mobilised support drawing on established policy and ideological reference points of Deng Xiaoping, stressing that law must develop in accordance with 'seeking the truth from the facts' and it must, therefore, derive from practical investigation and response to China's specific conditions of economic and social development so as to further the cause of 'socialism with Chinese characteristics'.

Zhang Youyu adumbrated what was essentially a mass-line epistemological perspective on the practical legal response to changing reality. He explicitly endorsed making separate laws first rather than engaging in premature comprehensive lawmaking, and indeed the new general principles responded selectively to what were regarded as the most pressing issues. Zhang acknowledged the general historical importance of Roman law, but he also claimed that there were overlapping commonalities as well as differences between three forms of civil law as they reflected three identifiable forms of commodity production, including the forms of precapitalist commodity production under Roman law, capitalist commodity production and socialist commodity production.

Implicitly following Mao's instruction to 'let foreign experience serve China', he advised against any indiscriminate and uncritical wholesale copying of any foreign comprehensive system or code. Zhang self-confidently claimed:

> In making our 'General Principles of Civil Law' we referenced foreign civil legislative experience including that of socialist countries and

> capitalist countries. But we did not adopt a dogmatic attitude of indiscriminate word-by-word copying [of this experience]. On the contrary we analytically investigated the merits and demerits of foreign civil law methods of organising commodity production and exchange in the making of our own legislative experience.[24]

According to Zhang, these principles not only gave new impetus to the protection of the personal and property rights of citizens and legal persons, but they also firmed up commitment to 'socialist spiritual civilisation' and the public ethics of society as against the inevitably 'negative factors of commodity economy'.

One member of the civil law drafting group and a leading CASS expert, Wang Jiafu, summed up seven major Chinese socialist characteristics of the new law in such a way as to emphasise its distinctiveness not only in relation to capitalist, but also other socialist, civil law. Firstly, the law recognised the reform emphasis on the coexistence of several forms of economy and ownership. While Articles 73 and 74 restated the pre-eminent position of socialist public ownership as consistent with current state constitutional and Party policy requirements, Articles 26, 28–29, 30–35, 51–53 and 41 and 48 apparently departed from foreign socialist convention to affirm the legal status of individual household industry and commerce, the joint operations of 'legal persons', Sino-foreign joint operations and foreign enterprises.

Somewhat redundantly, his second characteristic is summed up in the civil law 'taking reform as its soul' (*yi gaige wei linghun*). The third specifically *Chinese* characteristic is the law's response to policy which 'enlivens' enterprise. Fourthly, under the specifications of open door policy the law's attribution of legal person status to sino-foreign joint ventures and enterprise and foreign enterprise is touted as unique in the modern history of socialist civil codes. Fifthly, Wang claimed that the new law's scope for intellectual property rights is 'without precedent in world civil law history'.

While Wang explored several problems in the separation of ownership and operation, this attempted separation is listed under his sixth Chinese socialist characteristic, stressing legal protection of the interests of citizens and legal persons. And lastly, Zhang described how the law accords with Party emphasis on the combining of 'socialist material' and 'socialist spiritual civilisations'. The 'General Principles', for example, adhere to the emphases within 'socialist spiritual civilisation' on equality before the law, respect for the dignity of law and public ethics.[25]

In his powerful position, as both Secretary General of the NPC Standing Committee and Chairman of the NPC Law Committee, Wang Hanbin predictably reiterated that, even though it is incomplete, 'The civil code of our country is a socialist civil code serving the socialist base.'[26] In his introduction to the translation of the fourth draft of 1982, Professor William Jones of the University of Washington Law School earlier raised doubts as to such claims, suggesting instead that China has 'two distinct bodies of civil law', the first body including amorphous but practical policy and legal response to the exigencies of Chinese social life, and the second body composed of formal legislation and treatises on civil law which reveal an outstanding debt to German, as distinct from Soviet, civil law.[27]

Professor Jones added that Western law had achieved increasing influence in Chinese legislation, but that the latter did not, in effect, achieve the expected sinification of foreign experience which supposedly originates in the synthesis of theory and practice which fundamentally characterises 'socialism with Chinese characteristics'. Jones wrote:

> But instead of trying to study the law that was actually being used by Chinese, those preparing the codes seem to have taken over foreign law with very slight adaptations and imposed it on China. Little effort seems to have been devoted to trying to work out the principles of the actual law that was being used and to build a code on that basis.[28]

In his 1989 edited translation of a Chinese treatise on the general principles of civil law, Jones was even more emphatic in his insistence on the influence of Western law in China. He maintained that, despite the rhetoric of socialism in the 1986 'General Principles', the underlying substance not only reflected the underlying German concern for private autonomy but also an essentially capitalist economic philosophy:

> This is also, of course, the heart of classical [Western] economics: the individual intelligence making decisions as to economic activity – buying, selling, saving, manufacturing, etc. – all with the aim of maximizing his own interest…
>
> While the *Basic Principles of Civil Law* has a reference to the primacy of socialist ownership of the means of production…, there is very clear support for the notion that China's industrialization will be achieved by permitting individuals to make contracts on their own and to organize collective entities – juristic persons or corporations – that will act independently and in accordance with the market.[29]

In surveying the inherent tension between supposedly socialist rhetoric and legal substance focused on the self-interested calculations of juristic and natural persons, Jones concluded that China's jurists '…are perfectly conscious of what they are doing'.[30] The author, in his Beijing law faculty inquiries of September 1989, was not surprised to encounter Chinese objection to Jones' rendition of the motivation of China's legal circles. Beida comparative law expert, Shen Zongling, went so far as to suggest in an interview of 19 September that, even given the extensiveness of cross-system borrowing, there are still four distinctive legal systems in the world, the common law, civil law, Soviet and Chinese socialist legal systems. Shen is known for his disagreement with traditional Western sinological scholarship which treats Chinese law, not as socialist, but as part of 'Far Eastern Law'. On some issues he was prepared to dispute the relevance of Soviet law to contemporary China; however, the sudden loss of the Soviet Union is likely to have a serious impact on the wider international treatment of the socialist legal system as a distinctive component of comparative law.

The Chinese socialist characteristics within China's legal system may have been overstated by Chinese legal experts, and the increasing influence of Western legal experience is not in doubt, but emphases on harmony and mediation, for example, are still very pervasive and distinctive. Furthermore, development of Chinese legislation unquestionably reflects the particular substantive political and ideological concerns which have recently emerged in the Chinese context. Without a serious treatment of these discrete concerns the particular dimensions of legal response to policy and the internal resolution of disputes regarding the priorities and timing of legislation would be almost impossible to fathom.

Chinese theory has for a long time argued that commodity economy is not exclusive to capitalism. Even Mao, in sharp disagreement with Stalin, argued that the means of production can be subject to commodity production. In contemporary terms, there is no uniform political perception within China's legal circles. Support for either outright or qualified adaptation to Western legal experience, institutions and values varies significantly.

In the month of April 1992, two important Beijing symposiums reviewed the 1986 general principles and the newly minted Civil Law of Procedure of the PRC. The impact of the human rights debate was quite obvious. A major aspect of these discussions related to the spirit of the law and 'combining rights as fundamental with society as fundamental' (*quanli benwei yu shehui benweidi jiehe*), in light of the distinctions between capitalism and socialism.[31]

Some observers quickly seized the initiative to argue that subject equality and the free will of individuals were not exclusive to capitalist civil law. Jiang Ping, Vice-Chairman of the NPC Law Committee and Professor of the China University of Political Science and Law stated, for example: 'We need not treat "rights as fundamental" as if it were only a principle of capitalist civil law. Socialism wishes to strengthen and protect the rights of citizens and legal persons to participate in civil actions'.[32] Jiang believed that China's civil law did not take the 'individual as fundamental' (*geren wei benwei*). In his opinion, even in the modern development of Western civil law, absolute individualism was progressively qualified with reference to the interests of society and public and economic order.

The early 1990s debate witnessed new and strong support for the comprehensive codification of the civil code. Some legal experts again expressed reservation as to a continuing problem of the relation between law and policy. Articles Six and Seven of the 1986 legislation stressed that in those areas of civil relations where the NPC had yet to promulgate specific law, it is appropriate to follow state policy.

Article Seven reiterated a familiar policy orientation underscoring the importance of public ethics and the need to protect the state plan and the social economic order. Xu Guodong, writing in *Faxue yanjiu*, argued that the gaps in the civil law ought to be filled, and that Article Seven failed to provide legally precise guidance as to how to define, in law, activity which is deemed incompatible with public ethics and the social economic order. He wished to eliminate the state economic plan as a source of legal interpretation. He strenuously advocated the regular publication of state policy and noted a growing Supreme Court interpretative tendency to fill in the gaps left by Article Seven.[33]

In his symposium comments, Professor Zhao Xudong noted that the 1986 principles had failed to keep up with the rapidly changing economic situation particularly with reference to the private economy and the renting out and use of land with compensation. He too pointed to the use of the Supreme Court as a stopgap. While the general principles were contained within 156 articles in 1986 the Supreme Court had since issued 200 articles of judicial explanation.[34] The legal circles were always coming up with suggested revisions and expansions in every department of law and the legal sponsors of reform competed for attention within the NPC legislative timetable. Notwithstanding the issue of complete codification there was a steady and impressive development of civil law, and this represented a significant political commitment to reform and a much-needed response to the extraordinary changes which threatened to overwhelm contemporary Chinese society.

THE LEGAL RESPONSE TO NEWLY EMERGING INTERESTS

Economic reform and the open door in the 1980s created compressed and heady social change together with anomie and continual questioning as to the essential features of Chinese national character and the validity of Chinese cultural values in the context of modernisation. There was, in this period, a public fascination with the new and growing social scientific study of the changes within society, particularly with reference to family values, changing marital relations and the relation of the individual to society. And in response to rapid social change, there was an important new political focus on legislated rights and interests.

Marxist–Leninist theory still remained dedicated to the progressive interrelation of individual and collective interest, and the Party Conservatives still tended to neglect Marx's original focus on the liberation of the individual from alienation. However, social science analysis went so far as to suggest that American individualism in its concentration on the value of the individual's creativity need not simply be dismissed as excessive selfishness.[35] Some academic reformers, in ostensible support of Deng Xiaoping's 'emancipating people's minds' and 'seeking the truth from the facts', stressed the individual's self-confidence as distinguished from the traditional emasculation of individual initiative in the face of authority. They argued not only for new rationalism but also for the unleashing of individual creativity so as to spur on the process of development.[36]

The spirit of economic reform required the cultivation of creative adaptation to adversity, competiveness, and not just the old Party standby of hard work. A 1987 national survey of 4244 people from 364 cities purported to monitor changing attitudes with respect to family, social ethics, culture, ideology, work and political environment. Respondents were asked to select the leading attributes of the Chinese national character from a list of ten adjectives, including, 'industrious, frugal, realistic, humane, gregarious, intelligent, adventurous, conservative, obedient and concerned about face'. The survey interpreted the high response of younger teachers, engineers and students in favour of 'conservative', 'obedient' and 'concerned about saving face' as a matter of critical reaction to traditional passivity and fatalism which reinforced the notion 'those who are content with their lot are always happy.'[37]

A Californian Professor, Stanly Rosen, has extensively researched the Chinese student surveys of the 1980s to conclude that a 'decollectivization of morality' was afoot prior to Tiananmen. The progress of 1980s reform disrupted the traditional link between the state and students seeking career advancement, at the same time as students have become much more exposed to the influence of Western individualism. Rosen deduced a declining support for the regime and a change in moral attitude whereby Chinese youth was increasingly unwillingly to make moral judgements of others.[38]

In its struggle to achieve social stability, the Party contended with proliferating contradictions on several related fronts. While 'spiritual pollution' was flowing through the open door, the Party responded to the stunning re-emergence of negative feudal social phenomena such as sexually transmitted disease, rural infanticide, prostitution and trafficking in women by reviving ageless Chinese values such as honesty, hard work and plain living. It also had to meet the pervasive challenge of surviving traditional authority structures which reinforced conservative parochialism, authoritarianism and favouritism, and stood in the way of the development of the new attitudes needed to spark creative competition and enterprising spirit in the economy.

The Party self-consciously struggled to assert socialist spiritual civilisation as against bourgeois liberal side-effects of the open door and international exchange. Extreme individualism and crass, egoistic materialism were correlated with imported pornographic publications and videos, nudity and negativism in the fine arts, cultural nihilism in literature, blatant sexuality, public displays of affection, loss of filial piety, juvenile delinquency in neighbourhood streets and a cynical disrespect for elders. At least for some Chinese observers the last was most graphically portrayed in Wuer Kaixi's televised brazen lecturing of Premier Li Peng as 'Teacher Li' on 18 May 1989.

And on an even more personal level, many urban parents anxiously viewed the introduction of sex eduction classes into the middle-schools curriculum as 'uncivilised'. While Liu Dalin's extensive survey on sexual behaviour in modern China stressed widespread ignorance on the subject of sex, school administrators still had to contend with a student trend towards the public display of romantic affection. Stalk Party advice to women to 'lie back and think of Marx' was often perceived as prudish, and students frequently talked of 'moving love affairs from moonlight to sunlight'.

In the 1980s the Party regularly responded with ideological emphasis on modern socialist democracy and socialist legality; it also sought to enhance those traditional values which were selectively regarded as a matter of distinctive Chinese personality and which apparently offered some source of stability in the sea of change engulfing the Chinese family. The Party appropriated those values which seemed to reinforce 'socialism with Chinese characteristics' and even permitted a revival of the study of Confucian thought. While the Party also condemned feudalism and personality cult, it was, itself, condemned by dissidents who saw the monolithic Party as the very epitome of feudalism.

The Party chided impatient dissidents whose incessant demands for the radical re-structuring of Chinese society along Western lines allegedly demonstrated anti-patriotic sentiment. Not only octogenarian Party leaders, but many intellectuals were sceptical of the lavish eulogising of Western culture 'as if only foreign monks are capable of chanting the right scriptures'.[39]

Cultural and moral crisis has been most keenly felt in the realm of family relations. Where traditional mechanisms of mediation associated with *lisu shehui* (customary society) could not respond, law often assumed new responsibility. Even given the startling rise in the proportion of property protection cases, divorce cases still represented the greatest percentage of civil case listings.[40] Law has had to respond to an ever-growing problem of cultural identity which arose with the developing emergence of the nuclear family under the pressures of modernisation, the one-child family policy and challenges to 'socialist matrimonial morality' (*shehuizhuyi hunyin daode*). Reform opinion persistently argued against traditional norms which forced disaffected couples to remain married. Uninformed conservative opinion attacked Article 25 of the 1980 Marriage Law of the PRC for allowing divorce at the insistence of one party due to 'complete alienation of mutual affection'. Allegedly, Article 25 encouraged divorce and compounded the negative affect of liberal bourgeois 'sexual liberation' on the legal rights and obligations of socialist matrimony.[41]

Policy struggled with 'divorce is a shame' and, while there was growing concern over the stability of marriage, the law could not formally subscribe to traditional wisdom such as 'rather demolish 1000 temples than break a marriage', which considered divorce as antithetical to the fundamental values of society.[42] On the other hand, the courts increasingly faced citations of third persons involved in adulterous affairs. Also, in the context of escalating materialism some male spouses who enjoyed sudden opportunities of economic reform were no longer interested in their wives.[43] In some cases, the adulterous parties openly avowed their quest for 'pure love' (*chuncui aiqing*) and even mischievously cited Engels' saying, 'A marriage without love is immoral', in defence of their amorous excesses.[44]

With such spectacular change in society, the civil law took centre stage. The President of the Supreme Court, Zheng Tianxiang, in his NPC report of 8 April 1986, welcomed NPC consideration of the 'General Principles of Civil Law'. He traced the conspicuous rise – at least by Chinese standards – in violent crime to 'the sharpening of ordinary civil disputes'. He regretted the rise in divorce cases due to 'third party involvement' and 'young people's hasty attitude toward marriage and divorce'.[45] Wen Huifang, a judicial officer of the Supreme Court, explained that hasty urban marriage decisions could be traced to opportunist calculations to secure apartment space or job transfers, whereas in the countryside some women sought to marry out of the hardships of their birthplace.[46]

In the very midst of sensational economic modernisation, the forces of feudalism were still storming the socialist battlements of gender equality. While third persons blazingly proclaimed 'pure love', feudal notions of male superiority would simply not go away. With the growing uncertainties of employment and access to services, it was easy to call upon women to 'return to the kitchen'. Despite the two marriage laws, and despite Mao's revolution, not all of the dimensions of the traditional 'three obediences' – obedience to father before marriage, to husband after marriage, and to son after the death of husband' – had been swept into Marx's dustbin of history. Reformers targeted fallacious support for 'feudal practices in the guise of upholding justice and virtue' and condemned continuing traditional morality which encouraged indifference towards discrimination and the physical abuse of women. For them the declarations of new law were not enough for, as one newspaper commentator put it: 'Once a person, whether man or woman, is convinced that a model female should always submit meekly to maltreatment, modern law can have no place in their mind.'[47]

The advocates of new inheritance law claimed that a blow had been struck for sexual equality in Section 18 of the new Marriage Law detailing the equal rights of inheritance; however, the circumstances of economic reform were not always propitious. There was a revival of sentiment that women were more needed at home to deal with increasing family difficulties and that they should not compete with men in the modern technological sectors of the economy. Women were still *neiren*, or the women indoors who concerned themselves with the household while men struggled in the outside world. Women should 'return to their homes' so as to solve the social problems of the day was yet another permutation of the feudalistic notion, 'An ambitious husband for work and a beautiful wife for serving the family.'[48]

Controversy surrounding the law's response to marriage was also explicit in seemingly pedestrian argument over the positioning of the marriage law within the department of civil law. In a 1983 explanation of the distinctive departments of Chinese law to the Library of Congress Law Division, Renda Professor Zhang Jinfan merely noted that the marriage law had been given separate status so as to give it more prominence in the education of the general population.[49] However, with the promulgation of the 1986 'General Principles of Civil Law', marriage law was formally subsumed under the department of civil law.

Earlier reluctance to incorporate it into civil law is partly explained in the larger controversy over personal relations and property relations. Chinese theory had assimilated Soviet prejudice against this incorporation and repeated claims that socialist civil law cherishes social relationships whereas capitalist civil law highlights civil law relations as those between persons and things.[50] On the other hand, the early 1980s' attack on Soviet example and the new emphasis on commodity production justified a new relation between the marriage law and civil law department. In his text of comparative law, Shen Zongling, recorded, with some satisfaction, that Chinese legal philosophy had finally rejected the Soviet's 'simplified logic' which had established a separate departmental heading for marriage law so as to preserve personal relations from contamination with property and the commodity economy.[51] This particular development of the 'General Principles' was not without its critics. Shi Jichun of Anhui University's Law Department wrote, in typical protest, that subsuming of the marriage law into civil law would undermine its educational function and facilitate the 'infiltration' of the subversive principles of the commodity economy into the marital relations of the family.[52]

In this familial sphere of gender relations, as elsewhere in society, the law was officially sponsored as the means by which to ensure rights during a period of accelerated economic and social change. Whereas in the past problems of prostitution, female abduction and drug addiction were handled through Party-led mass campaigns, in the light of the elimination of the large-scale mass campaign and the ascending political importance of 'socialist legality', there is now a greater disposition to involve the legal system more extensively in the correction of such phenomena. However, despite the disappearance of the large-scale mass campaign, conceptual notions of mass-line politics are still important to the development of contemporary legal approach to problems of social control. There is a continuous emphasis on community participation in the legal system, as well as on mass-line coordination of society-wide education in the understanding of both the requirements and purposes of the law and the policy on which it is based.

While the rights of the individual citizen have received more attention in legal theory and law-making, the Party, in its particular historical preference for united-front tactics and related functional representation, has also given a distinctively Chinese corporatist emphasis to state-sponsored development of associational response to communities of interests.

After public security crackdowns in 1983 and 1989, two decisions banning prostitution and detailing severe penalties for the abduction and sale of women and children were passed at the 21st Session of the Seventh National People's Congress Standing Committee on 4 September 1991. Within two months of the founding of the PRC, all brothels were reportedly banned and closed, and prostitutes were put through the rigours of mass-line education and trained for work in socialist China. Later, the PRC declared that it had virtually eradicated all sexually transmitted diseases.

However, in the 1980s, 580 000 'prostitutes and whore-mongers' were detained, and prostitution has started to spread from the cities and coastal areas to some towns and rural areas.[53] Ideologically, prostitution has often been described as an 'ugly phenomenon of the old society'. This appears to neglect an emphasis on the related social history of treaty-port capitalism; however, the current spread of prostitution from urban coastal areas to rural towns certainly insinuates a qualified causal relationship between feudalism on the one hand, and economic reform and the open door, on the other.

The steady increase in the trafficking of women and children was also described as an 'ugly phenomena left over from the old society'. Internal Ministry of Public Security reference materials, forwarded to the 21st Session of the Seventh National People's Congress, indicated that revival of abduction and trafficking started in a few provinces including Sichuan in the early 1970s. The practice later spread regionally from major 'places of origin' such as Sichuan, Guangzhou, Guangxi, Yunnan, Hunan, Hubei and Shaanxi to 'major destinations' in Shandong, Hebei, Henan, Anhui, Jiangsu, Fujian and Guangdong. In 1986 public security agencies filed 1258 cases but that number climbed to 18 692 in 1990.

The Ministry of Public Security acknowledged that 70 per cent of these cases involved 'organized offenses' of gangs of three to four men at a minimum and that traffickers targeted a range of 'prey' including peasant women, urban women workers, girl students from college campuses or middle schools, women teachers and postgraduates and even foreign women.[54] While no explicit overall linkage between increased trafficking and reform was featured in this internal discussion, public security officials related relevant circumstances whereby traffickers deliberately sought to take advantage of 'women's state of mind'. Traffickers, for example, targeted women seeking a quick change in economic status with specious offers of 'job recommendations' and partnership in 'doing business'.

The Party leadership hoped to fill the gaps left in the Criminal Law which had not fully dealt with the recent revivals of prostitution and human trafficking. New law was urgently needed to detail criminal punishment for such offenses. As the new law on prostitution and whoring made its way through the revision process within the NPC Law Committee, its particular detail became increasingly stringent.

Article Two, sentencing for 'forcing people into prostitution', was revised slightly from 'up to ten years and not less than three years' to 'not less than five but not exceeding ten years'. The same article sought to provide clarification as to when such force results in such 'serious consequences' as to merit consideration of the death penalty and confiscation of property. 'Serious consequences' in the revision was elaborated as 'causing serious hurt, death, or other serious consequences to any one who is forced into prostitution'. The Law Committee also revised Article Four so as to increase the time of 'mandatory corrective legal and moral education' and productive labour which was to be imposed upon convicted prostitutes and their patrons from three to twelve months, to six months to two years.

The law-givers were obviously concerned with the social network sustaining prostitution and the need to ensure official integrity in the assiduous application of the laws guaranteeing the rights of women and children. The new measures on abduction and kidnapping stipulated that, depending on the seriousness of any alleged dereliction of duty on the part of state personnel responsible for the law's execution, they could now become liable to either administrative disciplinary action or prosecution under Article 187 of the Criminal Law. The prostitution law itself attacked the networking congenial to the spread of prostitution in Articles One, Two, Six, Seven and Eight. Personnel in the hotel, food and drink, cultural and entertainment and transport industries could be charged with 'organising others for prostitution', or 'assisting others for prostitution', or 'forcing others into prostitution'.[55]

Typically, Chinese Criminal Law likes to discriminate between principal and secondary criminal actors. Article One's rather unusual distinction between 'organising' (*zuzhi*) and 'assisting' (*xiezhu zuzhi*) differentiates for purposes of punishment between principals such as the pimps and the managers of brothels, or popularly the 'old chicks', from secondary characters who assist in introductions or facilitate the arrangements of the principals and their clients through the use of certain places of entertainment or even taxi-cab drivers offering tips as to local services.

The same NPC Standing Committee session passed related laws on the protection of minors. The first juvenile court had only been established in Shanghai's Changning District People's Court in 1984. Despite the promulgation of a compulsory education law on 12 April 1986, there has been an increasingly upward trend in the school drop-out rate which correlates with trends relating to increasing incidence of child labour, family breakdown and spectacular increases in juvenile crime. Juvenile delinquency and truancy went hand-in-hand. The average age of delinquents has been falling, and in the cities an estimated 70 per cent of criminals are juveniles.[56] Children of divorced parents were more likely to drop out of school and prematurely enter the labour force. Under the open door, Chinese youth were more exposed to pornography and violence. And, in the profit-seeking atmosphere of economic reform, child labour offered adult entrepreneurs an opportunity to cut their overheads.[57]

The Chinese system is geared to the extensive grass-roots deployment of techniques of neighborhood mediation in dealing with juvenile crime so as to relieve the pressure on the courts, but also to encourage constructive social action and education, but some experts complained that, just as in the United States, juveniles know they are too young to be punished by law and that this makes them more daring in their criminal activity. This argument suggested that the early tactical punishment of susceptible naive adolescents might prevent a future life of crime.[58]

Focusing on the rapidly changing social circumstances of juvenile crime as well as related adult responsibility, the proponents of new juvenile law ultimately stressed the need to emphasise the re-education, rather than the punishment, of young offenders. In fact, this emphasis triumphed in Article 38 of the 4 September 1991 Law of the PRC for the Protection of Minors, which reads: 'The policy of educating, helping, and redeeming minors who offend laws and commit crimes is to be pursued, and the principle of stressing education with punishment as a supplementary means is to be maintained.'[59]

In line with the model experience of the Changning District Juvenile Court, there was a great deal of discussion of the strategic implementation of the new law's purposes. The Shanghai experience emphasised the importance of an ongoing relationship between the juvenile court authorities and local women's associations and neighbourhood committees in the organisation of parental education and post-trial redemption.[60] The Shanghai municipal regulations, upon which the national legislation was largely based, noted in Article Two the 'common obligation of state agencies, people's associations, enterprise work units, schools and families' to protect minors, as well minors' own rights and obligations to education on self-protection.[61]

NPC Law Committee responded to pressure from the NPC Education, Science, Culture and Public Health Committee and to local authorities and departments to include in Article Three of the new national legislation reference to a broadly constituted coalition approach of state, society, schools and families in the elimination of juvenile delinquency and the protection of minors' rights. However, a simpler wording which merely referred to 'educating minors to become ethical, educated, and disciplined people with lofty ideals who can carry on the socialist cause' was elongated into the following windy, repetitious statement confirming 'socialist spiritual civilisation' against the inroads of capitalism and feudalism:

> The state, society, schools, and families are to give minors education in high ideals and morality, general education and education in discipline and the legal system, and education in patriotism, collectivism, internationalism, and communism; are to advocate the civic virtues of love for the motherland, for the people, for labor, for science and for socialism; and are to fight the corrosive influence of the capitalist, feudalist, and other decadent ideologies.[62]

The Committee did not entertain any mention of the need to propagate juvenile individuality, but the new law developed a notion of minors as having independent rights in law to 'human dignity' *vis-à-vis* any questionable behaviour of parents or institutions. In Articles 13 and 15, for example, schools are enjoined to 'give patient education' and are, on pain of administrative sanction, to desist from 'corporal punishments in obvious or disguised forms against underage students and children, or take other actions that infringe upon their human dignity'.

Article 30 spoke of upholding the 'personal privacy of minors' and the following reserved wording of Article 31 gives a rather interesting perspective on the relation of rights and obligations in China's changing society:

> No organization or individual is allowed to conceal or ruin the letters of minors. Except the public security organs or the people's procuratorates which may inspect such letters according to the legal procedures in the course of investigating criminal cases, and except parents or guardians who may open letters for minors who have no ability to do this, no organization or individual is allowed to open such letters.[63]

Underlying this particular focus was a hypersensitive concern over the extremist practices of Cultural Revolutionary politics which had often coerced minors to betray their 'capitalist-roader' parents. Such unnatural acts of forced filial betrayal outraged traditional Chinese moral sensibilities.

While the Communist Youth League, Young Pioneers, the women's federations, and the trade unions were all specifically named as having responsibility within this coalition of 'state, society, families and schools' for the dissuasion of any action infringing upon the rights of minors, this was, nevertheless, an unusually broad conception of collective responsibility which reflected government thinking on the need for 'comprehensive management of social control' in combating the urgent problem of juvenile delinquency. This politically emotional problem, in fact, was seen as pivotal to the very survival of the existing socialist state.

The Law Committee oversaw other revisions. Initial criticism concerning the lack of infant protection was partially met in Articles 8 and 52, focusing attention on the internationally embarrassing rural incidence of female infanticide through drowning. The Committee also made an unexplained adjustment to Article Ten's wording concerning parental and guardian obligations to 'stop minors from smoking, indulging in alcoholic drinking, roaming about, gambling, taking drugs, and prostitution'. The original wording, 'forbidden to lure, instigate, or force minors to take drugs or engage in prostitution' was dropped.[64]

The mix of criminal and civil law sanction was also given some priority. Responding to the concerns of the NPC Internal and Judicial Affairs Committee, several local authorities, judicial organs and leading experts, the Law Committee reworded Article 12 to stress the civil law legal responsibilities of parents and guardians who in light of failure to fulfil their supervisory responsibilities or violation of the legitimate rights of minors could become subject to civil suits under Article 16 of the 1986 General Principles of Civil Law. Also, unidentified members of the NPC Internal and Judicial Affairs Committee, the Education, Science, Culture, and Public Health Committee and local and judicial organs lobbied for the inclusion in the last chapter of explicit wording spelling out the limits of criminal responsibility under the Criminal Law.[65]

Article 52 of the approved new law made a blanket statement as to any person's liability to criminal prosecution for the infringement of the personal or other legitimate rights of minors. The Article makes specific reference to Article 182 of the Criminal Law dealing with abuse of minors by family members and specifies a range of sentencing of 'not more than two years of fixed-term imprisonment, criminal detention or control' in cases involving 'odious' circumstances. In the event of accompanying serious injury or the death of a minor a fixed-term prison sentence of two to seven years is stipulated. Article 182 includes a reservation that the question of abuse is 'handled only upon complaint'.[66]

The new circumstances of social change also involved significant controversy and lobbying over gender equality in the workplace and the law's failure to stipulate adequate provisions for the protection of women's personal and property rights. Typically, this area had through the 1980s been dealt with on an ad hoc basis whereby separate laws were formulated on a selective, reactive basis, but, after June 4, there was renewed momentum for a comprehensive legal strategy which resulted in the NPC's promulgation on 3 April 1992 of 'The PRC Law on Protecting Women's Rights and Interests'. The accented vocabulary of rights and interests, as distinct from past synthesis of rights and obligations, drew on the aforementioned national debate on human rights and symbolised an emerging new political vocabulary. NPC Standing Committee Vice-Chairman, Peng Chong, stressed in his 27 March report on Committee work the importance of the interrelationship of democracy and law and the protection of 'rights and interests' (*quanyi*).[67] The emphasis on gender equality was apparently so great that the issue of obligation was pretty much confined to a causal reference in Article 6. The new law lacked the usual separate section on rights and obligations and focused mainly on rights.

The new law was co-drafted by the All-China Women's Federation (ACWF), the Ministry of Civil Affairs, the All-China Federation of Trade Unions and leading experts, and Article 5's specific reference to the responsibilities of the ACWF, the trade unions and Communist Youth Leagues was consistent with united-front legal praxis relying on state and mass-line coordination for public education; however, a range of interesting concerns were aired in the panel sessions of the 22nd Session of the Seventh NPC Standing Committee.

Some panel members seemed to argue that the protection of women's rights and interests could not be considered as exclusive to the work of certain organisations and social groups, but must on the contrary involve the whole of 'citizen', as distinct from 'mass', society. Whereas Article 5 pointed to a more traditional mass-line state corporatist approach, the subsequent revised wording of Article 3 of the draft law highlighted the protection of rights and interests as 'a responsibility shared by the whole society'.[68]

Experts supporting a new comprehensive law argued that despite longstanding policy and constitutional law specifying the importance of sexual equality, women, during extraordinary economic development, were suffering from increasing discrimination at work and the lack of educational opportunity. Vice-Chairman of the Internal and Judicial Affairs Committee, Zou Yu, noted that while women accounted for a total population of 580 million, they constituted 70 per cent of the urban jobless and 70 per cent of China's 180 million illiterates. The statistics indicted the existing social welfare and educational systems, and Zou re-stated the case for sexual equality in all the spheres of politics, education, labour, property and social and marital activity.[69] While feudalism still helped account for the gap between oft-stated policy pronouncements and the socially inferior position of women, the principles of the new law were premised in the now widely accepted conclusion that women were not participating equally in the opportunities of economic reform. Reformers staunchly rejected the notion of 'returning to the kitchen' as a solution to rising problems of unemployment in the reform era.

While the new law was supposed to redress a situation whereby a patchwork of regulations had only incrementally targeted society-wide sexual inequality, some reservation was expressed in NPC panel discussion as to the law's overly sweeping nature, and it was suggested that the law sharply focus on the employment of women in state organs, social institutions and enterprises.[70] Despite panel discussion of the need to relax the retirement age for female professionals, the law failed to make either a recommendation of principle or a detailed stipulation in this area, but it incorporated, in its discussion of legal responsibilities, an elaboration of the principle of equality to include 'lawful rights in schooling, placement of graduates, awarding of academic degrees, and sending of students to study abroad'.[71]

The law reads like a social charter statement of general principle, and its high-profile policy pronouncements were politically consistent with the developing focus on human rights. The law's new policy vocabulary, however, still falls short in terms of extensive concrete regulation. Despite the 1986 incorporation of marriage law into civil law, this new law, with the exception of a generalised commitment in Article 52, did not systematically incorporate sections on legal responsibilities under the civil law. It re-affirms women's legal rights to common property, and at the level of principle, in Articles 30 and 50, subsection 5, it ostensibly addresses reform inequality in the countryside, emphasising equal rights in terms of the farming of responsibility fields, access to grain rations and land for housing construction.[72]

The new women's law did, however, provide guidelines which presumably could become significant in mediation and in the courts. Chapter Seven on marriage and family rights reflected the growing preoccupation with the legal complications of divorce settlement. In the event of continuing dispute over home ownership, the courts were instructed, in the absence of a formal marital agreement, to give 'favorable consideration to the rights and interests of the wife and children'. Article 44 lamely instructed that '...the husband should do all he can to help the wife solve her housing problem if they currently live in a house provided by the husband's organization'.

The text of the law brought together an impressive list of principles, for example, equal right to work, equal property rights, equal pay for equal work, rights to reputation, human dignity, privacy, freedom of person and protection against contractual termination on the grounds of marriage, pregnancy, maternity leave or lactation, but the last chapter, while it featured 'legal responsibilities' (*falu zeren*) and the protection of rights rather than the honouring of 'obligations' (*yiwu*), focused on remedial administrative discipline rather than the creation of justiciable rights. It also seemed to neglect any focus on a routine, strategic coordination of the courts with neighbourhood and mass organisation, as was the case in the law on the protection of minors.

The New China News Agency, in its endorsement of the new law, stressed that '...Women's involvement in political life is a symbol of their equal status with men.'[73] Women account for 21.3 per cent of the NPC Standing Committee membership. The new law generally touts the state's responsibility to ensure that women 'enjoy the same political rights as men', but, in Article 10, there was only the following vaguely construed generalisation: 'The National People's Congress and all levels of local people's congress should have adequate numbers of women deputies and should gradually raise the ratios of women deputies in them.'[74] There was no definition of 'adequate' or policy commitment to a particular schedule of appointment based upon sexual equality.

In the mid-1980s discussion of inheritance law one could already see the outlines of a debate concerning the growing need for the recognition of newly emerging interests and the protection of the rights of the marginalised and dispossessed sectors of Chinese society. Article 9 of the 1985 inheritance law, which concerned women's equal rights of inheritance, was designed to amplify the general commitment to equality in Article 48 of the state constitution. It was conceded that the law was needed as the inheritance rights of daughters and widows had not been well protected in the rural areas, and such rights were increasingly important in a context where the household was accumulating more funding and the social welfare responsibility of collective organisations was correspondingly diminishing.[75] The new inheritance law was generally hailed as it seemed to offer enhanced protection and favourable legal consideration of the rights of 'four kinds of people', namely, the old, minors, the sick and the disabled.

The rights of the disabled received unprecedented political and legal focus, and this was due in part to the early connection with Deng Xiaoping's handicapped son, Pufang. The national centre for the rehabilitation of the disabled was established in 1985. In 1987 the NPCSC endorsed the 1983 ILO Convention concerning the Vocational Rehabilitation and Employment of Disabled Persons. This was followed by the creation of a new mass organisation in March 1988, the Federation of Handicapped Peoples. Despite Deng Pufang's alleged involvement in a funding scandal, this focus continued and resulted in the 28 December 1990 'PRC Law for the Protection of Handicapped People' detailing the rights and interests of the handicapped, including the right of self-reliance through rehabilitation, education and employment.

The law represented a significant break from tradition. It was self-billed as a response to the UN World Programme of Action Concerning Handicapped Persons, and it was formally part of China's contribution to the UN Decade for the Handicapped, 1983–92. The state was to become more proactive in fostering the rights and interests of the handicapped, who were hitherto largely dependent upon familiar charity and ad hoc arrangements at their work units. Article 1 of the new law cited established principles of equality, participation and co-enjoyment. The law promoted an expressed philosophy of rehabilitation through special education and equal opportunity, which included quotas for the recruitment and hiring of the handicapped within state departments. The law appeared to give the handicapped legislated access to state funding as well as mass organisation assistance. Indeed, the competition for state funding has become part of an emerging new politics focusing on the legal protection of newly defined entitlements and related access to institutional resources.

While Article 7 appealed to people in society as a whole to manifest a 'socialist humanitarian spirit' towards the handicapped, Article 8 gave considerable emphasis to the corporatist linkage between government and mass organisation. The role of the China Federation of Associations of Handicapped People's was specifically spelled out in the law itself: 'The federation undertakes assignments the government entrusts to it; it carries out services for handicapped people and mobilizes social support for services needed by handicapped people.'[76]

The 1980s witnessed qualitative change in the syntax and vocabulary of Chinese politics, as rights and interests were increasingly formally entrenched within legislation and within lawfully sanctioned strategies to coordinate state and social organisation in the materialisation of rights and interests. Substantive, but not necessarily consistent, legal and political change occurred either within, or in spite of, feudalism and the surviving organisational traditions of one-Party dominance.

POLITICS AND THE CONTRADICTIONS OF LEGAL REFORM

In 1989 the Chinese press gave considerable coverage to a bizarre case in Gulan village in Guangxi Zhuang Autonomous Region. After a quarrel with her father-in-law, a peasant woman attempted to drown herself in a river. Her husband responded by dousing their house in gasoline and locking himself and his father inside. The situation was saved by Mediator Liao Yingping and two other villagers who dramatically gained entry into the house by pretending they were grandparents-in-law.[77] In-laws and family quarrels over housing, money and property issues have been increasingly featured in divorce cases, and this case received publicity in terms of official concern that civil disputes were increasingly leading to serious criminal violence. Reportedly, more than half the public security cases dealing with murder, arson, poisoning, bombing and serious injury stemmed from civil disputes.[78] Within fast-paced social and economic change, the family was stressed, but a solution was partly sought in the consolidation of the Chinese tradition of mediation.

Between 1982 and 1988 mediators apparently solved 50 million civil issues and helped save 680 000 lives threatened by suicide or homicide.[79] China's more-than-six-million mediators are elected at the community level. They receive popular legal education and, despite traditional emphasis on the importance of voluntary contributions to the community, increasingly they are given a modest stipend for their service to the community. The political reaction to Tiananmen included a re-assertion of the importance of mediation in light of the conflicting pressures of economic reform.

In the pre-June 4 neighbourhoods 'comprehensive management of public order' had suffered as distracted senior citizens, or the *laodaye* and *laotaitai*, scrambled for lucrative new economic opportunities and correspondingly spent less time on community service. In general formal terms, however, the new laws of the 1980s and 1990s have continuously supported mediation, not only in terms of neighbourhood response to family distress, but also in terms of the mediation of economic disputes concerning patents and property rights.

However, with the development of the legal system, there has been more agonising over the boundaries between mediation committees and the courts; for example, legal theorists and experts have argued over the legal and political status of mediation. Pro-mediation argument has focused on the need for more committee power which is justified in the democratic nature of the neighbourhood process and in the formal election of members. This argument included the point that the committee decisions should be legally binding unless the matter at hand is later referred to the people's courts.[80]

This boundary question points to the even larger issue of the relation of law and the legal system to non-judicial, politically coordinated society-wide action for purposes of what is formally known as *shehui zhian zonghe zhili* ('comprehensive management of public order', or 'comprehensive control of social order'). Mediation is only one, albeit significant, facet of this public order/public security dimension. The comprehensiveness of such management is practically all-inclusive; and it seems to include all that is, in the West, formally, if not always practically reserved for 'civil society'. It requires coordination of all individual and collective social and political effort to ensure public ethics and social discipline which will contribute to China's 'socialist spiritual civilisation'. It encompasses an entire continuum of legal force and mediation, including not only all policing and judicial processes, but also the related, coordinated organisation of legal culture and popular education in the law.

The contextual parameters and internal content of such control seem to be perpetually elastic as it progressively enrolls new policy emphases. Ma Jie, in writing of the duties of the sociologist, argues that the concept constitutes a philosophy of the modern world as well as social science theory with Chinese features, and, in his discussion of the emerging 'era of information' and 'era of comprehensiveness', he recommends the following viewpoint to his readership:

> only by putting comprehensive control into effect can we enhance our national strength. It is not only required by the times but also determined by the complex and comprehensive nature of the development of the objective world to run the state, administer the society and manage all undertakings in a comprehensive way.[81]

While this concept has a long historical association with Chinese Communist counterrevolutionary law, more recently it has coopted emphases on the post-Third Session of the Eleventh CCPCC strategy of 'there must be law, it must be followed, it must be strictly enforced and law-breaking must be investigated' (*youfa keyi, youfa biyi, zhifa biyan, weifa bijiu*), as well as emphases on citizen's rights and obligations and the new civil law protection of both public and private property.[82] However, the notion of control appears, on balance, to be conceptually biased in favour a unity of rights and obligations, which gives considerably more precedence to obligation than does the contemporary legal reform literature.

In the post-June 4 political reaction there was a renewed bid to preserve 'socialist spiritual civilisation' *vis-à-vis* the contemporary 'crisis of faith' (*xinxiang weiji*), and related internal pressures for 'complete Westernisation' (*quanpan xihua*). All judicial system personnel together with all members of state and mass organisation were urged to study the 2 March 1991 NPC Standing Committee decision on the strengthening of comprehensive management of public order. Now under the guidance and coordination of the Central Commission for Comprehensive Control of Social Order (*zhongyang shehui zhian zonghe zhili weiyuanhui*), this social control subsumes disparate, and sometimes conflicting, types of organisational activity including formal court proceedings and administrative disciplinary action. Under the rubric of comprehensive control, the explicit and politically directed coordination of mass organisations and the courts would seem to conflict with the formal Weberian notion of impersonal rational-legal authority. On a more concrete level, however, at least some Western experts would, for example, support a wider involvement of community associations in the legal system so as to protect the rights of minors.[83]

The ideological connection between socialist spiritual civilisation and rule of law was extensively explored in a major Shanghai conference in 1986.[84] No one bluntly raised the fundamental relation of these two seminal concepts as the antithesis of rule of law versus rule of man. Theoretically, the law had achieved supremacy over policy, and the entire Party was obliged to respect and observe the law, but this does not disguise the fact that this emphasis was, itself, part of the drive towards socialist spiritual civilisation.

Reform highlighted the need for a new legal culture to fight surviving feudal attitudes and to underwrite the lawsuit as a legitimate vehicle in the individual's attempt to assert the priority of rights and interests. Highlighting the need to escape the suffocating consequences of a political tradition which had reduced citizens to subjects, some dissident political science theorists went so far as to challenge 'mass society' (*qunzhong shehui*) and to argue for the creation of a new 'citizen society' (*gongmin shehui*). The latter was supposed to militate against the past pattern of 'politics is the management of state affairs' and the substitution of administrative method and action for law. The emerging Chinese notion of society entailed a new, but somewhat qualified, notion of the citizen as bearer of rights and as a participant in state life, but it did not explicitly endorse any conscious approximation to the civil society notion of autonomy.[85]

In orthodox theoretical and political terms, the rule of law is merely one subset within the larger conceptual matrix of socialist spiritual civilisation, hence, for example, Article 9 of the 3 April 1992 PRC Law on the Role and Position of Trade Unions notes that trade unions '...should conduct among staff members and workers education in patriotism, collectivism, socialism, democracy, rule by law, discipline, science'.[86]

The nebulous notion, spiritual civilisation, dates back to the turn of the century and predates Chinese Marxist vocabulary, and the usage of spirit or *jingshen*, essence, or the spiritual as distinguished from the material dimensions of existence itself suggests an important, but worrisome traditional element of absolute morality which cannot be explained within the contemporary terms of Chinese dialectical materialism. Indeed, in the aftermath of the Cultural Revolution, Chinese social science analysis warned of the need to replace 'spirit' in politics with predictable law. On the other hand, 'spiritual pollution' (*jingshen wuran*), as the antithesis of 'spiritual civilisation', seems to convey a morally vigorous Chinese perspective on Western problems of extreme individualism and materialism even in a time when so much emphasis is placed on the need to achieve wealth through the unleashing of entrepreneurial creativity.

Socialist spiritual civilisation eulogises revolutionary-cum-traditional virtues such as plain living, honesty, consistency in words and action, friendship and mutuality in common prosperity. The concept invokes the historical three workstyles of the Party, namely unity of theory and practice, integrating with the masses and 'self-criticism' which encompasses the aforementioned 'honesty' as the 'unity of words and deeds' (*yanxing zhiyi*). Within socialist spiritual civilisation socialist democracy and legality are interrelated with the moral concerns typically conveyed in the Party's traditional elliptical compounds such as *wu ai* (love of the motherland, people, labour, science and socialism) and *si mei* (beautiful thought, language, behaviour and environment). These concerns, in and of themselves, may reinforce an ongoing internalisation of centralised moral authority. Certainly, the Party's attack on feudalism and its economic and related legal reform policy emphases were not especially well squared.

Socialist spiritual civilisation encompasses an underlying conceptual paradox. It requires the triumph of the rule of law over the rule of man in the name of an all-encompassing policy of Chinese morality. The conceptual subordination of the rule of law to socialist spiritual civilisation may have been cause for some nagging trepidation in legal reform circles. Wang Shengxuan, for example, rather than repeating the formulation subsuming the rule of law under the rubric of socialist spiritual civilisation, preferred to make the rule of law the precondition of socialist spiritual civilisation. Wang put it this way: 'Only when everyone observes law, can we promote socialist spiritual civilisation and can we raise the entire people's communist morality.'[87] The central issue herein is one of comparative priorities – whether to focus on new laws which would eventually generate new citizen attitudes towards self-conscious participation in law and politics, or to focus on the development of socialist spiritual civilisation values which would underwrite the eventual development of law sustaining equality and the rule of law itself.

The conceptual bias of socialist spiritual civilisation, together with the society-wide authoritative approach of comprehensive control of social order, would seem to negate any serious development of a legally entrenched civil society. On the other hand, under the open door, the influence of Western legal concepts is truly significant, and while some elements of new law are explicitly designed to ensure Chinese values within a socialist moral order, the law has also elaborated new strategies in a response to a new structure of interests. The new interests, themselves, have taken advantage of the policy opportunities of economic reform to lobby for protective legal detail *vis-à-vis* traditional Party emphasis on flexibility and the avoidance of too many and too detailed laws. The gains of civil law, in this regard, are truly spectacular.

Chinese analysis has demonstrated an increasing awareness of the complexity of contemporary society. This society now constitutes a moral jigsaw puzzle. New values are commingling with deliberately refurbished old values. Contemporary social and economic transition and related legal reform are caught up in a number of simultaneous trends which derive from conflicting sources and reflect conflicting perspectives. Even as the post-Tiananmen reaction highlighted the threats of feudalism, bourgeois liberalism and the need for comprehensive management of public order, post-1989 law has continued the pre-1989 expansion of personal and property rights and encouraged the individual citizen to act as an autonomous legal subject under a newly developing principle of judicially enforced equality.

5 Law as the Contractual Predicate of Ownership Rights

Much of the Western discussion of 'civil society' turns on the importance of autonomous economic organisation and transactions in society. The related notion of the rule of law as a 'predicate' was introduced in the first chapter's discussion of Richard Thornburgh's Moscow remarks which featured the rule of law as due process facilitating the mediation of interests in the spirit of equal justice for all. Edwin Meese, in his advice to Premier Zhao Ziyang, added that due process has to uphold the centrality of ownership and the use and responsible conveyance of property as fundamental to modern legal culture.

Certainly, one cannot underestimate the centrality of the notion of ownership in contemporary Chinese politics. Emphases on public ownership of the means of production and distribution, based upon 'each according to his work', are almost always taken together as the central theoretical distinction between the socialist and capitalist systems; however, what is particularly important to the foreign observer is the response of law to the fast paced changes within China's 'interest structure' and to the development of a more complex system of ownership since late 1978.

Whereas, in 1978, the state-owned economy accounted for 56 per cent of the GNP, the collective economy 42 per cent, and other economies 2 per cent, by the end of 1991, these percentages had changed respectively to 40, 50 and 10 per cent. Similarly, the percentage of total industrial output value governed by compulsory government planning dropped from 95 to 16 per cent between 1979 and 1991 and, in the same period, the number of categories of production materials, allocated by central planning, were reduced from 256 to 20.

By December 1991 the number of private enterprises exceeded 100 000 and employed 1.75 million people. Also, in the period 1978–90 the percentage of the rural workforce employed in township and town enterprise grew from 9.5 to 22.1 per cent, and such enterprise is routinely described as the 'mainstay' of the rural economy. The rate of change in state enterprise can also be measured in terms of the effects of the policy assault on the 'iron rice bowl', or guaranteed employment. As of December 1991, 14 million workers, or 14 per cent of the state enterprise workforce, had already signed contracts with management as part of the process of liberating enterprise rights in terms of hiring and firing from the past state policy of guaranteed employment and equal pay for everyone. Reportedly, unemployment in urban state enterprise had reached 3 per cent, or 4.5 million out of a total of 45 million.[1]

Ma Hong, the eminent economist who currently directs State Council research on economic, technological and social development, noted that under the contemporary line of a socialist market economy, the past ownership system based upon a unitary public ownership of collectives and state-owned enterprise would evolve into a 'complex ownership system (stock and share system) based on the public-owned businesses'. Ma concluded:

> Thus, the establishment of incorporated enterprises is essential for developing a socialist market economy. Publicly-owned businesses should be the foundation of the incorporation system. This is a complex form of ownership under which enterprises under all sorts of ownership, all types of corporations, and everybody can be each other's shareholders.[2]

Ma not only stressed that enterprise decisions would be made by individuals and enterprise management instead of the government and society, but also that the different kinds of ownership would have to compete under the same rules rather than under the differentiated criteria of the past. While large and medium-size state enterprises are still expected to take the lead in the economy, the political leadership has concluded that this leading position would have to be reinforced through market competition. Emphasis on the structural changes accompanying a socialist market economy is likely to underwrite renewed political emphasis on the necessity of extending the principle of equal subjects before the law.

However, during his January 1992 southern tour, Deng Xiaoping not only endorsed market changes, but he also reiterated his socialist ideological position: 'SEZs bear the surname of "socialism" [i.e., She] rather than "capitalism" [Zi]. In terms of ...Shenzhen, public ownership constitutes the main body and foreign investment accounts for just one-fourth of the city's foreign investment.'[3] Since 4 June 1989, there has been controversy within the Western literature as to whether Thornburgh's predicate can possibly exist within the political and ideological limitatons of Deng's Chinese socialism.

Just prior to the Party's formal subscription to a socialist market economy, James Feinermann of the Georgetown University Law Centre, for example, raised serious doubt as to this possibility in the following manner:

> In China as well as in other Marxist–Leninist regimes, an entirely different perception exists of the rule of law and of the role of law in economic change or development. In keeping with Marxist-Leninist theory, these regimes have consciously downplayed the importance of the rule of law, denigrating this ideal as a tool of the ruling class in capitalist societies. In socialist countries, law is subordinated to the dictates of the ruling party, and there has been no independent judiciary with the power to subordinate party decisions to law.
>
> The role of law is also quite different from that in the West. Law (often in reality, party decisions) is frequently seen as a means to promote economic change or development, and not as something that develops as a result of changes elsewhere.[4]

Feinerman's bottom line is that the rule of law is not really viable until such time as the Party's all inclusive leadership is dismantled.

Also, Western sinological experts have not yet reached a definitive consensus as to the nature of the contemporary economy, the emerging structure of property relations and the related national policy intentions concerning the conditions of foreign investment. Robert Kleinburg's study of China's open door policy, for example, essentially concluded that the post-1979 reforms constituted neo-mercantilism rather than a liberal free trade regime.[5] Margaret Pearson, in her study of joint ventures and state control of foreign direct investment, projected a qualifying trend away from state control towards 'differential liberalization' which selectively enhances the operating autonomy of foreign and joint enterprise. Stanley Lubman's review of Pearson incidentally disputes her contention that the Chinese have tentatively sought due process or procedural regularity governing the substantive decisions of officials.[6]

Regardless of such commonly held reservations, there are a number of substantive trends in legal reform which do suggest a growing concern for due process and equal subjects before the law during the current period of change to China's three-tiered 'structure of interests' inclusive of state, collective and individual interests. Certainly in terms of theory and related legislation, this side of the rule of law debate has not been formally neglected. Even conservative advocates of legal reform believe in the establishment of legal principles for the division of economic power between the three types of economy: state collective and individually owned.[7]

While emphasising the continued importance of guide-like planning in concert with economic adjustment through the market, conservatives also accept that the stresses and strains of the transitional economy will require more dependence upon legal, as distinct from administrative, measures.[8]

The more aggressive advocates of civil and economic law development, on the other hand, have actively exploited the relationship between economic reform and the rule of law so as to reinforce their demands for new NPC law to deal with the new problems of contract within the economy and the deteriorating consensus which, in the early reform period, supported 'separation of ownership and management' (*liangquan fenli*).

During a 1991 seminar, sponsored by the editorial board of *Jingji fa* (Economic Law), Jiang Ping, President of Beijing's University of Politics and Law and Deputy Chairman of the NPC's pivotal Law Committee, decried the rule of man character of macro-level economic decision-making. He wished to employ law to restrict the overweening posture of personalised state administrative power. Without explicitly referring to power control theory, he targeted rule of man characteristics relating to arbitrary policy-making, and the lack of legal supervision, proper procedural restriction of power, and legal responsibility in state administration.

Jiang joined a chorus of critics who claimed that there is too much administrative freedom in the issuance of directives in substitution for law. Such 'directive-like regulations' (*shouquanxing guifan*), formulated in example terms of 'according to the decision of the State Council' or in exclusion clauses such as 'apart from the additional stipulation of the State Council', were interpreted as the manifestation of the rule of man.[9]

Commenting on Deng Xiaoping's new 'brilliant' theoretical insight into the liberation as well as the development of productive forces, three Shanghai legal experts, Zeng Jianmin, Sun Chao and Gu Changhao wrote in a 1992 issue of *Zhongguo faxue* that hitherto too many forbidden zones (*jinqu*), originating in the superimposition of the will of leaders over economic legislative thought, had inhibited the appropriate development of China's productive forces, and that, in the past, such legislation had fostered restrictions and obligations, as distinct from more progressive guidance and protection, in society's economic transactions. They related these forbidden zones to an over-emphasis on the class character of law, citing, for example, obstructionist conservative resistance to the law on joint ventures and the leasing of land in the coastal areas as indicative of a false opposition of socialism to capitalism.[10]

Borrowing from systems theory, Wu Shihuan interjected the rule of law debate into discussion of the perfection of the entire economic rule-of-law system. Rather than emphasising the correlation of the rule of man with feudalism *per se*, he focused on China's unfortunate assimilation of the Soviet experience of planned product economy. He warned that the perfection of the laws was not, in and of itself, sufficient to guarantee the rule of law. The number of laws produced could not stand alone as a measure of the rule of law. Wu hoped that with the transition from the old planned product economy to the planned and market commodity economies of the reform era the rule of law would take hold. From 1979 to 1990 there was extraordinary 'perfection' in terms of actual law-making, but the poor implementation of law was traced to the contemporary persistence of the rule of man. Laws and regulations pertaining to legal persons and ordinary citizens were often well implemented, but those which attempted to regulate the behaviour of senior Party and State officials were more often than not poorly implemented.

The NPC and its Standing Committee had approved 171 laws, 56 of which were economic laws and regulations. The State Council had issued and approved another 1297 state administrative relations, of which 860, or 66 per cent, related to economic matters. Wu cites an unidentified source to the effect that in a survey of selected localities only 10 per cent of the laws and regulations were well implemented. A further 30 to 40 per cent were generally implemented, but an astonishing 50 to 60 per cent were considered to have been either 'poorly implemented' or 'not at all implemented'.[11]

The difficulty in transcending past experience was paradoxically evident in Wu's own choice of words. Wu used the 'scientific' metaphor of engineering which had so clearly characterised the past era of socialist planned capital construction to describe the rule of law in the contemporary economic reform process. He discussed the rule of law in terms of three interrelated analytical levels of organisation and culture, inclusive of the economic rule of law system engineering (*jingji fazhi xitong gongcheng*), the economic legal system engineering (*jingji fazhi xitong gongcheng*), and the engineering system of economic law (*jingji faxitong gongcheng*). The largest category of economic rule of law system engineering builds on the other two less inclusive categories. It encompasses not only the widest dimensions of legal culture but also the underlying political and socio-ideological underpinnings of such culture. Wu points out that within an 'economic rule of law', law has to be conceptualised not only in terms of compulsory compliance in the predictable resolution of conflict, but also in terms of a social informational process which enhances prediction, coordination, inspiration, education and self-regulation in everyday economic activity.[12]

Wu's middle category of economic legal system encompassed the observance of economic law and the concrete institutional parameters of judicial practice, legislative and executive action, whereas his innermost category is narrowed to the economic law and regulations of those departments of law relating to the economy.[13] As indicated in the adaptation of Wu's translated diagram below, the lower levels are encompassed by the higher levels in an inverted conceptual pyramid:

Table 5.1 System engineering and the economic rule of law

System engineering of economic 'rule of law'
System engineering of economic legality
System engineering of economic law

As discussed in the last chapter, the legal circles have taken up the challenge of asserting the role of law in the resolution of the conflicts within society's changing interest structure. While Mao's theory formally laid equal emphasis on each of the three levels of interest, there was always a practical administrative assumption of the supremacy of the state's interest in relation to collective and individual interest.

The pioneers of legal reform, however, have been pushing towards a formal equality of interests in law. A more expansive notion of 'legal person' and the extension of the legal notion of subject equality is challenging the old administratively sustained hierarchy of interests. According to the existing Law of Economic Contract, the subject of economic contract is the legal person, which was defined in the 1986 General Principles of Civil Law as any organisation that has the ability of civil rights and action and independently enjoys civil rights and assumes civil duties according to law.[14]

Some of those advocating major revisions to the December 1981 Law on Economic Contract went so far as to sponsor presently non-legal person producers, such as private city and township enterprises, as proper 'subjects' of economic contract.[15] The importance of township enterprise is confirmed in the simple fact that it now accounts for approximately 22 per cent of national industrial output. The October 1992 14th Party Congress clearly indicated that state enterprise would have to compete with such market-based enterprise on the basis of equality.

During the early 1990s debates, one group of reformers argued that the subject of economic contract should include economic organisations, self-employed individuals and households, but exclude individual citizens as 'natural persons' (*ziran ren*). A second group wished to include citizens as bona fide 'subjects' of contract. This extension of legal person status might have considerable impact on continuing legal controversy over gender property relationships within the rural household. A third group emphasised that at least one of the parties to a contract would have to be a legal person.[16]

In the past, it was often assumed that Civil Law's overseeing of equal subject relations between legal persons would be circumscribed to economic relations relating to consumption as distinct from management relations in production. The 1986 NPC-endorsed division between civil and economic law departments based upon intersecting vertical-horizontal axes appears to be tenuous in terms of the potential decline in 'vertical' state-to-state enterprise relations and increasing attempts to circumscribe the state's interventions into enterprise organisation, and to supplant administrative regulation and exclusion clauses with legally explicit NPC law.

The original 1979 compromise, which sought more autonomy for state enterprise from within the sole ownership rights of the state, has run into continuing and deep opposition within legal reform circles, calling for the transfer of new ownership rights to state enterprise so as more effectively to facilitate their role in commodity production.[17] Such discussion has now become routine whereas, in 1979, it would have been regarded as ideological anathema.

During his famous southern-inspection tour of January 1992, Deng Xiaoping expanded upon his ideological notions of 'seeking the truth from the facts' and the 'emancipation of the mind' to attack abstract, counter-productive ruminations concerning the differences between capitalism and socialism. This provided for the conceptual endorsement of new theoretical distinctions between 'liberating and developing productive forces' and between 'interest-dominated social structure' and 'functional social structure', or 'social technology organization and management structure'.[18] The latter's focus on the achievement of efficiency and functionality has no social class. The reform is to liberate productive forces; and this liberation encompasses the transformation of social structure and the evolution of forms of ownership and systems of exchange and distribution. This is a bold and explicit extension of what the extreme left in the Cultural Revolution dubbed as the Liu Shaoqi/Deng Xiaoping 'theory of productive forces'.

In fact, in 1975, the Gang of Four's alleged theoretical brain, Zhang Chunqiao, clearly warned that the problem of ownership in form and reality had not been solved. He accused Party leaders of using assets which were formally owned by the whole people for self-interested purposes. Despite their often impeccable class credentials, Zhang believed that the members of a self-interested Party elite, or the 'new bourgeoisie', were using their

Party connections to create their own 'fortified villages' in the economy. His argument for the strong imposition of the dictatorship of the proletariat over the bourgeoisie was predicated in his central assumption that '...bourgeois right, which has not yet been abolished entirely in the system of ownership, is still prevalent to a serious extent in the relations between men and holds a dominant position in distribution'.[19]

In 'The Resolution on Certain Questions in the History of Our Party Since the Founding of the People's Republic of China', this alleged distortion of the meaning of 'bourgeois right' was rectified.[20] Apparently, the exchange of equal amounts of labour was a phenomenon under capitalism, but once under the socialist system of commodity production this exchange seemingly achieves a different and more salutary effect. As for Zhang's assumption of bourgeois right in the superstructure and the system of ownership in state and collective enterprise, this was dismissed as a wilful distortion of Marx's exposition on the bourgeois right. It was part of Zhang's own 'counter-revolutionary political line of "changing the dynasty"'.[21] The June 1981 decision merely noted the existence of commodity production and exchange under socialism; however, the Third Plenary Session of the 12th CCP Central Committee introduced for the first time the notion of a socialist commodity economy. The 13th National Party Congress in late October 1987 went further to entrench a new policy commitment to 'the state regulates the market and the market directs enterprise'.[22]

In his 25 October 1987 exegesis on 'socialism with Chinese characteristics', the new Party General Secretary, Zhao Ziyang, stressed the emergence of different interests in society and the evolving separation of ownership from enterprise management. This separation was to take on a variety of forms in its rejection 'of a self-enclosed natural economy', and Zhao endorsed the further development of 'horizontal economic ties'. To achieve appropriate separation, Zhao emphasised the importance of using 'legal means in the form of contracts to define the relations between the state and enterprises and between the owners and managers of enterprises'.[23]

In his 1992 argument supporting market socialism, Deng went beyond his earlier claim that China could rationally borrow Western management techniques on the basis of Mao's principle, 'let foreign things serve China', to argue that the functional social structures of capitalism and socialism are often the same. His focus on the autonomous development of enterprise management has underwritten a new emphasis on state enterprise as a legal person. The October 1992 14th Party Congress decisions relating to interest structure further emphasised the 13th Party Congress focus on the 'separation of state administration and enterprise' (*zhengye fenkai*), and paved the way for major changes in the relation between the state and large- and medium-sized state enterprise. The government was to shed its dominant role in economic relations. It was no longer to act as an economic entity, and state enterprise was to be freed from administrative affiliations.

The 14th National Party Congress focus on functional social structure originates in a developing critique of the failure of the institutional reforms of the 1980s. It is now acknowledged that state administrative agencies undermined the 1980s attempt to separate state and state enterprise. The Enterprise Law and the 13 April 1988 Law of the People's Republic of China on State-Owned Industrial Enterprises had provided a preliminary, but insufficient, basis for enterprise autonomy. The 1980s structural readjustment of state enterprise was caricatured as 'slogans without action'.

The 27 February 1988 State Council 'Provisional Regulations Regarding the Contracted Management Responsibility System' would seem to have deployed a mass-line concept of contractual relations which fostered social and political integration in favour of the planned direction of state enterprise. The editorial board of the journal *Zhongguo jingji tizhi gaige* (Reform to Chinese Economic Structure), for example, claimed that enterprise-contracted responsibility systems had contributed to worker solidarity and a politically enlightened understanding of state and worker interests during the 'turmoil' of June 4:

> By means of the contract system, it was possible to fulfill the enterprise's economic responsibility assigned by the state down to the work units at all levels so that an 'interest community', in which 'individuals committed themselves to groups, groups to workshops, and workshops to the enterprise', was formed within the enterprise. The broad masses of workers were fully aware of their responsibilities for the country, and understood it was also where their vital interest lay.[24]

Reformers, however, argued that, in the halting and incomplete 1980s 'separation', 'an additional tier of administrative organs between the government and enterprises came into being' as new large industrial companies performed both government and enterprise functions.[25] The 14th Party Congress reacted by calling for a rational division of functions.

Related programmes, initiated under Zhao Ziyang's late 1980s' leadership to create a professional civil service on the basis of a clear distinction between professional and political tasks and qualifications, had also stalled. Similarly, the past situation of state administrative regulation coopting law had been ineffectively addressed. Institution re-building and the division of functions now require specific law so as explicitly to challenge the rule of man. *Liaowang* commentary on the 14th Congress highlighted institutional reform in the following way:

> legislative work in institution establishment and administrative procedures should be augmented, and explicit stipulation can be made in legal forms regarding conditions for setting up institutions and procedures for the increase of reduction of institution establishment; on the other hand, separate legislation should be made regarding the specific laws governing institution establishment for various departments as well as the norm, functions, duties, and personnel establishment of every institution, while serving as a branch of law for various administrative institutions to work according to the law while changing the 'rule by man', which exists universally in administrative institutions.[26]

The emphasis on functional reform was aligned with the main theme of the Congress, namely, market socialism. Party General Secretary Jiang Zemin's political report highlighted Deng's 'emancipation of the mind' and repeated his argument that neither a planned economy equals socialism, nor a commodity economy, capitalism. Deng's theory of socialism with Chinese characteristics now formally incorporated a bold endorsement of 'socialist market economy' (*shehuizhuyi shihchang jingji*).[27]

Hence the Party has, since the famous Third Plenary Session, 11th Party Congress, negotiated the zig-zags, or the hair-pin turns, in a road which terminates with the market as 'the key mechanism to distribute all social resources'. The current line supersedes the Party's 1982 concept of 'keeping economic planning as the mainstay and supplementing it with market regulation'.[28] However, Jiang called for legal clarification of property rights within China's complex ownership system and attempted to clarify the relative position of different types of ownership, suggesting:

> In ownership systems, public ownership, including whole-people and collective ownership economies, is the dominant body, with individual, private, and foreign-capital economies as supplements. A variety of economic elements will develop together on a long-term basis. ...State-owned enterprises, collectives, and other kinds of enterprises will all enter the market and the leading role of state-owned enterprises will be realized through equal competition.[29]

Jiang was sensitive to the chaotic nature of new stock market projects. The government was already committed to the staged regional introduction of stock markets in 'three tiers', and, without specific elaboration, Jiang simply endorsed the helpful nature of joint stock companies.

Despite Tiananmen Square, and despite leadership anxiety over the collapse of socialism in Eastern Europe and the former Soviet Union, leftist rather than rightist political threats are still perceived as the greatest danger, and economic reform, even during the reaction to Tiananmen Square, has continuously worked to restrict the class dimensions of politics.

The Party's contemporary reform argument appears to represent a concerted theoretical attempt to empty the debate on the changing structure of interests and the related changes in the forms of ownership of any significant reference to class. Also, there is less ideological stress on the redeeming features of the 'easy co-ordination of the relations between various interests' and 'the realization of community interests' through public ownership and a more compelling political focus on the retarding influence of state ownership on enterprise participation in a commodity economy.[30] In terms of legal reform, accelerated ideological and policy change may well result in less focus on the vertical relations of economic law and the extension of the status of legal person to newly recognised interests. The combination of plan and market, which advocates of economic law have, up until very recently, regarded as central to the understanding of economic law, no longer enjoys such an extraordinary status as a political orthodoxy. Contractual relationships and the evolving new law on property relationships seem poised to fill the vacuum left by conventional state planning.

This prioritisation is partly reflected in inter-departmental wars over the placement of property law. CASS Law Institute's Professor Sun Xianzhong, for example, emphatically endorsed the extrication of property law from administrative law. He equated the past 'system of no compensation for land use' (*tudi wuchang shiyongzhi*) with the increasingly outdated 'product economy'. To his way of thinking, this economy had focused attention on administrative law relating to land protection and division and had ignored the dimensions of property relations concerning the relations of land use and ownership.

Focusing on the 12 April 1988 NPC revision of the State Constitution and Law on Land Management so as to facilitate the transfer and leasing of state land, Sun described the emergence of new property law and the current transition in the legal system relating to land in terms of the transition from a state planning model of resource management to the current model of property management, based upon the principle of compensation for the use of land as a valuable commodity, or *youchang zhuanrangdi yuanze*.[31] While Sun sought the extrication of property relations from administrative law, other legal opinion sought to cut property loose from the civil and economic law departments so as to constitute a more prestigious independent department of property law.[32]

Trial land leasing originally started in Shenzhen in 1987 and real estate has since started to receive increasing political priority especially at the behest of competing provincial and SEZ authorities anxious to consolidate the local policy significance of the new political focus on the socialist market. In October 1992 the China Real Estate Consulting Center was set up under the State Land Administration to provide an assessment of land prices, and compensatory costs of leasing, transfer and mortgaging of land and to facilitate the transfer of land use rights; however, there are serious disagreements between central state administration and local government over the ratio of lease income claimed by the central authorities who oversee state ownership of land.[33]

The proverbial change in political wind was apparent during Deng's southern tour of January 1992. On 10 January 1992, Deng's protégé, the no-nonsense Zhu Rongji, made a speech at a state-sponsored meeting concerning the national economic system reform which was widely circulated among legal circles. Zhu outlined his own understanding of the drafting of new regulations to implement the State Enterprise Law. The key to the drafting, in his view, was the transformation of enterprise management systems. He demanded that the coming regulations define ownership and the right of management with precise legal language, but Zhu also expressed concern that too much attention was being given to the decentralisation of power to enterprise and not enough attention was paid to the responsibility of enterprise directors for the loss of state-owned assets.

Zhu sternly admonished enterprise directors to take personal responsibility for losses. He expressed interest in the practice in some capitalist countries of establishing supervisory committees which brought together management experts, government, workers, and bank and enterprise representatives. Zhu, however, declined to support proposed new government organisation to exercise the prerogatives of state ownership, preferring instead the indirect exercise of state ownership rights at the macro-level through policy and law.[34]

The evolution of the legal theory and corresponding state law relating to the July 1979 'separation of ownership and management' has to be examined in detail in order to assess the extent of progress towards the use of law as a predicate in the contractual conveyance of property.

THE GREAT DEBATE OVER SEPARATION OF OWNERSHIP AND MANAGEMENT

In July 1979, the State Council passed its 'Regulations Concerning Expanding the Autonomous Rights of State Enterprises to Operation and

Management'. These regulations helped mark the theoretical ascendancy of the 'separation of ownership and management' over the 'leftist theses' of the Cultural Revolution. The new emphasis on enterprise autonomy of operation was considered to be a great reform in respect of the combination of planned and commodity economies. It reflected a move away from the old system of 'state ownership run by the state' (*guoyou guoying*), and 'collective ownership run by collectives' (*jiti suoyou jiti jingying*), and it challenged the 'theory of product economy' (*chanpin jingji lun*) and the related emphasis on 'plan is law' (*jihua qiushi falu*).

The separation of ownership and management was subsequently enshrined in the General Principles of Civil Law of 1986. However, in the civil law, this separation, immediately became the subject of intense criticism. Those who had supported the separation argued that the problems in the state-owned economy originated in the prevailing pattern of too much administrative intervention, but critics pointed out that the separation did not effectively deal with state ownership as a drag on state enterprise participation in the commodity economy, and that the law neglected state enterprise's independent status as a civil subject.[35]

Indeed, it was widely observed that the 1986 civil law chapter on right to ownership and rights to property, (*caichanquan*) had failed to stipulate any specific provision regarding 'right to things' (*wuquan*). It enshrined new enterprise autonomy in terms of the 'right of operation and usage' (*jingying shiyongquan*), and the 'right to contract out operations' (*chengbao jingyingquan*). State and collective enterprise, while under legal obligation to respect ownership by the whole people, formally acquired new freedom to contract out their resources and properties. While there was, in Soviet theory, precedent for the 'separation of ownership and management', the new requirements relating to usage and contracting out were featured as legal innovations confirming the unique validity of socialism with Chinese characteristics.[36]

The 1986 law's shortcomings in the area of *wuquan* (self right over things) and *tawuquan* (right to use other's property) can be inferred from the reconstructed diagram, below, which according to the mid-1980s research of Li Youyi and Qian Mingxing, illustrates the existing basis and the possible future development of civil law ownership and possession rights under the rubric, right over things. Items one through three, pertaining to rights of management, contracting out and land use, were addressed in the 1986 law, but Li and Qian argued for the civil law's extension into the virgin areas of loan and collateral.[37] Whereas items one through three facilitated rights concerning the usage and profiting of self-owned, or self-possessed assets, item five focused on the rightful access to common resources and assets in the collective context and items, for through seven, focused on the new legal definition of debtor-creditor rights and obligations in relation to mortgaging, debtor usage of property collateral and third party division of collateral.

Table 5.2 The civil law on 'right over things'

Self Right Over Things (*Ziwuquan*)

1. Right of Management (*jingyingquan*)
2. Right of Contracting Out (*chengbaoquan*)
3. Right to Land Use (*dijiquan*)

Right to Use Other's Property (*Tawuquan*)

4. Right-of-Way (*diyiquan*)
5. Mortgage Right (*diyaquan*)
6. Using the debtor's movable property as loan collateral (*zhiquan*)
7. Third Party retention of property due to debtor default (*liuzhiquan*)

Throughout the late 1980s legal reformers increasingly turned to deal with the questions which arose with the newly evolving dimensions of debtor-creditor relations. Also, legal reform critics were dissatisfied with the overly narrow determination of legal subjects, the lack of attention paid to the expansion of horizontal relations between equal civil subjects, and the law's inadequate reference to concrete issues regarding the contracting out of township enterprises to peasants and the contracting out of small state enterprises to collectives and individual citizens. The open door policy was served in that the 1986 law accorded foreign enterprise the same legal status as state enterprise, namely that of legal person; however, some critics were disappointed that while individual households and domestic small-scale enterprises were technically equal subjects before the law, they were actually disadvantaged in that they did not enjoy the same degree of equality as accorded the prestigious legal entity, the legal person.

They were arguably denied such status on the grounds that they lacked a solid organisational base. The strengthening of the legal position of the household *vis-à-vis* the state was controversial. Not everybody was convinced of the argument that the rural household contract responsibility system had demonstrated the policy superiority of the separation of ownership and responsibility.[38] From within the system of contracting out quotas to individual households, the production team had lost its responsibility for unified accounting in the name of greater economic efficiency and household control over the production factors of land and labour. This contractual reform was rationalised in terms of the augmentation of household rights to occupy the means of production from within a formal theoretical subscription to collective ownership of land. However, Zhang Hongyu, in his summary of current development, noted:

> the expectation that there will be a long-term scarcity of land among the peasants has caused short-term economic behavior and agricultural operations could not form an effective mechanism for investment and accumulation by itself. For example, under restraint of income, expectation, and risk, land as a limited production factor could not flow in a wider scope and be rationally allocated.[39]

While the Land Law's new stipulations for the contracting-out of land as a means of production encouraged legal reformers seeking the expansion of property law, the Minister of Agriculture had to remind the legal circles that the Land Law was actually a Land Management Law. In a country where there is intense use of every parcel of cultivatable land, there is growing concern over the use of land for non-agricultural purposes. Even state land-development companies have been caught profiting illegally from land speculation and sales.

Discrimination between the different dimensions of ownership became increasingly controversial in legal theoretical debates. Li Youyi and Qian Mingxing, for example, argued that the 'right over things' (*wuquan*) had to be incorporated into law governing state enterprise possession, usage and disposition of state-owned property. They regarded the rights to contract out as rights over things. State enterprise possession of things could not be operationalised without right over things. The latter, in their view, was superior to rights in debt law (*zhaiquan*) which, while providing some element of compensation under the civil law, did not provide serious protection against any illicit intervention by a third party such as a wilful state agency or political leader. *Wuquan*, on the other hand, would give the enterprise the right to demand the return of the original thing, the removal of third-party-inspired damages and or the prevention of damages during disputes over contracting-out operations.[40]

On the grounds that the law cannot tolerate two ownerships of the one and same thing, Li and Qian rejected argument that the state has state ownership and the state enterprises have 'ownership of the enterprise legal person' (*qiye faren suoyouquan*). The state by virtue of its planning responsibilities still enjoyed a partial right of usage and its taxation powers still meant some right to profit. On the other hand, they contended that the enterprise 'right of operation', consisting of a complete right to possession and partial rights of usage, profit and disposition of things owned by the whole people, could be considered a new type of 'right over things'.

Contracting out generated inevitable theoretical debate over the legal definition of ownership. The state gave state enterprise the right of operation but continued to enjoy an inalienable right of ownership. The state could still intervene to transfer fixed property among enterprises and to collect taxes according to law. On the basis of the combined planned and commodity economies, Lu Zhenbang, for example, suggested the following macro–micro distinction in sorting out the relation between ownership and operation:

> How is the relation between ownership and operating rights to be correctly handled in practice? First of all, at the macro level, the state must exercise fully its own exclusive powers and functions, and with regard to enterprise it will have to exercise appropriate control, administration and adjustment... the state will impose necessary control over the enterprise use of raw materials, plan, profit distribution and payment of taxes to the state.... Secondly, at the microlevel the state will loosen its control over the enterprises and enliven enterprise. The state allows the enterprises to enjoy a true right of control...to use every legal means for materialising their interests and goals. The state requires enterprise to self-accumulate, re-make itself, and self-develop its productive forces. The bankruptcy system will be instituted in accordance with the principle of 'the survival of the fittest'.[41]

Lu wanted to expand the state enterprise independent right of control (*zhibeiquan*) over state property (inclusive of rights of possession, usage, profiting from and transfer of state property) while retaining the state's ultimate right of sole possession (*duzhanquan*). On one side of the question, legal reformers argued against state ownership as a pure ownership which had no significant practical implication. Other reformers, like Lu Zhenbang, refused to endorse 'relative ownership' (*xiangdui suoyouquan shuo*), which implied enterprise property rights existed independently of the state's 'sole possession' of state property. His view fell within the limitations of the 'theory of right to management' (*jingyingquan shuo*).[42]

In June 1988, the State Council finally issued provisional regulations on the leasing out of state-owned enterprise assets. Qiao Lu's comparison of this law with the December 1989 Soviet law on enterprise leasing asserted that Chinese regulations, unlike Soviet law, stopped far short of attempting a transition in the forms of ownership.[43] Regardless of such disappointment, there was, nonetheless, a growing advocacy of legal person ownership within China's legal circles.

LEGAL PERSON OWNERSHIP VERSUS SEPARATION OF OWNERSHIP AND MANAGEMENT

Within the formulation of state enterprise autonomy under separation of ownership and management, iron-clad state ownership appeared to enjoy a theoretically impregnable position. The documentation of the 14th National Party Congress of October 1992, however, endorsed a theory of ownership function. From within the state's sole possession of state property, state enterprises are to command the concrete functions of ownership relating to the possession, use, the profiting from and disposition of state property.

A growing number of legal reformers have increasingly turned to the 'theory of ownership by legal person' (*faren suoyouquan shuo*), which allows state and enterprise property rights which are construed as legally independent of the state's right of sole possession. Also, this theory aggressively breaks with the orthodoxy of separation of ownership and management in its related policy emphasis on the creation of a share-holding system (*gufenzhi*) within state enterprise.

As we have noted, Jiang Zemin's October 12th report emphasised both the 'legal person' status of state enterprise as well as the 'value-preservation and appreciation of state-owned assets'. He then endorsed the perfection of the contracted managerial responsibility system and the rational expansion of 'enterprise groups'. Also, he described 'share-holding' as 'helpful in the separation of the government and enterprises, converting enterprises operational mechanisms, and collecting and accumulating social funds'.

Critics concede that initially the classic formulation of separated ownership and management may have facilitated a liberation of the forces of production, but now, under the qualitative development of economic reform, it is becoming a liability to the further development of the commodity economy. The adequacy of Section Two of the Enterprise Law guaranteeing to state enterprise management rights of possession, use and handling by law of state assets has been challenged with reference to generally recognised international attributes of ownership relating to the possession, use, profiting from and handling of owned assets. Critics argue, for example, that the state enterprise right of possession and right to achieve profitability is compromised by the state's 'sole possession' of state property.

Su Junzheng advances the following reasoning to argue that state enterprise cannot truly act as either an effective manager or independent legal person on the old basis of 'separation of management and ownership':

> Thirdly, who in state enterprise is the approved representative of ownership? If at the same time the factory manager has the right of

> enterprise management as the directors' representative of enterprise and the department responsible for work signs for contracting out and renting out, the factory manager and directors act as the representatives of management but not the representative of ownership. And if the factory manager and directors act on behalf of the enterprise and the state then obviously this disagrees with 'separation of management and ownership'.[44]

Su opined that the classical formulation separating management and ownership cannot provide for a real 'separation of state enterprise and administration' (*chengye fenkai*), and that state administrative attempts to represent enterprise deny its proper legal person status.

Su's opinion was largely shared by Xue Huizong of the Hubei Provincial Re-Structuring and Reform Office, who claimed that the first decade of state enterprise reform did not go all that smoothly due to the limitations imposed upon reform by the separation of management and ownership. Xue believed that independent and definite enterprise ownership is the only remedy for the short-term thinking of contemporary enterprise management. Xue knowingly encouraged the development of joint-stock companies realising that the resulting division of ownership interests into the ultimate ownership of stockholders, the manager's right to management, the ownership of legal person as exercised by the board of directors and the broker's right to engage in share buying and selling would frontally challenge established notions of ownership. He argued that the broker would serve as the medium between ultimate ownership and the ownership of legal person, and the enterprise would achieve a comprehensive internal integrity as the right of management and the ownership of legal person are internally integrated within the enterprise.

Xue advocated 'legal person's right of ownership' (*faren suoyouquan*) as the solution to the contemporary contradiction of the separation of management and ownership with reform, based upon an expanding commodity economy. The separation of management and ownership, he believed, had not only discouraged a flexible handling of state enterprise property, but it had also encouraged external state administrative interference and a pattern of ineffective administration to deal with the irregular actions of enterprise.[45]

As the forms of economic organisation proliferated in economic reform the proper identification of the status of legal person with clearly defined legal subjects became more problematic. Zhao Xudong of Beijing's University of Law and Politics, for example, wrote of the artificial transformation of private enterprises into collective enterprises and the artificial metamorphosis of collective enterprise into state enterprise at the expense of the property rights of citizens and the working masses.[46]

Zhao also noted that category of collective enterprise is itself imprecise, and that there are problems in the attribution of legal person ownership to either the working masses or to the collective economic organisation. In his view, the rough-and-ready distinction between urban collective enterprise and rural village or collective enterprise, which includes the cooperative store and credit cooperative as the major form of village collective enterprise, is probably too narrow. With reference to any so-called collective's history of incorporation, the source of collective property and the structure of labour relations and management, he distinguished between five possible categories including collective enterprise which originated from rural cooperatives.

Collective enterprise originating in rural cooperatives and now commonly referred to as 'big collectives' (presumably the Higher Agricultural Producers Cooperative) is distinguished in terms of cooperative members originally buying shares. The majority of this collective property, however, was generated through cooperative management of annual accumulation since the 1950s. Currently, most of the original cooperative members are no longer there and most of the staff have only a working relationship with the cooperative.

Zhao places in his second category rural cooperative stores and credit cooperatives which had historically undergone transformation into state economy during the zenith of the commune movement, only later to be returned back to their original collective enterprise status. The cooperative property, therefore, included many years of original accumulation as well as new injections of income from individual stockholders during the re-establishment of these enterprises as cooperatives. In this case, the workers are also cooperative members.

His third category encompasses village and small town cooperatives which vary in size from the original production team to brigade. The source of property in this case was economic organisation within the villages. It is assumed that there are no original cooperative members with shares, and that the working staff are mostly villagers from the local area.

Zhao's fourth category originates in Deng Xiaoping's 1980s remedial policy of urban employment. The property source of this urban collective enterprise lies in contributions made by Party and state organisation as well as state enterprise and mass organisation. While the latter presumably retain some element of ownership, this enterprise has increasingly gained more autonomy. It has also inevitably benefited from connections or (*guanxi*) with the contributing organisations. This type of enterprise deliberately sought to employ the children of parents working for the contributing agencies.

The fifth category of collective enterprise is constituted by town and city individual, industrial and commercial entrepreneurs. The property, in this case, originated solely with individual investment. The investors act as both managers and workers. The ownership nature of such organisations is still not clear, but current registration tends to place them under collective enterprise even though some such organisations may, under the 1989 regulations, more closely resemble private enterprise.

The specific problem of private enterprise masquerading as collective enterprise became euphemistically known as the 'red hat' phenomenon (*hong maozi*). Especially prior to 1987, when there was a lack of legal definition of the legal rights and responsibilities of private enterprise, private entrepreneurs piggy-backed off existing collective enterprise by using their names and accounts. In this way, they illicitly took advantage of the collective's legal status while escaping taxes and state supervision of their finances and salary scales. In short, they enjoyed windfall, illegal profits. Subsequent to new state rules distinguishing private enterprise in terms of its private funding, its autonomous form of management by individuals or family partnership, and its civil responsibilities including privately determined wage scales, these 'false collectives' (*jia tiji*) are being weeded out and re-defined as private enterprise, and their illicit profits have had to be re-distributed.[47]

The 1989 Interim Regulations on Private Enterprise of the People's Republic of China re-affirmed the State Constitution characterisation of private enterprise as complementary to socialist public ownership. Article 3 stipulated: 'The state protects the lawful rights and interests of private enterprises.'[48] However, the intent of Article 11 imposed a restrictive policy on such a supplementary economic formation which is only allowed to exist in so far as it contributes to selective state policies. This Article limited application for the opening of private enterprise to certain classes of people, including peasants in villages, 'waiting-for-job people' in the cities and towns, people who have resigned or quit other jobs and 'some retired people and others with the permission of the national law, regulations and policies'.[49]

The lack of uniform development of collective enterprise ownership has potentially generated a much bigger and legally vexing political situation. The separation of management and ownership in the household contract responsibility system has yet to provide a clear and consistent regime of ownership rights which responds to new commodity relationships. Zhao Xudong notes that there are two general answers as to who properly constitutes the subject of the property rights which are to be assigned to the various types of collective enterprise. While some experts assign ownership to the 'collective's working masses' (*laodong qunzhong jiti*) or the 'collective of the entire peasantry' (*quanti nongmin jiti*), others alternatively transfer ownership rights to the 'collective economic organisation' (*jiti jingji zuzhi*) or 'collective owned enterprise' (*jiti suoyouzhi qiye*). The proponents of the latter perspective argue that the law needs to ascribe ownership to specific economic organisation as a legal person.

Zhao Xudong anguishes over the lack of precision in law as to the basic definitions of 'working masses' (*laodong qunzhong*) and 'collective economic organization'.[50] In regard to village collective enterprise, he asks whether the working masses should include all the peasants in the village or only those who work in the enterprise. He has no answer as to what happens to the ownership rights of founding cooperative members if indeed the enterprise as collective economic organisation is assigned ownership status. There is no guidance as to how the latter can still enjoy legal person status if the ownership rights of founding cooperative members are recognised. The sorting out of contemporary property rights can have potentially explosive political and social consequences, and awareness of this reality certainly underlines the understandably cautious and evolutionary approach of the government to the new dimensions of law relating to questions of ownership.

CONCLUSION

Obviously there are going to be problems in the legal definition of property relations, but these should be assessed in the light of the phenomenal and taxing changes to China's structure of interests and in the light of genuine progress in legal thinking, which has crashed through traditional ideological barriers to further the development of subject equality and law on property ownership.

Especially in the light of all of the above difficulties, there is a credible ongoing attempt to define and protect ownership rights and to create the rule of law as a predicate in the mediation of newly emerging property interests under contractual law. This credibility is all the more significant when compared with the post-Soviet-Union Russian context where, despite the much wider dimensions of political and economic reform, law on private property and bankruptcy has yet to be effectively consolidated. Within the larger dimensions of such comparison, the Russian example might seem bolder, but it also seems to be a cold-water plunge into unknown depths. The Chinese legal reform has been more carefully staged, and yet it has also pushed up against the limits of traditional ideology. Its gradual recognition of newly emerging interests is part of a new evolving consciousness which thus far has avoided a final, frontal challenge to the existing political order.

Economic and legal reform will, nevertheless, generate new and cumulative political contradictions and controversies featuring the distinction between the rule of law and the rule of man. As many Chinese legal reformers as well as Western observers have pointed out, the very existence of law does not, in and of itself, guarantee the consolidation of the rule of law in the economy. However, the fact that the Chinese are undergoing a profound and unparalleled restructuring of economic institutions probably deserves more analytical patience in the West.

In fact, the law has been especially quick to deal with areas involving significant foreign investment whereas, according to Chinese legal reformers, in some crucial areas it lags behind significant changes to the domestic structure of interests and newly developing property relations. Ultimately, the interests of the foreign investor and the domestic legal reformer are entwined in the overall project to create what one observer so awkwardly described as an 'economic rule of law system engineering'.

The great transition in economy and society and the great transition towards a supporting rule of law is still an ongoing process. In his remarks concerning the 14th Party Congress emphasis on a socialist market economy, Wang Jiafu, Director of the CASS Law Institute, noted the need for a new drive towards the elaboration of legal regulation to carry out existing legal reform and the need for new law concerning communications, consumer protection, product quality, the regulation of the market, insurance, financial services and law to facilitate political re-structuring so as to further control over state administration and NPC supervision and representation.[51] Certainly, any sober, fair-minded evaluation has to recognise that the Chinese are still in the grips of an extraordinarily complicated transition in their evolution towards a system of multiple ownerships.

6 Politics and Criminal Law Change under Reform

INTRODUCTION

The stipulated nature of crime is changing under the contemporary reform of the legal system, and while the Criminal Law and Law of Criminal Procedure were only just promulgated in 1979, Chinese legal circles are already seriously engaged in an extensive discussion of a major revision of criminal law. These circles have routinely emphasised the centrality of the department of criminal law and the comparative depth of criminal law research in their discussion of the attempt to create the rule of law.

Among certain members of the criminal law research community, there is a focus on an expansive correlation of criminal law department norms and those of other departments. In commenting on this correlation, Wang Yong and Zhao Bingzhi once placed the following gloss on Rousseau's dictum, 'The criminal law is fundamentally not so much a special law as it is the punitive force of all law':

> We can argue that in between the norms of criminal law and the norms of right and wrong [in other law], there is a structural relationship such that the latter is prerequisite to the establishment of the former, and the former is the guarantee of the latter's materialisation[1]

The 1980s rule of law debate focused on both the invigoration of criminal procedure and the expansion of guaranteed rights in response to Cultural Revolutionary legal nihilism and the requirement for predictability in the midst of economic reform and the extension of commodity production and market relations. As the social, rather than the class nature of law was highlighted in the new era of economic reform, it became politically acceptable to argue that the law must hedge the arbitrary expression of state power; and correspondingly there was a developing focus on the notion of equality before the law.

The open door fostered a comparative perspective on the procedural dimensions of criminal law development, and economic reform relatedly fostered a notion of autonomy suggestive of civil society. However, the developing political focus on the limitation of arbitrary state power and the procedural application of a principle of equality before the law conflicted with a contemporaneous indigenous political focus on the comprehensive management of social control. As the policy implications of the open door and economic reform took hold, there was also a growing substantive concern over the inevitably negative consequences of the external challenge to domestic socialist spiritual civilisation. This awareness was heightened in light of the events of Tiananmen Square which so vividly confirmed the potential for instability and axiological crisis within China's contemporary transitional society. Thus, within the very modernising context of economic reform, the development of new criminal law has reflected a strongly indigenous substantive concern which tends to modify the law's new-found procedural strength with the flexible application of severe punishment so as to ensure public order and comprehensive management of social control.

Together with the formal political focus on the 'four cardinal principles', the open door and economic reform are central emphases within the prevailing Party orthodoxy stressing 'one centre and two basic points' (*yige zhongxin, liangge jiben dian*). The extended formulation, namely, 'one center, economic construction, and two basic points, the four cardinal principles and upholding the general policy of reform, opening to the outside world, and rejuvenating the economy', was endorsed in the 13th National Party Congress of 1987 and, subsequent to June 4, it was immediately re-affirmed in Deng Xiaoping's critical speech of 9 June 1989 and more recently at the October 1992 14th National Party Congress.[2]

On 9 June Deng acknowledged that the 'crux of the current incident' constituted a 'confrontation between the four cardinal principles and bourgeois liberalization', but he explicitly denied any suggestion that the Party's judgement had suddenly become leftist. From the perspective of October 1992, it appears as somewhat ironic that Deng stated on 9 June 1989 that while, in future, there could be policy adjustments favouring either the state plan or the market economy, there would be no basic change in the policy of coordination between a planned economy and a market economy. Also of significant relevance to this discussion of the criminal law reform is Deng's 9 June reference to his early 1980s advice to Guangdong comrades to the effect that they '...should persevere with reforms and openness, and on the other hand, they should deal severely with economic crimes'.

In its rejection of leftism and in its ongoing emphases on economic reform and opening, the Party leadership was reluctant to draw an explicit and direct correlation between the open door and economic reform, on the one hand, and particular rises in the rate of criminal activity on the other. However, even in the midst of the extraordinary response of legal reform and thinking to the newly emerging structure of interests, there was a reflexive pressure which favoured 'comprehensive management of social control'. The rapid extension of the death penalty and the 1980s focus on the incorporation of criminal law norms in non-criminal law both revealed a deep underlying anxiety over the potential lawlessness of Chinese society in the grip of profound value change.

THE DEATH PENALTY IN THE REFORM YEARS

The extent of this substantive concern became explicit in two rather striking NPCSC decisions on 2 September 1983.[3] The 'Decision Regarding the Severe Punishment of Criminal Elements Who Seriously Endanger Public Security' modified the stipulated maximum punishments, set out in the 1979 Criminal Law, so that the death sentence could be applied despite apparent lack of criminal law sanction. The NPC decisions extended the death penalty to apparently serious cases of harm to public security, so that not only 'ringleaders of criminal hooligan groups' but also those who organised secret superstitious sects to carry out 'counterrevolution', those who injured state personnel, those who engaged in the traffic of human beings, those who forced women into prostitution, and those guilty of 'imparting criminal methods' in serious cases suddenly became vulnerable to the death penalty.

A second decision, 'Decision Regarding the Procedure for Rapid Adjudication of Cases Involving Criminal Elements Who Seriously Endanger Public Security', modified various time limits set out in Articles 110 and 131 of the Law of Criminal Procedure so as to facilitate rapid sentencing of serious offenders. The Decision explicitly subscribed to quick action '...where the main criminal facts are clear and the evidence irrefutable and the people's indignation is very great...'. The 1979 stipulated time limit for appeal, for example, was shortened from ten to three days, and hence procedural requirements were flexibly superseded in cases involving great public indignation.

The open door and economic reform have furthered the influence of foreign legal experience; however, notwithstanding official claims to the contrary, the social implications of such policies would also seem to have politically filliped a latter-day Chinese Legalism which rather deliberately construes the necessity of law as an educational deterrent against criminal deviance and which correspondingly emphasises the nature of criminal law punishment. In short, in a time of increasing Western influence and domestic 'crisis of faith' (*xinyang weiji*), there is a somewhat paradoxical reliance on the death penalty, even in the contemporary circumstances of reform stressing the social as distinct from the class nature of law.

There is really very little significant debate as to whether or not to abolish the death penalty, but the 2 September 1983 decisions did precipitate debate on the application of the death penalty across the various categories of crime in the Criminal Law. Reformers predictably focused on the incongruence of Chinese and international norms on capital punishment and the need to restrict, rather than to expand, these categories.

Also, reformers explicitly decried counterrevolution as a political and not a legal concept. In April 1989, reform went so far as to call for the revision of the counterrevolutionary provisions of the Criminal Law and the reduction of the scope of the death penalty. However, the focus on social control is especially noticeable in the contemporary approach to Criminal Law, and, even among otherwise-progressive legal circles, there is a widely shared strong belief in the deterrent effect of capital punishment. China's law experts have occasionally replied to Western human rights agencies that, in fact, China's use of the death penalty is humane and rooted in the principle of 'killing less'. While some observers have noticed that contemporary Western public opinion has increasingly favoured restoring capital punishment, very few observers have directly commented on past liberal US Supreme Court decisions which viewed capital punishment as cruel and unusual punishment.[4]

The question of leniency or severity in the circumstantial application of the criminal law has always been a question of direct policy response to the prevailing official understanding of objective circumstances. In the classical art of Chinese politics and law, for example, too much leniency can result in 'a little benevolence towards a crook interferes with the great benevolence [owed the people]' (*xiaorenzhe darenzhi zei*). Also, Chinese 'judicial independence' – it will be recalled – only implies the exclusion of Party Committee involvement from court proceedings. Otherwise it formally respects the Party's guidance of the legal system for the purposes of achieving the comprehensive management of social control.

Many legal reformers have, themselves, argued that capital punishment is legitimately necessary to assuage the anger of the community. It is frankly accepted as a deterrent. Its redeeming social implications are made explicit in the execution of criminals by a bullet to the head as witnessed by the assembled masses. There is the common, if not cynical, parlance, which is often cited alike by political and legal authorities who highlight the deterrence provided in Criminal Law, namely, 'kill the chicken to frighten the monkey' (*sha ji xia hou*), or 'execute one to warn a hundred' (*sha yi jing bai*).

Conversely, community solidarity and united front political calculation sometimes requires a policy of 'less killing' (*shaosha zhengce*), and leniency for followers whose good intentions were manipulated only by a handful of alleged malcontents. Under the glare of international media exposure, and in the context of internal leadership dispute over the Party's approach to China's student intellectuals, leniency recently became the optimal policy factor in the 1990–1 trials of June 4 activists.

Since 1989, some legal reformers have had the temerity to challenge the conceptual validity of criminal law reasoning which highlights the imposition of the death penalty in order to assuage extreme popular resentment against specific criminals. They cite the lack of any objective measure of such resentment; however, Kang Runshen countered, in a 1991 issue of *Zhengfan luntan* that while *sha yi, jingbai* reasoning should not in the current period constitute a major consideration, it is still a factor which is justified in its beneficial social effects and in its mass-line consideration of popular resentment and community involvement in the legitimation of the justice system.[5]

In the context of calls throughout the 1980s to revise the Criminal Law so that it more closely approximates the purposes of economic reform, there has been both criticism and support for a more extensive incorporation of Criminal Law norms in non-criminal law which is applied in economic reform activity. While some reformers have been concerned about the failure of the criminal law to respond positively to the new course of economic reform, others are concerned that the criminal law has not reinforced the state against unacceptable capitalist activities.

There have been ongoing attempts to de-criminalise formerly questionable market economic activity which, as late as the early 1980s, would have been commonly regarded as illegal. Beginning in 1983 the State Council's Legal System Bureau began the laborious task of checking the estimated post-1949 50 000 regulations of the State Council, central ministries and governments of provinces, municipalities and autonomous regions to identify and rescind regulations on the books contradicting contemporary reform policy on finance, insurance, taxation, trade marks and free markets.[6]

In the early 1980s, anything to do with private enterprise still had dubious legal status. There were, for example, no rules as to what might be regarded as legitimate business expense, or commission, but there was a growing political focus on official corruption. There was public and official antipathy towards 'leather-bag companies' (*pibao gongsi*) or companies which, for example, brought together buyers and sellers for a fee. Chinese traditional culture despised the self-interested pursuit of profit at public expense, and in the more contemporary ideological terms of Mao's regime, such companies apparently add no real value to production. Despite newly acquired policy sanction, tertiary services are even now struggling for recognition against a hostile public attitude and legal interpretation of their apparently unacceptable capitalistic features.

Through the early to mid-1980s, there was not only criticism of the Criminal Law's failure to back up new economic law with appropriately criminal law punishment, there was also serious controversy as to the appropriate strategy by which to expand the criminal law categories relating to serious economic crime. While legal reformers exhaustively argued the importance of criminal law revision so as to adapt to the changing circumstances of the new commodity economy, those most apprehensive over a related loss of social control, and the need for strong campaigning against serious economic crime stressed the specious tendency to defend illegal behaviour with reference to economic reform. This tendency is, for example, allegedly manifest in official arguments that 'to perpetrate a crime is to perform meritorious service'. Supporters of economic reform were charged with putting 'pioneer laurels' on the heads of criminals who masqueraded as 'meritorious persons'.[7]

Over the 1980s, even given the immediate reaction to the Tiananmen Square event, the imposition of the death penalty for counterrevolution declined significantly, whereas there was an extraordinary imposition of the death penalty to deal with serious economic crime. Ironically, there is a greater *conceptual* reliance on the death penalty under Deng Xiaoping than under the Mao Zedong regime of the mid-1950s. The 1980s' discussion of economic crime emphasised changes in the economy and the need for transition in the legal system, but Party policy has been at cross-purposes as economic reform precipitated conflicting, contemporaneous emphasis on rational procedural authority as well as on 'combining flexibility and principle' and 'combining punishment and leniency'. In his 1987 analysis of these conflicting trends, an American professor of law, Stephen Davis, commented that the expansion of the death penalty '...runs counter to the spirit of the new criminal laws designed to enhance regularized adjudication and protection against erroneous judgements'.[8]

In the 1988–9 legal reform debate on revision to the 1979 Criminal Law there were qualified disagreements over the 1980s extension of the death penalty. Legal experts such as Gao Xijiang and Luo Hua were prepared to consider modest contraction of the death penalty. The supporters of such contraction pointed to world trends in the reform of criminal law, and they raised objection to the reliance on the 1982–3 NPCSC decisions as the means for expanding death penalty categories. In his case for revision, Gao Xijiang, for example, noted the current 15 articles of criminal law and 14 NPCSC decisions mandating the death penalty, and argued that

NPCSC decisions regarding criminal law should be nullified in favour of a related revision of the Criminal Law. This contradicted the conservative argument that NPCSC action accorded with a justified principle of flexibility and that with the achievement of public order and social stability it would be easier to change NPCSC decisions as distinguished from changing the Criminal Law as a fundamental law.

Gao Xijiang argued that the doubling of categories in the 1980s conflicted with the world trend. On the other hand, he backed away from a drastic contraction which might undermine the state's response to serious crimes and cause an adverse public outcry affecting the credibility of the legal system. Not only did he subscribe to reduction of the death penalty for the crime of counterrevolution, he also wished to delete the death penalty under the NPCSC decision regarding those who teach others how to commit serious crime. However, he moved in the opposite direction in his support for the inclusion in the Criminal Law of the death penalty for fraud.

Another legal expert, Luo Hua, wrote in favour of the restriction of death penalty categories, arguing that in light of the international trend to limit or eliminate the death penalty, the image of China's criminal law had been tarnished with such a blatant extension of the death penalty and that this, on the contrary, undermined the comprehensive management of social control. In order to achieve good effect, Luo contended that the effective use of the death penalty in the achievement of social control would have to comply with the principle of fitting the punishment to the crime. Luo's bold ideas on revision of the Criminal Law included the elimination of 'public surveillance' (*guanzhi*) and the elimination of the special provisions on counterrevolution in favour of a new, non-political conceptual category of crime, namely, endangering state security (*guoshizui*). Also, Luo opined that the Criminal Law itself need not reference 'taking Marxism–Leninism, Mao Zedong Thought as guidance', as this was inappropriate to the format of departmental law, and as the four cardinal principles had already been enshrined in the state constitution.[9]

In China there is also emphasis on the death penalty with two-year reprieve as a uniquely rehabilitative legal aspect of 'socialism with Chinese characteristics'. This separate category of death penalty has been internally criticised at various times since 1957. Wang Yong, in his notes on the history of criminal law research, referred to a stage of research between 1957 and 1976 when advocates of the structural theory of crime critiqued both the death sentence with two-year reprieve (*sihuan*) and forced labour as anachronisms of Chinese feudal society. Such reformist advocacy was, in the Gang of Four period, rejected as part of the alleged conspiracy to restore capitalism.[10]

The contemporary argument for retention even now rests upon Mao Zedong's Yenan theory of contradiction accentuating the political importance of rehabilitation or 'transformation'. The two-year reprieve is seen as advancing the policy of less killing and is regarded as an appropriate compromise in cases where there is no significant public outcry against the criminal. Mao's conservative theory treats this category of death sentence as only one aspect of a broader range of means to achieve comprehensive management of social control. Politically, Mao at times was prepared to argue the importance of severe punishment in light of the principle ('little compassion [for the individual criminal] opposes great compassion [owed the people]'). At other times Mao expediently subscribed to less killing as an eminently practical political exercise, reinforcing social control which can neither rationally nor politically be achieved on an exclusive principle of 'ruling the country by criminal punishment' (*yixing zhi guo*).[11] Although Mao was flattered by Taiwan comparison of himself with the vicious unifier of Chinese history, Qin Shihuangdi, he was not at all philosophically committed to Legalism as the preeminent approach to the establishment of a durable political power.

A legal scholar at the Northwestern University of Politics and Law, Wang Changxue, has explained that the two-year reprieve is currently extended in relation to the following ten criteria:

1. The crime did not involve serious harm to the interests of the state and people.
2. The criminal was not a ring leader of an organised group.
3. The criminal turned himself in, confessed, reported other crimes or otherwise performed some 'meritorious service' (*ligong baoxian*), including reporting on counterrevolutionary organisation, helping ward off a grave accident, or the creation of invention which significantly contributes to the economy.
4. The criminal has not incurred significant public indignation for his crime.
5. The criminal belongs to a category which has been formally designated in policy as a category to which 'less killing' applies.
6. The crime belongs to the category of non-antagonistic contradictions among the people, and the victim committed wrongs which provoked the criminal to murder.
7. The criminal is mentally handicapped.
8. The criminal is a ringleader of a group of criminals, but his exemption from immediate execution is politically expedient in the splitting-up of the other members of the group.

9. The criminal can serve as an informant.
10. Criminals who are later found to have deserved immediate execution on the basis of new evidence, but who have, since conviction under the two-year reprieve, demonstrated repentance.[12]

When taken together these criteria certainly reveal the calculated utilitarian dimensions of Chinese criminal law thinking.

Beida criminal law expert Wang Zhongyi pointed out in 1991 that the death penalty with two-year temporary suspension, pending subject repentance, constitutes a dualism fostering both the deterrent force (*weishe li*) which characterises the death penalty as supreme punishment, and the 'transforming function' (*gaizao gongneng*) of ordinary criminal punishment.[13] The psychology of impending execution is not only mobilised so as to expedite the individual criminal's repentance, but more importantly it confirms the political legitimacy of Mao's original notion of rehabilitative transformation as a necessary component of the comprehensive management of social control.

The contemporary contradictions of criminal law reform were revealed in the recommendations of a spring 1989 research group for NPC revision of the 1979 Criminal Law. While the Chairman of the group, Ciu Qingsen, publicly advocated the elimination of the concept of counterrevolution from the text of the Criminal Law and the reduction of the scope of the death penalty, other members of the group wanted the expansion of the death penalty to include crimes of serious fraud and forgery.

This is in line with a general, if not objective, tendency to ascribe extraordinary significance to material goods, especially state property, and with the leadership's political focus on corruption as it adversely affects the legitimacy of the regime and its policies which have facilitated commodity production, rural specialised households, city private enterprise, state enterprise autonomy and foreign investment. The group also recommended the inclusion in the criminal code of new crimes relating to the illegal transference of land, falsification of occupational credentials, damage to mineral resources, patent infringement, unauthorised diversion of public funds, prostitution, drug abuse, serious environmental pollution and the sale and publication of pornography.[14]

On the eve of Tiananmen Square, China's political and legal circles were focusing not only on serious economic crime involving profiteering, fraud and embezzlement, but also spectacular rises in the percentage proportion of juvenile crime and serious offences in the totalled crime figures. A survey of the proportion of juvenile crime in China's 22 major cities showed a steady increase from 18.1 per cent in 1972, to 22.4 in 1973 and 31.2 in 1976, up to anywhere between 60 and 70 per cent in 1988.[15] Juvenile delinquents were becoming increasingly involved in serious family violence and, as discussed in Chapter 4, there was a growing concern over the spread of prostitution, drug smuggling and the trafficking in human beings which has resulted in newly legislated severe punishment in the post-June 4 period.

There was also a rise in serious offences, inclusive of murder, robbery, theft, larceny and rape, which called for severe sentences ranging from immediate execution, to death with two-year reprieve, to life imprisonment. 'Serious crimes' had increased by 65.7 per cent between 1987 and 1988.[16] In the first three months of 1989, for example, 94 800 criminals were sentenced, and this was a rise of 10 per cent over the same period in 1988, but the number of severe sentences, involving death, death with a two-year reprieve [the Chinese claim that 99 per cent in this category have their sentences commuted to fixed-term or life imprisonment] and life imprisonment increased by nearly 17 per cent over the same period in 1988.[17]

The Western human rights offensive has often focused on China's death penalty, political crime, administrative detention and the explicitly circumstantial application of criminal law punishment in the violation of the rights of the individual citizen. In fact, in light of this focus, some Western authors are of the opinion that China is not even at the point of struggling to achieve a legitimate rule of law. This focus will be examined herein with special emphasis on the legal reform debate concerning comparative criminal law response to counterrevolution and serious economic crime.

COUNTERREVOLUTION AS A DECLINING ASPECT OF CRIMINAL LAW

The changing focus in contemporary Chinese Criminal Law is especially apparent in the continuing erosion of support for the law on counterrevolution.[18] This law has enjoyed seminal symbolic relevance. It acts as a cornerstone in Mao Zedong's class theory relating to the dictatorship of the proletariat, particularly as this theory discriminates between 'non-antagonistic contradictions' among the people and 'antagonistic contradictions' between the people and the class enemy.

The 1990–1 trials of leading activists of the 1989 democracy movement thrust the Chinese law on counterrevolution back into the international spotlight. Hong Kong Professor Carlos Wing-Hung Lo, for example, notes that the trials provided 'a solid basis for a sound assessment of the mainland Chinese legal system' so that CCP leaders' commitment to democratic values could be assessed along with the extant political commitment to 'monolithic rule'.[19] However, what is not particularly well known in the West is that, just prior to the June 4 event, the NPC had scheduled a major revision of the related State Constitution and Criminal Law provisions of counterrevolution. Counterrevolutionary crime (*fangeming zui*) was to be replaced by 'crime endangering state security' (*weihai guojia anquan zui*).

A compelling legal argument amplifying policy emphases on economic reform and the open door was mustered against the retreating proponents of class struggle. One can already see, in the drafting of the 1979 Criminal Law, an important, but graduated political reaction to the way in which counterrevolution was maliciously bandied about in the Cultural Revolution period. As early as 1983 there was consideration of amendment to the law on counterrevolutionary offences, and this reaction became increasingly powerful through the 1980s and resulted in the formal scheduling of this law for NPC revision.

Contrary to US State Department reporting, the debate has continued even in the context of post-Tiananmen Square legal fallout. Some reformers have concentrated upon a careful reiteration of the pre-June 4 1989 argument for revision, while others have focused on the narrowing of the law's application with reference to those involved in the Tiananmen Square event. In the opinion of the author, the argument against this category is unlikely to go away, particularly in light of the inexorable logic and uncontrollable political implications of accelerated economic reform and the open door.

During the heady and violent early 1950s campaign to suppress counterrevolutionaries, the issue of counterrevolution was fundamentally a question of policy. Theoretical discussion of the nature of law deliberately highlighted Mao's principle of combining principle and flexibility and the struggle against the class enemy. 'Predictability', as distinguished from 'flexibility', in law was not then, as it is now, such a serious concern. As confirmed in Patricia Griffin's study of pre-1949 counterrevolutionary crime, flexibility was frankly an essential matter of political expedience:

> The Communists viewed flexibility as a positive attribute necessary to respond to a changing revolutionary situation, and purposely built it into their legal system through imprecise legal codes, frequently changing laws and flexible interpretation of laws.[20]

Combining severe punishment with leniency, as recently highlighted in the 1990–1 trials, has its origins in Mao's late 1930s united-front political tactics to isolate the 'hard-core of reaction'. Mao self-consciously used 'dual struggle' to discriminate between different kinds of enemy and both to cooperate and struggle with wavering popular elements of the national united front against the Japanese. Mao claimed that he would only execute the most heinous traitors to the national cause, and for explicit purposes of domestic political unity, he supported 'killing none and arresting few'.[21]

Mao's utilitarian approach elaborated upon a distinction between the people's distant, or 'general enemies' (*pubian yuantou*), and the 'immediate enemies' (*zhijie yuantou*). During the anti-Japanese war, the latter consisted of 'small counterrevolutionaries', or 'small Chiang Kai-sheks' who, at the local level, actually carried out violent crimes against the people and were, therefore, the immediate targets of popular indignation. The former, however, were 'big counterrevolutionaries', or big 'Chiang Kai-sheks' such as Emperor Pu Yi and Chiang's generals. In Mao's view, they may all have actually deserved the death penalty, but they were not an immediate target of local people's anger; and they had not directly and concretely harmed the people. Rather than killing them, Mao advised that they 'transform' themselves. If their crimes did call for the death penalty they were to receive the death penalty with a two-year reprieve.

This logic is a little suggestive of the practical tendency of Confucian officialdom to protect its own members from the harshness of penal punishment, but it does not formally reinforce the contemporary emphasis on severity for the 'ringleader' as distinguished from the 'follower'. Commenting on whether or not Mao's distinction results in the awarding of different punishments for the same crime, Gao Daohui claimed that Mao's selective approach was not necessarily inconsistent with a principle of equality. Gao maintained that punishment had to vary in relation to different social conditions. In this view, the law legitimately responds to the objective situation in society. The same kind of crimes in fact had resulted in different degrees of social harm under different social conditions, and the requirement that 'punishment fit the crime' (*zuixing yizhi*) had to be interpreted in the light of these differences.[22]

Mao's utilitarian dialectics deliberately synthesised two conflicting opposites so as 'to use leniency and severity to support each other'. The two qualities not only depend upon one another for their mutual identification, but they had also to integrate within policy characterised by 'leniency without ignoring severity, and being severe without forgetting about leniency'. Again, there is herein an explicit political calculation of social control. On the one level, Mao's strategy of 'dividing and breaking up criminals' (*fenhua wajie fangzui fenzi*) seeks to educate and reform the majority of criminals, while, on another level, there is a targeting and isolation of a supposed minority of intransigent criminals which requires the swift application of severe punishment.[23]

The 1990–1 trial emphasis on leniency is expressed in a somewhat-awkward political distinction between the majority of activists who were simply misinformed and manipulated, and the 'ringleaders' (*shouyao fenzi*) and those who organised and led counterrevolutionary groups, *zuzhi lingdao fangemin jituan*. The great mass of students who joined in the reciting of anti-government slogans were not, therefore, accused of counterrevolutionary crime. Premier Li Peng explained that such leniency draws from Mao's theory on antagonistic and non-antagonistic contradiction. Severe punishment was to be meted out only to the ringleaders who allegedly sought to overthrow the regime and socialism, and to those who had committed acts of violence which were liable to criminal law punishment.

Leniency was predictably offered to students who had taken part in demonstrations and fasting and who had committed extremist acts and made extremist statements which were not by definition criminal.[24] Presumably, such a policy did not imply exemption from disciplinary action under the 1 January 1987 NPC 'Regulations governing Offenses Against Public Order of the People's Republic of China' which detailed non-criminal minor offences concerning minor disturbance to the social order, obstructing public safety, infringing upon the rights of citizens and trespassing on public or private property.

Li Peng's leniency accorded well with established Chinese historical revolutionary perspective and contemporary legal argument. An authoritative gloss on Mao's combining severe punishment with leniency can be found in Gao Mingxuan's leading university text on the criminal law which extensively highlights Mao's 1956 explanation in 'On the Ten Major Relationships'.[25] In his particular dialectical understanding of revolution and counterrevolution Mao referred to critical liberal opinion which had criticised his 1951 suppression of counterrevolutionaries as unnecessarily severe, and he countered: 'Had it not been for the campaign of suppression, the people would not have approved our present policy of leniency.'[26] Mao, on the other hand, rejected any comparison with Stalin's purges of the 1930s, just as he had done in Yan'an in the early 1940s.

Mao Zedong's earlier correlation of the killing of counterrevolutionaries with killing wartime captives was reiterated in 1956. In his April 1956 speech Mao referred to the fact that there was no need of a law stipulating that no counterrevolutionary in the Party or state need ever be executed, as there was already in place '...a policy for internal observance which need not be made public, and all we need do is carry it out as far as possible in practice'.[27] Perhaps, Mao was thinking of the vulnerability of great leaders in light of the denunciation of Stalin when he observed: 'Probably no one is free from mistakes, only some make more and some less, and once they do they need help'.[28] Mao referred to the Yan'an distinction between making mistakes and committing counterrevolution and he asserted, in contradistinction to Stalin's way of doing things: 'For revolution, it is always better to have more people'.[29]

In stressing the circumstantial need for leniency in 1956, Mao exuded a calculated utilitarianism which originated with his united front politics:

> We don't have [counterrevolutionaries] executed, not because their crimes don't deserve capital punishment, but because such executions would yield no advantage. If one such criminal is executed, a second and a third will be compared with him in their crimes, and then many heads will begin to roll. This is the first point. Second, people may be wrongly executed. Once a head is chopped off, history shows it can't be restored, nor can it grow again as chives ... The third point is that you will have destroyed a source of evidence. You need evidence in order to suppress counterrevolutionaries.[30]

Mao's gratuitous underscoring of evidence may be less than reassuring, but his reluctance to 'chop off heads' seems to invoke Confucian imperial thinking as to the finality of the death penalty and the need for elaborate appeal and direct resort to the Emperor for its confirmation.

In light of such political and legal caution, the flagrant accusations of counterrevolution in the Cultural Revolution seem quite extraordinary. However, perhaps it is even more startling that after the promulgation of the new criminal law of procedure, in the very midst of Deng Xiaoping's reform, there was a relaxation in the required Supreme Court review of the death penalty. Article 144 of The Law of Criminal Procedure of the People's Republic of China, which came into effect on 1 January 1980, flatly stipulated: 'Sentences of death are to be approved by the Supreme People's Court'.[31] However, under the authority of a 1983 Supreme Court circular, high courts at the provincial level are, themselves, under circumstances where either the high court is the court of second instance, or there is no appeal by either the defendant or procurator, empowered to finalise the death penalty.[32]

The Criminal Law of 1979, including its special provisions on counterrevolution as crime which, due to its exclusive origins in 'antagonistic contradiction', constituted the most grave harm to society, was pulled together, after repeated attempts at drafting, in an urgent response to the political ramifications of the Cultural Revolution. Peng Zhen, a senior leader of the drive for post-Cultural Revolution legal reform, had himself been detained without warrant by a radical mass organisation. Many in China's senior leadership had been unceremoniously paraded through the streets in peaked dunce caps with placards slung from their necks proclaiming their counterrevolutionary crimes.[33]

Cultural Revolutionary 'flexibility' seemingly had no natural or legal limits. The Minister of Coal, Zhang Linzhi, was beaten to death for his counterrevolutionary activities. During the power seizures, leaders were arrested without warrant and subjected to kangaroo court proceedings, and concurrent physical and verbal abuse. Their homes were ransacked. Their relatives were subjected to brutal psychological abuse in the Red Guard search for incriminating evidence of counterrevolution. The Party, in its subsequent analytical summary of events, acknowledged that there had been a tragic confusion of 'people' with the 'enemy' and 'non-antagonistic' with 'antagonistic contradictions'.[34] Increasingly, the Party elite began to realise that the political and legal category of 'counterrevolution' constituted a double-edged sword.

As a result of Cultural Revolutionary violence the crime of ideological crime was labelled as a leftist evil perpetrated under the 'feudal fascism' of the Gang of Four. And, even before the completed drafting of the new Criminal Law and Criminal Law of Procedure, there was swift passage of new regulations on the formal requirements of arrest and detention. The NPCSC passed on 23 February 1979 'Regulations of the People's Republic of China Governing the Arrest and Detention of Persons Accused of Crimes'. This was the beginning of a general institutional offensive against Cultural Revolutionary nihilism which focused on the elaboration of criminal law procedure and the restoration of the institutional principle, *fen gong fuze huxiang zhiyue*, which presumed an interactive system of procedural checks and balances between the courts, public security and procurators.

The Beijing Journal, *Xiu shi bao*, hailed the newly promulgated regulations regarding arrest as they reinforced established constitutional rights *vis-à-vis* Cultural Revolution 'rampages'. Noting the Gang of Four destruction of the legal system, the Journal referred to the timely nature of the regulations in light of the following:

> A small handful of counterrevolutionary criminals opposed to our revolutionary legal system unscrupulously violated the citizens' civil rights of the inviolability of personal freedom and dwelling. They injured anyone they wished to injure, and arrested anyone they wished to arrest... many innocent people were persecuted to death.[35]

Also, in 1979 the Party Central Committee endorsed the removal of ignominious labels of the 'four kinds of elements' which had been coercively applied during the trumped up class struggles of the Cultural Revolution. Apparently, this involved a review of the previous imprisonment of hundreds of thousands. The labels of 'landowner, rich peasant, reactionary and bad element' were to be removed from all but 'a very small number who persist in the reactionary standpoint'. A dissident, Xiao Min, responded with an article in *Siwu luntan* (5 April Forum) attacking the 'unscientific' wording of such policy which in effect had 'the force of law'.

While Xiao's article looked forward to the transcendence of artificially created class struggle and decried the political competition to seize ever-larger numbers of class enemies, it attacked conventionally worded policy which failed to clarify what was meant by 'a very small number':

> Any number can be simultaneously small and large. Therefore, the terms 'large number' and 'small number' cannot accurately express the numerical concept. Our policies are, in fact 'laws' to be enforced by the 'lower level'. The solemnity of laws requires that the regulations and articles be worded scientifically, accurately and rigorously, so that there are no loopholes and no way to interpret them subjectively. When such simple daily life words as 'large' and 'small' are employed in a document with the force of law, it will only furnish openings for some people.[36]

The thirty-third and final draft of the new criminal law, promulgated on 1 July 1979, incorporated a fairly rigorous, if somewhat incomplete, political response to the legal nihilism of the Cultural Revolution. The new law did not entail the repudiation of counterrevolutionary crime. Rather the Party claimed to make the concept more narrow and more precise. The new law was debated on June 27–30 both at the NPC and the Chinese People's Political Consultative Committee, where deputies sought greater clarification on the definition of 'counterrevolutionary offence'.

Liaoning University Professor Song Zexing, for example, emphasised the conceptual importance of actual harm to society so as to insure that reactionary thinking and erroneous statements would not be treated as counterrevolutionary offences. The NPC Law Committee responded to the emphasis on social harm by inserting the phrase, 'which jeopardizes the People's Republic of China' in between 'any act' and 'for the purpose of overthrowing the political power of the dictatorship of the proletariat and overthrowing the socialist system is a counterrevolutionary offence'. The new wording regarding such acts was compared to the offence of high treason in the criminal codes of other countries.

In a related response to the Gang of Four's opportunistic usage of counterrevolution, discussion focused on the gang's indiscriminate tendency to bring false charges against innocent people. In response to Rong Yiren, one of pre-liberation China's biggest capitalists, the NPC inserted into the law a principle of compensation for economic losses stemming from malicious false charges.[37] Deputy Zhao Chaogou, a well-known journalist in the 1940s, spoke of the new importance assigned to the personal and democratic rights of citizens in light of past accusations of counter-revolution, but he too laid his stress on the clarification, rather than the elimination, of the legal concept of counterrevolution:

> Now the criminal law gives a clear definition of a 'counterrevolutionary': only one who commits an action with the purpose of overthrowing the political power under the proletarian dictatorship and the socialist system can be considered a counterrevolutionary. Moreover, the law also stipulates that no person is allowed to be framed and persecuted by any method or means. All these provisions, laid down after summing up the bitter lessons of the past, will effectively protect the democratic rights of citizens.[38]

Perhaps the possibility of leftist resurgence and retribution was still too real but, in 1979, at the onset of economic reform, no one was prepared to challenge frontally the legal notion of counterrevolution. In legal theory, 'flexibility' was still thought to be a positive attribute, and analogy was carried forward into the new law. Article 79 simply stated:

> A crime that is not explicitly stipulated in the Special Provisions of this Law may be determined and punished according to the most closely analogous article of the Special Provisions of this Law, but the matter shall be submitted to the Supreme People's Court for approval.[39]

A leading participant in the drafting and a member of the Party Central Committee's Politics and Law Group, Gao Mingxuan, elaborated on Article One's reference to Marxism–Leninism–Mao Zedong thought as a 'guide'. While, in the West, the 1954 State Constitution had often been positively cited in terms of its emphasis on legal development as opposed to mass-line justice, Gao cited Mao's endorsement of the 1954 Constitution as an admirable combination of 'flexibility and principle'.[40] Also, Gao insisted that 'no crime without a law and no punishment without a law' had to be upheld along with a continuing emphasis on 'flexibility'. The latter was one of the five central requirements of Mao's thought on legal development, which also included objective criteria in establishing criminality and punishment, the correlation of punishment with the severity of the crime, emphasis on class struggle and dictatorship and adherence to 'seeking the truth from the facts'.[41]

'Flexibility' was deliberately built into the new draft law in terms of deliberately vague wording such as 'when the circumstances are serious' in Article 94. According to Gao, this was necessary to crime-fighting and the protection of the people from crime. Article 103 endorsed the imposition of the death sentence for crimes, outlined in Articles 98, 99 and 102, if 'the harm to the State and people is especially serious and circumstances especially odious'.[42] No specific guidance was given as to the determination of what is and what is not 'serious' because, as Gao argued, judicial personnel need some latitude if they are going to combat crime efficiently in a vast country with such a diversity of local conditions.

'Flexibility', therefore, reiterated the circumstantial interpretation of the law in 'accordance with time and place' (*yinshi zhiyi and yindi zhiyi*).[43] This does not of course address the question as to at what point such flexibility becomes less necessary in the light of improvements in national communications.[44]

Despite the blatant political misuse of counterrevolution in the Cultural Revolution, and again in the characterisation of the April 5th Movement of 1976 as counterrevolutionary, as well as strongly felt reservations within the Party leadership itself as to the potential use of the concept to discredit the revolutionary credentials of Party leaders, the category of counterrevolutionary crime passed from the 1951 law into the new 1979 criminal law. Ironically, the Party still needed this category of law in order to punish the Gang of Four. Calls for revision were then limited to the need for more precise definition and a narrowing of the scope of counterrevolutionary offences. However, the distinction between action and ideas still continued to pose conceptual problems and, in the subsequent development of the 1980s reforms, there was more substantive criticism of the new Criminal Law's special provisions on counterrevolution.

Although the Party had clarified that no one could be tried for ideological crime, and negative personal opinion and internal consciousness which criticised the regime and its socialism could no longer be considered as instances of counterrevolution, the new Criminal Law still included in the second section of Article 102 an emphasis on the propagation of counterrevolution.

The question as to how to distinguish such propagation from the constitutionally guaranteed right of free speech was featured at the trial of the famous dissident, Wei Jingsheng. Wei was tried in 1979 under the old law of 20 February 1951. In his own defence, he emphasised the distinction between mistaken ideas which inevitably come with democratic freedom of expression and counterrevolutionary propaganda. Mao himself had made a similar distinction, but only with limited internal reference to state and party cadres. Regardless of his original unflattering criticism of Deng Xiaoping, Wei's defence cleverly appealed to the emphasis on objectivity within Deng's own logo, 'seeking the truth from the facts', and insinuated a relation between the underlying logic of law on counterrevolution and the Gang of Four's political manipulations of the notion of counterrevolution.[45]

The journal *Tansuo* (Exploration) was originally the locus of Wei's alleged propagation, and it editorially commented on Wei's defence drawing attention to 'flexibility' in law:

> to guarantee completely the rights of freedom of thinking and freedom of speech, laws in their most ideal form should be able to distinguish between speech and acts of violence and distinctly stipulate that speeches expressing people's ideas and opinions should not constitute any crime; otherwise, even the strictest laws will become highly 'flexible'.[46]

Writing in *Tansuo*, Lu Lin relatedly raised a fundamental question of objectivity in law and politics. He critiqued Article 90 which stipulates that counterrevolutionary crime includes 'actions which are for the purpose of overthrowing the political power of the dictatorship of the proletariat and the socialist system', and he asserted that there is no firm criteria for the judgement of action which is subjectively human:

> The press has discussed the meaning of these actions and held that since words, either spoken or written, only express ideas, a 'guilty' verdict should never be passed on account of words. As to 'action', however, the explanation is also ambiguous. The propagation of an ideology or doctrine can be treated as an 'action'. Anyway, all activities are carried out by human beings, so it is the human element that has decisive effect. In other words, there is no firm criterion.[47]

The lack of legally definable criteria certainly bothered some reformers in China's legal circles. Kang Liqun, for example, commented on the related issue of the 'object' (*keti*) of counterrevolutionary crime. The law's emphasis on protecting the dictatorship and socialist system as object created ambiguity which the law itself could not easily handle. Kang did not hesitate to point out that the Gang of Four had attempted to justify their political actions in terms of the protection of proletarian dictatorship, and he suggested that the law should not be denigrated in questionable justifications of changing political outcomes.[48] The new Criminal Law had only just taken effect when intrepid reformers began fundamentally to question the law's relation to politics.

Even in the full glare of international publicity, Deng Xiaoping's leadership refused to compromise insisting that Wei's action or propagation constituted a criminal act. In response to the Spring 1989 signature campaign to release Wei Jingsheng, the Beijing Municipal Higher People's Court addressed several Beijing University electors and re-stated the 1979 logic to the effect that Wei was tried, not for ideological crimes, but for illegal action: 'The so-called ideological crime means punishing people's criminal ideas in ideology as if they were actual criminal acts. Such is the method of feudalism and fascism....The law of our country punishes acts, and not ideas.'[49]

Whereas Wei Jingsheng had been tried under the older 1951 law, the Gang of Four were publicly tried under the new law in a televised special court proceeding by order of the NPCSC. In the opinion of one of the trial judges, Fei Xiaotong, the trial itself constituted '...a lesson, vivid and profound, on the rule of law'. The trial, which was nevertheless extensively criticised internationally, was billed internally as a convincing attempt to move China out of feudal society where government is 'government by an individual or certain individuals and never by law'.[50] Domestic publicity surrounding the trial emphasised that even the once high and mighty would have to submit to equality before the law. Zhang Youyu, Director, Institute of Law, CASS, and Jiang Hua, President of the Supreme Court, stressed the trial's rigorous application of the rules of evidence under the new Criminal Law of Procedure to prove criminal motive and purpose of overthrowing political power.[51]

The proceedings highlighted the existence of a counterrevolutionary clique. Mao's obstreperous wife, Jiang Qing, in a defiant outburst claimed that she had indeed ordered the struggle-and-criticism against the Head of State, Liu Shaoqi. And as for the alleged illegal order to search Liu's house in violation of the State Constitutional guarantee of personal rights, she taunted her accusers and proclaimed: 'House searches were a deviation from the main current, but if you "smash the four olds", of course you have to search houses–that's revolutionary behavior!'[52]

While the political leadership at the point of trial wished to prosecute for counterrevolutionary violence, it was also attempting to respond to the abusive accusations of counterrevolution which had characterised Cultural Revolution politics. Deng Xiaoping's political commitment to build up the legal system drew to a significant extent from his own bitter experience of Cultural Revolutionary legal nihilism. The trial focused attention on the distinctions between the rule of law and rule by man, and the *Guangming ribao* dutifully editorialised on the trial's significance as a victory of the revived legal system over 'feudal fascism':

> And furthermore, they [the Gang of Four] used the power they had appropriated to themselves, and in their illegal machinations wilfully trampled underfoot our Constitution and our laws, doing their utmost to reintroduce the infamous inheritance which had permeated feudal dictatorship, namely 'replacement of law by power' and 'replacement of law by personal pronouncements', so as to institute their regime of feudal fascism. They did not want to see or hear evidence.... They did not care for judicial procedures, but ransacked homes, sent people to prison and inflicted cruel punishments. They would execute people without trial.[53]

In dealing with Mao, the trial applied Mao's own circumstantial distinction between mistakes and counterrevolution. Mao had made political mistakes, whereas the Gang of Four had broken the criminal law. The concept of counterrevolution was, nevertheless, unwieldy and double-edged. It increasingly attracted the critical attention of China's legal reformers. Legal criticism of counterrevolution as a legal rather than a political concept was filliped by changing political perspective on the economy, and the developing Party criticism of Mao's own confusion of antagonistic and non-antagonistic contradictions.

Under this theory, counterrevolution is generally an exclusive matter of antagonistic contradiction, and it was considered to be the most harmful type of crime in so far as it encompassed a direct contradiction between the class enemy and the people. As has already been seen, the treatment of counterrevolutionaries varies circumstantially in relation to the leadership's political calculations, and leniency, as well as severity have been theoretically entwined in the deliberate dialectics of Chinese criminal law. The transparent subjectivity of such a politically volatile exercise has been progressively exposed over time. While some reformers explicitly challenged counterrevolution as a political rather than a legal concept, others continued their efforts to modify the actual legal significance of the concept.

Professor He Xin, in his charted study of contradiction and counterrevolutionary crime, noted that even though Articles 91–102 all relate to antagonistic contradiction, a distinction could be made between major and minor counterrevolutionary crime. Such minor crime might only require public surveillance and would require more leniency than serious economic crime or violent crime involving arson, rape and murder.[54]

The 10 June 1981 NPCSC decision seemingly gave more procedural protection to those accused of counterrevolution than to those accused of other types of serious crime. The latter stipulated that Supreme Court approval would not be necessary to deal quickly with criminals who 'seriously disrupt social peace and order, such as murderers, robbers, rapists, bomb throwers and arsonists'. High-level provincial people's courts could act in the last instance and mete out the death sentence without reference to the Supreme Court, but the same decision reiterated that death sentences, meted out to counterrevolutionaries, would still require People's Supreme Court approval in accordance with the PRC Law on Criminal Procedure.[55]

With the evolving 1980s codification of the law and the continuous attempts to enhance the law's 'lofty dignity', there was robust controversy over the underlying concept of counterrevolutionary crime, as it relates to legal theory and the new Criminal Law concerning the essence of criminality and 'object' (*keti*) and 'purpose' (*mudi*). Standard textual explanations of the objective criteria of criminality define object as 'the socialist relations' protected by the criminal law and endangered by the actions of the accused or subject. The 'object' is one of four necessary components of criminality which also include the physical elements, the accused and the mental elements.[56]

The physical elements include the consequences of action, the means, the time and place, and the mental elements, which only loosely correspond to Western *mens rea*, encompass intention, negligence and purpose. 'Intention' (*guyi*) can be either direct or indirect intention, *zhijie guyi* or *jianjie guyi*. In a case, for example, where A shoots B in the head with the intent to kill B there is direct intention, but where A intends one action, which then sets in train a series of related events resulting in the unexpected consequence of B's death, then indirect intention is manifest.

However, with the mental elements relating to counterrevolutionary crime, legal theory had accentuated the special character of such crime by exclusively invoking 'purpose' (*mudi*) which can only relate to direct intention. The controversy over the wording of Article 90 in the Criminal Law highlights the importance of purpose in the phraseology, 'all acts endangering the People's Republic of China committed with the purpose of overthrowing the political power....', and Articles 100, 101 and 102 refer to 'whoever for the purpose of counterrevolution' (*yi fangeming wei mudi*).[57] The question of purpose was later highlighted in post-June 4-reformer attempts to narrow the interpretative significance of the counterrevolutionary law in the judgement of student demonstrators.

In the years immediately before Tiananmen Square reformer legal opinion boldly asserted that counterrevolution is a 'political' rather than a 'stringent' concept of law.[58] Article 90's stress on the purpose of overthrowing the dictatorship and socialism was challenged for its lack of clear legal interpretation of objective reality. While there was no direct reference to the Wei Jingsheng case, the issue similarly spotlighted the tension between Article 45 of the State Constitution, guaranteeing freedom of speech, and Article 90 of the Criminal Law. Regardless of the formal rejection of ideological crime, the Criminal Law had not provided an effective gloss as to how to draw the legal line between the promotion of healthy criticism of bad government and an act of disseminating counterrevolutionary propaganda.

Legal reformers proposed that the conceptual category of purpose and Chapter One special provisions relating to counterrevolution be dropped in favour of expanded language concerning state security and the categories of crime discussed in Chapters Two and Three relating to 'endangering public security' and 'undermining the socialist economic order'. On 2 June 1989 the country's leading national law daily, *Fazhi ribao,* editorialised on the need for revision, citing the practical difficulties of legally interpreting purpose and object in the proving of counterrevolutionary crime.[59] The *Fazhi ribao* contended that the meaning of 'crime of counterrevolution' is neither stable, nor 'scientific'. This category of crime was construed as in conflict with Deng Xiaoping's open door and 'one country, two systems' strategy *vis-à-vis* Hong Kong. Also, the past Soviet decision to abandon this category was duly noted, as were current difficulties in achieving extradition, given international reaction to China's explicitly political language of counterrevolution.

The paper argued that the distinction hardly seemed worthwhile, noting that, despite the conceptual distinctiveness of *'mudi'*, the punishment for counterrevolutionary homicide is the same as that for homicide. Specific proposals for revision were advanced. Article 90 was to be deleted and to be replaced with new wording relating to intent to damage the national interest and security. The crimes, detailed in Articles 91–7 were to be retained, but the wording, 'purpose of counterrevolution' was to be struck out. The same words were to be deleted from Article 100 which highlights crime endangering public security and personal safety. Deletions were recommended along with additions detailing new categories of crime concerning the national interest and security, assassination, propagating war, inciting nationalities and selling state secrets.

In October 1989, professors at the People's University in Beijing indicated to the author that in light of the serious political implications of Tiananmen Square, revision was no longer a priority. Gao Mingxuan even suggested that the change of wording from 'counterrevolutionary crime' to 'crimes endangering state security' was not all that substantive, as the issue in either case turns on the security of the state.[60] However, the continuing controversy over the contemporary relevance of counterrevolutionary crime was readily apparent at a post-June 4 national seminar on the criminal law. He Bingsong, as a standard bearer for the conservatives, attacked the pre-June 4 revision argument as 'dangerous'. In his attempt to rebut Jiang Ping and Liang Hua, he argued that the counterrevolutionary rebellion in Tiananmen Square had conclusively proven the need for such law even in the 'primary stage of socialism'.[61]

The pro-revision argument once again drew attention to the declining rate of counterrevolutionary crime in relation to the rising rate of crime relating to public order and economic crime. Firm statistics on counterrevolutionary crime have not been freely circulated. However, on 2 April 1991 the Supreme People's Court reported that the majority of officials prosecuted for involvement in Tiananmen Square had already been released. A total of 715 officials had been prosecuted for serious violent offences involving beating, burning and homicide, and of this number 72 had been prosecuted for attempts to overthrow the regime.[62]

Table 6.1 Countrywide Procuratorial approved arrests in 1987

Type of crime	*Total*	*Arrests**	*Arrests***
All categories	357 056	336 101	20 955
Counterrevolution	501	501	----
Harming public security	10 417	9 603	814
Damaging social economic order	8 399	6 251	2 148
Infringing citizens' personal and democratic rights	81 960	9 511	2 449
Violation of property	213 089	20 1737	11 352
Disrupting order of social administration	37 450	37 450	----
Harming marriage and the family	1 215	217	998
Dereliction of duty	2 748	----	2 748
Other	1 277	831	446

* Arrests as approved by the Procuratorate upon Public Security request.

** Arrests decided by the Procuratorate on its own initiative as provided for under Article 51, Criminal Law of Procedure.

Source: Wang Zhongfang, *Zhongguo shehui zhian zonghe zhilidi lilun yu shijian* (Theory and Practice of Comprehensive Management of Public Order of China) (Beijing: Qunzhong chubanshe, 1989) p. 464..

A preliminary sense of the relative proportion of counterrevolutionary crime to other types of crime, under Part II, Special Provisions of the Criminal Law, may be gleaned from the 1987 chart of nationwide arrests (Table 6.1). The 1987 comparative significance of counterrevolutionary crime in relation to crime involving the violation of property rights is extraordinary. The former accounted for only 0.14 per cent of total procuratorial arrests, whereas the latter accounted for 59.6 per cent of the same total.

Prior to Tiananmen Square, there was growing concern in legal circles as to the changing statistical configuration of crimes committed. In 1988, serious crime had increased by 65.7 per cent over 1987, and theft accounted for 80 per cent of the 827 000 crimes reported for 1988. Commenting on the 1988 statistics, Yu Lei, Deputy Minister of Public Security, pointed his finger at an estimated transient population of 50 million and acknowledged sharp increases in crime particularly in those large cities most affected by the open door policy.[63]

Although these rates were exceptionally low by international standards, Yu doubted whether China could return to the extraordinarily low domestic crime rates of the 1950s and 1960s when there was little commodity economy and very little contact with the outside world. What is perhaps more politically important here is not the relative international rates of comparison but mounting domestic apprehension over what appears to be a stark change in the enjoyment of security of person and property. Nostalgia for the past achievement in public order is likely to feed a more conservative emphasis on the need for greater social control as coordinated through Party leadership and as reinforced in campaigns for socialist spiritual civilisation.

Commenting on a 14 per cent increase in the criminal caseload of the first quarter of 1989, President of the Supreme People's Court noted that 94 800 criminals had been sentenced and that there had been a 17 per cent increase in the death sentence and death sentence with a two-year reprieve over the same period in 1988.[64]

In response to the figures showing a long-term decline in counterrevolutionary crime, He Bingsong single-mindedly countered that, regardless of the declining statistics, the qualitative impact of counterrevolutionary crime on socialism was patently obvious. He explicitly invoked Deng Xiaoping's authoritative support for 'one central task and two basic points', but he placed his emphasis on the four cardinal principles. He also attempted a less-than-compelling rebuttal of all of the arguments cited in the 2 June 1989 *Fazhi ribao* editorial.

In early 1990, Liang Huareng and Zhou Songsheng replied to He. Their tone was somewhat conciliatory, but again they insisted that counterrevolution was simply unwieldy as a matter of law. They protested that they certainly had no intent to weaken the State response to forces hostile to socialism. They believed, on the contrary, that the proposed name-change to 'crimes endangering state security' would enhance the State ability to respond legally to problems of disorder. They claimed that distinguishing criteria for the classification of crime is derivative of an emphasis on what object has been infringed, and the proposed focus on state security would create the needed legal precision. Rather than challenging the underlying premise of flexibility, they enlisted flexibility in support of a name-change which, after the fashion of 'seeking the truth from the facts', would bring the law more effectively in line with reality. They reassured He and his conservative political backers that the proposed revision was merely a matter of 'form' (*xingshi*), and that the new form, 'crimes endangering state security' would not substantively change the relation of law to society.[65]

Such theoretical qualification as to 'form' may have weakened the pre-June 4 argument that the criminal law had to change in response to a qualitative change of social and political context from the pre-1949 base area wartime struggle, and the early 1950s establishment of the revolutionary regime, to the 1980s focus on economic reform in the 'primary stage of socialism'. Liang and Zhou still referenced this change, but they somewhat incongruously argued that, in 1990, the changing times required no more than a change of form. At the same time, they observed that what might be considered counterrevolution in China might well be considered revolution in other countries. In contrast to He, they chose to emphasise the basic point of economic reform and the open door within 'one central task, two basic points'. They suggested that counterrevolutionary crime conflicted with the open door policy, and more specifically with the essence of 'one country, two systems' and future coordination of the different laws of the PRC, Hong Kong and Taiwan.

The legal circles had, nevertheless, to deal with the very sensitive political problem of legally trying Tiananmen-Square activists. Supreme Court opinion called for a very careful distinction between qualitatively different kinds of contradictions, the establishment of purpose and the strict adherence to the boundaries between crime and non-criminal activity. While ideological crime had been presumably erased from the criminal law, the question of establishing the ideological disposition of the subject still had to to considered in the legal determination of purpose. While critically hostile Western human-rights opinion may have very little interest in following the internal legal logic of the trials, it is, nonetheless, quite important to our understanding of the internal dynamic of legal thinking and to any assessment of the potential for revision of the law within the practical limits of prevailing legal and political reality.

Liu Mingxing's legal opinion on the legal identification of the crime of counterrevolutionary instigation, for example, reviewed a case of a 17-year-old high-school student who, upon hearing during his afternoon calligraphy class, 'Down with X [presumably Deng Xiaoping]' replicated the same slogan in his calligraphy exercise book. Liu opined that there was no evidence of previous counterrevolutionary thought and that, therefore, there was no purpose. He quickly added that the student certainly needed ideological education.[66]

Liu also noted the case of a young worker who forged an identity as a military official and wrote senior leaders a letter warning them of dire consequences should they give the order to fire in the Square. Liu reasoned that there was no indication of a purpose to overthrow the government, and that the confused and misinformed student had only sought to avoid the potentially violent implications of a direct confrontation with military authority.

Liu sought to exclude from criminal law consideration of counterrevolutionary offences several categories of action. He distinguished between a vague opposition, in words and deeds, to the people's democratic dictatorship and a pointed opposition to upholding the four cardinal principles. He suggested exemption for people who, due to their confusion while under the influence of bourgeois liberalism, spread words exaggerating the comparative advantages of capitalism over socialism. Even if they had participated in demonstrations, he thought they ought to be exempt from the special provisions unless they were important organisers of counterrevolutionary instigation.

Liu also advised that a careful distinction had to be made between counterrevolutionary crime and 'similar crime' (*xiangyangzui*). He seemed to blunt the influence of the NPCSC decision of 2 September 1983 when he contended that subjects who, during the turmoil, had spread confusion by inciting superstition among the masses, could not be construed as having propagated counterrevolution. Liu further distinguished between instigation of counterrevolution which purposefully sought the overthrow of the state and socialism, and insult or libel which was aimed at particular persons.

On the other hand, Liu's exercise in legal reasoning cited an example of three offenders in Beijing who had defaced the portrait of Mao Zedong as a clear case of counterrevolutionary sabotage as stipulated in Article 100 of the Criminal Law. He used this case to discriminate between sabotage and instigation. In contrast to the portrait case, student demonstrators in Beijing and Shanghai had taken the flags down at government buildings to mourn fellow students who had died during the Beijing demonstrations. Liu opined that this could not be interpreted in light of the more serious provision on sabotage as there was no deliberate damage done to the object, namely, the national flag, and there was no clear establishment of purpose, as in the Beijing portrait case. However, Liu was not altogether charitable in his assumption that the students in the flag cases were guilty of a 'counterrevolutionary arrogance' (*fangeming qiyan*), which amounted to an incitement of others to participate in counterrevolutionary action.[67] One might reasonably expect that Western human rights analysis will treat such legal reasoning as arcane casuistry.

The inherent elastic property of principles such as flexibility, and indeed 'combining severe punishment with leniency', was amply demonstrated in the post-June 4 trials of leading dissidents. In the immediate aftermath of June 4, when the leadership was attempting to re-consolidate its power, severe punishment was applied against workers, beginning with the execution of three men in Shanghai who, on 6 June, had allegedly set fire to a train which had crashed through a barricade killing six people.[68] The 2 September 1983 NPCSC regulations permitting the speedy trial of criminals who '...commit heinous acts greatly endangering public security' were expeditiously applied in the trial of the workers who had 'endangered public security' as distinguished from having committed a crime of counterrevolution.

In reporting on the November 1990 to February 1991 trials of students and intellectuals, the Chinese press was less than scrupulous in reporting the details concerning what Criminal Law articles were used in each trial, but the press did underscore the conceptual application of 'combining punishments with leniency'.[69] One can extrapolate from the nature of the event itself the authorities' inclination to apply Articles 90, 95, 98 and 102 with respect to the instigation of counterrevolution. On 26 January, Liu Xiaobo was convicted of spreading 'counterrevolutionary propaganda', but he was 'exempted from punishment', and commended for 'meritorious service'. Although he had allegedly violated Article 102 in inciting the masses to resist State law, this action was mitigated by his organisation of students to withdraw from the Square, and '...he prevented thugs from using weapons'.[70]

Wang Dan, who was number one on the State's list of 21 top student organizers, was tried under Articles 90 and 102, but he received leniency and was sentenced to four years in prison. Article 98 stipulates a sentence of not less than five years; however, Article 59 allows for a reduced sentence under this prescribed minimum. Apparently, Wang had not only confessed, but the Chinese authorities alleged that he had assisted the State in pointing out other offenders – and such 'service' can justify the application of Article 59. Guo Haifeng, a leader of the Beijing Autonomous Students Federation, was given a 'light sentence' (*cong jing*) of four years under the loosely worded Article 58 which merely refers to warranted circumstances. The Criminal Law itself fails to provide explicit definition as to the different types of circumstance which apply under the two different articles, 58 and 59. As for Wang and Guo, they were released early on 17 February 1993 in what was widely interpreted in Western media as a gesture to the International Olympics Committee and the new presidential administration of Bill Clinton.

The late May Students Federation position calling for the evacuation of the Square may have had an impact at Guo's trial. Reportedly, martial law troops had captured Guo and three associates who were allegedly in possession of incendiary bombs, but Guo later repented and confessed and his action had had 'no serious consequences'.[71]

On the other hand severe punishment was meted out to Cheng Ziming and Wang Juntao, of the Social and Economic Sciences Research Institute, and presumably their respective 13 years' sentences reflected the formal distinction between supposedly confused students and the behind-the-scenes ringleaders who had served as the real instigators. Also, leniency requires a confession, and Cheng and Wang both refused to oblige. Moreover, their Institute was connected with Zhao Ziyang, and Robin Munro of Asia Watch has suggested that their trials politically served to confirm a conspiracy to establish a 'second headquarters' within the Party.[72]

The difficulties of legally interpreting the special provisions on counterrevolution in the trials of those involved in Tiananmen Square confirm the pre-June 4 legal argument concerning the irrational and explicitly political nature of such anachronistic law. The controversy is not over. Such law conflicts with the overall trend towards rationality in China's legal reform. Such rationality has been incrementally asserted in economic reform, where it must also compete with a focus on political stability, public order and social control.

ECONOMIC REFORM AND THE CHANGING NATURE OF CRIME

Economic reform has generated important opportunities for the development of law and the consolidation of its 'lofty dignity', but the relation between criminal law and social control has also been accentuated in the politics surrounding the social implications of economic reform. Criminal law research focused on the growing lack of alignment between prevailing criminal law and contemporary policy. China's legal reformers had to deal with the twisted complexities of 'credits [referring to the policy benefits associated with economic reform policy predicated in 'seeking the truth from the facts'] turning into crimes' (*yougong bian youzui*), and 'crimes turning into credits' (*youzui bian yougong*).[73]

Even as the proponents of Criminal Law revision attacked the law on counterrevolution, they called for the multiplication of the categories of crime relating to the changing social circumstances of the economy. While some reformers pointed out that there was solid precedent in Western legal experience for the extension of criminal law norms into non-criminal law, the drastic extension of the death penalty into categories of serious economic crime more probably originates in a widely held domestic assumption concerning the efficacy of this penalty as a deterrent.

Regardless of the formal policy commitment to 'killing less', in the early to mid-1980s campaigns against serious economic crime there was a much greater resort to 'swift and heavy punishment'. While there was no frontal attempt to discredit the new procedural law, there was, nevertheless, a 'rush to justice' which disturbed some of the more progressive-minded members of China's legal circles.[74] Late 1980s discussion of revisions to the 1979 Criminal Law revealed a growing conflict in the theoretical and policy reaction to the developing priorities of economic reform. Gao Xijiang, for example, in an article in *Faxue pinglun*, wrote of the need to widen the debate on the contemporary relevance of the Criminal Law. In his opinion, while there was no need for the detailed stipulations on counterrevolution in the light of the evolution of Chinese society, there was a growing need for more concrete Criminal Law stipulations concerning theft, smuggling, speculation and profiteering. Gao wanted the Economic Law rather than the Criminal Law to take up much more slack on the question of economic crime.[75]

Luo Hua, in his review of proposals for revision of the Criminal Law, suggested that, despite NPCSC regulations, there was still confusion and contention over the subject status of enterprises and associations involved in speculation, profiteering, smuggling and bribery, and he argued that the Criminal Law should clarify that such subjects have legal responsibility as legal persons.[76] According to the account of Sun Qian and He Yong, this issue precipitated a heated debate between advocates of 'positive' as opposed to 'negative theory' (*kendingshuo* versus *foudingshuo*).

Established negative theory maintained that a legal person, unlike the natural person, in law does not have flesh and bones, and that criminal responsibility can only be borne by those who have physically committed the crime in question. Otherwise, if legal persons were punished innocent members of the corporate legal person could become liable to criminal punishment. Reformer advocacy of the British and American criminal law example, which, in effect, subscribed to 'positive theory', triggered suspicion in the minds of those who argued that China's so-called legal persons formed part of the material base for the transition from socialism to communism. They believed that it would be ideologically reprehensible to penalise such progressive institutions.[77]

Sun and He wanted an alternative Chinese socialist solution to the lack of consistency in the legal response to economic crime. While, in theory, the legal person was to bear responsibility for economic crime in terms of bearing the costs of fines and compensation for social harm caused, and, if necessary, the law would single out the responsible natural person for criminal law punishment, in practice, too often the legal person was fined, but the criminally responsible personnel were let go, or the criminally responsible personnel were punished, and the legal person escaped fine.

This controversy was rendered all the more complex in that foreign capitalists had, in the economic reform, become legal persons. And, while in Chinese legal theory and politics there has always been a very strong insistence on China's sovereignty, there has also been some disinclination to apply the full rigour of Chinese criminal law to American and European nationals, in order to avoid compromising the trade and investment benefits of the open door policy in international disputes over the legitimacy of the Chinese legal system.

Advocates of the criminal law responsibility of the legal person nevertheless appeared to gain the upper hand. While calling for an expansion of the criminal law to include new punishments for new crime, such as the suspension or stoppage of enterprise operations for rectification or the disbanding of the legal person, the research office of the Higher Court of Guangdong Province argued that in so far as a legal person commits crime which essentially furthers the interests of an organisation, as distinct from the pursuit of personal gain accruing to a natural person, then the punishment should be lighter for such a legal person.[78]

Many legal reformers argued that the established notion that the Criminal Law only deals with 'natural persons' (*ziran ren*) had to be overcome, as there was a pressing need to expand the scope of the objects protected under Criminal Law.[79] In the context of the transition away from 'taking class struggle as the key link' towards new emphases on reform, the open door and the promotion of productive forces and commodity production, the change of the Criminal Law's scope related, in theory, to the changing standards underlying the evaluation of the social harm caused by crime, and the move away from emphasis on the political to the economic consequences of crime. Like many others, Luo Hua also noted that the Criminal Law had only twenty articles which clearly sanctioned the use of fines as punishment. He believed that this scope had to be significantly enlarged to deal with the proliferation of economic crime.[80]

Gao Mingxuan's comments on the need for revision also responded to changing economic reality. He argued that the Criminal Law had yet to catch up with the developing need to protect the legitimate development of the 'three types of capital enterprise' (*sanzi qiye*) namely private enterprise (*getihu*), joint Chinese-foreign enterprise, and solely owned foreign enterprise. Existing criminal law had failed to respond effectively to new crimes relating to the making of counterfeit foreign currency, the manufacture of fake or bad quality products, the forging of patents, use of substandard measurements, bankruptcy and advertising fraud, industrial espionage, and the wanton destruction of mineral, water and vegetation resources.[81]

Gao joined with another senior Criminal Law expert, Zhao Bingzhi, to summarise contemporary trends in criminal law research and the need for Criminal Law revision.[82] Writing shortly before the Tiananmen Square event, Gao and Zhao pointed to a prevailing sentiment that the development of productive forces had superseded the class struggle as the central task, and dictatorship and the suppression of the class enemy could no longer act as the pivot of Criminal Law which, in the current period, had to play a more extensive role in the provision of social guarantees for the personal, property and democratic rights of citizens.

Gao and Zhao opined that a commodity economy had not, in and of itself, created a new pattern of economic crime. On the contrary, it had created positive conditions for the improvement of the material base of society which would ultimately serve to help reduce social tendencies towards serious economic crime. On the other hand, the two authors seemed to argue that the rising trend of serious economic crime is threatening the healthy development of the new commodity economy.

Criminal law research generally concluded that the Criminal Law has to incorporate private economy into the objects to be protected under a newly revised criminal law. The past political censure of 'wealth has no compassion' (*weifu buren*) is deemed inappropriate to the social values sustaining the new commodity economy. Distinguishing *ziyouxing* (criminal punishment relating to freedom) and *caichanxing* (punishment involving property) the Gao–Zhao summary suggested that the criminal system of punishment which had given exclusive weight to the deprivation of freedom had to be adjusted so as to give new weight to punishment which incorporates the deprivation of property through fines and public confiscation.[83]

Within the same summary, there was an argument for a 'mild criminal law' (*huandedi xingfa*), which would moderate emphasis on scientific comprehensive management against crime with the active promotion of the citizen's democratic and personal rights. While the Criminal Law's underlying philosophy of punishment generally called for 'socialist humanism' (*shehuizhuyidi rendaozhuyi*), the summary emphasised the need for severity so as to insure the principle of equality before the law as against any special privilege in the treatment of state personnel who heinously use their official position to commit crime.

Two new broad methodological approaches are suggested in this summary of criminal law research. It is recommended that the Criminal Law be overhauled in relation to changing circumstances rather than incrementally responding as problems arise due to the inconsistences among NPCSC 'separate criminal laws' (*danxing xingshi falu*), and the inconsistences between criminal law norms within the Criminal Law and the criminal law norms within non-criminal law departments. Ad hoc NPCSC response to policy priorities emphasising the stringent and immediate control of serious economic crime, such as in the 8 March 1982 and 9 September 1983 regulations concerning economic crime and public order, was criticised as inconsistent with the strengthening of the Criminal Law.

Critics divided over the assessment of contemporary experience of extending criminal law norms into non-criminal law. Some reformers objected to the resulting inconsistency and the need to achieve a more stable basis for dealing with new crime within the Criminal law itself.[84] Some advocates of the development of economic law, on the other hand, focused on the need for flexibility and the Criminal Law's lack of expedient response to the changing demands of the economy. They contended that the Economic, as distinguished from the Criminal, Law could respond more quickly to changing patterns of crime within the economy.[85] Also, some of China's most senior experts on Criminal Law argued for the incorporation within the Criminal Law of new categories of crime relating to hijacking, the sale of poisonous products, medical malpractice, fraudulent advertising, insurance and bankruptcy fraud, child labour, computer theft of property and information, destruction of rare water and animal resources, advertising fraud, incest, the intentional propagation of sexual disease, destruction of rare water and animal resources, the use of drugs, etc.[86]

There was in economic reform a proliferation of new forms of economic opportunity as well as general confusion in the legal distinction between legitimate and illegal activity: for example, the media in the 1980s publicised techniques to domesticate legally protected black bears so as to harvest their bile for sale for medical purposes. Originally, this was promoted to reduce the killing of the wild black bear for bile; however, the popularisation of such farming resulted in cruel practices and increased poaching on an endangered species. Similarly, would-be entrepreneurs became so interested in the smuggling of the giant panda for its fur that the Supreme People's Court, in a July 1978 circular, required sentences, including 10 years fixed imprisonment, life imprisonment and even death for bear killing and smuggling, or the sale of one giant panda skin.[87] A new NPCSC law on the protection of wildlife finally went into effect on 1 March 1989.

To cite yet another interesting example of the changing nature of crime in relation to the dynamics of economic reform and the open door, the legal circles focused on the need for new and tighter laws on drug smuggling, transportation and manufacture. The major problem was identified as transit drug trafficking. Geographically, this was concentrated in Yunnan province which borders on the 'golden triangle' with Burma, Laos and Thailand, and in Guangdong which served as a conduit for the international export of drugs from Hong Kong and Macao.

The tactical response of the Chinese authorities was reportedly complicated by their own 'accommodating and magnanimous practice towards the entry of foreigners, overseas Chinese, visitors from Hong Kong, Macao and Taiwan since the adoption of the open policy'.[88] Unsympathetic Western analysis has suggested that the Chinese are overly sensitive to the history of the nineteenth century Opium Wars and that charges against foreigners 'blunt the willingness of China's anti-drug officials to confront a long-hidden problem openly and realistically…'.[89] The Chinese, however, are quite open in their criminal law focus on severe punishment for drug-related offences.

Domestic criminal law authorities have focused on the rising number of drug addicts among China's youth, and the legal circles have already turned their attention to the potential for domestic drug production. These circles, for example, divided into three opinion groups on the question of whether it was necessary to incorporate a new crime of 'growing original narcotic plants' (*zhongzhi dupin yuan zhiwu*) into the law. The groups apparently disagreed on the issue of object. A more liberal-minded group called for only limited administrative punishment, arguing that the real action lay in trafficking and international smuggling, and that small-scale village production was largely confined to remote rural areas where the locals had an innocuous tradition of growing narcotics only for their own consumption.

On the opposite side of this law-and-order spectrum, a hardline second group recommended that plant growing should be conceptually equated with making drugs as a serious criminal act. In the self-described middle of this spectrum, a third group rallied for supplementing extant law with a specific crime of 'growing original narcotics plants', which was to be distinguished from the more serious crime of 'drug-making'. This position claimed that administrative punishment had not stopped the spread of the practice, and there was concern that what was originally a benign village pursuit could easily turn into a much larger unwanted economy which would have dire consequences for social order.[90]

On 28 December 1990, the NPCSC duly passed a decision on the smuggling, sale, transporting and manufacturing of drugs; however, senior legal reformers criticised the legislation for adding to the continued procedural confusion over drug-related crime.[91] The new law's Article Two, nevertheless included the compromise distinction between the 'manufacturing' of drugs, and 'growing original narcotics plants'.

The law coopted a qualified emphasis on administrative detention in a quantitative response to peasant poppy cultivation, but also emphasised the criminalisation of such illicit large-scale horticulture. Article Six stipulated not more than five years' imprisonment and fines for the growing of at least 500 and not less than 3000 poppy plants. Those caught growing less than the 500 minimum were subject to fine and administrative detention of 15 days.[92] While noting that the NPC Law Committee had made no fundamental changes to the draft decision on banning drugs, Song Rufen, Vice-Chairman of the Committee, reported to the NPCSC on 27 December 1990 that the Committee had made changes to the stipulated punishments in Articles Two and Three, which in effect represented a strong law-and-order message. The original wording, for example, prescribed for those convicted of smuggling, transporting or manufacturing more than 2000 grams of opium or more than 100 grams of heroin, life imprisonment or the death penalty, but the revised wording provided less room for tolerance by dropping the prescribed amounts to more than 1000 grams of opium and 50 grams of heroin, and stipulating 15 years, life imprisonment or death.[93]

On yet another serious front, there was, in the mid-1980s, a national outcry over the production of phoney medicines and sub-standard food products. Ironically, the quality of the national drink, *maotai* – the libation most popularly associated with open door diplomacy – deteriorated as entrepreneurs expanded their profit margins by watering down their famous product.

The failure to incorporate pharmaceutical administration into the legal system was also publicly acknowledged with great regret. In 1985, national media exposure was given to the public burning of medicines produced in Fujian's Jinjiang area. The illicit production of 45 Jinjiang factories had been allowed to pass by local authorities. The *Renmin ribao* also noted cases of self-employed producers who used industrial alcohol in the production of spirits and the widespread official approval of false products and the failure of local authorities to mete out appropriate Criminal Law punishment to factory directors and managers. Often, upon discovery, these officials experienced minor administrative discipline and/or fines, but they retained their posts.[94] On 1 July 1985 a new NPCSC law on pharmaceutical management came into effect which included new standards for licensing, testing and packaging of medicinal products.[95] Public health departments were empowered to mete out administrative punishments, and it was re-affirmed that officials who grossly neglected their duties could be criminally charged with 'dereliction of duty'.

The literature on criminal law revision has been especially indignant over inconsistent treatment in law of official 'embezzlement' (*tanwuzui*). There is no doubt that economic reform created proliferating opportunities for official corruption in the 1980s. State officials were perceived to be in an extraordinary position to exploit the differential between state-priced and market-priced goods. The media correlated corruption with the coexistence of 'a primitive market system with old and excessively authoritarian economic, political and cultural systems'.[96]

The death penalty was often used to create an example of cadres during the 1980s campaigns against serious economic crime. For example, during one day's docket in December 1989, the Guangdong higher court dealt with the cases of Yu Xilun, Wang Weicheng, Chen Shaogeng, Li Yibing, He Guozhen, Fu Zhaoshen, Dong Fang. Yu, the Party Secretary of the Guangdong Provincial Medicine Company, and Wang Weicheng, the company's deputy director of planning received life sentences for accepting bribes in excess of 7000 yuan. Chen Shaogang, a company pharmacist, was given a 10-year term, and Li Yibing, a company business chief, received 5 years. The four allegedly falsified their records to cover-up the sale of large amounts of valuable Chinese herbal medicine at artificially low prices to a Hong Kong businessman in exchange for three colour television sets, three refrigerators, three cameras, two bicycles and cash totalling 23 000 yuan. The object, in this case, amounted to an estimated loss to the state of HK 10 million dollars.

On the same day, He Guozhen, an accountant of the Shengang Credit Society, *Conghua Xian*, and his accomplice, Fu Zhaoshen, were sentenced to death for stealing 322 000 yuan. The Court also gave a death penalty with two-year reprieve to Dong Fang, the deputy manager of a Guangdong building materials company for accepting bribes valued in total at 42 000 yuan. Dong had allegedly extorted 13 900 yuan in cash, and he had acquired 20 television sets and 19 cassette recorders in exchange for 1800 tons of cement and 8500 square metres of glass. This object, or loss to the state, was costed out at 108 000 yuan.[97]

Proposals for criminal law revision encompassed an especially strong remonstrance regarding the need to reinforce equality before the law and the related principle of establishing punishment which fits the crime. Many legal reformers stoutly contended that officials who take advantage of public trust and use their position for self-enrichment should be punished more severely than a common thief who might have stolen the same amount. Suggestions for revision of the criminal law almost always included emphasis on the elimination of the crime of embezzlement, which applies only to officials. This categorisation was popularly thought to have led to gross leniency for officials and abuse of judicial practice. There was a growing public consciousness of examples of officials getting off with an administrative slap on the wrist, and the legal circles vociferously called for the application of the full force of the Criminal Law's punitive applications against corrupt officials, including the firm application of the death penalty in cases involving large sums of money.

Again, public and legal attitudes are historically informed. There is herein a compelling modern parallel with the imperial, or feudal, disjuncture between failed Confucian official moral example and abusive judicial practice by which officials freed themselves from the more onerously punitive dimensions of the criminal law. Officials, in other words, self-servingly subscribed to a modern day equivalent to the Confucian prescription, *dezhu xingfu* (ethics are primary and criminal punishment secondary).[98]

Incensed legal reformers were outraged at official violation of socialist property. They underscored the fact that the minimum amount for embezzled funds, as set under the crime of embezzlement, was set at a much higher minimal amount in comparative reference to other categories of property crime involving theft and fraud. According to the NPCSC's 'separate criminal laws', punishment for embezzlement was scaled to the amount 2000 yuan, and the death penalty could be invoked in relation to bribes amounting to 50 000 yuan, whereas the criminal law relating to theft of only two to three hundred yuan could fetch imprisonment, and the theft of 10 000 yuan could result in the death sentence.[99]

Despite the continuing symbolic significance of counterrevolutionary crime in the 1980s, China's political and legal circles were much more concerned with the Criminal Law's response to the changes in society wrought by economic reform. The question of official corruption was fundamentally tied to the crisis of faith, and official corruption, more than the occasional sporadic acts of counterrevolution, preoccupied the minds of those engaged in the revision of the Criminal Law.

CONCLUSION

The changing nature of crime in the recent reform years reflects a very complicated transition in China's society and economy. Under the painful happenstance of rapid societal change and attendant axiological crisis, China's legal circles have been struggling with the question as to how to ensure a routine realisation of the principle, *nullum crimen, nulla poena sine lege,* (no crime, nor punishment without law).

Notions of the law's predictability and the importance of socially guaranteed protective procedure have been highlighted in the more rational circumstances of reform, especially as these circumstances contrast in almost everyone's mind with the legal nihilism of 'class struggle as the key link'. The growing parallel between the Chinese and Western patterns of criminal procedural activity seem quite striking, and perhaps this is consistent with the growing First World presence within China's developing economy.

With the open door policy, there has been significant Western influence on the legal thinking of reformers who are engaged in the comparative study of criminal legal development. One cannot discount the growing significance of Western influence on Chinese legislation; on the other hand, there is obviously a Chinese dimension to the Chinese effort to ensure social control in this difficult period of societal transformation. The focus on assuaging public indignation is an ongoing cultural factor of traditional 'substantive rationality'; and it is difficult at this stage to guage accurately the extent to which this perspective ranges beyond the law-and-order mindset of the political leadership to find sympathetic support throughout changing contemporary society.

These conflicting influences and perspectives account for what is apparently an inconsistent approach to the death penalty and the inconsistent weighting of counterrevolution and serious economic crime. In terms of the Weberian sociology of law, there is an ongoing and uneven adjustment in the relative weights assigned to formal and substantive rationality in response to the tensions within China's newly emerging economy and society, and the related internal challenge to Chinese political culture which originates in the developing structure of interests.

7 Hong Kong and the Rule of Law across 'Two Systems'

Hong Kong's fast-unfolding transition from colonial administration to a 'high degree of autonomy' under the 'direct leadership' of the Chinese central people's government has already provided significant opportunity for the comparative reading of the international contents of the 'rule of law'. Deng Xiaoping's formula, 'one country, two systems' (*yiguo liangzhi*) optimistically assumes that two different legal systems and legal cultures can operate on the basis of different systemic conceptions of society and economy, and can cooperatively co-exist within the confines of a single sovereignty.

As the entry in *Blackwell's Encyclopedia of Political Science* indicates, 'rule of law' is 'open textured', and certainly it has inferred significantly different emphases in different constitutional settings. However, it is not uncommon for experts, trained in the British Common Law system, to presume that the rule of law invokes specific systemic assumptions in terms of judicial, as opposed to legislative, interpretation of the law, the centrality of *stare decisis* and the general applicability of precedent as generated in particular case law. These characteristics are thought to reinforce judicial independence and the limitation of arbitrary state behaviour through limitations imposed by the courts. This perspective does not seriously consider whether there are any other viable means by which to ensure a system of checks and balances circumscribing undesirable state behaviour. Without this kind of judicial independence, it presumes that it is impossible to contemplate the development of the rule of law.

Philip Baker and Berry Hsu discuss the relation between the Common Law tradition and Hong Kong's Basic Law. For the rule of law to take hold they require the real manifestation of seminal 'attitudes and behaviour patterns' such as the 'individual and legal rights, the Rule of Law, judicial independence, the adversary system and independent legal profession, the jury system, and the right of silence and presumption of innocence' as typical of the Common Law.[1] These co-authors assume that despite the formal authoritarian dimensions of Hong Kong's colonial administration, the rule of law has been practiced in Hong Kong in terms of practical application of equality before the law, legal protection of the individual against unlawful arrest, detention, search and imprisonment and the citizen's access to courts in the challenge to the acts of executive authorities.[2]

This kind of heavily qualified comparison is not entirely convincing, as it neglects the comprehensive assessment of the influence of the continental legal tradition on China's legal system, and it also fails to explain the formal PRC procedural subscription to some of these same principles across the various departments of PRC law. There is no gainsaying the existence of self-conscious distinction between 'judicial independence' (*dulidi sifa*), which invokes the Western political tradition of 'separation of powers', and the more limited Chinese idea of *shenpan duli*, implying the freedom of the day-to-day judicial process from inappropriate political influence. However, does the concept of the rule of law necessarily invoke the 'energetic expression of judicial power' as the very 'proclamation of the separation of powers'? In his authoritative study of the future of law in Hong Kong, Professor Raymond Wacks regards the judicial review of executive and legislative acts as the essence of, or the 'true meaning of the Rule of Law'.[3] Also, it is often presumed that Hong Kong's contemporary legal system and culture is essentially British. Western comparative Hong Kong-PRC analysis is not particularly interested in pinpointing shared reference points in traditional Chinese legal culture.

Obviously comparison should encompass the growing cross-cultural complexity of the Chinese legal system, the relative capacity for foreign borrowing and the practical implications for the future PRC and Hong Kong legal systems. There is, for example, little current political support for the PRC's adoption of a Chinese-style system of precedent, but the case has been repeatedly made within Chinese legal-circle debate for active consideration of such a system in so far as it represents a rational continuity with China's imperial legal tradition.[4] Also, the development of a new provincial legislative personality has encouraged legal debate as to the relation between the formal and 'informal' constitutions, and this could have implications for Hong Kong's legal autonomy.[5]

PRC PERSPECTIVE ON LAWS AND 'SYSTEMS'

Deng Xiaoping's policy, 'one country, two systems', directly raised the political issue of the compatibility of the PRC and Hong Kong legal systems in light of the larger and even more elementary question as to the coexistence and compatibility of socialism and capitalism within one country. Theoretical speculation within PRC legal circles thereupon proceeded to dispute the tendency of traditional Chinese socialist legal theory to place capitalism and socialism in absolute and exclusive opposition.[6]

Theoretical debate often amplified the economic reform argument, favouring commodity production in the primary stage of socialism and the supplementary development of individual ownership and private enterprise within the national socialist economy as sanctioned in the 1982 State Constitution. In fact some scholars proposed a significant revision of this Constitution so that it would even further reflect the realities of economic reform, the importance of the market, the decline of the commune and the growing position of individual economy and international investment. The extension of established dialectical emphasis on the unity of theory and practice and the corresponding distinctiveness of socialism with Chinese characteristics highlighted the historical appropriation of capital in the Mainland, the current position of public ownership as the mainstay in the overall national economy and the appropriateness of the dual strategy of 'enlivening from within and opening on the outside' (*dui nei gao huo, dui wai kaifang*) as part of the response to the contemporary contradiction between China's backward productive forces and China's modern aspiration to improve upon the material and cultural conditions of everyday life.[7]

Chinese Marxist theoreticians contended that under 'one country, two systems' the will of the working class would still be reflected in the laws of the Mainland, but while the laws of the Hong Kong Special Adminisrative Region (HKSAR) would reflect the will of Hong Kong's 'bourgeois ruling class', these laws could not threaten the socialist system given the enormous state power of the Mainland and the historical destruction of bourgeois rule therein.[8] Essentially, the rules of united front were to apply in Hong Kong. Any contradictions would be treated as benign and historically necessary differences within a unity. These contradictions were innocuous 'non-antagonistic' contradictions within the people.[9]

On the Mainland side, there was often happy optimism that the NPC could formally make laws for the capitalist system in Hong Kong and that inter-system differences would be tolerated on the basis of Zhou Enlai's Bandung notion of peaceful coexistence and its diplomatic corollary of 'seeking common ground while preserving differences' (*qui tong cunyi*).

In the early 1980s, the Mainland professional legal literature referenced the notion of *yiguo, liangzhi, sanfa* (one country, two systems and three legal systems), thus highlighting the future relationships of three distinctive legal systems in Hong Kong, Taiwan and mainland China. More recently the same literature has discussed 'four [legal] territories, one country (*siyu, yiguo*), referring to the distinctive legal territories of Hong Kong, Macao, Taiwan and the Mainland.[10]

In an increasingly complex and contradictory world wherein state sovereignty is becoming more permeable, the relations of distinctive legal systems has become a pressing practical political issue. The consultative process in Hong Kong which paralleled the drafting of the Basic Law, for example, compared the relationship of the Basic Law to PRC law with the relationship between European Community Law and that of its member states.[11] The gap between 'systems' was presumed to be more profound than in the European–UK case. The accommodation of the British Common Law system to the supremacy of European Community Law, and its relation to the continental tradition, has not to the same extent raised any question as to the survival of the rule of law in the UK. In contrast, the Western media has on occasion viewed the 'one country, two systems' in the starkest of terms – in terms of the possible loss of the rule of law and its devastating impact on the future prosperity and stability of Hong Kong.

The consultative process sponsored by the Consultative Committee of the Basic Law (CCBL) generated discussion and reports on the issues regarding the lasting integrity of Hong Kong's Common Law system and future conflict of law between the legal jurisdictions of the HKSAR and the mainland which, under Deng's policy, must co-exist within the same sovereignty.

The final report of the CCBL's Special Group on Powers of Interpretation and Amendment of the Basic Law outlined the significant differences in point form. Within the Hong Kong system the legislature enacts legislation and the courts interpret this legislation and thus they 'declare the meaning of the law'. Judicial interpretation of specific cases by the Court of Appeal becomes binding on all Hong Kong courts. Courts may invalidate law which has been improperly passed or contravenes superior legislation. Unlike in the PRC, there is neither legislative nor executive interpretation of the law. In the PRC, however, 'judicial interpretation', which is sometimes the prerogative of the procuracy as well as of judges, is delegated by the legislature and while such interpretation is gradually acquiring increasing practical importance, in theory it does not have an ultimate binding effect.[12] More importantly, there is a strong emphasis on the general powers of the Standing Committee of the National People's Congress (NPCSC) to interpret the law.

Presently the power to interpret the Basic Law under its Article 158 is consistently vested with the NPCSC, and the outspoken advocate of democracy for Hong Kong, Martin Lee, has stated in Legislative Council debate that he believes this Article 158 is 'completely at variance' with the Hong Kong Common Law notion of judicial independence and that it '...may lead to the failure of the "one country, two systems" policy'.[13] The International Commission of Jurists basically reiterated Lee's position: 'There can be no independence in a judiciary which has to look to the government for the interpretation of the laws relevant to matters under its jurisdiction'.[14]

While Article 8 of the Basic Law formally speaks to the preservation of the Common Law system, the Basic Law is, itself, the product of competing and contradictory tendencies. The PRC has, for example, insisted on upholding the NPC powers of interpretation and amendment to the Basic Law. Hong Kong politics, on the other hand, have highlighted the judicial independence, composition and competence of Hong Kong's new Final Court of Appeal, the exact definition of central and SAR powers and the legal protection for human rights in Hong Kong before and after 1997.

THE BASIC LAW AS HONG KONG'S 'MINI-CONSTITUTION'

The development of the post-1997 rule of law will have to relate to Hong Kong community support for the Basic Law as the constitutional instrument which defines the relationship between the Hong Kong and Beijing governments and their respective jurisdictions. While the massive Hong Kong reaction to Tiananmen Square generated a new interest and a sudden alarmed response to last-minute changes to the final draft of the Basic Law, the constitutional status of the Basic Law, particularly in its relation to the PRC State Constitution of 1982, has not been the subject of continuous community-wide concern in Hong Kong.

Pragmatic political considerations have alternatively focused on the implications of Mainland policy and leadership change. Certainly, any suggestion that the Hong Kong side might pressure for amendment to the 1982 Constitution so as to clarify further the significance of Article 31 in relation to other parts of the same constitution and further to entrench the constitutional status of Hong Kong is widely seen as unrealistic.

In Hong Kong there is, nonetheless, frequent reference to the Basic Law as a 'mini-constitution'. Even Ji Pengfei, one of the most senior PRC architects of the Basic Law, recently deferred to this internal political characterisation in a commemorative reference to Hong Kong's 'mini-constitution' (*xiao xianfa*). In his speech of 5 April 1992, Ji candidly acknowledged a worrying lack of enthusiasm for the Basic Law:

> Since the promulgation of the Basic Law various circles in the Mainland and Hong Kong have done of lot of work in terms of public pronouncement, popularisation and explanation, and this has achieved some good social results. But we ought to recognise that in the coming realisation of the HKSAR's mini-constitution, there are still marked gaps in the

> necessary levels of universal support for the basic law, and whether we speak of the Mainland or Hong Kong, people are still lacking in enthusiasm for the Basic Law. These circumstances with regard to the pushing through of one country, two systems and the implementation leave a lot to be desired.[15]

Perhaps even more worrying is the almost universal and formally correct assertion in the Chinese legal literature that the Basic Law is not in and of itself a constitutional law.[16] The Basic Law is not a local law (*difang fagui*); it was passed by the NPC under Article 31 of the State Constitution. Within the categorisation of PRC law, however, basic law is still inferior to constitutional law.

While the socialist system is fully endorsed in the wording of the PRC's 1982 constitution, Hong Kong's capitalist system is indirectly guaranteed under a Basic Law which is passed under the authority of Article 31 of the same constitution. Furthermore, the constitution as a whole reflects a well-established constitutional interpretation of the 'multinational unitary state' which restricts legislative power to the NPC and projects a very narrowly defined centrist relation between the Centre and regions.

Quite apart from any happy political reference since the early 1980s to Deng's policy of 'one country, two systems', the historical evolution of Mainland constitutional legal theory has yet to provide a congenial basis for the interpretation of the high degree of autonomy which is confirmed to Hong Kong in its Basic Law. Chinese sensitivity as to any possible Hong Kong challenge to China's sovereignty in Hong Kong has made negotiation of this dilemma difficult. Any advocacy of federal arrangements is thus treated as an hostile challenge to China's sovereignty and flies in the face of the history of revolutionary struggle against the feudal and imperialist forces which sought to undermine the unity of the modern Chinese state.

In his study of comparative constitutional development, Mainland scholar Liu Nanping frankly approached this dilemma as it influenced debate between the Hong Kong and Mainland members of the Basic Law Drafting Committee:

> The Hong Kong members of the draft committee generally hold that the Basic Law should clearly state which articles of China's constitution are applicable in Hong Kong. They argue that Article 31 of the Constitution cannot in and of itself clarify the legal status of the Basic Law. But the Mainland members have argued that it is Article 31 which provides a legal basis for the Basic Law.[17]

While he could not see how the demands of the Hong Kong members could possibly be met, Liu believed that their anxieties were understandable, and he seemed to agree that the Basic Law has insufficient support in Article 31.

In various interviews with several of China's legal experts at the Chinese Academy of Social Sciences, the Beida and Renda Law Faculties and the University of Politics and Law, the author was consistently told that the issue of Basic Law validity under Article 31 was not really a problem. Any qualms were answered with a ringing endorsement of the National People's Congress exclusive legislative power to do what it wants.

A high-powered Beijing legal forum on the Basic Law responded more specifically, citing Article 31 as a 'proviso' in legal theory. The Basic Law met the constitutional requirements for drafting and promulgation, and Article 31 can be construed as an exception which allows for departure from general principles of socialism cited elsewhere in the Constitution.[18]

For some Hong Kong observers the NPC's exclusive power is altogether too real in light of the NPC's power to interpret and amend the Basic Law as re-affirmed in Articles 158 and 159 of the Basic Law, itself. But to make the two systems work the NPC has seemingly obfuscated its own constitutionally enshrined exclusive legislative power under Article 58 of the Constitution, and turned a blind eye to the inter-system differences on questions of judicial interpretation and independence. It would seem that on the PRC side policy has politically run ahead of constitutional law in the practical realisation of 'one country, two systems'.

In fact, the compatibility of the Basic Law and the PRC constitution was thoroughly aired in the local consultative process which accompanied the drafting of the Basic Law. In a consultation report of the Consultative Committee of the Basic Law (CCBL), Hong Kong opinion on the need to amend the PRC Constitution so as to ensure clear understanding of the status of the Basic Law was duly noted, particularly with respect to Article 5 of the 1982 State Constitution which insists that no law [including 'basic law'] shall contravene the Constitution. Under section 3.4.4 of the report the following view was recorded:

> The Basic Law is the highest form of law only at a local level and is not equivalent to the Constitution, hence contradictions between the Basic Law and the Constitution cannot be resolved by amending or redrafting the Basic Law but rather by amending or redrafting the Constitution.[19]

Virtually the same position was adopted in the 1992 International Commission of Jurists' report which was described in Beijing's authoritative *Fazhi ribao*, (Legal Daily) as 'a pretext to keep Hong Kong under British administration'.[20]

Sections 3.3.1 through 3.3.4 of the CCBL report detailed some of the obvious points of difference between the wording of the Basic Law and the PRC Constitution of 1982, as indicated in Table 7.1.

Table 7.1 The 1982 PRC State Constitution and the Basic Law

Chinese Constitution	*Draft Basic Law*
Article 1: The People's Republic of China is a socialist state under the people's democratic dictatorship led by the working class and based on the alliance of workers and peasants. The socialist system is the basic system of the People's Republic of China. Sabotage of the socialist system by any organization or individual is prohibited.	*Article 4*: Socialist system and policies shall not be practised in the Hong Kong Special Administrative Region and the existing capitalist system and way of life shall not be changed for 50 years.
Article 24: The state...educates the people in patriotism, collectivism, internationalism and communism and in dialectical and historical materialism; it combats capitalist, feudal and other decadent ideas.	
Article 19: The state promotes the nationwide use of Putonghua	*Article 4*: ...the existing... way of life shall not be changed for 50 years.
Article 25: The state promotes family planning so that population growth may fit the plan for economic and social development.	*Article 36*: The freedom of marriage of Hong Kong residents and their right to raise a family freely shall be protected by law.
Article 49: Both husband and wife have the duty to practice family planning.	
Article 34: All citizens of the People's Republic of China who have reached the age of 18 have the right to vote and stand for election....	*Article 25*: Permanent residents of the Hong Kong Special Administrative Region who have reached the age of 21 shall have the right to stand for election as prescribed by law.[21]

The PRC's concern to maintain sovereignty meant all along that there could be no challenge to the NPC's position *vis-à-vis* Hong Kong. Somehow the maintenance of Hong Kong's prosperity and stability had to be made to square with the national unity and territorial integrity of the PRC under its unitary system. The NPC not only was to promulgate the Basic Law, but it would become responsible for its interpretation and amendment. Furthermore, while the impressive extent of Hong Kong's high degree of autonomy was emphasised many times, any references to federalism, or of Hong Kong acquiring 'residual power' were continuously rebuffed.

Xiao Weiyun, the Deputy Director of the Beida Law Faculty and a key mainland Basic Law drafter, for example opined:

> According to the stipulations of the Basic Law, Hong Kong's high degree of autonomy is much greater than that of the nationality autonomous regions [such as Tibet and Inner Mongolia]....
>
> In many respects the HKSAR in its high degree of autonomy will be able to exercise greater power than that exercised by member states within federal states.[22]

Albert H.Y. Chen, a China law expert at the University of Hong Kong, agreed with the repeated Mainland view as to the comparatively sweeping dimension of Hong Kong's 'high degree of autonomy', noting:

> the SAR's autonomy is very high indeed from the comparative perspective. The significant fact in this regard is that almost no member states of federal states or autonomous governments in unitary states exercise complete autonomous powers over all of the following crucial matters of government – finance and taxation, monetary affairs, the issue of currency, customs, entry and exit controls, external trade relations, basic areas of law such as criminal law, criminal procedure, civil law, and civil procedure – where the SAR will exercise full autonomy over these.[23]

Chen went on to describe the reservation over defence and foreign affairs as 'of a minimal nature' in light of the above substantive comparison; however, this area has become much more controversial since the promulgation of the Basic Law.

Chen also noted that the reservation of residuary powers by member states of a federation is not an exclusive feature, as federalism could just as well reserve such power to the central government.[24] While Dr Chen, in an informal discussion with the author, expressed general satisfaction with the final outcome of the Basic Law draft, his written discussion of Centre–SAR relations notes that in a unitary, as contrasted with a federal, context, autonomous areas are not 'directly protected by the constitution'. In theory, such autonomy derives from national legislation and may, therefore, be withdrawn through mere legislative, as distinct from constitutional, amendment.[25]

In fact, the final draft of Article 159 of the Basic Law stipulates a very arduous amendment process. The NPC Standing Committee, the State Council and the HKSAR must together propose bills of amendment. The HKSAR Chief Executive and two-thirds of Hong Kong regional delegates to the NPC and two-thirds of the HKSAR Legislative Council must consent in order to initiate an amendment.

During the consultation process some Hong Kong observers argued the merits of 'residual power theory', suggesting that its focus on an explicit division of powers between centre and region was of practical interest even if the HKSAR could not be construed as an independent sovereign unit.[26] Xiao Weiyun was suspicious of any such comparison of the unitary and federal system, and his warning against residual power theory was couched exclusively in the reservation of power to member states:

> As for what is meant by the Basic Law's stipulation of a 'high degree of autonomy', the right of high degree of autonomy is granted by the National People's Congress, it is not inherent to the HKSAR and hence this high degree of autonomy is still local in nature. This kind of autonomy is not a complete autonomy, a 'high degree' and 'complete' are two different things...Some people think that the powers which are not stipulated by the Basic Law should belong to the HKSAR, this 'residual power theory' is the theory of the federal system...This theory is inappropriate to our unitary state.[27]

Frequent protestation as to the immutability of China's unitary system should not distract from the very real possibilities of informal and even formal constitutional response to the growing legislative capacity of the Chinese provinces. There is a new qualitative pattern of regionalism at large within the PRC which is becoming manifest in the complicated contexts of economic reform, decentralisation, market commodification, reduced central planning, regional competition for foreign investment and challenge to Party legitimacy and functions. But there is no emerging consensus as to the implications of this institutional devolution on the future status and operation of the Basic Law in Hong Kong.

POTENTIAL SYSTEM MODIFICATION UNDER 'ONE COUNTRY, TWO SYSTEMS'

Western, if not always local, opinion has usually presumed that there already exists in Hong Kong a 'rule of law' and, although this rule of law is not specifically cited, Article 8 of the Basic Law undertakes to preserve the existing common law, rules of equity, ordinances, subordinate legislation and customary law 'except for any that contravene this Law, and subject to any amendment by the legislature...'.[28] The Attorney General's Chambers has, in response, accelerated the process of sanitising the explicitly 'colonial' wording of existing ordinances so as to ensure their continued acceptance beyond 1997.

The Basic Law itself, however, does pose a number of potentially difficult problems of interpretation which will probably affect Centre–HKSAR constitutional relations. The issue of what national law would have validity within the regional confines of the HKSAR was not entirely resolved in the formula offered in Articles 18, 19 and 159, and Annex III.

Prior to final drafting of these Articles, the CCBL report revealed a wide range of opinion as to what to do with national legislation under Hong Kong's 'high degree of autonomy'. Those who sought maximum independence from Beijing urged that the Basic Law include stipulations that, with the exception of Article 31, all other provisions of the 1982 constitution should not apply in the HKSAR. Those who disagreed described the relation between the Chinese Constitution and the Basic Law as that of 'parent' to 'subsidiary' legislation. Blanket exclusion of the effect of the Chinese constitution in Hong Kong would, therefore, be theoretically impossible as subsidiary legislation cannot govern parent legislation.

Some opined that the Basic Law should give elaborate definition to the powers of local autonomy and any residual matter would then revert to the authority of the Chinese Constitution. This position was metaphorically described in terms of the sun's rays:

> Hence, some people compare the Basic Law to an umbrella and the Chinese Constitution to the sun. The sun is shining all over the territory of China but its rays cannot penetrate the area sheltered by the umbrella, i.e., the Basic Law. In other words, the provisions concerning the SAR and its scope of autonomy will be implemented in accordance with the Basic Law and not with the provisions of the Chinese constitution. In areas not stipulated by the Basic Law, the relevant provisions of the Chinese Constitution will be automatically applied.[29]

The final draft ultimately adopted a compromise whereby those provisions of the Chinese constitution which are to be construed as applicable within Hong Kong's autonomy would be specified in Annex III to the Basic Law. Six relatively uncomplicated reservations were set out in the existing Annex which relate to common-sense issues of foreign affairs and defense, but Article 18 leaves open the possibility of future deletion and addition to this list. The list is in the keeping of the NPCSC which, on consultation with its own Basic Law Committee and the HKSAR 'government', may add or subtract provisions 'relating to defence and foreign affairs as well as other matters outside the limits of the autonomy of the region...'.[30]

The wording of the Basic Law is such that it seems to allow for either a strict or loose construction of NPCSC powers to extend Mainland laws into the HKSAR. The potential for such extension was highlighted in Legislative Council debate over the invitation of overseas judges to sit on Hong Kong's future Final Court of Appeal (FCA). Those who wished to preserve Hong Kong flexibility in making such invitations 'as required' argued that judicial continuity and independence was on the line in that Article 82 of the Basic Law explicitly stipulated that the Court of Final Appeal 'may as required [*ke genju xuyao*] invite judges from other common law jurisdictions'.[31] Attorney General Jeremy Mathews attempted in Legislative Council debate to put a particular spin on the article's interpretation by suggesting that the wording did not imply 'may as **it** [i.e., as the FCA] requires'.[32]

In Legislative Council debate, Simon Ip and James To featured the journal opinion of Wu Jianfan, one of the mainland members of the BLDC. Wu apparently argued that if Hong Kong's Legislative Council failed to endorse the Joint Laison Group 4:1 formula for the 'localisation' of the FCA judgeship, whereby only one judge would hail from a foreign jurisdiction, then China still had the power under Article 83 to set up the FCA after 1997. This specific Article reads: 'The structure, powers and functions of the courts of the Hong Kong Special Administrative Region at all levels shall be prescribed by law.'[33] Wu reportedly argued that such law included laws enacted by the NPC and applied to Hong Kong through Annex III.[34]

Those Councillors who supported flexibility based on Article 82 tiptoed round the contentious issue of localisation and 'Hong Kong people ruling Hong Kong'. Councillor Tam Yiu-chung supported the JLG 4:1 proposal and argued for Simon Ip's motion for flexibility. He called for a genuine legal approach and regretted attempts to politicise the FCA issue. He did not mince his words: he singled out two explicitly political reasons for the preference for more overseas judges, namely a lack of confidence in local judicial personnel and the fear of Chinese interference with judicial independence.[35]

Speaking for Ip's motion, James To argued that the overseas judges would lend international prestige to the FCA. Without the overseas component he believed that it would not have the same stature as the Privy Council and purely local FCA judgeship would then '...undermine the confidence of the people of Hong Kong as well as investors in the rule of law'. To was careful to suggest that as local judges would be more familiar with local systems and customs they might even 'be more capable of mastering the rule of justice', but he advised: 'we should also make sure that these local judges have ...the ability to ensure that the principles of common law are correctly applied in Hong Kong'.[36]

Even more significantly, the issue of the centre's legal prerogative was highlighted in the specific wording regarding the central control over foreign affairs and defence. Historically, the Common Law approach allowed for judicial interpretation of 'acts of state' and 'facts of state', but this was countermanded in the exclusion clause of Article 19 which reads: 'The courts of the Hong Kong Special Administrative Region shall have no jurisdiction over acts of state *such as* defence and foreign affairs.'[37] This wording included the woolly notion 'such as' which has attracted the critical comment of the International Commission of Jurists as an 'unnecessary ambiguity'.[38]

This issue was originally a point of contention in the consultative process. Hong Kong objection followed along these lines: 'Some opinions are against the incorporation of the expression "other affairs", which are the responsibilities of the Central People's government as it is too broad to afford a clear definition. Moreover, the *Joint Declaration* only mentioned defence and foreign affairs.'[39]

The final ambiguous wording attracted an extended exegesis by Martin Lee in the Legislative Council as to the Common Law definitions of acts of state and facts of state. Lee was especially chagrined in that the Basic Law deprived the courts of a rightful opportunity to decide whether or not an act is or is not in fact 'an act of state'.[40] The wording of Article 19 gives exceptional power to the Chief Executive who will certify whether indeed any particular act is an act of state. This unreserved use of executive authority may be seen in some quarters as very undesirable since the Chief Executive is, under Article 43, dually accountable to the HKSAR *and* the Central People's Government.[41]

Martin Lee preferred facts of state, which under Common Law narrowly consists 'in matters, the determination of which is solely in the hands of the executive' and which are restricted to whether a state of war exists or whether the principles of diplomatic immunity apply to particular individuals. Lee regretted that the more restrictive wording, facts of state, which appeared in the second draft of the Basic Law had been dropped from the final draft.

Notwithstanding problems of exact interpretation as to 'such as' and 'acts of state', the Basic Law encompasses a whole set of vexatious problems relating to the retention of Hong Kong's international personality and ability to carry on independently after 1997 with its existing international memberships and commitments. According to Lee, the Common Law definition of an act of state is 'a prerogative act of policy in the field of foreign affairs performed by the Crown in the course of a relationship with another state or its subjects'. Under Article 151 of the Basic Law it is stipulated that the HKSAR '...may on its own, using the name "Hong Kong, China", maintain and develop relations and conclude and implement agreements with foreign states and regions and relevant international organizations in the appropriate fields, including the economic, trade, financial and monetary, shipping, communications, tourism, cultural and sports fields'.[42]

The promulgation of the Basic Law was supposed to be, in and of itself, a confidence-boosting measure which would instil mutual trust and the confidence of the Hong Kong people in the future of Hong Kong beyond 1997; however, the Basic Law came out after the Tiananmen Incident. Immediately prior to the Incident the proposed changes to counterrevolutionary law were tabled for NPC approval and were rationalised in reform terms of the open door policy and 'one country, two systems'; however, the Party's Tiananmen Square strategy spotlighted the notion of counterrevolution and very few observers in Hong Kong were prepared to accept the Beijing leadership's claim that the students had acted illegally. Whereas the Tiananmen disturbances of 1986 had resulted in Beijing reassurances that there would be no future emulation of the Mainland struggle against bourgeois liberalism within Hong Kong's separate capitalist system, the 1989 situation was viewed in Beijing with deep alarm in the light of the ability of Hong Kong dissident political organisations to affect the internal course of Mainland politics.

The PRC reaction to Mainland student protest was to stress the legality of martial law. In reply to student argument in 'defence of the dignity of our Constitution', the *Renmin ribao* noted that the scope of Article 35, which confirmed freedoms of speech, assembly, process and demonstration, was reasonably limited by Article 51 which stipulated that citizens' exercise of their freedoms '...may not infringe upon the interest of the state, of society, and of the collective, or upon the lawful freedoms and rights of other citizens'. The disruption of Gorbachev's historic state visit was regarded as a violation of Article 51.[43]

While two Hong Kong drafters dropped from the BLDC explicitly to protest the Tiananmen Square event, the Mainland drafters then dug in their heels on the issue of Hong Kong interference in Mainland politics and wanted explicit reference within the final draft of the Basic Law as to the respective HKSAR and NPC responsibilities for 'subversion' (*dianfu*) and 'turmoil' (*dongluan*). In response to CCP Secretary-General Jiang

Zemin's warning that Hong Kong not be used as a base for 'subversion', the then Governor of Hong Kong, Lord David Wilson, replied: 'We here in Hong Kong prize and attach great importance to our freedoms under our own legal system....We don't wish, we don't intend that Hong Kong should be used as a base for subversion. We do intend that our own freedoms should be preserved.'[44]

In Hong Kong the right to speak out against the Chinese government and its record of human rights became a quintessential matter of the rule of law itself. Martin Lee, for example, associated the cause of the United Democrats of Hong Kong with the rule of law: '...we saw the shameful letter of the political adviser to the New China News Agency in October 1989 in which he stated the government was willing to compromise the rule of law in deference to good relations with China'.[45]

In the Legislative Council's debate on the NPC's promulgation of the Basic Law, Martin Lee derided the last minute inclusion of a clause on subversion into Article 23:

> Subversion is a term foreign to the common law system which shall continue to apply to Hong Kong, and this particular crime can neither be reconciled with the values nor the precedents of the common law system. Such an effort to take a communist law concept and impose it upon a common law system undermines the non-political nature of the Hong Kong courts.[46]

In fact, Beijing's response to 'internationalisation' and the perceived Hong Kong political challenge to PRC sovereignty reflected political pressure within the NPCSC membership and the Democratic Party membership of the Chinese People's Political Consultative Committee for a more flexibly worded clause against 'any interference with the socialist system on the mainland'.[47] Suggested verbiage relating to 'wanton interference' was challenged in Hong Kong observation as to the term's inexact legal implications and the possible future challenge to Hong Kong's judicial independence. Hong Kong legislators argued that the term 'interference' was infinitely malleable, and that it would create confusions of jurisdiction as Hong Kong lawyers would never know for sure what cases belonged to Mainland jurisdiction.[48]

At the time of the BLDC's final decision, Miss Maria Tam, a Hong Kong drafter, noted that the inclusion of 'subversion' in Article 23, which stressed the responsibility of the HKSAR to 'enact laws on its own to prohibit any act of treason, secession, sedition, subversion against the Central People's Government' was essentially a compromise between Mainland and Hong Kong drafters.

The BLDC as a whole had refused to interpret the clause as in conflict with Chapter III's explicit endorsement of freedom of speech. Dr Rayson Huang, the Co-Convenor of the BLDC SubGroup on Centre–HKSAR relations, acknowledged the influence of the June 4 event, noting at the same time that the term's inclusion in the final draft was 'a reintroduction of a previously abandoned idea'. And the Mainland Co-Convenor of the same Group, Shao Tianren, asserted: 'The term is widely employed in common law systems and continental law systems, in capitalist and socialist countries.'[49]

Nevertheless, it is not altogether clear how Mainland law and theory distinguishes 'subversion' from 'sedition' (*shandong panluan*). While 'subversion' is used infrequently, 'sedition' has well-established connotations in Common Law reference to speech and writing which calls for violence and disorder so as to arouse disaffection against the sovereign, the encouragement of changing law by unlawful means, and the raising of discontent among Her Majesty's subjects and hostility between different classes of subjects. While a vague parallel might be found in Section Two of Article 102 in the PRC's Criminal Law's special provisions concerning counter-revolution, there is no explicit reference therein to the word 'sedition'. However, Article 92 does require life imprisonment for those 'who plot to subvert [*yinmou dianfu*] the government or dismember the state'.[50]

The Basic Law's Article 23 also included a requirement that the future HKSAR 'prohibit foreign political organizations or bodies from conducting political activities' and this was of immediate importance in light of the setting up of a local office of the Paris-based Federation for a Democratic China in Hong Kong.[51] Dr Rayson Huang claimed that this provision was similar to provisions in Hong Kong's own Societies Ordinance which empowered the Registry of Societies to refuse registration of any local groups with overseas links. Under the discretion of British colonial administration, however, this Ordinance, which was originally designed to deal with the expansion of the criminal triad organisation, was extended to include undesirable political organisations.[52]

While Mainland opinion stressed that it would be the future HKSAR which would determine the law with reference to subversion, this should not distract from the firm assertion of PRC sovereignty in Article 18 of the Basic Law which stipulates that the Central People's Government 'may issue an order applying the relevant national laws in the region' in the event of 'turmoil which endangers national unity or security and is beyond the control of the government of the region'.[53] The PRC's central government will decide if such an exigency exists, and it can do so without consulting the HKSAR. This departs from the Annex III formula which at least requires some form of consultative protocol in the case of either adding to or subtracting from the specific listing of national laws which are to apply in Hong Kong under normal circumstances. The International Commission of Jurists has interjected that as a general rule it is the responsibility of the government directly affected to determine whether it has lost control in an emergency. The Commission characterised this dimension of Article 18 as 'Draconian'.[54]

PROTECTING HONG KONG'S HUMAN RIGHTS WITHIN 'ONE COUNTRY'

There is no need to stress the conceptual relation between the rule of law and the limitation of the state in the lawful guarantee of human rights in contemporary Western political thought. Regrettably, in Hong Kong, as elsewhere in the West, there has been little discernible reaction to the national debate on human rights within the PRC, as it was described in Chapter 3. Little sympathy has been extended to reform-minded legal circles within the PRC on the subject; however, there has been tremendous trepidation, especially since Tiananmen Square, over the potential loss of human rights in the transition from British colonial administration to a 'high degree of autonomy' under China's direct leadership.

The human rights issue was originally reviewed at length by one of the five sub-groups of the Basic Law Drafting Committee which recommended the wording of Chapter Three of the Basic Law, 'Fundamental Rights and Duties of the Residents'. At least some of the Hong Kong Basic Law drafters may have felt that Chapter Three '...serves as a Bill of Rights within the Basic Law'.[55] However, the Hong Kong government, reeling in the highly charged context of post-Tiananmen Square anxiety, gave more immediate priority to an earlier plan to legislate a human rights bill. This was a pre-emptive tactic to ensure both the generation of new pre-1997 case law precedent and the clear definition of rights in the context of local 'public emergency'.

The drafting of human rights legislation was a popular government initiative within the Legislative Council, but it immediately ran into difficulties relating to format and its constitutional relation to the Basic Law. Certainly, Mainland constitutional theory, which has all along supported a notion of positive law, has yet seriously to consider restraining the legislative powers of the NPC so as to place human rights out of reach of domestic political change. Thus far the State Council has only issued a white paper on the subject of human rights, and the practical effect of related legislation awaits future analysis.

The Mainland Co-Convenor of the BLDC Sub-Group on Rights and Duties, Wang Shuwen, advised that Article 8 of the Basic Law would support laws previously in force so as to protect the Common Law tradition, but he was also emphatic that the Article would not lend any support to certain laws as supreme over others. The Hong Kong Co-Convenor of the same group, retired Appeal Court judge Simon Li Fook-sean, agreed: 'I have never heard about certain law being supreme over another in the history of the British legal system....As far as the Basic Law is concerned, it has no such power.'[56]

The government did not need to be advised of the need for convergence of its human rights legislation with the Basic Law but, in its desire to accelerate the creation of pre-1997 judge-made case law which could respond to a single piece of written law in the protection of civil rights, it wrestled with the seemingly intractable problem of entrenchment. Selina Chow, as the governor of the Legislative Council ad hoc group on the draft Bill of Rights, set out the dilemma:

> Given the supremacy of the Basic Law as Hong Kong's constitution at the change of sovereignty, a status which no one disputes and which China makes sure repeatedly that no one forgets, there does not seem to be any other option open to us except the one presently proposed, that is, a form of so-called indirect entrenchment by mirroring Article 39 of Chapter 3 of the Basic Law with an amendment in the Letters Patent ...The group accepted that while the Bill does not technically enjoy supremacy, clauses 3 and 4 of the Bill together ensure a special status for the Bill over existing and all future legislation by requiring the courts to interpret all legislation consistently with the Bill.[57]

Mrs. Chow's view was supported by the Attorney General who referenced expert legal opinion that entrenchment and supremacy 'can only be achieved by a sovereign nation'. He had no hope of an agreement between the two sovereign members of the JLG; therefore, the only available option was 'special status' through amendment of the Letters Patent.[58]

Despite the Administration's protestations that a deliberate relation was created between the Basic Law's Article 39 and the proposed ordinance, this convergence is somewhat questionable in light of that Article's reference to both the International Covenant of Civil and Political Rights (ICCPR) *and* the International Covenant of Social, Economic and Cultural Rights (ICESCR). The Hong Kong business community was not prepared to accept the costs of the latter's content any more than it was prepared to accept any potentially costly liabilities arising from a proposal to include inter-citizen rights into the Ordinance wording. Indeed, some of the government's leading constitutional experts regard the ICESCR as a political statement which lacks any pretence of justiciability. The neglect of the second international covenant certainly reflected Western and PRC differences of opinion on the content of human rights.

Interestingly, the International Commission of Jurists ignored this point in its assertion of the compatibility of the Bill of Rights Ordnance with the Basic Law.[59] Alternatively one might even argue, as did China's own *bête noire*, Martin Lee, that some of the terms of the Basic Law are more progressive than is the Hong Kong Bill of Rights Ordinance. In Legislative Council debate, Martin Lee predictably chose his words so as to emphasise the supremacy of the Bill, but he also noted that many of the rights offered in the ICESCR are already found in the Basic Law, and he repudiated the Government's attitude:

> The Government has failed to support its contention that all the rights guaranteed by this second Covenant – such as the right to form independent trade unions, the right to academic freedom, and the right to education – 'in general are not rights that can be easily enforced in the courts'.[60]

CCBL debate over rights and obligations had already revealed a similar viewpoint to the effect that political rights, as detailed in the ICCPR, could be more effectively materialised than ICECSR rights, which could 'only be gradually materialized through development of society and economy'.[61]

The final text of the Basic Law adopted the form if not the substance of Mainland theory relating to the unity of rights and duties. It also modestly reflected PRC Constitutional concerns regarding the legal protection of social welfare and retirement benefits under Article 36 of the Basic Law. The Basic Law does not expressly enshrine 'equal pay for equal work', 'right and duty to work' and 'the right and duty to receive education', but, in several substantive areas, it goes beyond the rights and freedoms of the PRC Constitution in that it offers Hong Kong residents the right to strike, the freedoms of international travel and emigration, freedom of academic research and the right freely to raise a family.

On behalf of the Administration, the Chief Secretary, Sir David Ford, replied to the criticisms of several Legislative Councillors repeating the assertion that rights outlined under the ICESCR were 'different in nature'. It was this difference which originally necessitated the historical separation of rights into two international covenants. Here he could have easily referred to Cold War debate between the socialist and capitalist delegates of the United Nations. Not only in his view were many of the rights in the ICESCR 'not capable of legal definition', but State Parties need only realise such rights according to their available resources. Finally, it was clearly stated that debate as to the selection of rights from the ICESCR would have entailed such exhaustive and prolonged debate that it would have seriously impeded enactment of the present human rights legislation.[62]

The Chinese side, which has occasionally questioned the authority of the Legislative Council as it is consultative and still part of the colonial governing apparatus, responded with cold hostility to the promulgation of the new legislation, indicating that the legislation's final disposition would rest with the future SAR government.

Given the Chinese-side rejection of a supreme law or bill of rights which would challenge the Basic Law's own supremacy, the Hong Kong government opted for a mere 'ordinance' (*fa'an*), but it was no ordinary ordinance. It required an amendment to the Hong Kong Letters Patent so that the wording of all past and future legislation must consistently honour those elements of International Covenant on Civil and Political Rights which had been agreed to under Britain's signature in 1976 and which, with reservations concerning national self-determination and universal franchise, had supposedly come into force in Hong Kong.[63]

Perhaps, one of the politically most contentious areas of convergence lies in the area of derogation. Article 39 of the Basic Law not only indicates that provisions of the two international covenants as well as international labour conventions which were previously applied in Hong Kong 'shall remain in force', but that these rights and freedoms 'shall not be restricted unless as prescribed by law'.

Presumably, under Article 18, such legal prescription might include 'relevant national laws' in the instance of uncontrollable turmoil. The notion of derogation under the PRC Constitution's Article 51 asserts that the citizen's enjoyment of freedoms and rights '...may not infringe upon the interests of the state, of society and of the collective, or upon the lawful freedoms and rights of other citizens'.[64] At the very least, dissident Hong Kong opinion may legitimately question the elasticity of the Mainland view of 'interests of state'.

The eminent PRC constitutional expert, Gong Xiangrui, wrote that, while there is considerable agreement between Chapter III of the Basic Law and the broad declarations of substantive rights in Hong Kong's bill of rights, different notions of human rights characterise the two systems, and 'first and foremost is the priority of benefit allocation'. While there is some doubt as to the continuing viability of the traditional structure of interests in China, Gong correctly pointed out that in Chinese theory there has been an ascending priority of individual, collective and state, whereas in the Western theory this order is reversed.[65] Professor Gong was also very frank in his opinion that the Hong Kong legislature is not a 'representative legislature and the amendment to the Letters Patent, which gave the Bill "superior status", will cease to have legal effect at midnight on 30 June 1997'.[66]

Hong Kong's Bill of Rights Ordinance copies the rationale, 'public emergency which threatens the life of the nation', straight from the ICCPR. The International Commission of Jurists did not give full consideration to the PRC's repeated endorsement of the principles of the ICCPR, and its willingness to accept the continued applicability of the ICCPR and ICSECR to post-1997 Hong Kong, but it acknowledges that the 'nation' in such a context must be construed as China. The Commission's report, nevertheless, discounts China's sovereignty as it favours interpretation which suggests that as long as the PRC is not actually a signatory to the ICCPR the question of emergency and related derogation must apply to 'the context of Hong Kong alone'.[67]

Substantive objections relating to entrenchment, the absence of provision for inter-citizen rights, the temporary freezing of six key ordinances relating to law and public order and the absence of reference to the ICSECR were raised over the course of debate, but the Legislative Council was disposed to give the legislation its final blessing.

THE RULE OF LAW IN HONG KONG'S CHANGING POLITICS

As indicated earlier in the introductory chapter, theoretical speculation has often highlighted the vital correlation of the rule of law and democracy. This correlation has also been featured in the theories of reforming legal and political circles of the Mainland. In Hong Kong, however, colonial administration has developed the British Common Law and the rules of equity in the absence of formal democracy, and this seems to conflict with conventional Weberian assumption as to the contemporaneous development of law and market capitalism. Indeed, the contradictions of Hong Kong as a 'borrowed place in a borrowed time' only multiply on closer examination.

Prominent Hong Kong sociologist, Lau Siu-kai, in his discussion of Hong Kong's rule of law points out that while, in theory, law-making and the application of laws reflect an arbitrary bureaucratic will, in practice, the bureaucracy has been 'restrained in its legal power by the need to take into consideration the prevailing legal norms in England, the customary practices of the Chinese people, the vested interests of the bureaucracy itself, and the political imperatives of the times'. In Lau's view the law acquired a degree of legitimacy within the larger community in terms of the bureaucracy's willingness to conform to its own rules.[68]

In the past, the stability and international acceptability of Hong Kong's legal system was counted as an important aspect of the colony's spectacular commercial success. Not surprisingly, in its review of the Basic Law provisions for representative government, the OMELCO Standing Panel on Constitution Affairs concluded in 1987: 'Without direct elections there could still be democracy and the rule of law must be maintained regardless of whether there are direct elections.'[69]

Regardless of OMELCO's conclusions, the question of the constitutional relationship between Hong Kong and the Mainland has commanded much less political attention than one might expect, given the frequency of past government and media allusion to the importance of the rule of law as a foundation of prosperity and stability. Also, regardless of historic Western criticism of the PRC's marked subscription to 'policy as the soul of law', many in the bureaucracy, or for that matter in the Legislative Council, subscribe to a pragmatism which self-consciously focuses on the policy level and the importance of the changing leadership lineup in Beijing. Perhaps, this is a peculiar form of 'rule of man-ism'. At any rate, during the drafting process very few people in Hong Kong were concerned with the theoretical and constitutional arguments, and instead there was a popular focus on the policy of 'one country, two systems' as it related to Hong Kong's practical needs.[70] The disregard of apparent legal nicety and the formal constitutional relationship of Centre and region may reflect the hard political lessons learned in the early 1980s' negotiations with the Chinese, but it bodes ill for the consolidation of the post-'97 rule of law. Such pragmatism could possibly have an enervating effect on the development of Hong Kong's future rule of law.

Indeed, if one assumes that Hong Kong has over the years consolidated the rule of law under the Common Law, the following conclusion of the International Commission of Jurists is somewhat difficult to explain: 'The rule of law is not seen as a guarantee of Hong Kong's future as it is felt that there is no certainty that it will be observed by China after 1997'.[71] The Hong Kong reaction to the events of Tiananmen Square was deep and wide-ranging, and yet it seldom featured the integral relation between democracy and the rule of law.

In the 4 December 1991 Legislative Council debate on the composition of the Final Court of Appeal, Dr Samuel Wong did speak of 'a duty to teach the Mainland about justice and rights in an advanced society'.[72] One must note, however, that there has been no suggestion of systematic liaison with the reform-minded political circles in Beijing which have sponsored the notion of the rule of law in opposition to the rule of man.

During the same debate the well-known 'democrat', Szeto Wah, obliquely raised the distinction between 'rule of law' (*fazhi*) and 'rule of person' (*renzhi*) in terms of a consideration of the racial origins and passports of judges as part of the issue of 'Hong Kong people ruling Hong Kong',[73] but the ongoing political debate concerning the necessity of more direct election to the Legislative Council seldom included a systematic emphasis on the rule of law.

The Council debate on the composition of the Final Court of Appeal raised the issue of the future of the rule of law particularly in relation to investor confidence in Hong Kong, but it also demonstrated the ongoing concern for policy rather than law itself. Some members of the Legislature were even reluctant to engage in debate which they regarded as 'untimely' and counterproductive. They wished to avoid renewed confrontation with China just after some measure of mutual confidence had been restored with the negotiation of the Sino–British memorandum on the thorny issue of the new airport.[74]

As far as the government was concerned, the issue 'boiled down' to whether one or two foreign judges would sit on the Final Court of Appeal, and such a nit-picking exercise could not be construed as a matter of high principle which might possibly impact on the future of Hong Kong's judicial independence and rule of law.[75]

Such pragmatism is, however, open to criticism in so far as it fosters a cynical fatalism which discounts local political argument concerning the need to preserve the established notion of the rule of law as a waste of energy. Fear over confrontation with China might lead locally to less of a confident, self-standing commitment to the resolution of Hong Kong's problems. This is what is behind Martin Lee's criticism of an attitude which he described in terms of 'you ought to take what is given and not complain' (*ni lai shun shou*).[76]

The pressures of localisation, whereby Hong Kong may be expected to become more Chinese after 1997, adds to this complicated conceptual mix yet another related dimension which invokes sinological comment on the underlying nature of Chinese society in Hong Kong and its particular perspective on the British legacy of the rule of law. The sociology of Professor S.K. Lau has, for example, focused attention on 'utilitarian familialism', connoting the individual's attempts to place his familial interests above the interests of society and others in the pursuit of materialistic interest.[77] Under this view the law is seen as an instrument of the family business agenda rather than as a community-wide project. Lau and Kuan attempted to survey the 'uneasy marriage between the modernity of civic liberties and the tradition of situational morality', and their following conclusion is especially noteworthy:

> the reception of the common law system in this rather atypical Chinese society has proceeded largely on an instrumental, utilitarian and

> egocentric basis, whereas the philosophical and ethical foundation on which the legal system operates still contains traces of traditional Confucian and familistic considerations.[78]

While the International Commission of Jurists focused on one man, one vote as the only proper democratic process, British colonial administration had historically treated functional representation as viable, efficient and even democratic. Moreover recent survey work has confirmed the Hong Kong public's ambivalence towards modern political parties which are often seen as playing a self-interested adversarial role in politics.[79]

While there are obvious differences in the conceptual origins of the British and Chinese notions of functional representation and in the contrast between Communist mass-line united-front-style politics and Hong Kong colonial practices requiring the cooptation of preferred elites, the notion of functional representation was historically more relevant to Hong Kong's political transition than direct democracy based upon one man, one vote. The focus on colonial functional representation may have even facilitated an earlier pattern of Sino-British agreement in the drafting of the Basic Law. The Chinese side was quite willing to extend not only executive-led administration, but to perpetuate the existing pattern of functional representation. However, the current Governor, Chris Patten, has spoken out strongly on the relationship between the rule of law and representative democracy. His strategy of separating out Legco and Executive Council membership and broadening the base of functional election so as to achieve a greater pattern of Legco democracy and direct election prior to 1997 conflicts with the PRC focus on more evolutionary expansion of direct elections after 1997.[80]

In trying to come to terms with the rule of law between systems it is perhaps still necessary to assess the significance of a common Chinese cultural variable. In an interview with the author Wang Gengwu, Vice-Chancellor of Hong Kong University and new member of Hong Kong's Executive Council, distinguished Western and Chinese views of the law as a matter of 'first' as opposed to 'last resort' in the resolution of conflict within society. Certainly, the differences between the two systems should not obscure the potential influence of an underlying Chinese cultural commonality. To put the issue in its starkest terms, is it possible that Hong Kong's Common Law Tradition itself is a pearl-encrusted veneer which overlays a substantive Confucian philosophical preference for an informal community-based moral resolution of problems?

This is perhaps to over-dramatise the dichotomy of policy and leadership, on the one hand, and the imposition of law on to society on the other;

however, this question curiously invokes the Mainland argument over the relation of the rule of law and the rule of man. Those who adhered to a middle viewpoint in PRC debates argued that the rule of man highlights the human dimensions of society, and that it is not identical with 'rule by one man' or 'rule by the individual'. In their view the rule of law could not be achieved unless it was humanistically synthesised with such a rule of man. This perspective quite naturally reflected the desire to find genuinely Chinese solutions to contemporary Chinese problems in the light of Chinese history and social development.

Noting that legislation can only be effective if it is brought into line with actual social practice, Hong Kong Legislative Councillor Lam drew the attention of his colleagues to the familiar observation of Mencius: 'Laws alone cannot bring themselves into practice.'[81]

One can dissect the Legislative Council debate on the Bill of Rights Ordinance in this light. Some members who stood guard at the gates of the Common Law Tradition were appalled that some of their fellow Councillors would not only place law and order in antithesis to the justiciable realisation of human rights, but they would also treat human rights as an East-versus-West issue.

There was in the debate repeated reference to the 'question of balance' so that the justiciability of human rights not interfere with the struggle against corruption and police duties in maintaining law and order, especially in the light of a growing public outcry over a growing crime wave generated by Guangdong criminal gangs who were criss-crossing the border. Widespread public concern over law and order may still yet generate incipient Legalist tendencies which resist the progressive limitation of government in favour of the extension of human rights beyond the minimal standards set in the ICCPR. In response to such anxiety, Martin Lee cited international experience and the position paper of the Hong Kong Bar Association which maintained that the 'application of the ICCPR' would not 'undermine the efficacy of law enforcement agencies'.[82]

Andrew Wong regretted the 'fallacious view' expressed even within the sober confines of the Legislative Council: 'The human rights concept Chinese people hold is radically different from that of the West.'[83] While he countered that Hong Kong had benefited from exposure to Western concepts of human rights as well as of the rule of law itself since 1841, other Members noted the general public's apathy towards the Bill of Rights Ordinance, Britain's lack of public education on the subject and the government's lackadaisical implementation of ICCPR requirements since 1976.

Debate over the Heung Yee Kuk traditional rights, or succession rights of male indigenous villagers to common ancestral property, as confirmed in the New Territories Ordinance and in the Basic Law itself, featured the tension between Western and Chinese concepts. Some members stood ready to give precedence to human rights provisions on gender equality; however, 'speaking for the ordinary citizen', Mrs Fong expressed deep concerns as to the possibility of confrontation with China and as to the preservation of traditional Chinese culture. She asked: 'What is this Bill anyway?' And she affirmed: 'I treasure Hong Kong's existing living environment.'[84] The 'living environment' of the New Territories may in fact be a lot more complicated than what is suggested in Mrs Fong's rhetorical remarks.

As Hong Kong undergoes the actual mechanics of transition, the judicial process and law enforcement agencies will undergo greater strains in coping with an enlarged pattern of localisation just at a time when the issue of cultural identity is likely to play an increasing role in local politics. Hong Kong's particular Common Law Tradition has already undergone some change in the local political response to the 1997 deadline. Whether within a few years the new trend to make human rights justiciable in relation to a single piece of legislation will make an important impact on the public mind and local politics is still questionable, particularly in light of general cynicism as to China's position on the Bill of Rights Ordinance. Once Chinese sovereignty becomes an actual reality in Hong Kong local politics may undergo significant change, and pragmatism may triumph over the advocacy of transparency and direct elections *vis-à-vis* functional representation.

Despite British adherence to *pacta sunt servanda* and somewhat unrealistic claims that Britain will still have responsibility to ensure the implementation of the Joint Declaration, the Chinese role will dramatically increase as the British factor declines. 'Internationalisation' is likely to become an anachronistic issue in local politics, and the pace of internal democratisation could possibly become more closely linked to the process of PRC political reform. After 1997, Hong Kong will be more exposed to the PRC dynamic of centre-region politics. The local rule of law will no longer have a British leg to stand on, and despite the promise of the Basic Law ostensibly guaranteeing the preservation of a different system as well as the British Common Law tradition, minus its colonial trimmings, there is likely to be change in the relation of law to changing Hong Kong society.

As the British constitutionalist Sir Ivor Jennings once pointed out, the rule of law concept is larger than the sum of rules which adjusts legal relationships and limits sovereign power: it expresses the ethical consensus of the community as to elementary distinctions between right and wrong, and it is, itself, an expression of a public attitude which incorporates individual self-discipline in favour of a sense of community welfare.[85] Basic underlying assumptions as to the specifically necessary relation between the individual and society in the creation of the rule of law will be tested in post-1997 experiment with 'one country, two systems'. In Hong Kong, just as in the PRC as a whole, there is likely to be an ongoing dynamic which places the tension between rule of law and rule of man in the changing cultural response to the complexity of social change.

8 Conclusion: Before and After Tiananmen Square

The 'rule of law' concept is 'open textured'. What is more, the physical establishment and social materialisation of the rule of law is an ongoing struggle in any state. The rule of law has become politicised in international debate, and the debate on its comparative contents can influence states. The contemporary Chinese debate on the rule of law has been informed by such comparison, but this debate was not precipitated by a new and insightful re-reading of the texts of Aristotle, Locke, Montesquieu and Dicey.

The political origins of the Chinese debate lie specifically in the internal reaction to the politics of the Cultural Revolution, the rejection of 'class struggle as the key link', related political support for the modernisation of the economy, and the self-explanatory critique of contemporary 'feudalism' in Chinese society. Contained within the aforementioned critique there was an important rejection of Legalism, which facilitated a new fundamental distinction between rule *by* law and rule *of* law. While some conservative Party members do continue to subscribe to an 'instrumentalist' approach to law, the CCP leadership, as a whole, has formally endorsed the rule of law, as distinct from rule by law.

China's socialist rule of law is self-consciously defined within a synthesis of Western Marxist ideas and practical Chinese experience. This synthesis, highlighting China's concrete conditions, constitutes an explicit ideological formulation, but it has a range of complex political and social implications which have not yet been fully identified and formally understood even within China itself.

Needless to say, Western sinological comparative analysis has been very impressed with the achievements of Chinese civilisation and is relunctant to prescribe fundamental regime change in the name of 'Westernisation'. Its focus is on a specifically Chinese perspective in the context of the contemporary vicissitudes of internal social and cultural change. In post-Cold War Western human-rights commentary, however, there is a much greater predisposition to assess China's progress towards the rule of law in light of a fundamental discussion of the relative merits of liberal versus socialist democracy and the capitalist versus socialist economic systems. In their support of the Western concept of the rule of law, some critics may simply dismiss any Chinese attempt to conceptualise and operationalise the 'socialist rule of law' as an intriniscally flawed enterprise. Such ill-fated emulation might be described in the Chinese term of 'drawing a tiger with a cat as a model' (*zhao mao hua hu*).

In the international lists of disagreement there is, for example, the International Commission of Jurists who explicitly claim, as in the 1965 ICJ Declaration of Bangkok, that the rule of law can only reach its highest and fullest expression under the liberal democratic norms of Western-style representative democracy.[1] This same sentiment animates the 1992 report on Hong Kong, *Countdown to 1997*. On the other side of the lists, at least some cautious Western exponents of sinogical study will contend that unqualified Westernisation of China's domestic political and value structures could exacerbate the contemporary crisis of faith and accelerate a counterproductive pattern of political disintegration which could well lead to a new variant of the rule of man.

The actual contemporary status of Chinese legal reform, in its relation to the conceptualisation and materialisation of the rule of law, requires a comprehensive weighting of interacting domestic and international factors. In reaction to the traumatic persecution of the Cultural Revolution, the Chinese political leadership suddenly became aware of its own tendencies towards rule by law, rule of man and feudalism. This qualitative change in internal political consciousness was critical to the political recognition of the rule of law as a seminal characteristic of modernisation. The internal debates of China's legal circles on the content and materialisation of the rule of law has helped generate a growing interest in the international comparative history of the rule of law. The study of the rule of law is supported in the evolving convergence between Chinese and Western sinologies. The concept of the rule of law has been supported despite open disagreement with Western emphases on judicial independence and the separation of powers.

The open door and economic reform policies significantly focused political and legal attention on the application of the principle of equality in the legal mediation of conflicting social interests. In the relation of law to society, there is a deepening tension which has yet to achieve effective dialectical and political resolution within Chinese legal theory and policy understanding. Increasing corporatist interest in legal protection and continuing corporatist involvement in the making of the law conflicts, willy-nilly, with the growing challenge to the implicit hierarchy in the traditional structure of interests and in the manifestation of autonomous economic activities of private capital and international investment.

Western sinological study has not yet figured out just how these competing tendencies will intersect. At the macro-analytical level, for example, Arthur Rosenbaum has argued that the internal systemic transformation of the party–state and contemporary emergence of civil society are 'interrelated' but 'distinct' processes:

> A fundamental change in the organization and operation of state power in China most likely will facilitate greater social autonomy but does not necessarily mean the acceptance and institutionalization of civil society. Conversely, the rise of civil society and of more autonomous social groups is often seen as a precondition for a transition from authoritarianism to democracy, but by itself it does not guarantee the dismantling of existing authoritarian political structures.[2]

On the other hand, current Western human-rights advocacy has politically focused on the importance of censoring the negative features of China's political system, and this has helped obscure the underlying continuity in Chinese legal reform and legislation. Much of this volume's coverage and interpretation of post-June 4 legal reform and debate factually disputes the following conclusion of the US State Department report on 1990 Chinese human-rights performance:

> After the 1989 crackdown, however, the tightening of political and ideological controls seriously undermined these reforms [i.e., the 1980s legal reforms], and closed off debate on the relative merits of 'rule by man' and 'rule by law' [perhaps 'rule of law' is meant herein] and set back China's efforts to build a modern autonomous judicial system.[3]

Indeed, there was a limited conservative reaction focusing on the absolute necessity of political unity and stability; however, China's legal circles continued a significant debate on the rule of law. There was no conceptual retreat back to rule by law and the instrumentalist notion of law as an aspect of state administration. At least at the level of policy and theory, the distinction between rule of law and rule by law held.

Carlos Lo, in his perceptive assessment of Deng Xiaoping's difficulties in attempting to deal with this distinction, commented:

> Deng's ideas on law had unparalleled significance in Chinese history because he provided a leadership that saw the positive value of law and that brought to an end the legal nihilism enshrined in the notion of the 'two whatevers'.

But Lo also contends that Deng, in his response to Tiananmen Square, pursued the rule of law in an expedient fashion without comprehensive reference to the entirety of the political framework and without the benefit of a coherent theoretical formulation. In short, Deng's Tiananmen view 'bent in the direction of expediency' in the practical political correlations of party leadership, democracy and law.[4]

During the 1989 sequence of events, the last-minute attempt to switch the political action away from the Party towards a reform-based NPC failed, and Deng's re-assertion of leadership ominously suggested the return of the 'great helmsman' to Chinese politics. In the middle of Gorbachev's visit, Zhao Ziyang revealed, not so inadvertently, that Deng, despite his self-acclaimed lack of formal position, still acted as 'helmsman'. Western critics often interpreted this as a relapse back into the rule of man as distinct from government of law, and, in the wake of post-June 4 reaction, the issue became too sensitive for explicit internal reform comment. Although no one dared comment critically on Deng's role, there was a continuing focus on the abstract problems of feudalism and rule of man.

Predictable official opinion viewed Tiananmen Square student action as illegal and politically misguided in its false opposition of socialist legality to democracy. However, China's recorded human-rights performance in Western monitoring sunk to an extraordinary low which in some cases put the PRC on par with the world's worst human-rights abusive regimes such as Burma and Iraq.[5]

Whatever the true extent of post-June 4 setback, legal reform continued to make important strides in both theory and legislation, for the original political reasons for the 1980s debate and related legislation on the rule of law were still politically valid within the Party leadership itself. After June 4 major gains were made in the expansion of administrative and civil law, in the extension of 'equal subjects' and the development of new property law, not to mention the remarkable recognition of the terminology of human rights and the passage of related human-rights legislation.

Inevitably, political reaction highlighted 'counterrevolution' and 'peaceful evolution'. The Party was caught up in the contradictions of its own making. While the Party sought to impose the rule of law on Chinese history, Chinese history imposed itself on the Party. The Party did not resolve this persisting contradiction, but it did not abandon its original endorsement of legal reform. This continuing endorsement cannot be properly explained on the basis of antithetical extremes, or the contention that neither the rule of law nor human rights can possibly be advanced within so-called totalitarianism.

The assumption of the immutability of the Leninist state and its inability to achieve attributes of modernisation such as technical rationalisation, functional specialisation and organisational complexity has been convincingly critiqued in Richard Baum's review of the Brzezinski–

Huntington thesis, or 'iron law of Leninist monocracy', which, in the 1960s, discounted any suggestion of East–West post-industrial convergence.[6] Certainly, this thesis has failed to provide an adequate conceptual basis for understanding contemporary Chinese political and legal change, and much of this volume's review of changed legal thinking and related legislation suggests that substantive progress has occurred even within the limitations and self-contradictions of contemporary Chinese political leadership.

A major *Renmin ribao* editorial of 26 July 1989 reviewed the Tiananmen event, defending the Party's decision not to retract the 26 April editorial. It described the student protest as a 'turmoil' and disputed the legality of the students' autonomous union for Beijing universities and colleges. In its conclusion, this editorial returned to the reasoning which had originally highlighted the rule of law as the antidote to any re-occurrence of the Cultural Revolution:

> Legal construction must be strengthened in China now. Only by doing so will officials at various levels be ensured to be under the effective supervision of the broad masses while citizens can be confident of enjoying more democracy and freedom without harming the interests of the State and other people. To strengthen legal construction is also the best way to avoid the reappearance of a 'cultural revolution' tragedy.[7]

The Cultural Revolution has spawned both new interest in the rule of law as well as a reactive, or reactionary, perspective on the absolute priority of political stability and unity. While the formal post-June 4 terms of political re-structuring have been narrowed, the political implications of economic and legal reform continue to proliferate and to impact on the development of the legal system.

Peng Zhen's report on the revised state constitution of 1982 reiterated a longstanding Party perspective: 'Freedoms and rights with absolutely no restrictions have never existed in the world.'[8] Post-June 4 official interpretation predictably re-asserted the classical formulation of 'unity of rights and obligations' in rejecting the Tiananmen students' 'defence of law' and lamented the alleged irony that the Constitution was trampled upon by 'good and honest students' who misguidedly defended the dignity of the Constitution.

Student reference to the defence of Article 35 of the State Constitution, which among other things guarantees freedoms of speech and demonstration, was predictably countered with reference to Article 51 which stipulated that the exercise of rights 'may not infringe upon the interests of the state, of society, and of the collective, or upon the lawful freedoms and rights of other citizens'. Article 51 purportedly came into play in light of the disruption of the official memorial programme for Hu Yaobang on 22 April and the later cancellation of the grand welcome ceremony for Mikhail Gorbachev.[9]

In a *Jiefangjun bao* editorial comment on Jiang Zemin's National Day speech in October 1989, Fang Li attacked the 'elite politics' of student activists who allegedly wanted democracy for themselves, first, and at the expense of the worker–peasant alliance. The editorial lectured student dissidents on the proper correlation of the 'socialist legal system' with 'socialist democracy':

> the socialist legal system can be established and developed only after the working class and laboring people have taken over the political power and won their democratic rights. At the same time, socialist democracy cannot be consolidated and perfected without the guarantee of the socialist legal system. Therefore, it is erroneous and very harmful to set democracy against the legal system, to hold that the legal system will restrict democracy, and to deviate from the legal system in striving for democracy.[10]

In the post-June 4 era, there are continuing disagreements within political and legal circles as to which points within 'one centre, two basic points' require primary emphasis. The hardcore interpretation of one centre, two basic points has meant that comparatively less attention could be formally ascribed to qualitative democratic reform, but this should not obscure the far-reaching political and legal implications of economic reform itself.

The so-called economic rule of law, for example, incorporates a qualitative political implication in its required legislative delimitation of the power of state administration. Irrespective of whether or not this implication is explicitly derivative of Western power control theory, it is intimately connected to the issue of government of law, and not of man. Subscription to the 'socialist market' has contributed to the formal supercession of *liangquan fenli*, separation of management and ownership, and the developing theory of state enterprise as a 'legal person'. 'Law as a tool of state administration' has increasingly been identified as a liability in the new era of socialist market economy. While Party conservatives may entertain 'instrumentalist' assumptions about the use of law in the economy, the struggle for the rule of law is entwined with multi-dimensional implications of reform which are often at odds with rule by law and rule of man.

In a January 1990 national conference on court work, both Jiang Zemin and Li Peng stressed the importance of popularising legal knowledge and raising the general level of citizens' consciousness of the law. Citing hostile foreign forces and the dangers of peaceful evolution and the Party's focus on stability, Premier Li, nevertheless, affirmed the continuation of reform emphases on the open door' policy and the strengthening of the legal system:

> Foreign hostile forces will not stop their attempt to stage a 'peaceful evolution' in China....Under these circumstances, China should on the one hand continue its reform and opening policy and on the other strengthen its legal system. While increasing exchanges with foreign countries, China should prevent the infiltration of decadent things.[11]

In the light of this central leadership support, the second five-year programme for the popularisation of legal knowledge was launched for the specifically stated purposes of increasing citizen ability to handle affairs according to law and to 'promote the management of business in light of the law and gradually bring various kinds of economic activities into the legal sphere'.[12]

In the midst of acute Party anxiety over the collapse of Soviet and East European socialism, reform forces were still able to place human rights at the top of the State Council's agenda in November 1991. Conservatives finally foreclosed Politbureau consideration of an amnesty for the Tiananmen Square dissidents, but the conservative ideologue, Deng Liqun, was unable to form a 'Leading Group Against Peaceful Evolution' within the Party Central Committee.[13] Moreover, while Party conservatives were able to stall the NPC revision of the Criminal Law special provisions on counterrevolution, they could not force the pro-revisionists to recant their arguments.

In the post-June 4 reaction, there was a heightened leadership concern over the 'comprehensive management of public order', but there was also continuing emphases on the use of administrative procedural law to ensure power control. The Civil Law survived June 4 reaction, and there has been continuing expansion of 'equal subjects' before the law. Leftist rather than rightist deviations continue to receive the greatest leadership priority. Conservative reaction has progressively petered out. It has a progressively diminishing theoretical and policy base from within which to work.

Debate within China's legal circles has continued in much the same way as before June 4 with emphasis on the consolidation of a Chinese socialist version of the rule of law. Chen Chunlong, for example, in his post-June 4 eulogy to the rule of law noted that the rule of law is the prerequisite to political stability and socialist politics. The 'will of the people' (*renxin*) is to be legally guaranteed in the 'control of public power' and the stipulation of rights and obligations.[14]

Writing in the June 1991 issue of the journal of the University of Political Science and Law – a school which had been seriously implicated in the June 4 student movement – Zhang Guicheng criticised the continued influence of feudal patriarchicalism and the Confucian rule of man. Once again, he set out the underlying thinking of Aristotle and Montesquieu on the rule of law which required state agencies and officials to use their powers only in accordance with formally published law and the application of the principle of equality before the law. Without giving his endorsement, Zhang also described Montesquieu's 'separation and balance of powers' (*quanli fenli he zhiheng*). He conceded that for a long time after the founding of the PRC there was a negative tendency simply to dismiss the rule of law as bourgeois. He argued that the socialist rule of law currently requires socialist democracy and the Party leadership's strategy of 'mutual checks and balances' (*xianghu hexuo xianghu zhiyue*) so as to combat the inherent and arbitrary trend towards the over-concentration of state power in modern Chinese history.

Zhang also wrote that the historical development of the rule of law is contemporaneous with the development of productive forces and that the regulation of the economy by law is pivotal to the development of national economy. He stressed that, in China's particular case, all three means of managing the economy – namely, economic, administrative and legal – require a continuous process of legalisation. Zhang eschewed the arbitrary nature of past administrative and economic regulation of the economy, but he stopped short of the notion that the rule of law required the transformation of the Party's pre-eminent position within the state. Deng's new directives on the liberation of productive forces and socialist market are likely to accentuate the developing political emphasis on the need for a rule of law to deal with the new demands for legal mediation within China's changing structure of interests. If anything, there is an increasing focus on the legal mediation of disputes which would formerly have been resolved on the exclusive basis of the dictates of state planning and Party guidance.

During an international symposium on the rule of law and social and economic development in Beijing in October 1991, Western and Chinese legal experts initially agreed that the modern rule of law originates in commodity economy and democratic politics which respond to developments in science and technology. Drawing on familiar official argument underlying socialism with Chinese characteristics, some of the Chinese participants, however, strenuously objected to Western participants' particular distinction between *xingshi fazhi* (rule by law) and rule of law, which assumed the superiority of commodity production, based exclusively upon private ownership and Western-style democratic pluralism.

Replying to this allegedly patronising critique of China's legal system, they might well have referred to *The Blackwell Encyclopaedia of Political Science* to the effect that the rule of law is open textured. Western opinion once again protested Chinese subscription to 'cultural relativist' argument. The Chinese once again argued against one model and one standard by which to define rule of law. They claimed that, from within Chinese socialism, they had a legitimate interest in 'government of law' as distinct from the rule of man and that socialist, as distinct from capitalist commodity production also needed a rule of law so as to coordinate interest relations and equally protect all legally defined interests.[15]

Since 4 June 1989, Chinese comparative legal scholarship has continued to claim that there is no single perfect model of the rule of law which must apply in all national contexts. Li Long, of Wuhan University's Institute of Law, for example compared the models of ancient Greece, the former Soviet Union, Germany, France and China. Li argued that, although the Chinese Legalism had coined the rule of law, its meaning related to the technique of governing, or 'using law to rule the state' (*yifa zhi guo*), or what Wang Liming had earlier termed 'rule by law'. In Li's view, the Legalist rule of law had three chief characteristics, namely, an internal essence which related to rule of man, focus on the function of law in government by the state, and emphasis on severe punishment. On this basis, Li favourably referenced Aristotle's disagreement with Plato's focus on the rule of man, and the Aristotelian emphases on law made by the people, the impartial application of law, its stable content *vis-à-vis* changes of ruling personalities, and the clear expression of norms in the law.

On the other hand, Li Long harshly criticised the Soviet rule of law and Gorbachev's new thinking. Apparently, Gorbachev's abstract notions of democracy and freedom had helped undermine the clear expression of the norms of socialism in the Soviet rule of law. Interestingly, Gorbachev,with hindsight, commented in a Stanford University address on the Russian capacity for extremist politics and put the contemporary inability to establish a Russian rule of law in longterm perspective: 'We are burdened by our dark heritage – absence of a political culture, disrespect for the law and a hostility to those responsible for the preservation of order.'[16]

Li continued his comparison with a discussion of the French rule of law, citing important gains in 1980s French legal theory on the materialisation of the ideas of legal order, the limitation of the state by law and development of the content of existing law in light of theory and the perfection of legal techniques. Not surprisingly, he insisted that China's rule of law would have to reinforce both socialism with Chinese characteristics and one central task and two basic points, but he did single out for attention three points for improvement of China's rule of law, namely, emphases on legal order, the lawful delimitation of state power, and the improved relation between law and new technology.[17]

Disjuncture between formally stated intention in law and the consistent practical application of the law is to be expected in any political context. In fact, contemporary Chinese Marxist theory itself insists that there is always a gap between legally entrenched rights and the materialisation of rights in society. The empirical assessment of progress in the Chinese struggle for the rule of law is, nevertheless, quite daunting.

Western human-rights monitoring has yet to come up with a universally acceptable measure of the practical implementation of human-rights legislation throughout targetted domestic societies. It remains as an explicitly European extension of natural law reasoning. Western human-rights monitoring is not set up to assess comparative human-rights performance in light of distinctive legal and political cultures. In China's case, the West's emphasis is certainly not on dialogue between equals. Such monitoring is more or less censorial in its explicit attempt to achieve behavioural modification. It has not systematically identified and supported the positive elements of Chinese legal reform; and it has not even provided a systematic assessment of the affects of Western influence on Chinese society and its legal system.

The changing Chinese societal context reflects differing trends which, at one and the same time, respond to demand for 'comprehensive management of public order' and mass-line focus on community mediation, and the implications of economic reform which demand the benefits of the 'predictability' of law. There is no ready agreement either within or without China as to the optimal balance between community and legal system effort in the resolution of Chinese social and economic conflict. In the meantime, the Chinese continue to claim that their considerable achievements in human rights have gone unrecognised. They emphasise, for example, that security against violence is a basic matter of the enjoyment of human rights and that China still has, by any international standards, an extraordinarily low crime rate.[18]

Whether we are discussing the rule of law or civil society, such notions cannot simply be imported, uncrated and reconstituted in Chinese society; they have to have indigenous supports within the public mind and within the society-wide application of law in the mediation of interest conflict.

American law professors, Lawrence Friedman and Stewart Macaulay, essentially agreed with Sir Ivor Jennings that the rule of law is a practical moral understanding, the significance of which ranges beyond the mere statement of a set of rules. They contended that a comprehensive analysis of a working legal system would have to encompass structural, cultural and substantive components which would include a wide-ranging set of the interconnecting variables. The latter range across the forms and processes of existing institutions, 'the values and attitudes which bind the system together and which determine the place of the legal system in the culture of the society as a whole', as well as the actual content of law, statutes and decrees and the application of such in the interaction of the rulers and ruled.[19]

As we have seen, China's legal circles are increasingly advocating a similar multidimensional approach in their theoretical opposition of the contemporary notion of the rule of law to feudalism and cultural autocracy. Related debates assume the centrality of rights and equality before the law and condemn the one-dimensional nature of imperial law in its focus on the protection of the state interests and 'cultivating oneself in order to obey heaven'.

There are continuous and unresolved tensions within the contemporary Chinese struggle to define and materialise the rule of law, but it must also be emphasised that a retreat back into the heyday of policy as the soul of law is increasingly unlikely. There has been qualitative departmental development of law and substantive progress *vis-à-vis* the self-conscious identitification of traditional impediments to modern legal culture, such as 'ethics and law are inseparable', 'judiciary and administration are inseparable', and 'combining all types of law into one'.

This volume has focused largely on an explanation of the legal thinking of China's legal circles, as they have self-consciously responded to the changing political context, but one may well ask, in the context of rising regionalism, a crisis of faith and the imminent passing of the last of the revolutionary generation of leaders, whether central institutions will be able to strengthen progress towards the rule of law. Will the death of the last of the 'helmsmen' be marked by a general retreat into corruption, administrative breakdown and possibly rule by the 'man on horseback'?

A Chilean 'man on horseback', Augusto Pinochet, once bluntly told those who wished to send his military officers to jail for human-rights abuses: 'The day they touch me or...my men, the rule of law is over.'[20] In China's recent past, the CCP was able to squelch politically any militarist tendencies. The politicisation of the PLA, inclusive of its subordination to Party democratic centralism and the cooperation of its top leaders within the Party leadership, helped to guarantee army acceptance of the subordination of military modernisation to the larger goals of national economic development as set by the Party's civilian leadership.

The 14th Party Congress reiterated Party leadership over the army, but is it possible that the PLA could become more politically unstable under economic reform and the socialist market than under Mao? At the same time the military becomes a stakeholder, if not a vested economic interest group, the traditional Party-based safeguards against a *coup d'état* may have been weakened as the crisis of faith becomes more and more aggravated within China's economic and social transformation.

The currently anticipated transition in supreme leadership may certainly highlight once again the relation between rule by law and rule of law. While the memory of the Cultural Revolution is still politically powerful, the final dénouement of the revolutionary generation is momentary. Succeeding leaders will not have the same stature. They will not enjoy the same degree of informal authority and political support throughout China's major institutions. Their ability as national leaders to resort to the rule of man may well be circumscribed in the ongoing crisis of faith and the rise of regional elite politics.

At least the proponents of the rule of law within China's legal circles have reached an important crossroads. They have engineered a historically significant evolution in Chinese legal thinking in response to societal change and the evolving requirements of economic reform. They have had significant influence on the drafting of new law in response to the changing structure of interests. In spearheading legal reform, China's law scholars appear, at first glance, to fill the role that Max Weber assigned to the *legal honoratriores* (legal scholars) who in European legal history fostered the practical dimensions of legal thought along with a 'formal' as explicitly distinguished from a 'substantive rationality'.[21]

On the other hand, within China's reform legal circles, many scholars are in conflict in terms of their own personal correlations of law with society. While they are often sympathetic to newly emerging interests, they are also very committed to law and order and the underlying 'substantive' dimensions of morality and ideology. While some reformers eagerly embrace Western terms of reference, there are many others who still regard the Weberian differentiation between formal and substantive rationality with an instinctive caution which originates in their native philosophical expectations and their formal Marxist–Leninist training in the law.

Moreover, throughout society, there is a continuing 'legal blindness', which is readily acknowledged by both the legal and political circles of leadership. Even so, the Party leadership stands ready to attempt to legislate a new legal culture into existence. The fast track has been endorsed on the basis of Deng Xiaoping's personal authority and on the basis of a longstanding conviction as to the importance of mass-line organisational experiment and praxis. The extent of new legislation may have already reached the point of saturation where it will become popularly difficult to assimilate any new legal changes in a time of increasing legal, political and cultural stress. While some scholars loudly complain of the law's inability to catch up with qualitative changes in the economy and society, state-sponsored societal change through legislation has been fast and furious. The 'lofty dignity' of the law could easily become a casualty of social change. New legal consciousness requires accumulated social practice and a careful husbanding in the routine application of widely understood and accepted laws, but the circumstances of social change are bewildering and extraordinary.

While the gains in the Chinese struggle for the rule of law need to be properly identified and understood, this struggle has yet to resolve the integral paradox between a new political focus on the rule of law and a reflexive tendency to genuflect before the rule of man and the necessity of political unity.

In 1989, Deng Xiaoping rejected neo-authoritarianism and endorsed the rule of law, but then he personally assumed Mao's role as 'helmsman'. The paradoxical implications of this contradiction were revealed in April 1991 when Deng Xiaoping was reportedly involved in a minor car accident. His Mercedes-Benz entered a Beijing intersection at the same time as an ambulance carrying a state prosecutor and a pregnant prisoner. When horrified public security officers hesitated as to the right of way, Deng's car quite naturally claimed precedence only to crash in the middle of the intersection with the ambulance. No one was hurt, but rule *by* law seemingly prevailed as the driver of the ambulance was immediately arrested, his licence plates removed and his vehicle confiscated.[22]

The CCP gave its benediction to the principle of equality before the law, and the Party and State Constitutions both require that Party leaders, as well as all institutions, obey the law. The Party Constitution, in theory, cannot override the State Constitution, but while respecting the law, the Party still claims a role in the 'guidance' of overall legal and constitutional development. While Party is also committed to the legal mediation of conflicting interests, it is not yet ready to accept the open-ended involvement of China's senior leadership in politically sensitive lawsuits.

Continuing controversy is likely as to whether Deng Xiaoping's institutional strategy of mutual cooperation and restriction can, in comparison with the Western separation of powers, provide a sufficiently viable institutional base for the extension of the rule of law. However, with the explicit decline in the political significance of class struggle, there has been substantive progress in legal thinking and even in the evolving independent status of law.

Conceptually, law is no longer a mere adjunct of the political superstructure, as implied in 'policy as the soul of law'. With the important exception of NPC legislation regarding the death penalty, there has been no significant Party trend towards the politically capricious change of formal legislation. On the other hand, government of laws, and not of men is still ideologically and politically extrapolated from within an all-inclusive socialist spiritual civilisation, which contemporaneously emphasises legal culture, legalisation and politically organised comprehensive management of public order.

There are encouraging signs of new legal practice in the economy. Furthermore, in legal thinking and legislation, impressive documented qualitative gains have been achieved in the Chinese struggle for the rule of law, but for many observers the real litmus test is whether the law can be openly and equally applied against senior leaders and their progeny.

In the course of a 1992 interview, the elder statesman of Singapore, Lee Kuan Yew, ranged across the relation between Eastern and Western values and the PRC's related need to create a complete legal system and respect for the law at all levels of government. Lee claimed that Singapore had preserved traditional Confucian values and the related decorem of the five relationships, while at the same time it had dealt effectively with the problems of modernisation through the application of Western rational legal method. When an alert reporter inquired if, in dealing with corruption at the highest reaches of government, this apparently innocuous synthesis entailed a contradiction 'between feelings and sensibility in the course of law enforcement', Lee replied in all candour:

> It is a difficult thing to take action to deal with a friend or minister you have known for many years. But if no action is taken and he is allowed to go unpunished, the whole system could be ruined and our clean administrative system...reduced to nothing. If the prime minister carries out abnormal interference to prevent a high-level person who has close relations with him from being punished according to law, this cannot be kept secret absolutely. As a matter of fact, he is guilty of a more serious crime because of his position. Therefore, no matter how difficult it is, I would submit this matter for legal action and would not stand in the way.[23]

Hopefully, Lee would not just stand aside but would also take a rigorously pro-active position in supporting the administration of justice on the basis of equal justice for all under the law. Lee apparently aspired to something more than 'good person politics'. The interview, however, did not touch on the sensitive issue as of what would happen in the case of Lee's own indiscreet violation of the law. Indeed, what would happen if Lee's limousine crashed into an ambulance? Would his personally endorsed subscription to the Confucian five human relationships conflict with the principle of equality before the law?

Lee clearly emphasised the seminal correlation of ruling by moral example and good government. This might possibly be construed as originating in a Confucian preference for *shenjiao*, by which a moral elite teaches by personal example in public life, and certainly this appears to give rise to a baffling contradiction. To what extent is the authority of the teacher compatible with the assumptions of representative democracy and the rule of law? Is a contemporary version of rule by man necessary to the moral materialisation of the rule of law? Lee showed no apparent anxiety about the negative ascriptive features of traditional political culture, or what the PRC scholars have focused on as feudalism, and his position appears to correspond with the middle position of Zhang Guohua and Zhang Xin, as discussed in Chapter 1: 'In that we have good men and good laws then we have good rule.'[24]

The contemporary 'theory of combining rule of law and rule of man' (*fazhi renzhi jeihe lun*) appears to be a reformer adaptation to the classical Confucian emphasis on 'sageliness within and kingliness without'. The sage-king (*shengwang*) taught and ruled by self-example. Moral demonstration was philosophically seminal to good government. The latter was an exercise in rectifying behaviour; hence Confucius' advice to Zhi Kang in the *Analects*: 'To govern means to rectify. If you lead on the people with correctness, who will dare not to be correct?' And when Zhi Kang somewhat indelicately suggested the need to 'kill the unprincipled for the good of the principled', Confucius rejoined: 'Sir, in carrying on your government why should you use killing at all? Let your *evinced* desires be for what is good, and the people will be good.'[25]

The predictability of autonomous law was not at issue. Law within this tradition was formally accorded only a supplementary role in government. The decorum, underlying the 'rule of virtue', was philosophically anterior to law (*fa*). Xunzi's *lifa jiehe*, or the combining of *li* and *fa*, was not intended to promote the priority of legal development per se. The modern theory of combining the rule of law and rule of man, as espoused by some of China's most senior legal historians, argues that a better compromise is possible – one which would more appropriately enhance the dignity of law. In their simultaneous subscription to the humane dimensions of government and to the rationality of law, they no longer focus so intently on causing the people not to become involved in litigation.

This reformist position seeks a philosophical justification in the 'golden mean'. It is the contemporary re-statement of a late nineteenth century reform attitude. Liang Qichao, as one of the most well-known sponsors of modern liberalism in contemporary Chinese history, provided a memorable exposition of this 'middle way' in the following extract from his trenchant critique of Legalism:

> If political habits are not fostered, if political morality is not stabilized, then even if China had the best Constitution in the world it would be only a scrap of paper. Is not this an illustration of the truth that 'The law cannot stand by itself', and 'Disorder prevails in spite of the existence of a perfect law'? Therefore a final conclusion might be drawn from the words of Hsuntze [Xunzi], 'There are men who govern, but there are no laws that govern.' Or, to strike a middle way, no one could be more moderate than Mencius when he says, 'goodness alone is not sufficient for government; law alone is not capable of applying itself'. The claim which the Legalist school makes, 'to govern by law is as easy as lifting a thing and then putting it down', cannot be accepted by men of the least intelligence.[26]

The rule of law is not as easy as 'lifting a thing', but government of law, and not of men arguably depends upon appropriately humane leadership thinking, human commitment to open and democratic government and personal moral example. This modern attempt to combine the best of rule of law and rule of man appears to go one step beyond the cautionary logic of Aristotle who, in his description of law 'as intelligence without appetition', placed his emphasis on the law's ability to check undesirable behaviour in the quest for good government. In reacting to tyranny, Aristotle stressed the substitution of rational principle for what the Chinese call rule of man; however, China's legal historians more often than not operate within a conceptual circle of optimism which always returns to the same initial point, namely, that rational principle orginates with the moral expression of human character within society.

The contemporary incorporation of the rule of law within the Party's modern day notion of socialist spiritual civilisation raises the same difficult question as to the proper relation between the law and the moral development of society. In the sinological explanation of Chinese political culture and the considered application of Weberian social science notions to the comparative development of the rule of law, we are perennially forced to come to terms with practical politics and the ambiguous overlap of competing 'ideal types'. The latter is, of course, well recognised in Weberian analysis, which acknowledges both the positive and negative charismatic tendences within modern rational–legal institutionalisation.

Legal challenge to the most senior leaders of any state is deeply traumatic and politically rare even in the celebrated Western constitutional context of the separation of powers. Irrespective of all the unsung progress that has occurred within contemporary Chinese legal reform, until such time as China's embyronic rule of law is demonstrated in a clear legal challenge to supreme political authority, international observers will doubt Chinese intentions and will remain sceptical as to the extent to which the rule of law has substantively modified the informal, ascriptive dimensions of feudal or patriarchal authority and the inherent Chinese tendency to resort to moral autocracy and the rule of man. The interpretation of contemporary Chinese legal and political development has not become any easier, but defining moments in modern Chinese history, such as Tiananmen Square, do require significant and properly balanced analysis. In contributing to such analysis, Western sinological assessment may still respond to charges of 'cultural relativism' with a comprehensive and well informed understanding of the political and legal cultural continuities and discontinuities in the Chinese struggle for the rule of law versus rule by law.

Whereas traditional sinology self-consciously resisted the conceptual hegemony of Western ideas, selective human-rights monitoring currently tends to reinforce more explicitly hostile Western analysis which has a long list of preconditions to impose before any progress in the Chinese struggle for the rule of law can be properly acknowledged. The Chinese must emulate Western 'civil society'. In conceptualising human rights, they must embrace the European natural law tradition. They must dismantle the Party and institutionalise Western-style representative democracy. They must subscribe to judicial independence, particularly as it has evolved out of the separation of powers and as it relates to seminal importance of precedent and judicial interpretation of case law.

Alternatively, the Chinese struggle for the rule of law may be placed on the reform continuum of discrete reaction and response to domestic political culture and international influence. The present contradictions between indigenous and external legal cultures within China's tentative and nascent rule of law are likely to become more profound and complex under the conditions of new openness and rapid internal economic and social transformation.

While the Party continues to insist on comprehensive management of public order, especially in the coordination of the courts with mass organisation so as to deal with the ramifications of new interests and the changing nature of crime within society, it has made a new and sustained attempt to withdraw from court proceedings. The procedural dimensions of the Criminal Law represent a vast improvement over the past. Also it is significant that the law on counterrevolution has been frontally challenged as anachronistic and legally irrational.

Also, in legal theory and related legislation there is an emerging focus on human rights and the correlation of rights and obligations in law. The bureaucratic authority of state administration has been openly challenged in the development of Administrative Law. The latter has begun to confront traditional resistance against lawsuits, and it is explicitly premised in the need to check arbitrary and inefficient state authority.

Moreover, there is a self-conscious response to compensate for the diminution of Civil Law and the near absence of rights-bearing subjects within the traditional legal system. Civil Law, in its response to the changing structure of interests, is acquiring a more solid infrastructural presence within the judicial process, and its advocates have fostered the extension of equal subjects to an unprecedented degree. Despite deep Conservative anxiety over the fate of Chinese socialism, property law is becoming a real category of law.

This new predicate focuses on the law's predictability and the principle of equality before the law. It represents a qualitative breakthrough, and yet it is still likely to operate within a Chinese syntax which self-consciously synthesises flexibility and principle. Certainly, indigenous cultural political assumptions tend to work against a strict bifurcation of the substantive and procedural dimensions of the law, but this should not distract our attention from the growing interaction of Chinese and Western legal ideas and the most progressive reform within the entire span of China's legal history.

Appendix: NPC/NPCSC New Law 1979–1991[1]

Title	Time of Passage
Forest Law of the PRC[2] (trial implementation[3])	23.2.1979
Arrest and Detention Act of the PRC	23.2.1979
Election Laws of NPC and Local People's Congresses of the PRC	1.7.1979
Organic Law of Local People's Congresses and Local People's Governments of the PRC	1.7.1979
Organic Law of People's Courts of the PRC	1.7.1979
Organic Law of People's Procuratorates of the PRC	1.7.1979
Criminal Law of the PRC	1.7.1979
Criminal Procedural Law of the PRC	1.7.1979
Law of the PRC concerning Sino–Foreign Joint Ventures	1.7.1979
Environment Protection Law of the PRC (trial implementation)	13.9.1979
Act of Academic Degrees of the PRC	12.2.1980
Temporary Lawyers Act of the PRC	26.8.1980
Guangdong Province Special Economic Zone Act of the PRC	26.8.1980
Nationality Law of the PRC	10.9.1980
Marriage Law of the PRC	10.9.1980
Taxation Law of the PRC concerning Sino–Foreign Joint Ventures	10.9.1980
Personal Income Tax Law of the PRC	10.9.1980
Temporary Act of the PRC on Punishing Violations of Military Service	10.6.1981
Economic Contracts Law of the PRC	13.12.1981
Taxation Law of the PRC concerning [Wholly] Foreign Owned Enterprises	13.12.1981
Civil Procedural Law of the PRC (trial implementation)	8.3.1982
Compensation Act of the PRC concerning Land Expropriated by the State	4.5.1982

[1] Sources: Guo Daohui, *Zhongguo lifa zhidu* (China's legislative system) (Beijing: Renmin chubanshe, 1988); and *Xinhua yuebao* (New China monthly), 1987–1991. This list of 'national legislation' includes laws, *fa* and *falu*, as well as *tiaoli*, acts. It does not include NPCSC resolutions, decisions and regulations.

[2] Italics, in this list, indicate laws that were passed by the whole session of NPC. Normal type face is used for the laws that were passed by NPCSC.

[3] Law, prior to 1983, which was designated as 'trial implementation' refers to law which requires experimentation and related leadership consensus. Three of the four laws so designated have been superseded by law of the same title.

Maritime Environment Protection Law of the PRC	23.8.1982
Trade Mark Law of the PRC	23.8.1982
Antiques Protection Law of the PRC	19.11.1982
Food Hygiene Law of the PRC (trial implementation)	19.11.1982
Constitution of the PRC	4.12.1982
Organic Law of NPC of the PRC	10.12.1982
Organic Law of State Council of the PRC	10.12.1982
Maritime Traffic Safety Law of the PRC	2.9.1983
Law of the PRC concerning [Government] Statistics	8.12.1983
Patent Law of the PRC	12.3.1984
Water Pollution Prevention and Treatment Law of the PRC	11.5.1984
Fire Fighting and Prevention Act of the PRC	11.5.1984
Minorities–Regions Autonomy Law of the PRC	31.5.1984
PRC Military Recruitment and Service Law	31.5.1984
Forestry Law of the PRC	20.9.1984
Medicine Administration Law of the PRC	20.9.1984
Accounting Law of the PRC	21.1.1985
Law of the PRC concerning Economic Contracts Involving Foreign Parties	21.3.1985
Inheritance Law of the PRC	10.4.1985
Grassland Law of the PRC	18.6.1985
Measurements Law of the PRC	6.9.1985
Resident Identification Cards Act of the PRC	6.9.1985
Foreigners' Entry and Exit Law of the PRC	22.11.1985
Citizens' Border Exit and Entry Law of the PRC	22.11.1985
Fishery Law of the PRC	20.1.1986
Mineral Resources Law of the PRC	19.3.1986
General Principles of the Civil Law of the PRC	12.4.1986
Mandatory Education Law of the PRC	12.4.1986
Law of the PRC concerning [Wholly] Foreign Owned Enterprises	12.4.1986
Land Administration Law of the PRC	25.6.1986
Foreign Diplomatic Privileges and Immunity Act of the PRC	5.9.1986
Administrative Punishments Act of the PRC concerning Public Security Offenses	5.9.1986
Law of the PRC Concerning Border Health Inspection	2.12.1986
Post Administration Law of the PRC	2.12.1986
Enterprise Bankruptcy Law of the PRC	2.12.1986
Custom Law of the PRC	22.1.1987
Technology Contracts Law of the PRC	23.6.1987
Air Pollution Prevention and Treatment Law of the PRC	5.9.1987
Archives Law of the PRC	5.9.1987
Organic Law of the PRC concerning Rural Residents Committees	24.11.1987

Procedural Rules of NPCSC of the PRC	24.11.1987
Water Law of the PRC	21.1.1988
Law of the PRC concerning Enterprises Owned by the Whole People	13.4.1988
Law of the PRC concerning Sino–Foreign Cooperative Enterprises	13.4.1988
PLA Officer Ranks Act of the PRC	1.7.1988
State Secret Protection Law of the PRC	5.9.1988
PLA Officer Service Act of the PRC	5.9.1988
Wild Animals Protection Law of the PRC	8.11.1988
Land Administration Law of the PRC[4]	29.12.1988
Standardisation Law of the PRC	29.12.1988
Import and Export Goods Inspection Law of the PRC	21.2.1989
Contagious Diseases Prevention and Treatment Law of the PRC	21.2.1989
Procedural Law of the PRC Concerning Administrative Law Suits	4.4.1989
Procedural Rules of NPC of the PRC	4.4.1989
Law of the PRC on Public Assembly, Procession and Demonstration	31.10.1989
Organic Law of the PRC concerning Urban Residents' Committees	26.12.1989
Environment Protection Law of the PRC	26.12.1989
City Planning Law of the PRC	26.12.1989
Military Facilities Protection Law of the PRC	23.2.1990
Basic Law of Hongkong Special Administrative Region of the PRC	4.4.1990
Law of the PRC concerning[5] *Sino–Foreign Joint Ventures*	4.4.1990
National Flag Law of the PRC	28.6.1990
Copyright Law of the PRC	7.9.1990
Railway Law of the PRC	7.9.1990
Returned Overseas Chinese and Relatives of Overseas Chinese Protection Law of the PRC	7.9.1990
Foreign Consulate Privileges and Immunity Law of the PRC	30.10.1990
Handicapped People Protection Law of the PRC	28.12.1990
Procedural Law of the PRC for Concluding Treaties	28.12.1990
National Emblem Law of the PRC	2.3.1991
Civil Procedural Law of the PRC	9.4.1991
PRC Tax Law Concerning[6] *Enterprise with Foreign Investment and [Wholly] Foreign-Owned Enterprises*	9.4.1991
Tobacco Monopoly Law of the PRC	29.6.1991

[4] This is a re-enacted version of the 1986 land administration law.

[5] This is a re-enacted version of the 1979 Law concerning Sino–Foreign Joint Ventures.

[6] This law superseded the 1980 taxation law concerning Sino–foreign joint ventures and the 1981 taxation law concerning (wholly) foreign owned enterprises.

Water and Soil Conservation Law of the PRC	29.6.1991
Law on Protection of Minors of the PRC	4.9.1991
Law concerning Animal and Plant Inspection at the Borders of the PRC	30.10.1991
Adoption Law of the PRC	29.12.1991

Notes and References

1 The Chinese Struggle for the Rule of Law

1 Jerome Cohen drew this conclusion in 'The Criminal Process in the People's Republic of China: An Introduction', *Harvard Law Review*, vol. 79, no. 3, Jan. 1966, p. 470. Richard Baum extensively analyses this distinction. See fn. 15 below. Charles Burton comments on Deng Xiaoping's 'rule by law' in terms of efforts to minimise 'the discretionary authority of the lower-level bureaucracy' and the 'mechanisation' of the Party Centre's specific policies. Charles Burton, *Political and Social Change in China since 1978* (New York: Greenwood Press, 1990) p. 31.

2 'Top Judge Feels Law Has Made Big Gains', *China Daily* (hereinafter CD) 3 Oct. 1989, p. 4.

3 Liu Han, 'Zhengzhi tizhi gaige yu fazhi jianshe' (Political re-structuring and the establishment of the legal system) *Faxu yanjiu*, no. 1, 1988, p. 8.

4 US Committees on Foreign Relations and Foreign Affairs of the Senate and House of Representatives, *Country Reports on Human Rights Practices for 1990* (Washington, DC: Government Printing Office, 1991) p. 849.

5 Li Long, 'Fazhi moshi lun' (On models of the rule of law) *Zhongguo faxue* (Chinese Legal Science) no. 6, 1991, pp. 29–35.

6 Zhang Guicheng, 'Lun fazhi' (On rule of law) *Zhengfa luntan* (Tribune of Political Science and Law) no. 6, 1991, pp. 13–8.

7 '"Supremacy of Law" Rejected', *China Daily Report*, 12 November 1991, p. 12.

8 See Shao-chuan Leng, Hungdah Chiu, *Criminal Justice in Post-Mao China* (Albany: State University of New York Press, 1985) p. 7.

9 See, for example, John F. Copper, Franz Michael, Yuan-li Wu, *Human Rights in Post-Mao China* (Boulder & London: Westview Press, 1985) p. 5. The authors 'readily admit' to a 'western bias' in their focus on Western-defined 'human rights' concepts, p. xi. Their view in some respects might be contrasted with that of Suzanne Ogden who later argued that the Third Plenum constituted a 'watershed' marking 'the demise of "leftist" influence' and a 'positive step forward' in legal development. Suzanne Ogden, *China's Unresolved Issues* (Englewood Cliffs, NJ: Prentice Hall, 1989) pp. 228–9.

10 Rodger Beehler discusses the question of relative emphasis in 'Waiting for the Rule of Law', *University of Toronto Law Journal*, vol. XXXIVIII, 1988, p. 298.

11 Ann Van Wynen Thomas & A.J. Thomas, Jr., *A World Rule of Law* (Dallas: SMU Press, 1975) p. 4.

12 See F.R. Cristi's discussion of this advice in 'Hayek and Schmitt on the Rule of Law', *Canadian Journal of Political Science*, vol. xvii, no. 3, September 1984, pp. 521–2.

13 'Law is the Cornerstone of Progress', *CD*, 22 August 1987, p. 4.

14 Richard Thornburgh, 'The Soviet Union and the Rule of Law', *Foreign Affairs*, vol. 69, no. 2, 1990, p. 14.
15 Richard Baum, '"Modernization" and Legal Reform in Post-Mao China: the Rebirth of Socialist Legality', *Studies in Comparative Communism*, vol. xix, no. 2, Summer, 1986, pp. 70–2.
16 Franz Michael, 'Law: A Tool of Power', *Human Rights in the People's Republic of China* (Boulder & London, Westview Press, 1988) p. 33.
17 Li Buyun, *Fazhi, minzhu, ziyou* (Legal system, democracy and freedom) (Chengdu: Sichuan renmin chubanshe, 1985) p. 133.
18 For a gloss of the Congress terminology see Zhang Zhengde, 'Womendi mubiao shi shehuizhuyi fazhi guo' (Our objective is to create a rule-of-law state) *Xiandai faxue* (Contemporary Legal Studies), no. 5, 1988.
19 'Communique of the Third Plenary Session of the 11th Central Committee of the Communist Party of China', 22 December 1978, *Peking Review*, no. 52, 29 December 1978, p. 14.
20 Ibid., p. 14.
21 Deng Xiaoping, *Selected Works of Deng Xiaoping* (Beijing: Foreign Languages Press, 1984) p. 158.
22 Zhang Zhengde, 'Womendi mubiao shi shehuizhuyi fazhi guo' (Our purpose is a socialist rule of law country) *Xiandai faxue* (Modern Law Science) no. 5, 1988, p. 13.
23 As cited in 'China's Socialist Legal System', *Beijing Review* (hereinafter *BR*) no. 2, 12 January 1979, p. 26. Dong attributed the lack of societal respect for law to 'petty bourgeois fanatacism' and the extension of the early '50s mass campaign style of thinking which had only been necessary in the first years of the 'people's republic'. Dong Biwu, *Dong Biwu zhengzhi falu wenji* (Dong Biwu's collected works on politics and law) (Beijing: Falu chubanshe, 1985) p. 486.
24 Zhang Guohua, 'Zai faxue lingyu bixu jinchi he fazhan makesizhuyi' (In legal studies we must firmly grasp and develop Marxism) *Guangming ribao*, 10 December 1986, p. 3.
25 Sun Guohua, for example, warned that any notion of 'renovation' can only apply from within the requirements of Marxism–Leninism. See Sun Guohua, 'Woguo faxue jichu lilundi xiandai he qianjing' (The present circumstances and future prospects of basic Chinese legal theory) *Faxue jikan* (Law Studies Quarterly) no. 4, 1986, p. 10.
26 See, for example, Yuan Chengdi, 'Shehuizhuyi fa ye yingyou gongsi fazhi fen' (Socialist law should also have the distinction between private and public law) *Faxue jikan*, vol. 30, no. 4, Oct. 1986, pp. 22–4. Yuan attacked uninformed opinion predicated in Soviet experience and Leninist rationalisation which assumed that the development of 'private law' is exclusive to the 'bourgeois legal system'.
27 See Ronald C. Keith, 'Transcript of Discussions with Wu Daying and Zhang Zonglin Concerning Legal Change and Civil Rights', *China Quarterly* (hereinafter *CQ*) no. 81, March 1980, p. 115.
28 See Constitution of the People's Republic of China, 4 December 1982, in *Fifth Session of the Fifth National People's Congress* (Beijing: Foreign Languages Press, 1983) p. 11; and *The Criminal Law and the Criminal Procedure Law of China* (Beijing Foreign Languages Press, 1984) p. 116.

29 Fei Xiaotong, *A Great Trial in Chinese History* (Beijing: New World Press, 1981) preface, pp. 7, 9.

30 Peng Zhen, 'Several Questions Concerning Political and Judicial Work', *Hongqi* (Red Flag) no. 9, 1 May 87, p. 3, FBIS, 6091.

31 See Anthony Dicks' analysis in 'The Chinese Legal System: the Reforms in the Balance', *CQ*, no. 119, Sept. 1989, pp. 542–3.

32 Peng Zhen on the legal system', *Xin Hua*, 5 April 1986, in FBIS-CHI-86-066, 7 April 1986, vol. 1, no. 066, p. K8.

33 See analysis of Peng's speech in *Fazhan shehuizhuyi minzhu jian quan shehuizhuyi fazhi* (Develop Socialist Democracy and establish socialist legality) (Beijing: Falu chubanshe, 1988) p. 123.

34 Zhang Yongmin, 'Strengthening the legal system is a pressing need in reform of the economic system', *Hongqi*, no. 14, 16 July 1986, in JPRS-CPS-84-068, 15 October 1984, p. 33.

35 Li Buyun, 'Certain questions concerning the relationship between Party policies and state laws', *Faxue jikan*, no. 3, July 1984, in JPRS-CHS-84-068, 15 October, p. 33.

36 The essentials of this debate were tentatively reported in Ronald C. Keith, 'Chinese Politics and the New Theory of the "Rule of Law"', *CQ*, no. 125, March 1991, pp. 109–118. These three positions were outlined by Zhang Guohua and Li Buyun in my Beijing interviews on 21 and 22 September 1989. I raised the issue in September–October 1989 during meetings with the following experts on legal reform and the 'rule of law': Beida law professors Gong Xiangrui (constitutional expert), Zhang Guohua (president, Chinese Legal History Association), Sheng Zongling (expert in comparative law); Renda law professors Sung Guohua (senior theorist), Wu Lei (vice-general manager, Criminal Procedural Law Institute), Tong Rou (senior civil law expert), Gao Mingxuan (senior criminal law expert and vice-president, China Law Society), Han Yusheng (vice-dean, Law Department); Wu Daying (director, Institute of Political Science, CASS); Li Buyun, CASS Institute of Law and a general editor of *Faxue yanjiu*; Liu Han, CASS Institute of Law; Xu Chongde, vice-president, Political Science Association and Constitutional Law Society; Yao Keming, Beijing Higher Peoples's Court Judge and director of the courts' research department; Wang Huaran, deputy general-secretary, All-China Lawyer's Association. See Lu Shilun, Liu Xin, '*Lun renzhi he fazhi*' (On rule of man and rule of law) *Faxue yanjiu* (Studies in Law), no. 5, 1979, p. 27.

37 Fan Mingxuan, '*Women yinggai paoqi fazhi he renzhidi ti fa*', *Faxue* (Studies in Law) no. 4, 1980, p. 64.

38 Mao stated in 21 August 1958: '[We] can't rule the majority... by relying on law. The majority... [can be ruled] by the cultivation of [good] habits.' See Roderick MacFarquhar (et al.) (eds), *The Secret Speeches of Chairman Mao* (Cambridge and London: Harvard University Press, 1989) p. 424

39 Zhang Guicheng, 'Lun fazhi', p. 14.

40 For example see Lu Shilun, Liu Xin, '*Lun renzhi he fazhi*' (On rule of man and rule of law) *Faxue yanjiu* (Studies in law) no. 5, 1979, p. 27.

41 Gao Yu, 'Neo-Authoritarianism: Does it Represent a "Spirit," or a "Rat"?', *Jingjixue zhoubao*, 12 March 1989, p. 1, in FBIS-CHI-89-058, 28 March 1989, p. 30.

42 See Sun Liping, 'The Present Authority Crisis and Its Cause', *Jingjixue zhoubao*, 12 March 1989, p. 5, in FBIS-CHI-89-058, 28 March 1989, p. 32–3.
43 18 September 1989 Beida interview with the author.
44 Zhang Xin, *Zhongguo fazhizhi xianguang ji gaige* (Conditions and reform of China's legal system) (Singapore: Mingbao chubanshe, 1989) p. 16.
45 Li reiterated this in his 22 September 1989 interview at CASS. Also see Li Buyun, *Fazhi, minzhu, ziyou*, pp. 121–6.
46 Li Buyun, *Fazhi, minzhu, ziyou*, pp. 122, 124, 134.
47 Wang Liming, '*Yi fazhi guo bushi fazhi*' (A rule-by-law state does not equal the rule of law) *Renmin ribao*, 27 February 1989.
48 Li Buyun discusses the relevance of these expressions, *Fazhi, minzhu, ziyou*, p. 127.
49 Sun, in his 26 September 1989 discussions with the author, emphasised that after June 4 the new Party Secretary General Jiang Zemin endorsed '*fazhi*' as 'rule of law'. For his usages of *fazhi* see '*Chuji duanjiedi fazhi: gainian he tedian*' (The legal system in the primary state: the concepts and its characteristics) *Falu xuexi he yanjiu* (Legal Studies and Research) no. 6, 1988, pp. 15–19.
50 'Lesson about Law', *CD*, 17 July 1986, p. 4, and 'Top figures attend Party law lectures', *CD*, 4 July 1986, p. 1.
51 Yang Yujing in *Zhengfa luntan*, Oct. 1987.
52 Gao Gao, 'Improve the Social Control System Taking the Rule of Law as the Main Body', *Jingjixue zhou bao*, 12 Mar 89, p. 5, FBIS-CHI-89-058, 28 March 1989, p. 32.
53 Ni Zhengmao, '*Lun zhengzhi tizhi gaigedi fanzhi xuyao*' (The requirements of the legal system in political restructuring), *Faxue jikan*, Chongqing, no. 2, 1987, pp. 3.
54 See Zhang Xin, *Zhongguo fazhizhi xianguang ji gaige*, p. 15.
55 See 'Wang Hanbin Explains the Principles of Civil Code', FBIS-CHI-86-078, 23 April 1986, *China Daily Report*, p. K7.
56 Li Buyun, Wang Hanqing, 'Adhere to the Principle that all Men Are Equal Before the Law…', Hongqi, no. 12, 16 June 1986, in *China Report: Red Flag*, JPRS-CRF-86-015, 7 August 1986, p. 46.
57 Deng Xiaoping, *Fundamental Issues in China Today* (Beijing: Foreign Languages Press, 1987) p. 146.
58 See, for example, Li Maoguan, 'Why "Laws Go Unenforced"', *BR*, no. 37, Sept. 11–7, 1989, p. 17.
59 See Yao Jianguo (ed.) (*Beijing Review*, comp.), *Construction of the Legal System* (Beijing: New Star Publishers, 1991) pp. 9–10.
60 Liu Zhaoxing, Ji Lin, '*Shehuizhuyi chuji jieduan fazhi jianshe ruogan lilun wenti yanjiu*' (The study of several problems of building the legal system in the primary stage of socialism) *Faxue yanjiu*, no. 5, 1988, pp. 85–9.
61 See Deng Xiaoping, *Deng Xiaoping wenxuan* (Selected works of Deng Xiaoping) (Hong Kong: Sanlian shudian/ Renmin chubanshe, 1983) p. 137. There are several overviews of Deng's view of the 'rule of law'; for example, see Wang He, '*Shilun Deng Xiaopingdi fazhi jianshe sixiang*' (Examining Deng Xiaoping's thought on the rule of law) in Yue Zong & Xin Zhi (eds.) *Dui Deng Xiaoping yu lilun yanjiu huibian* (Collection on Deng Xiaoping and theoretical research) (Beijing: Zhonggong Dangshi ziliao chubanshe,

1988), pp. 183–206, and Liu Peng, '*Fazhi sixiang*', (Legal thought) in Zhang Lansun and Liu Peng (eds.) *Deng Xiaopingdi sixiang lilun yanjiu* (Theoretical research of Deng Xiaoping's thought) (Beijing: Zhongguo shuji chubanshe, 1988), pp. 104–18.

62 Deng Xiaoping, *Selected Works of Deng Xiaoping* (1975–82) p. 158.

63 Li Buyun, Wang Hanqing, 'Adhere to the Principle that All Men Are Equal Before the Law', op. cit., p. 43.

64 Zhang Youyu, *Guanyu shehuizhuyi fazhidi ruogan wenti* (On the problems of the socialist legal system) (Beijing: Falu chubanshe, 1982) pp. 125–6.

65 Zhao Ziyang, 'Advance Along the Road of Socialism with Chinese Characteristics', *BR*, no. 45, 9–15 Nov., 1987, Documents, p. 43.

66 *Fagui* is translated as 'law' or 'regulation' but it has less significance than NPC or NPC Standing Committee law, *falu*. See Tao-tai Hsia and Constance Johnson, 'Lawmaking in China, Part I', *East Asian Executive Reports*, Jan 1987, p. 6.

67 The origins of the ideological formulation are discussed in Ronald C. Keith, '"Egalitarianism" and "Seeking the Truth from the Facts" in the People's Republic of China', *Dalhousie Review*, vol. 63, no. 2, Summer, 1983, pp. 325–9.

68 For a discussion of Mao's mass line 'pragmatism' see Ronald C. Keith, 'Mao Zedong's View of Modernity', in Anthony Parel and Ronald C. Keith (eds.) *Comparative Political Philosophy: Studies Under the Upas Tree* (New Delhi, Newbury Park and London: Sage Publications, 1992) pp. 102–4.

69 Mao Zedong, *Selected Works of Mao Zedong*, vol. V (Beijing: Foreign Languages Press, 1977) p. 248.

70 This relation of policy-making and execution to time and space is discussed in Mao Zedong, *Selected Works of Mao Zedong*, vol. V, p. 230.

71 Tao-tai Hsia & Wendy Zeldin, 'Recent Legal Developments in the People's Republic of China', *Harvard International Law Journal*, vol. 28, no. 2, Spring, 1987, p. 263.

72 Tao-tai Hsia, Wendy Zeldin, 'Recent Legal Developments in the People's Republic of China', p. 264. For Zhang Youyu's remarks see, '*Weishenma zhiding jei bu "minfatongze"*' (Why establish this category of the principles of civil law) *Guangming ribao*, 6 August 1986, p. 3.

73 Richard Baum,'Modernization and Legal Reform in Post-Mao China: The Rebirth of Socialist Legality', op. cit., p. 102. Also see Derk Bodde, Clarence Morris, *Law in Imperial China* (Cambridge: Harvard University Press, 1967) p. 31.

74 'Explanation of the Law on Administrative Procedure', *Renmin ribao*, 10 April 1989, pp. 2, 3, FBIS-CVHI-89-083, 2 May 1989, p. 100.

75 Interview with the author at the Beijing Higher People's Court, 20 September 1989.

76 As discussed in Chapter One of Lin Sen, 'Chinese Provincial Economic Legislation and the New Pattern of Decentralization', Ph.D. dissertation, University of Calgary, March 1993.

77 Wu Daying and Li Yanming, '*Shehuizhuyidi gongheguo shi dianfu buliaodi*' (The question whether the socialist people's republic is a subverted form) *Renmin ribao*, 9 September 1989, p. 6.

78 Fan Zhongxin, '"Neo-Authoritarianism" Described, Refuted', *Renmin ribao*, 6 March 89, p. 5, FBIS-CHI-89-047, 13 March 1989, p. 34.
79 Uli Schmetzer, 'Sorcery, Slavery are Back in Vogue', *Calgary Herald*, 26 July 1991, p. A5.
80 *BR*, no. 2, June 14–20, 1991, p. 4.
81 'Lawyers Busy in rural Areas', *CD*, 14 May, 1987, p. 3.
82 China, *The First Session of the Seventh NPC of the PRC* (25 March–13 April, 1988) (Beijing: Foreign Languages Press, 1988) p. 48.
83 China, *The Constitution of the People's Republic of China* (Beijing: Foreign Languages Press, 1983) p. 24.
84 C.V. James (ed., CASS comp. and trans.), *Information China*, 3 Vols. (Oxford, New York, Beijing: Pergamon Press, 1989) p. 434.
85 Wang Shengxuan, '*Lun shehuizhuyi faludi cunshou*' ('On honouring socialist law'), *Shanxi daxuebao* (Journal of Shanxi University) no. 1, 1987, p. 77. For raportage see '*Falu yu jingshen wenming jianshe*' (Establishing law and spiritual civilization) *Qunyan* (Masses Speak) no. 4, 1986, pp. 2–9.
86 See 'China Works to Eliminate Illegal Marriages', *BR*, no. 19, 8–14 May 1989, pp. 25–8.
87 See Wen-hui Tsai, 'Mainland Chinese; Marriage and Family Under the Impact of the Four Modernizations', *Issues and Studies*, vol. 24, no. 3, March 1988, p. 116.
88 See 'Law Helps to Change Daily Life, *CD*, 9 May 1987, p. 4.
89 William Jones, 'Civil Law in China', *Chinese Law and Government*, vol. XVIII, Spring 1985–Fall/Winter 1985–6, p. 8.
90 Yuan Chengdi, '*Shehuizhuyi fa ye yingyou gongsi fazhi fen*' (Socialist law should also distinguish between public and private law) *Faxue jikan*, vol. 30, no. 4, 1986, pp. 22–4.
91 Meng Qinguo, '*Jingji tizhi gaige shiqidi minshilifa*' (Civil legislation in the period of economic restructuring) *Zhongguo shehui kexue* (Social Science in China) no. 6, 1988, p. 57.
92 Ding Jimin, '*Jingyingquan yu suoyouquan*' (The rights of operation and ownership) *Faxue yanjiu* (Studies in Law), no. 1, 1987, pp. 12–17.
93 These lines of argument were present during an NPC-sponsored symposium to mark the fifth anniversary of the General Principles of Civil Law. See Wang Hanbin et al., '*Renzhen shishi minfa tongze he minshi susongfa*' (Seriously implementing the General Principles of Civil Law and the Civil Suits Procedural Law) *Zhongguo faxue*, no. 4, 1991, pp. 22–31.
94 Zhao Ziyang, *China's Economy and Development Principles* (Beijing Foreign Languages Press, 1982) pp. 76–7.
95 Cooper, Michael and Wu, *Human Rights in Post-Mao China*, p. 52.
96 For an extended analysis of the arguments for and against the revision of the law on counterrevolution see Ronald C. Keith and Lin Zhiqiu, 'To Revise or Not to Revise China's Law on Counterrevolution', *China Information*, vol. V, no. 4, Spring, 1991, p. 24.
97 See Li Li and Li Shaoping, '*Shenhua gaige yu xingfa xiugai*' (Deepening Reform and Revising Criminal Law) *Xiandai faxue* (Modern Law Science) no. 5, Oct. 1988, pp. 10–11.

98 For an overview of these revisionist ideas see Gao Mingxuan and Zhao Bingzhi, '*1988 nian xingfaxue yanjiu jinzhang gailan*' (Brief sketches on the developing study of criminal law) *Zhengfa luntan*, no. 3, 1989, pp. 1–8.

99 For comment on this see Fu Siming, '*Lue lun "yiguo liangzhi" yu xianfa*' (Preliminary discussion of 'one-country, two-systems' and the constitution *Faxue*, no. 12, 1988, pp. 66–8.

100 Zhao Bingzhi, '*Lue tan "yiguo liangzhi" shiji Gang, Ao, Tai fanzuidi xingshi zeren*' (Preliminary exploration of criminal responsibility of criminals in Hong Kong, Macao and Taiwan in the period of 'one country, two systems') *Faxue zazhi* (Law Magazine), no. 6, 1988, p. 9.

101 Joseph Y.S. Cheng (ed.) *Hong Kong: In Search of a Future* (Hong Kong, Oxford, New York: Oxford University Press, 1984) p. 120.

102 *Hong Kong Standard*, 1 April 1989, pp. 1, 8.

103 *Wen wei po*, Hong Kong, 31 March 1989, p. 1, in FBIS-CHI-89-063, 4 April 1989, p. 35.

2 The Rule of Law within Comparative Legal Cultures

1 Derk Bodde, 'Feudalism in China', in Ruston Coulborn (ed.) *Feudalism in History* (Hamden, Conn.: Archon Books, 1965) p. 52. Also see Ronald C. Keith, 'Law and Society in Confucian Thought', in Anthony Parel & R.C. Keith (eds.) *Comparative Political Philosophy: Studies under the Upas Tree* (New Delhi, Newbury Park, London: Sage, 1992) pp. 80–2.

2 Wang Shiming, '*Zhongguo yu XiOu zaoqi fengjian zhengzhi zhidu butong moshi xingcheng yuanyin*' (The causes underlying the formation of different models of early feudal political systems in China and Western Europe) *Shehui kexue* (Social Science), no. 4, 1986, p. 46.

3 Here I cannot agree with the suggestion that the usage of 'feudalism' itself represents a 'totalitarian' impulse. Vivienne Shue, *The Reach of the State* (Stanford: Stanford University Press, 1988) p. 25. More extended commentary can be found in Suzanne Ogden's interpretation of Chinese 'feudalism', *China's Unresolved Issues. Politics, Development and Culture* (Englewood Cliffs, N.J.: Prentice Hall, 1989) pp. 93–7.

4 Jerome Cohen, 'The Criminal Process in the People's Republic of China: An Introduction', *Harvard Law Review*, vol. 79, no. 3, January 1966, p. 470.

5 Yu Ronggen, '*Zhongguo guyou fawenhua jiqi zai jintiande weizhi*' (The current position of China's ancient legal culture) *Xinan shifan daxue xuebao* (Journal of the Southwest Normal School) no. 4, 1986, p. 7.

6 Zhang Jinfan et al., '*Zhongguo gudai falu lungang*' (An outline of China's ancient legal culture) *Zhengfa luntan*, no. 5, 1991, p. 59.

7 Jiang Weide, '*Cong Hanlu kan wuoguo gudaidi minshi lifa*' (Our ancient civil legislation from the perspective of the Hanlu) *Neimenggu daxue xuebao* (Journal of the University of Inner Mongolia) no. 1, 1987, pp. 93–7.

8 For the 12th CCPCC Resolution of 28 September 1986 see *BR*, no. 40, 6 Oct. 1986, Documents, p. v.

9 For an example of such Chinese Weberian analysis see Sun Liping, 'The Present Authority Crisis and its Cause' in *Jingjixue zhoubao*, 12 March 1989, p. 5, FBIS-CHI-89-058, 28 March 1989, p. 32.

10 'Top Figures Attend Party Law Lectures', *China Daily* (henceforth *CD*) 4 July 1986, p. 1.
11 Excerpted in 'People Must See Laws as Freedom', *CD*, 5 Jan. 1988, p. 4.
12 The issue is explored in Xunzi's '*Jundao*' (Way of the prince). See Zhang Guohua et al., (eds.) *Zhongguo falu sixiang shi* (History of Chinese legal thought) (Beijing: Falu chubanshe, 1982) p. 117.
13 Xunzi as quoted in Derk Bodde, Clarence Morris, *Law in Imperial China* (Cambridge: Harvard University Press, 1967) p. 22.
14 As quoted in Hyung Kim, *Fundamental Legal Concepts of China and the West* (Port Washington, N.Y.: Kennikat Press, 1981) p. 4.
15 Liang Zhiping, '*Cong "liruyufa" kan Zhongguo dudai falu*' (Looking at ancient Chinese law from the perspective of 'ritual entering law') *Wenshi zhishi*, (Knowledge of History and Culture), no. 1, 1987, p. 88.
16 Zhang Jinfan, Zeng Xianyi, '*Renzhi yu fazhidi lishi pouxi*' (Historical analysis of rule of man and rule of law) *Faxue*, no. 5, 1979, p. 34.
17 Confucius, '*Lunyu*' (Analects) in *Sishu* (The four books) (Macao: Juwendangshu, 1962, Book II) p. 146.
18 Confucius, '*Daxue*' (Great Learning) in *Sishu*, Book I, p. 25.
19 Wang Liming, '*Dui fajia "fazhi" shuo zhiyi*' (Questioning the legalist argument for 'rule of law') *Zhongguo faxue* (Law Science in China), no. 4, 1991, pp. 116–19. Wang may have misinterpreted Liang. Liang rated Legalism highly for its pre-modern attempt to use law to set timeless, impersonal standards, but more importantly Liang could not abide Legalism, for, while it laid claim to equality before the law, it gave the ruler an unqualified legislative authority. See Liang Qichao, *History of Chinese Political Thought during the Early Tsin Period* (New York, AMS, 1969 reprint of 1930 edition) p. 132–5.
20 Herlee G. Creel, *Chinese Thought from Confucius to Mao Tse-tung* (Chicago: University of Chicago Press, 1975) p. 153.
21 Tang Zhongmin, '*Han Feizidi falu sixiang*' (Han Feizi's legal thought) *Xiandai faxue*, no. 6, 1988, pp. 55–7.
22 As cited in Herlee Creel, *Chinese Thought from Confucius to Mao*, p. 154.
23 For text see Burton Watson (trans.) *Han Fei Tzu* (New York: Columbia University Press, 1964) p. 105.
24 Fung Yu-lan, trans. by Derk Bodde, *A History of Chinese Philosophy*, vol. 1 (Princeton: Princeton University Press, 1983) p. 313.
25 Hyung I. Kim, *Fundamental Legal Concepts of China and the West: A Comparative Study*, op. cit., p.7.
26 Quoted and analysed by Tang Zhongmin, '*Han Feidi falu sixiang*' (Han Fei's legal thought) *Xiandai faxue*, no. 6, 1988, pp. 55–7.
27 These systematic distinctions are discussed by Liu Shuguang, '*Lun rujia sixiang dui Zhongguo fengjian faludi yingxiang*' (The influence of Confucian thought on China's feudal law) *Zhengfa luntan*, no. 2, 1986, pp. 61–6; and in Zhang Jinfan et al., *Zhongguo fazhi shi*, (History of the Chinese legal system) (Beijing: Qunzhong chubanshe, 1989) pp. 210–11.
28 See Liu Guangan, '*Gudai "shuxing" kaolu*' (A Brief examination of the ancient 'buying out of penalties') *Zhengfa luntan*, no. 6, 1985.
29 He Xiaorong, '*Fazhi xiandaihuadi guannian zu'ai ji qi wenhua beijing*' (Conceptual obstructions to the modernization of the legal system within

cultural context) *Xibei zhengfa xueyuan xuebao* (Journal of the Northwest Institute of Politics and Law) no. 1, 1987, pp. 5–8.

30 William C. Jones, 'Studying the Ch'ing Code – The Ta-Ch'ing Lu li', *The American Journal of Comparative Law*, vol. 22, 1974, p. 356.

31 Liu Zuoxiang, '*Shilun falu wenhuadi cengci jiegou*' (Preliminary comment on the structural layers of legal culture) *Xibei zhengfa xueyuan xuebao* (Journal of the Northwest Institute of Politics and Law) no. 1, 1988, pp. 12–16.

32 Jiang Xun, '*Zhongguo falu wenhuadi xiandaihua*' (The modernisation of China's legal culture) *Faxue* (Legal Studies) Shanghai, no. 7, 1987, pp. 12–15.

33 Ding Xueliang, '*Xiandaihua lilundi yuanyuan he gainian goujia*' (The origin and conceptual framework of 'modernisation theory') *Zhongguo shehui kexue* (Chinese Social Science) Jan. 1988, pp. 65–78.

34 Shen Zongling, *Bijiaofa zonglun* (An outline of comparative law) (Beijing: Beijing daxue chubanshe, 1987) pp. 340–1.

35 Zhang Jinfan and Lin Zhong, '*Zhongguo gudai falu wenhua lungang*' (An outline of China's ancient legal culture) *Zhengfa luntan* (Tribune of Law and Politics), no. 5, 1991, p. 61.

36 Zhou Weijia, 'A comparison of several aspects of Chinese and American legal thought and practice', *Shehui kexue* (Social Sciences) no. 7, 1987, p. 73.

37 Liang Zhiping, '*Faziran yu ziranfa*' (Law following nature and natural law) *Zhongguo shehui faxue*, no. 2, 1989, pp. 209–23.

3 The Conceptualisation and Materialisation of Human Rights

1 Benkan pinglunquan, [journal commentator], '*Shenru kaizhan renquan yu fazhidi lilun yanjiu* (To delve deeply in the study of human rights theory and the legal system) *Zhongguo faxue*, no. 3, 1991, p. 4.

2 Quoted from 'rule of law' entry in Vernon Bogdanor (ed.) *Blackwell's Encyclopedia of Political Science* (Oxford: Basil Blackwell, 1991) p. 548. Dicey's three meanings can be found in his chapter on the nature and general application of the rule of law, *Introduction to the Study of the Law of the Constitution* (London: Macmillan, 10th edition, 1964) p. 187–96.

3 Li Buyun, '*Lun renquandi sanzhong cunzai xingtai*' (On the three extant forms of human rights) *Faxue yanjiu*, no. 4, 1991, p. 16.

4 Human Rights Watch, *Human Rights Watch: World Report 1990*, January 1991, p. 359.

5 US Department of State, *Country Reports on Human Rights Practices for 1991*. Report to Committee on Foreign Affairs, House of Representatives, and Committee on Foreign Relations, Senate, Washington, DC, February 1992, pp. 809–10.

6 Ibid., p. 827.

7 US Department of State, *Country Reports on Human Rights Practices for 1990*, Report to Committee on Foreign Affairs, House of Representatives and Committee on Foreign Relations, Senate, Washington, DC, February 1991, p. 860; and US Department of State, *Country Reports on Human Rights Practices for 1991*, p. 826.

8 For the Chinese on their own UN positions see their 'white paper', 'Human Rights in China', Information Office, State Council, November 1991, in *BR*, no. 44, 4–10 November 1991, pp. 42–3.

9 See, for example, Liu Wenzong, '*Zong guojifa lun renquan he Meiguodi "renquan waijiao"*' (Human rights and American 'human rights diplomacy' from the point of view of international law) *Renmin ribao*, 5 October 1992, p. 5. Liu cites an American source indicating that the the US has signed only 4 out of 20 international treaties on human rights. Hurst Hannum (ed.), *Guide to International Human Rights Practice*, 2nd ed. (Philadelphia: University of Pennsylvania Press, 1992) pp. 280–6 indicates that the PRC has signed 6 and the US 4 of 13 major international conventions.

10 Edward Lawson (in cooperation with the UN Centre for Human Rights), *Encyclopedia of Human Rights* (Washington, DC: Taylor & Francis Inc., 1991) p. 185.

11 For a detailed view of American 'peaceful evolution', see Rui Bian, 'Tactics used by the West in promoting "peaceful evolution"', *Ban Yue Tan*, 25 October 1989, pp. 57–9, in FBIS-CHI-90-004-S, 5 January 1990, p. 17.

12 '*"Renquan wu guojie" shuo pouxi*' (Analyse talk of 'human rights without state boundaries') *Renmin ribao*, 8 November 1991 (overseas edition) p. 2.

13 See Bai Guimei's usage, '*Lun xinyidai renquan*' (On the new generation of human rights) *Faxue yanjiu*, no. 5, 1991, pp. 1–6.

14 Statement by H.E. Mr. Li Peng, at the UN Security Council, 31 January 1992, *Bulletin*, Embassy of the PRC in Canada, p. 4.

15 Statement by H.E. Mr. Li Peng, at the UN Security Council, 31 January 1992, *Bulletin*, Embassy of the PRC in Canada, p. 4.

16 'UN council bows to China over human rights issue', *Calgary Herald*, 31 January 1991, p. A12.

17 See, for example, 'Beijing hits back over human rights', *South China Morning Post*, hereinafter *SCMP*, 2 November 1991, p. 1.

18 Xu Xianming, '*"Jiben quanli" si*' (Analysis of 'basic rights') *Zhongguo faxue*, no. 6, 1991, p. 27.

19 Xu Goujin, '*Guojia luxing guoji renquanyiwudi xiandu*' (The limits to the international human rights obligation of states) *Zhongguo faxue*, no. 2, 1992, pp. 16–18.

20 Wu Weidong et al., '*Lun requandi yishi xingtai biaozhun yu falubiaozhun*' (On ideological and legal standards of human rights) *Zhongguo faxue*, no. 1, 1992, pp. 21–5.

21 For example see Xiao Weiyun and Wei Dingren, *Xianfa xue gailun* (Introduction to Constitution Studies) (Beijing: Beijing Daxue chubanshe, 1985) pp. 273–4; and Li Lin et al., '*Yi Makesizhuyi wei zhidao shenru yanjiu renquan lilun*' (Deepening research on human rights theory under the guidance of Marxism) (Human rights symposium summary) *Faxue yanjiu*, no. 5, 1991, pp. 17–18; Zuo Yu, Shu Sheng (pseudonyms) '*Renquandi jiben neihan: renquan yu gongminquan*' (The basic connotation of human rights: human rights and citizen's rights) *Zhongguo faxue*, no. 6, 1991, p. 17.

22 Joseph Needham, *The Shorter Science and Civilisation in China: Vol. 1* (London: Cambridge University Press, 1978) p. 304.

23 Liang Zhiping '*Faziran yu ziranfa*' (Law following nature and natural law) *Zhongguo shehui kexue* (Social sciences in China) no. 2, 1989, in Faxue, no. 4, 1989, pp. 139–51.

24 H.G. Creel, *Sinism: A Study of the Evolution of the Chinese World View*, pp. 2, 17, as cited in Hyung I. Kim, *Fundamental Legal Concepts of China and the West: A Comparative Study* (Port Washington, NY: Keenikat Press, 1981) p. 28.

25 See Schwartz on Joseph Needham's views in *Science and Civilization in China* (Cambridge: Cambridge University Press, Vol. 2, 1956) p. 247 in Benjamin Schwartz, *The World of Thought in Ancient China* (Cambridge, Mass: Belknap Press of Harvard University Press, 1985) p. 364. For a lengthy treatment of 'correlative cosmology', see John B. Henderson, *The Development and Decline of Chinese Cosmology* (New York: Columbia University Press, 1984) passim.

26 Derk Bodde, Clarence Morris (eds), *Law in Imperial China* (Philadelphia: University of Pennsylvania Press, 1973) p. 4.

27 Liang Zhiping, '*Faziran yu ziran*', op. cit., p. 150.

28 Li Buyun, '*Lun renquandi sanzhong cunzai xingtai*' (On the three extant forms of human rights) *Faxue yanjiu*, no. 4, 1991, p. 13.

29 Li Buyun, '*Fadi liangchongxing yu jiben maodun*' (On the dual nature and basic contradictions of law) *Faxue*, no. 6, 1992, p. 20.

30 Li Buyun, '*Lun renquandi sanzhong cunzai xingtai*', op. cit., p. 17.

31 Li Lin (et al.), '*Yi Makesizhuyi wei zhidao shenru yanjiu renquan lilun*' (Deepening human rights theoretical research under the guidance of Marxism) *Faxue yanjiu*, no. 5, 1991, p. 14. Further distinctions were apparent in later discussion concerning the relation between substantive 'actual human rights' and 'procedural human rights', *chengxuxing renquan*, including for example the rights to ask for evidence in court and the right to open trial. See Sun Xiaoxia, '*Lun falu chengxuzhongdi renquan*' (On lawful human procedural rights), *Zhongguo faxue*, no. 3, 1992, pp. 39–45.

32 On the condemnation of Fang see, for example, 'Behind the banner of human rights – commenting on Fang Lizhi's ballyhoo on the question of human rights', *Liaowang*, (Overseas) 25 December 1989, pp. 8–9, FBIS-CHI-90-003, 4 January 1990, pp. 14–17.

33 These views were reported in Li Lin et al., '*Yi Maksizhuyi wei zhidao shenru yanjiu renquan lilun*', op. cit., p. 15.

34 Zhang Xipo and Han Yanyu, *Zhongguo geming fazhi shi (1921–1949)* (China's Revolutionary Legal History) vol. 1 (Beijing: Zhongguo shehui kexue chubanshe, 1987) p. 37.

35 On political rights which accrue to 'people' and 'citizens' see Andrew Nathan, 'Political Rights in Chinese Constitutions' in R. Randle Edwards, Louis Henkin, Andrew Nathan, *Human Rights in Contemporary China* (New York: Columbia University Press, 1986) pp. 96–100.

36 Zhang Guangxin and Shi Peixin discuss this era in '*Makesizhuyi renquanguan jiqi zai woguodi shijian*' (The Marxist view of human rights and human rights practices in China), *Shehui kexue* (Social Sciences) no. 4, 1990, p. 33. The pre-1949 united front legislation of the border region governments offered a range of different usages and perspectives on 'human rights'. In the Shanganning Border Region, for example, the rights of the

'people' [*renmin*] were featured whereas in the Shandong regulations the character, *ren*, used in 'human rights' seems to have implied both 'national citizens', *guomin*, and 'people', *renmin*. The Shandong human rights regulations featured democratic equality, the four democratic principles of election, dismissal, establishment of government by popular will and referendum as well as freedom of person and militant resistance to Japan, freedoms of abode and movement, freedoms of speech, creativity, publication, assembly, association and correspondence and freedoms of conscience, religious belief and political participation. See Zhang Xipo and Han Yanyu, *Zhongguo geming fazhishi*, op. cit., p. 49.

37 Xiao Weiyun & Wei Dingren, *Xianfa xue gailun*, op. cit., p. 263.

38 Xu Chongde, *Zhongguo xianfaxue* (Studies in Chinese constitutional law) (Tianjin: Tianjin renmin chubanshe, 1986) p. 191.

39 'Notes on the Human Rights Question', *BR*, no. 45, 9 Nov. 1979, p. 19.

40 Li Buyun, '*Lun renquandi sanzhong zun cai xingdai*', op. cit., p. 11.

41 Peng Zhen, 'Several questions on the socialist legal system', *Hongqi*, no. 11, 2 November 1979, FBIS-CHI-79-229, 27 November 1979, vol. 1, no. 229, p. L3.

42 See Ye Jianying, 'Report on the revision of the constitution', 1 March 1978, in *BR*, no. 11, 17 March 1978, p. 19.

43 China, *The Constitution of the People's Republic of China* (Beijing: Foreign Languages Press, 1983) p. 33.

44 Henkin, 'The Human Rights Idea in Contemporary China: A Comparative Perspective', tends to jump over these apparently atypical articles so as to stress the larger point that the constitution when it comes to rights suggests no limitation on what the law may provide. See *Human Rights in Contemporary China* (New York: Columbia University Press, 1986) p. 31.

45 'Supreme Court Authorities Address Press Law', *Zhongguo jizhe*, no. 1, 15 January 1989, pp. 6–9 in FBIS-CHI-89–078, pp. 37 & 41.

46 Li Buyun, '*Falu yu ziyou*' (Law and freedom) *Hongqi*, no. 22, 1981, p. 16.

47 Robert C. Tucker (ed.), *The Marx–Engels Reader* (New York & London: W.W. Norton, 1978) p. 42.

48 Andrei Y. Vyshinsky (ed.), *The Law of the Soviet State* (London: Macmillan 1948) p. 636.

49 Zuo Yu, Shu Sheng (pseudonyms), '*Renquandi jiben neihan: renquan yu gongminquan*' (Basic connotations of human rights: human and citizen's rights) *Zhongguo faxue*, no. 6, 1991, pp. 14–22.

50 'Human Rights in China', Information Office, State Council, *BR*, no. 44, Nov. 4–10, 1991, p. 16.

51 Ibid., p. 13.

52 '*Zhongguodi renquan zhuangkuang*'(Human rights conditions in China) *Renmin ribao*, 2 November 1991, p. 5.

53 'Human Rights in China', *BR*, no. 44, Nov. 4–10, 1991, p. 9.

54 Sun Xiaoxia, '*Quanli benweishuodi jiben quandian, fangfa he linian*' (The foundation, method and idea of rights as fundamental) *Zhongguo faxue*, no. 4, 1991, pp. 48–53.

55 Wei Shaoying, '"*Quanli yiwu yizhixing*" *pingxi*' (Review on the unity of rights and obligations) *Faxue pinglun* (Law Review), no. 5, 1988, pp. 8–11, in *Faxue*, no. 1, 1989, p. 57.

56 Zhang Wenxian, '*Lun faxuedi fanchou yishi, fanchou tixi yu jishi fanchou*' (On basic, ideological and systemic categories in legal studies) *Zhongguo faxue*, no. 3, 1991, p. 7.
57 See Zhang Shangzhuo, 'Protect Rights and Interests, Strengthen Management-Exploring the Guiding Ideology of the Legislation of the Press and Three Other Laws', *Renmin ribao*, 6 January 1989, p. 5, in FBIS-CHI–89-007, p. 26–7.
58 Ibid., p. 27.
59 Du Danzheng, Director, China's Press and Publications Administration, disclaimed reports of fundamental disagreement over 'freedom of the press' and cited argument over whether or not to include press law within an onmibus law on publication as the main reason for the 1980s delays in NPC consideration of the press law. 'Press Law Draft to Go before NPC' *CD*, 13 February 1989, p. 3.
60 'Press Freedom Helps Stability', *CD*, 30 March 1989, p. 4.
61 Wang Renzhong, 'Limits of Journalism Reform under Deng Xiaoping', Communication Studies, unpublished University of Calgary M.A. Thesis, August 1993.
62 'An Important Basis for Establishment and Management of Public Organizations', *Renmin ribao*, 9 November 1989, p. 6, in FBIS-CHI-89-230, 1 December, 1989, p. 14.
63 See 'Regulations Issued on Social Organizations' *CD*, 1 November, 1989, p. 3. The Chinese text, '*Shehui tuanti dengji guanli tiaoli*' (Regulations for the registration and management of social organizations) is in *Renmin ribao*, 9 November 1989, p. 6.
64 Standing Committee Members Wang Wei and Tao Dayong, for example, argued that conditions were not ripe for the law's passage. 'Draft Law Opens for Discussion', *BR*, No. 29, 17–23 July 1989, p. 9.
65 See 'New Draft Law in People's Benefit', *CD*, 27 October 1989, p. 3.
66 US. State Department, *Country Reports on Human Rights Practices for 1990*, p. 855.
67 'Forum held on assembly, demonstration law', *Renmin gongan bao*, 8 December 1989, p. 3, in FBIS-CHI-009-S, 12 January 1989, p. 17.
68 'Rallies, Demonstration Law Revised', *Xin Hua*, 25 October 1989, in FBIS-CHI-89-205, 25 October 1989, p. 12.
69 'Beijing Adopts Rules for Demonstration Law', *Xin Hua*, 20 December, 1989, FBIS-CHI-89-249, 29 December 1989, p. 21.
70 See English text, 'PRC Law Governing Assemblies, Parades, and Demonstrations', *Xin Hua*, 31 October 1989, FBIS-CHI-89-210, 1 November 1989, pp. 16–9. Chinese text, '*Zhonghua renmin gongheguo jihui youxing shiwei fa*' (Law on assembly, procession and demonstration) *Renmin ribao*, 1 November 1989, p. 1.
71 Ye Jianying, 'Report on the Revision of the Constitution', 1 March 1978, *PR*, No. 11, 17 March 1978, p. 18.
72 Tan Hongkai, 'New Law on Mass Rallies Took 10 years of Effort' *CD*, 26 December 1989, p. 4.
73 Pitman Potter, Editor's Introduction, *Chinese Law and Government*, vol. 24, no. 3, Fall, 1991, pp. 4–5.

74 As cited in 'Court Can Check Government Power', *CD*, 26 January 1988, p. 4. Professor Gong gives his views at length in Gong Xiangrui (ed.), *Xingzhengfa yu xingzheng gaosufa* (Administrative law and administrative procedural law) (Beijing: Falu chubanshe, 1989) passim.
75 Jiang Bixin, 'What Sorts of Things Can Administrative Lawsuits Be Lodged against in China', *Zhongguo xinwenshe*, 10 September 1991 in FBIS-CHI-91-183, pp. 25–6.
76 'Comments on Law', Beijing, *Xin Hua*, 31 March 1989, FBIS-CHI-89-063, 4 April 1989, p. 21.
77 'Regulations on Rights Infringement Promulgated', Beijing Domestic Service, in FBIS-CHI-90-007, 10 January 1990, p. 21.
78 According to the reporting of Yang Haikun in '*Jinnianlai woguo xingzhengfaxue lilundi zhuyao jianshu*' (Major achievements in the theory of contemporary Chinese administrative legal studies) *Jiangsu shehuikexue* (Jiangsu Social Sciences), no. 3, 1991, reproduced in *Faxue*, no. 7, 1991, p. 56.
79 This is in accordance with the estimation of Ying Songnian and Ma Huaide, who have reported on the future direction of administrative law theory and legislation, '*Xiang xindi gaofeng maijin: jiushinian woguo xingzhengfaxue zhanwang*' (Marching up a new peak: a prospective on China's administrative legal studies in the '90s) *Zhongguo faxue*, no. 2, 1992, p. 10.
80 Yang Haikun goes into detail in '*Dangqian guanyu xingzheng faren wentidi lilun tantao*' (An inquiry into the current problem of administrative legal person) *Hebei faxue* (Hebei Legal Studies, Shijiazhuang) no. 3, 1991, p. 1.
81 Wang Hanbin, 'Explanation of the Law on Administrative Procedure', Second Session, Seventh NPC, 28 March 1989, FBIS-CHI-89-083, 2 May 1989, p. 101.
82 These conventional dualisms are, for example, found in Zhu Weijiu of the CASS Institute of Law, '*Jianlun xingzhengdi jiben yuanze*' (A brief discussion of the basic principles of administrative law) *Faxue yanjiu*, no. 1, 1989, p. 9.
83 See, for example, remarks of Le Debao as quoted by Wang Ganyi, 'New Law Will Give People More Rights', *CD*, 13 April 1989, p. 4.
84 Li Fuhai, '*Zhongxi xingzheng susong jiben lilun zhi bijiao*' (A comparison of Chinese and Western theories of administrative lawsuits) *Faxue yanjiu*, No. 1, 1991, pp. 29–36.
85 Wang Hanbin on the relation between judicial authority and administrative power, 'Explanation of the "Law on Administrative Procedure", FBIS-CHI-89-083, 2 May 1989, p. 99.
86 Ibid., p. 102.
87 'Wang Hanbin Holds Press Conference', Beijing, 29 March 1989, FBIS-CHI-89-060, 30 March 1989, p. 14.
88 Ibid., p. 15.
89 Law to Sue Government...', *CD*, 29 March 1989, p. 1.
90 See, for example, Wang Ganyi, 'New Law Will Give People More Rights', *CD*, 13 April, 1989, p. 4; 'An Important Step in Building Democratic Politics', *Renmin ribao*, 10 April 1989, p. 1, in FBIS-CHI-89-068, 11 April

1989, p. 14–5. On the importance of procedural law to human rights see Sun Xiaoxia, '*Lun falu chengxuzhongdi renquan*' (On human rights in legal procedure), *Zhongguo faxue*, no. 3, 1992, pp. 39–45.

91 See the opinion of Professor Jiang Ping, President, China University of Political science and Law, Beijing, 'Law Termed "Disaster"', *Xin Hua*, Beijing 29 March 1989, FBIS-CHI-89-059, 29 March 1989, p. 8.

92 Yang Haikun, '*Jinnianlai woguo xingzhengfaxue lilundi zhutao jianshu*' (Major achievements in recent Chinese administrative law theory) *Jiangsu shehui kexue* (Jiangsu Social Sciences) no. 3, 1991, in *Faxue*, no. 7, 1991, p. 57.

93 See, for example, Zhou Weiping et al., '*Woguo xingzheng faxue ruogan lilun wenti yanjiu zongshu*' (Summaries of several theoretical research problems in Chinese administrative law) *Zhongguo shehui kexue*, no. 4, 1991, pp. 28–40, in *Faxue*, no. 9, 1991, p. 58.

94 Supreme People's Procuratorate Work Report', *Renmin ribao*, 13 April 1991, pp. 3, 5, FBIS-CHI-91-115, 14 June 1991, p. 72. Yang Haikun's advocacy of the democratisation of administrative law provides a slightly different statistic. During 1979–89, 60 per cent of all laws and regulations concerned economic legislation whereas only 4 per cent of such law related to citizens' democratic rights. Yang Haikun, '*Woguo xingzhengdi minzhuhua, kexuehua fazhan zhanwang*' (A prospectus on the democratisation and scientification of China's administrative law) *Zhongguo faxue*, no. 2, 1992, p. 27.

4 Civil Law and Civil Society under a 'Socialist Rule of Law'?

1 John K. Fairbank, *China: A New History* (Cambridge, Mass.: Belknap Press of Harvard University Press, 1992) p. 257.

2 Martin Whyte, 'Urban China: A Civil Society in the Making?', in Arthur Rosenbaum (ed.), *State and Society in China* (Boulder: Westview Press, 1992) footnote 8, pp. 98–9.

3 Fairbank, *China*, pp. 429–430.

4 Fairbank, *China*, p. 432.

5 Barrett McCormick, Su Shaozhi and Xiao Xiaoming, 'The 1989 Democracy Movement: A Review of the Prospects for Civil Society in China', *Pacific Affairs*, vol. 65, no. 2, Summer, 1992, p. 187.

6 Thomas Gold, 'Party-State Versus Society in China' in Joyce Kallgren (ed.), *Building a Nation-State: China After Forty Years* (Berkeley: Center for Chinese Studies, China Research Monograph, No. 37) p. 150. Thomas Gold, 'The Re-Surgence of Civil Society in China', *Journal of Democracy*, Winter, 1990, p. 25.

7 Whyte, 'Urban China: a Civil Society in the Making', op. cit., p. 77.

8 See McCormick, Su and Xiao, 'The 1989 Democracy Movement: A Review of the Prospects for Civil Society in China', op. cit., p. 196.

9 Meng Qinguo, '*Jingji tizhi gaige shiqidi minshilifa*' (Civil legislation in the period of economic restructuring) *Zhongguo shehui kexue*, no. 6, 1988, p. 56.

10 Ibid., p. 57.

11 Zhou Ming, '*Lun quanli yu yiwudi jizhong guanxi*' (On the various relations of rights and obligations), *Faxue*, no. 8, 1992, p. 15.
12 Zhang Jinfan, '*Lun Zhongguo gudai minfa yanjiu zhongdi jige wenti*' (On several problems concerning research into China's ancient civil law) *Zhengfa luntan*, no. 5, 1985, pp. 1–13.
13 'Civil law Has Key Role…' as cited in *CD*, 13 September 1983, p. 4.
14 See, for example, 'China's Civil Laws to Enter a New Stage', *CD*, 12 April 1986, p. 5.
15 This debate was summarised in 'Chinese Jurists Challenge Traditional Legal Concepts', *CD*, 10 June 1986, p. 4.
16 See the comments of one China's most senior jurists, Zhang Youyu, in 'Jurist Answers Questions on Civil Procedure Law', FBIS-CHI-82-051, 16 March 1982, vol. 1, no. 051, p. K3 and the *Renmin ribao* editorial, 'Strengthen the Building of the Legal System, Facilitate the People's Litigations', *Renmin ribao*, 11 March 1982, p. 4, in FBIS-CHI-82-051, 16 March 1982, vol. 1, no. 051, p. K1.
17 See, for example, Jiang Ping, '*Shehuizhuyi shangpin jingji yu minfa tiaocheng*' (On socialist commodity production and civil law readjustment) *Zhengfa luntan*, no. 5, 1987, pp. 43–9.
18 Strengthen the Building of the Legal System…', op. cit., 11 March 1982, p. K1.
19 Ibid., p. K2.
20 Zheng Yongliu, '*Zhongguo nongmin falu yishidi xianshi bianqian*' (Contemporary change in the legal consciousness of China's peasants) *Zhongguo faxue*, no. 1, 1992, pp. 94, 99.
21 'An Important Step toward the Strengthening of the Legal System', *Renmin ribao*, 17 April 1986, p. 2, in FBIS-CHI-86-078, 23 April 1986, vol. 1, no. 078, p. K12.
22 'Law Committee Suggests Changes', *Xin Hua*, (New China News Agency) 12 April 1986, FBIS-CHI-865-071, 14 April 1986, vol. 1, no. 071, p. K10.
23 Ibid., p. K11.
24 Zhang Youyu, '*Weishenme zhiding jeibu "minfa tongze"*' (Why establish this department, 'General Principles of Civil Law') *Zhongguo faxue*, 1986, no. 4, pp. 3–10, in *Falu* (later *Faxue*) no. 8, 1986, p. 17. Wang Jiafu, '*Yibu juyou Zhongguo tesedi minfa tongze*' (The general principles of civil law as having Chinese characteristics) *Faxue yanjiu*, no. 3, 1986, pp. 7–11.
25 Zhang Youyu, "*Weishenme zhiding jeibu "minfa tongze"*", *Faxue*, no. 8, 1986, p. 18.
26 'Wang Hanbin explains principles of civil code', *Xin Hua*, 16 April 1986, FBIS-CHI-86-078, 23 April 1986, p. K6.
27 William Jones, 'Civil law in China', *Chinese Law and Government*, vol. xviii, no. 3–4, Fall/Winter, 1985–6, p. 10.
28 Ibid., p. 11.
29 William Jones, *Basic Principles of Civil Law in China* (New York: M.E. Sharpe, 1989) p. xvi.
30 Ibid., p. xviii.
31 For example, see the remarks of Liang Huixing at the CASS symposium of 5 April 1991 in Sun Xianzhong, '*Minfa tongzedi huigu yu zhanwang*

(Retrospective and prospectives on the General Principles of Civil Law) *Faxue yanjiu*, no. 3, 1991, p. 86.

32 Wang Hanbin et al., '*Renzhen shishi minfa tongze he minshi susongfa*' (Seriously implement the General Principles of Civil Law and the Civil Procedural Law) *Zhongguo faxue*, no. 4, 1991, pp. 22–31, herein, p. 26.

33 Xu Guodong, '*Minfa tongze guidingdi minfa yuanyuan*' (Sources of civil law as stipulated in the General Principles of Civil law) *Faxue yanjiu*, no. 1, 1991, pp. 76–8.

34 Zhao's remarks are reported in Sun Xianzhong, '*Minfa tongzedi huigu yu zhanwang*', op. cit., p. 88.

35 See, for example, 'America Individualism', *CD*, 22 February 1988, p. 4.

36 Vice-President of CASS, Zhao Fusan, who later chose to remain in Paris after June 4th, stressed the linkage between individualism and development, 'The Future Culture of Socialist China', *CD*, 2 August 1985, p. 4.

37 'Survey Analyses National Character', *CD*, 28 September 1987, p. 4.

38 Stanley Rosen, 'Students and the State in China: the Crisis in Ideology & Organization', in Arthur Rosenbaum (ed.), *State and Society in China* (Boulder: Westview Press, 1992), pp. 172–73.

39 See 'Traditions Appraised', *CD*, 14 April 1989, p. 5.

40 Changes in divorce rate and the underlying reasons are discussed in 'Divorce in China', *BR*, no. 36, 7–12 September 1992, pp. 28–30.

41 For example see 'How divorce can be avoided', *CD*, 27 October 1983, p. 4.

42 'Rising Divorce Rate Is Held Not "Serious"', *CD*, 14 November 1985, p. 4.

43 Gail Hershatter looks at rural couples who, despite similar status, undergo disaffection as the result of one party's economic success. "Making a Friend: Changing Patterns of Courtship in Urban China', *Pacific Affairs*, vol. 57, no. 2, Summer, 1984, p. 248.

44 'Rising Divorce Rate Is Held Not "Serious"', op. cit., p. 4 and Wang Chunyuan and Chen Zheguang, '*Zhengque chuli jiehunyin jiating wenti*' (Correctly handle the matrimonial problems of the family) *Hongqi*, no. 5, 1982, p. 38.

45 Report on the work of the Supreme Court, *Xin Hua*, 19 April 1986, in FBIS-CHI-86-081, 28 April 1986, vol. 1, no. 081, p. K12.

46 'Rising Divorce Rate Is Held Not "Serious"', op. cit., p. 4. A survey of 179 divorced couples in Xuhui District, Shanghai showed that 91 couples planned to use their marriage certificates to secure more spacious housing. See 'Analysis of Divorce Cases', *CD*, 16 August 1985, p. 4. The latter point was not sustained in a national survey of the marriage attitudes of rural youth which cast doubt on the continuance of the past trend of girls from the mountain areas wanting to marry men on the plains or seeking boyfriends in the cities. The survey argued that rural girls were more confident of rural prosperity and no longer sought large quantities of betrothal gifts. It also claimed that young married couples were reacting against the traditional principles of filial piety to equally honour the parents of both parties. 'Young People Change Ideas on Marriage', *CD*, 27 January 1986, p. 1.

47 See Chen Si, 'Female Equality', *CD*, 30 June 1989, p. 4.

48 Drive Urges Women to Stand up for Rights', *CD*, 27 February 1989, p. 1 and 'Women in China: Words Tell It All', *CD*, 19 March 1986, p. 6. 'Woman's Role in Society Debated', *CD*, 8 March 1988, p. 1.

49 See Jeanette l. Pinard, *The People's Republic of China: A Bibliography of Selected English-Language Legal Materials*, Law Library, Library of Congress, 1985, p. 7.

50 See, for example, William Jones (ed.), *Basic Principles of Civil Law*, p. 31.

51 Shen Zongling, *Bijiaofa zonglun* (Outlines of comparative law). (Beijing: Beijing daxue chubanshe, 1987), p. 413.

52 Shi Jichun '*Woguo minfa tongze yu waiguo chuantong minfa tongzedi bijiao*' (Comparison between the General principles of China's civil law and the traditional general principles of foreign civil laws) *Shehui kexue* (Social Sciences, Shanghai) no. 7, 1986, p. 24.

53 'Security Ministry Cracks down on Prostitution', *Xin Hua*, 6 September 1991, FBIS-CHI-91-175, 10 September 1991, p. 31.

54 'CCP Internal Document on People-trafficking', *Chiushi nientai*, Hong Kong, 1 November 1991, pp. 29-31 in FBIS-CHI-91-230, 29 November 1991, pp. 29–30.

55 For the Law Committee's revisions see 'Song Rufen Reviews Draft Laws', *Xin Hua*, 3 September 1991, in FBIS-CHI-91-172, 5 September 1991, pp. 27–8. The translated text of the law is available in English in FBIS-CHI-91-172, 5 September 1991, pp. 28-30; and the Chinese text, '*Quanguo renmin daibiao dahui changwu weiyuanhui guanyu yanjin yinpiaochangdi jueding*' (NPC Standing Committee decision on prostitution and whoring), is in *Zhonghua renmin gongheguo xinfa huibian* (Compendium of New PRC Law) vol. 3 (Beijing: Zhongguo fazhi chubanshe, 1991) pp. 15–20.

56 This figure has often appeared in the press, but the statistical cohorts are seldom clearly identified in such generalisation. Commenting on the total prison population of 1.1 million in 1991, Minister of Justice Cai Cheng, noted that 44.9 per cent were under the age of 25 and 79.4 per cent under the age of 35 'Official Discusses Prisons, Reforming Criminals', *Xin Hua*, 17 September 1991, in FBIS-CHI-91-181, 18 September 1991, p. 16.

57 'Child Labour Is a Serious Problem', *CD*, 17 August 1989, p. 4; 'Shenzhen Firms Illegally Hire Child Labour', *CD*, 4 August, 1988, p. 3.

58 'Tougher Laws Urged to Curb Juvenile Crime', *CD*, 3 December 1985, p. 4.

59 'Law of the PRC on the Protection of Minors', *Xin Hua*, 4 September 1991, FBIS-CHI-91-174, 9 September 1991, p. 39. Chinese text, '*Zhonghua renmin gongheguo mochengnianren baohu fa*' (PRC law on the protection of minors), in *Zhonghua renmin gongheguo xinfa huibian*, 1991, vol. 3, pp. 3–14. For other pre- and post-1949 legislation in this area see *Funu he mochengnianren falu baohu quanshu* (The complete volume on the legal protection of women and minors) (Beijing: Zhongguo jiancha chubanshe, 1991), pp. 1184–209.

60 'Juvenile Delinquency Poses a "Major" Problem', *Liaowang* (Overseas) no. 34, 26 August 1991, p. 20 in FBIS-CHI-91-175, 10 September 1991, pp. 29–31.

61 '*Shanghaishi qingxiaonian baohu tiaolie*' (Shanghai municipal regulations on the protection of minors), *Jiefang ribao*, 2 July 1987, p. 1.
62 'Law of the PRC on the Protection of Minors', op. cit., p. 36.
63 Ibid., p. 38.
64 'Song Rufen Reviews Draft Laws', op. cit., p. 27.
65 'Draft Law for Minors', *Xin Hua*, 29 August 1991 in FBIS-CHI-91-170, 3 September 1991, p. 31.
66 *The Criminal Law and the Criminal Procedural Law of the PRC* (Beijing: Foreign Languages Press, 1984) p. 61.
67 Peng Chong, '*Quanguo renmin daibiao dahui changwu weiyuanhui gongzuo baogao*' (Work report to NPCSC) in *Xin Hua yuebao*, no. 4, 1992, p. 50.
68 'PRC law Protecting Women's Rights and Interests', *Xin Hua*, 7 April 1992, FBIS-CHI-92-072S, 14 April 1992, p. 17. Chinese text, '*Zhonghua renmin gongheguo funu quanli baozhang fa*' (PRC law on the guaranteeing of the rights and interests of women) *Xin Hua yuebao*, no. 4, 1992, pp. 42–4.
69 'NPC Body Gathers to Debate New Legislation', *CD*, 26 October 1991, p. 1. The comparative position of Chinese women has been an area of contention. The Women's Federation surveyed 42 000 subjects in its reaction to a 1988 Western survey which claimed that in terms of attitude towards male and female infants, rates of male-female schooling, attainment of high position, etc., China ranked abysmally at 132nd in the world. See Stanley Rosen, 'Women and Reform', *China News Analysis*, no. 1477, 15 January 1993, pp. 1–10.
70 'Panel Discussions on Women's Law', *Xin Hua*, 26 October 1991, in FBIS-CHI-91-208, 28 October 1991, p. 31.
71 Chapter Eight, Section Six, 'PRC Law Protecting Women's Rights and Interests', op. cit., p. 20.
72 On the difficult issues of equal 'property rights' see Johnathan Ocko, 'Women, Property, and Law in the PRC', Rubie Watson & Patricia Ebrey (eds.) *Marriage and Inequality in Chinese Society* (Berkeley: University of California Press, 1991) pp. 313–46. Ocko establishes a lack of legal clarity as to provisions of premarital property and surveys the persisting 'feudal' attitudes which undermine the inheritance rights of widows and daughters. Also, Myron Cohen argues that there is a wide gap between the practical realities of family ownership in the villages and the law's formal requirements of equality. See Myron Cohen, 'Family Management and Family Division in Contemporary Rural China', *CQ*, no. 130, June 1992, p. 368.
73 'Law to Further Protect Women's Rights', *Xin Hua*, 30 December 1991, FBIS-CHI-91-250, 30 December 1991, p. 21.
74 Ibid., p. 18.
75 See Zhang Yongen, '*Yibu juyou Zhongguo tesedi jichengfa*' (Inheritance law with Chinese characteristics) *Faxue jikan*, no. 3, 1985, p. 35, and Zhang Zhoujiang, '*Shilun caichan jichengquandi zhuti*' (Examination of the subject of the right of property inheritance) *Faxue* (*Renda*) no. 1, 1987, pp. 59–60.
76 The PRC Law for the Protection of Handicapped People', *Xin Hua*, 29 December 1990, FBIS-CHI-91-003, 4 January 1991, p. 23.

77 'Community Mediators Heal Family Discord', *CD*, 18 March 1989, p. 1.

78 See, for example, 'Mediators Urged to Help Cut Crime', *CD*, 14 July 1988, p. 4.

79 'Mediation System Resolves Legal Disputes', *CD*, 10 October 1989, p. 4, 'Mediation System Helps Deter Crimes', *CD*, 2 November 1989, p. 4.

80 'People's Mediation Needs Improvement', *CD*, 22 December 1986, p. 4.

81 Ma Jie, *Zhongguo shehui zhian zonghe zhili yanjiu* (The study of China's comprehensive control of public security) (Beijing: Falu chubanshe, 1990) p. 6.

82 See, for example, Wang Zhongfang, *Zhongguo shehui zhian zonghe zhilidi lilun yu shijian* (Theory and practice of comprehensive management of public order in China) (Beijing: Qunzhong chubanshe, 1989), pp. 419–27.

83 See, for example, '*Zonghe zhili da you zuo wei renmin fayuan can yu shehui zhian*' (Comprehensive social control is of great service to the people's courts involvement in social order) *Fazhi ribao*, 3 March 1992, p. 1. Both Wang Zhongfang and Ma Jie devote separate chapters to juvenile deliquency in their respective discussions of the comprehensive control of the social order. Wang Zhongfang, *Zhongguo shehui zhian zonghe zhilidi lilun yu shijian*, op. cit., pp. 443–58; Ma Jie, *Zhongguo shehui zhian zonghe zhili yanjiu* (The study of China's comprehensive control of public security) (Beijing: Falu chubanshe, 1990) pp. 171–97.

84 For raportage see '*Falu yu jingshen weming jianshe*' (Establishing law and sprititual civilisation) *Qunyan* (The Masses Speak) no. 4, 1986, pp. 2–9.

85 Liu Zhiguang and Wang Suli, '*Zong "qunzhong shehui" zou "gongmin shehui"*' (From 'mass' to 'citizen society') *Zhengzhi yanjiu* (Political Studies Research) no. 5, 1988, pp. 1–5.

86 '"Text" of Law on Role, Position of Trade Unions', *Xin Hua*, 7 April 1992, in FBIS-CHI-92-072-S, 14 April 1992, p. 9.

87 Wang Shengxuan, '*Lun shehuizhuyi faludi cunshou*' (On honouring socialist law) *Shanxi daxuebao* (Journal of Shanxi University) no. 1, 1987, p. 77.

5 Law as the Contractual Predicate of Ownership Rights

1 For a selective discussion of these changes see 'Market Economy', *China Daily*, 20 October 1992, p. 4; 'Number of Private Enterprises Exceeds 100,000', Beijing, *Wenzhai bao*, 1 December 1991, p. 1 in FBIS-CHI-91-247, 24 December 1991, p. 38; Li Hong, 'Firms will Get Greater Freedom to Manage', *CD*, 13 December 1991, p. 1, FBIS-CHI-91-241, 16 December 1991, p. 51.

2 'State Council's Ma Hong's Comments', *Xin Hua*, 14 October 1992, FBIS-CHI-92-200-S, 15 October 1992, p. 21.

3 See Wang Congbiao, 'Deng Xiaoping and the Shenzhen Special Economic Zone', *Liaowang* (Overseas), no. 39, 28 September 1992, pp. 3–7, FBIS-CHI-92-198, 13 October 1992, p. 15. Jiang Zemin reiterated this point in his October 1992 political report to the 14th National Party Congress, FBIS-CHI-92-198-S, 13 October 1992, p. 25.

4 James V. Feinerman, 'Economic and Legal Reform in China, 1978–91', *Problems of Communism*, vol. xl, Sept./Oct., 1991, p. 66.

5 Robert Kleinburg, *China's 'Opening' to the Outside World* (Boulder, San Francisco, & Oxford: Westview Press, 1990) passim. In my own discussion of the relation between 'self-reliance' and the 'open door' I have tended to favour the same emphasis; however, the 14th National Party Congress decision supporting the extension of coastal legislative privileges concerning foreign investment to all provinces under 'open door in all dimensions' suggests that the current emphasis on 'self-reliance' is becoming even less meaningful. See Ronald C. Keith, 'The Origins and Strategic Implications of China's "Independent Foreign Policy", *International Journal*, vol. xli, no. 1, Winter 1986–5, pp. 126–7; and Ronald C. Keith, 'The Asia-Pacific Area and the "New International Political Order": The View from Beijing', *China Report*, vol. 25, no. 4, 1989, p. 347.

6 Stanley Lubman's review of Margaret M. Pearson, *Joint Ventures in the People's Republic of China: The Control of Foreign Direct Investment under Socialism* (Princeton: Princeton University Press, 1991) in *CQ*, no. 130, June 1992, p. 433.

7 See, for example, Yang Ronghao, '*Taolun jingji fenquandi zhuyao falu yuanze*' (Discussion of key legal principles in the division of economic powers) *Jingji fa* (Economic Law), no. 2, 1992, pp. 37–41.

8 See Sun Wanzhong, *Jiaqiang jingji lifa shijian jingji guiding xietiao fazhan* (Strengthening economic legislation, realising the development of a stable, coordinated economy) *Jingji fa*, no. 6, 1991, p. 25.

9 Summaries of seminar participants' remarks in '*Guanche qi zhong quanhui jingshen, jia kuai jingji fazhi jianshe*' (Carry out the spirit of the seventh plenary session of the National Party Congress, increasingly and quickly establishing the system of economic law) *Jingji fa*, no. 3, 1991, p. 4.

10 Zeng Jianmin, Sun Chao, Gu Changhao, '*Shehuizhuyi fazhi bixu you luyu jiefang he fazhan shengchanli*' (The socialist legal system has to favour the liberation and development of the productive forces) *Zhongguo faxue*, no. 4, 1992, pp. 8–9.

11 Wu Shihuan, '*Jiji kaizhan fazhi xitong gongchengdi yanjiu*' (Positively develop the study of the economy's rule-of-law system) *Jingji fa*, no. 3, 1992, p. 26.

12 Ibid., p. 27.

13 Ibid., p. 25.

14 See Zhang Guilong, '*Xiugai jingji hetongfadi ruogang yijian zongshu*' (Summary of opinion on the revision of the law on economic contract) *Jingji fa*, no. 1, 1991, p. 19.

15 Kuang Aimin, '*Xiugai "jingji hetongfa"di ruogan sikao*' (Thoughts on the revision of the 'Law on Economic Contract') *Jingji fa*, no. 2, 1991, p. 94.

16 Zhang Guilong, '*Xiugai jingji hetongfadi ruogan yijian zongshu*', op. cit., p. 19.

17 See Kang Deguan and Xu Xiaosong, '*Guo you qiye gongsihuazhi yanjiu*' (The study of the transformation of state enterprise into companies) *Zhongguo faxue*, no. 3, 1992, pp. 32–8.

18 Wu Yuanliang, 'On the dialectics of liberating and developing productive forces', *Renmin ribao*, 18 September 1992, p. 5 in FBIS-CHI-92-191, 1 October 1992, p. 39.

19 Zhang Chunqiao, 'On Exercising All-Round Dictatorship Over the Bourgeoisie', *Peking Review*, no. 14, 4 April 1975, p. 8.
20 Chinese Communist Party, *Resolution on CCP History (1949–1981)* (Beijing: Foreign Languages Press, 1981).
21 Shi Zhongquan, 'What Is Meant by "Bourgeois Right"?', *BR*, 28 December 1981, p. 20.
22 According to an interview with leading economist, Liu Guoguang, in Dong Ruisheng, 'Why Should a Socialist Society Practice a Market Economy', *Liaowang* (Overseas) no. 39, 28 September 1992, pp. 7–9 in FBIS-CHI-92-200, 15 October 1992, p. 29.
23 Zhao Ziyang, 'Advance Along the Road of Socialism with Chinese Characteristics', *BR*, no. 45, 9–15 November 1987, p. 34.
24 'Questions and Answers on Reform', *Zhongguo jingji tizhi gaige*, no. 8, 23 August 1989, pp. 7–9, FBIS-CHI-89-196, 12 October 1989, p. 52.
25 Liu Jinghuai, 'China to carry out comprehensive institutional reform', *Liaowang* (Overseas) no. 38, 21 September 1992, pp. 3–4 in FBIS-CHI-92-199, 14 October 1992, p. 18.
26 Ibid., p. 20.
27 See Jiang Zemin's report to the 14th National Party Congress, Beijing Central Television, 12 October 1992, in FBIS-CHI-920198-S, 13 October 1992, p. 30.
28 See 'Socialist Market Economy – A New Trend in Reform', *BR*, no. 35, 31 Aug.–6 Sept., 1992, p. 7.
29 Jiang Zemin's political work report to the 14th National Party Congress, Beijing Central Television, FBIS-CHI-92-198-S, 13 October 1992, p. 31.
30 The quoted aspects were highlighted by Dong Furang, Director of Institute of Economics, CASS, 'Socialist Countries Diversify Ownership', *BR*, no. 40, 5 October 1987, p. 20.
31 Sun Xianzhong, '*Guoyou tudi shiyong quan zizhan guanlidi falu zhidu chuyi*' (Preliminary opinion on the legal system for the property management of state land use) *Zhongguo tudi kexue*, 1991.9.6-9, *Jingji fa*, no. 6, 1991, p. 89. For an introduction to the 'department' of land law see Zhang Zixi (et al.), '*Tudi fa tixi chutan*' (A preliminary exploration of the system of land law) *Jingji fa*, no. 6, 1991, pp. 83–8.
32 Li Changqi refers to the advocacy of independent property law in his discussion of four different schools of thought on the development of a basic economic law, '*Kuanyu zhiding "Zhonghua renmin gongheguo chiben jingji fa" di jige wenti*' (Several problems on the drafting of the "Basic Economic Law of the People's Republic of China") *Jingji fa*, no. 3, 1992, pp. 34–9.
33 For example, see 'Perplexities in Real Estate – Notes on Covering `Reform of Land Use System in Guangdong and Fujian', *Xin Hua*, Beijing, 8 October 1992, FBIS-CHI-92-199, 14 October 1992, p. 32.
34 Zhu Rongji, '*Guanyu zhiding zhuanhuan qiye jingying jizhi tiaolidi jige wenti*' (Several regulatory problems concerning the transformation of enterprise management mechanisms) *Zhongguo faxue*, no. 4, 1992, pp. 3–7.
35 Guo Feng, '*Zhongguo minfaxue lilun zai gaigezhongdi fazhan he fanrong...*' (The development and flourishing of Chinese civil law theory during the reform era...) *Faxue*, no. 11, 1988, p. 67.

36 Xiang Chuyi, '*Minfa tongzedi Zhongguo tese*', (On the Chinese characteristics of the Law on the Principles of Civil Law) *Zhongguo faxue*, no. 3, 1986, pp. 3–9.
37 Li Youyi and Jian Mingxing, '*Woguo minfa wuquan tixi chutan*' (A preliminary inquiry into the right over things in China's civil law) *Beijing daxue xuebao*, (Beijing University journal) no. 1, 1987, p. 120.
38 See Ding Jimin, '*Jingyingquan yu suoyouquan*' (The rights of management and ownership) *Faxue yanjiu*, no. 1, 1987, pp. 12–17.
39 Zhang Hongyu, 'China's land system transformation and adjustment of agricultural structure – reviewing China's rural reform and development since 1978', *Liaowang* (Overseas) 25 November 1991, pp. 16–17 in FBIS-CHI-91-241, 16 December 1991, p. 53. Also, see 'NPC Examines Draft Land Law', *BR*, no. 26, 30 June 1986, p. 7.
40 Li Youyi and Qian Mingxing, '*Woguo minfa wuquan tixi chutan*', op. cit., p. 120.
41 Lu Zhenbang, '*Lun minfa suoyouquan yu jingyingquan*' (On ownership and operation rights in the civil law) *Faxue yu shijian*, no. 2, 1987, in *Faxue*, no. 5, 1987, p. 68.
42 In 1988 Guo Feng identified five current theories relating to ownership and operation, namely, the theories of 'relative ownership', 'ownership by legal person', 'ownership function', 'management rights', 'user benefits'. See Guo Feng, '*Zhongguo minfaxue lilun zai gaigezhongdi fazhan he fanrong...*', op. cit., pp. 66–7.
43 Qiao Lu, '*ZhongSu qiye zulin jingyingdi falu bijiao*' (Comparison of Chinese and Soviet Enterprise Law on Leasing and Management' *Jingji fa*, no. 3, 1991, pp. 47–51.
44 Su Junsheng, '*Lun faren chanquan zhidu*' (On the system of legal person property rights) *Jingji fa*, no. 5, 1991, pp. 30–1.
45 Xue Huizong, '*Faren suoyouquan pingjie*' (A review of the legal person's right of ownership) *Jingji fa*, no. 5, 1991, pp. 27–30.
46 Zhao Xudong, '*Jiti qiye faren yanjiu*' (The study of collective enterprise as legal person) *Jingji fa*, no. 1, 1991, pp. 73–80.
47 See, example, Wang Jinding, '*Guanyu jingli "jia jiti" qiyedi ruogan falu wenti*' (Several legal problems relating to the management of 'false collectives') *Jingji fa*, no. 2, 1992, pp. 71–3.
48 'Interim Regulations on Private Enterprise of the People's Republic of China', *BR*, 6–12 March 1992, p. IX.
49 Ibid., p. X.
50 Zhao Xudong, '*Jiti qiye faren yanjiu*', op. cit., pp. 74–5.
51 '*Shehui kexuejie taolun dui Zhongguo mianlindi xin keti*' (Social science circles discuss new problems facing China) *Renmin ribao* (Overseas) 28 October 1992, p. 3.

6 Politics and Criminal Law Change under Reform

1 Wang Yong and Zhao Bingzhi, '*Lun feixingshi faluzhongdi xingfa guifan*' (On the criminal law norms in non-criminal law) *Faxue pinglun*, vol. 27, no. 1, 1988, p. 40.

2 See Deng Xiaoping '*Zai jiejian shoudu jieyan buduijun yishang ganbu shidi jianghua*'(Speech at the time of receiving the senior officers of the capital martial law troops) *Renmin ribao*, 28 June 1989, p. 28. For English text see 'Deng Talks on Turmoil on June 9', *China Daily*, 28 June 1989, p. 4.
3 For English and Chinese texts of the two decisions see *The Criminal Law and the Criminal Procedural law of China* (Beijing: Foreign Languages Press, 1984) pp. 241–9.
4 See, for example, Cheng Baoshu, '*Sixing wenti yanjiu*' (Research into the problem of the death penalty) *Faxue yanjiu*, no. 3, 1985, pp. 35–41.
5 Kang Runsen, '*Lun Mao Zedong dui maliezhuyi sixing lilundi chuangzaoxing fazhan*' (On Mao Zedong's creative development of Marxist-Leninist theory on the death penalty) *Zhengfa luntan*, no. 6, 1991, pp. 29–32.
6 'State Drops Old Laws', *CD*, 11 August 1988, p. 3.
7 For example, this phenomena is discussed in the 1986 work report of the President of the Supreme People's Court, Zheng Tianxiang, 8 April 1986, Sixth NPC, in FBIS-CHI86-081, 28 April 1986, vol. 1, no. 081, p. K 8.
8 Stephen Davis, 'The Death Penalty and Legal Reform in the PRC', *Journal of Chinese Law*, vol. 1, no. 2, Fall 1987, pp. 304–5.
9 Gao Xijiang, '*Guanyu xiugai xingfa zhidao sixiang fangmiandi jige wenti*', (On several problems regarding revision to the guiding thought of the criminal law), *Faxue pinglun*, (Legal Science Review) no. 1, 1989, pp. 1–3; Luo Hua, '*Guanyu xiugai he wanshan Woguo xingfadi ruogan shexiang*' (Tentative ideas on the revision and improvement of China's criminal law) *Faxue pinglun*, no. 1, 1988, pp. 4–10.
10 Wang Yong, '*Dui guo xingfaxue yanjiudi fansi–du "xin Zhongguo xingfaxue yanjiu zongshu"*' (Reflections on Chinese criminal law research on reading *The General Survey of Research in New China's Legal Science*) *Zhongguo shehui kexue*, no. 3, 1988, p. 171.
11 See Guo Daohui's discussion of Mao on 'less killing', '*Lun juyou Zhongguo tesedi sixing zhidu*' (On possessing a death penalty system with Chinese characteristics) *Zhongguo faxue*, no. 4, 1984, p. 109.
12 Wang Changxue, '*Sixing huanqi zhixing zhidu chutan*' (Preliminary study of the system of death penalty with reprieve) *Xinjiang shehui kexue*, no. 5, 1988.
13 Wang Zhongyi, '*Woguo sihuan zhidudi falu xingzhi chutan*' (Comments on the legal nature of China's system of death penalty with two-year reprieve) *Faxue yanjiu*, no. 5, 1991, p. 43.
14 'Revision of the Criminal Law Urged', *CD*, 6 April 1989, p. 3.
15 'Changes in Society Cause Crime Rise', *CD*, 21 June 1988, p. 4.
16 'China Faced Sharp Rise in Crime during '88', *CD*, 24 January 1989, p. 1.
17 'Criminal Caseload Rises by 14 per cent', *CD*, 9 May 1989, p. 1.
18 The ensuing discussion of 'counterrevolutionary crime' is an expanded and updated version of the analysis in Ronald C. Keith and Lin Zhiqiu, 'To Revise or not to Revise China's Law on Counterrevolution', *China Information*, Leiden, vol. 5, no. 4, Spring 1991, pp. 24–41.
19 Carlos Wing-Hung Lo, 'Trials of Dissidents of the 1989 Democracy Movement: The Limits of Criminal Justice under Teng Hsiao-p'ing', *Issues and Studies*, vol. 28, no. 2, Dec. 1992, p. 24.
20 Patricia Griffin, *The Chinese Communist treatment of Counterrevolutionaries: 1924–1949* (Princeton, NJ: Princeton University Press, 1976) p. 6.

21 Mao Zedong, '*Lun zhengce*', (On policy) *Mao Zedong xuanji* (Selected works of Mao Zedong) vol. 2. (Beijing: Renmin chubanshe, 1969) p. 725.
22 Gao Daohui, op. cit., p. 109.
23 See the unpublished M.A. thesis of Lin Zhiqiu, 'Politics and the "Autonomy" of the Chinese Criminal Justice System, 1978–1988', University of Calgary, April 1989, p. 93.
24 'Li outlines policies regarding protesters', *CD*, 3 July 1989, p. 1.
25 Gao Mingxuan, senior editor, *Xingfaxue* (Criminal Law Science) (Beijing: Falu chubanshe, 1981) p. 33.
26 Mao Zedong, 'On the Ten Major Relationships', *Selected Works of Mao Zedong*, vol. V. (Beijing: Foreign Languages Press, 1977) p. 298.
27 Mao Zedong, op. cit., p. 300.
28 Mao Zedong, op. cit., p. 302.
29 Mao Zedong, op. cit., p. 302.
30 Mao Zedong, op. cit., pp. 299–300.
31 *The Criminal Law and the Criminal Procedure Law of the People's Republic of China* (Beijing: Foreign Languages Press, 1984) p. 160.
32 For discussion of this high court power see Ni Shouming, '*Sixing fuhe chengxu bushi yiqie sixing anjiandi bijing chengxu*' (Supreme Court procedure for the review of the death penalty is not the required procedure for every death sentence) *Faxue yanjiu*, no. 1, 1989. Some observers were quite critical of the procedural dimensions of high court review; for example, see Xiao Shengxi, '*Sixing fuhe chengxu shijianzhongdi jige wenti*', (Problems in the procedure of death penalty review) *Faxue yanjiu*, no. 3, 1986, pp. 56–8.
33 See Harry Harding's description in Denis Twitchett, John K. Fairbank (eds), *The Cambridge History of China*, vol. 15 (Cambridge: Cambridge University Press, 1991) p. 174.
34 Chinese Communist Party, *Resolution on CPC History (1949–81)* (Beijing: Foreign Languages Press, 1981) p. 34.
35 Observe "PRC Regulations on Arrest and Detention"', *Qiu shi bao* (Seek the Truth Journal) no. 4, 1 March 1979, p. 1, in *China Report*, FBIS, JPRS 73922, 27 July 1979, p. 44.
36 Xiao Ming, 'Wording of policy with the force of law must be scientific', *Siwu luntan*, no. 7, 11 March 1979, pp. 17–20, in *China Report*, FBIS, 6080 CSPO: 4005.
37 'Government laws changed at NPC, CPPCC Deputies' suggestion', *Xin Hua*, 8 July 1979, *China Report*, FBIS, 25 July 1979, pp. 85–6.
38 'Shanghai NPC deputies praise new criminal law', *Xin Hua,* 27 June 1979, *China Report*, JPRS 73881, FBIS, 23 July 1979, p. 83.
39 *The Criminal Law and the Criminal Procedure Law of the People's Republic of China* (Beijing: Foreign Languages Press, 1984) p. 32.
40 For example, see Shao-chuan Leng and Hungdah Chiu, *Criminal Justice in Post-Mao China: Analysis and Documents* (Albany: State University of New York Press, 1985) pp. 7–13. Gao's remark is in Gao Mingxuan, *Zhonghua renmin gongheguo xingfadi yunyu he dansheng* (The conception and birth of the criminal law of the People's Republic of China) (Beijing: Falu chubanshe, 1980) p. 17.
41 Gao Mingxuan, op. cit., p. 178.

42 *The Criminal Law and Criminal Procedure Law of the People's Republic of China*, English text, p. 39.
43 Gao Mingxuan, op cit., p. 134.
44 During the author's group discussion with Zhang Zhonglin in 1979, Zhang emphasised that procedural rights such as freedom from detention within a specified time period and speedy trial would have to vary in light of extremely poor communications in areas such as the remote parts of Qinghai province. Ronald C. Keith, 'Transcript of Discussions with Wu Daying and Zhang Zhonglin Concerning Legal Changes and Civil Rights', *CQ*, no. 81, March 1980, p. 120.
45 For Wei's comments on counterrevolution during his defence, see *Siwu luntan*, 21 October 1979, *China Report*, JPRS no. 74764, 13 December 1979, pp. 49–50.
46 *Tansuo*, September 1979, pp. 34–42 in JPRS 74764, 13 December 1979, p. 31.
47 Lu Lin, 'The masses and the criminal law' in *Tansuo*, 9 September 1979, pp. 34–42 in *China Report*, no. 42, p. 30, JPRS 74764, 13 December 1979.
48 Kang Liqun, '*Tantan biaoshu fangemingzui qinfan ketidi wenti*' (Discussing the expression of the object in the crime of counterrevolution) in *Neimenggu shehui kexue* (Inner Mongolian Social Sciences) no. 2, 1981, pp. 59–61.
49 See '*Beijing ribao* on Wei Jingsheng's case', in *Beijing ribao*, 6 March 1989, pp. 1–2 in FBIS-CHI-89-050, 16 March 1989, p. 23. Also see Han Mingzhu (ed.), *Cries for Democracy* (Princeton, NJ: Princeton University Press, 1990), pp. 23–4. In his 25 September 1987 NBC interview, Zhao Ziyang repeated the official line, namely that Wei had not been jailed for criticising policy and leadership. As cited in Andrew Nathan, *China's Crisis* (New York: Colombia University Press, 1990) pp. 88–9.
50 See Fei Xiaotong's preface to *A Great Trial in Chinese History* (Beijing: New World Press, 1981) pp. 7, 9.
51 For example, see 'Jiang Hua Reports on the Trial of the Lin-Jiang cliques', *Xin Hua*, 8 March 1981 in *China Report*, no. 172, p. 37, JPRS, No. 77631, 20 March 1981.
52 David Bonavia, *Verdict in Peking* (New York: R.B. Putnam's & Sons, 1984) p. 32. Jiang was referring to the slogan, 'eradicate old ideas, culture, customs and habits'.
53 'A great victory for the socialist legal system' in *Guangming ribao*, 25 January 1981, p. 1, in *China Report*, no. 173, pp. 15–16, JPRS, no. 77645, 23 March 1981.
54 He Xin, '*Guanyu lianglei butong maodunxingzhidi fanzui wenti*' (On problems concerning the nature of crime relating to the two different types of contradiction) *Zhengfa luntan*, no. 4, 1987, pp. 70–4.
55 See Chim Kim(trans), *The Criminal Procedure Code of the People's Republic of China and Related Documents.* (London: Sweet & Maxwell, 1989) p. 129.
56 See, for example, Gao Mingxuan (ed.), *Xingfaxue*, p. 107.
57 *The Criminal Law and the Criminal Procedure Law of China* (Beijing: Foreign Languages Press, 1984) Chinese text, pp. 90–1.
58 See for example, *Xin Hua*, 5 April 1989 in FBIS-CHI-89-065, 6 April 1989, p. 35.
59 *Dui "fangemingzui" di xiugao jianyi'* [Proposals for revision of 'counter-revolutionary crime') *Fazhi ribao* (Law Daily) 2 June 1989, p. 3.

60 From Ronald C. Keith's discussions with Sun Guohua, Gao Mingxuan, Wu Lei, Xu Chongde, Tong Rou and Han Yusheng at the Law Department of People's University, 26 September 1989. In a separate discussion with Li Buyun on September 22nd, Li indicated that the ultra-leftist manipulation of 'class struggle as the key link' had once again rejected the challenge to argument concerning the 'scientific' credibility of 'counterrevolutionary crime'. He suggested that, while the academic issue might indeed by affected by the June 4th event, the debate would, nevertheless, continue.

61 He Bingsong, '*Yige weixiandi jueze*' (A dangerous choice) in *Zhengfa luntan*, (Tribune of Political Science and Law) no. 2, April 1990, pp. 69–75.

62 Charles Greer (ed.), *China, Facts and Figures Annual, 1992*, vol. 16 (Gulf Breeze, Florida: Academic International Press, 1992) p. 296. One regrets that the statistics for 1989 in the appendices of 1990 *Zhongguo falu nianjian* (China law yearbook) (Chengdu: Law Yearbook of China Press, 1990) p. 995 exclude without explanation the 1989 figures on the total arrests for counterrevolution.

63 'China Faced Sharp Rise in Crime during '88', *CD*, 24 January 1989, p. 1.

64 'Criminal Caseload Rises by 14 per cent', *CD*, 9 May 1989, p. 1.

65 Liang Huaren and Zhou Songsheng, '*Lun fangeminglei zuimingdi xiugai*' (On improving the categories of counterrevolutionary charges) *Zhengfa luntan*, no. 4, 1990, pp. 65, 68.

66 Liu Xingming, '*Lun dui dongluan he baoluanzhong fangeming shandongzuidi jueding*' (Focusing on the crime of inciting counter-revolution during the turmoil and rebellion) *Zhengfa luntan*, no. 1, 1990, p. 9.

67 Ibid., p. 11.

68 *Renmin ribao* (Overseas) 16 June 1989.

69 For example, see *Renmin ribao* (Overseas) 28 January 1991.

70 *BR*, no. 5, 4–10 February 1991, p. 27.

71 Ibid., p. 26.

72 *Globe and Mail*, Toronto, 13 February 1991, p. A9.

73 See Wang Yong, '*Dui woguo xingfaxue yanjiudi fansi*' (Reflections on Chinese criminal law research) *Zhongguo shehui kexue*, no. 3, 1988, p. 174.

74 For an informative discussion of the tension between procedure and the Party's mass line politics in this campaign see Lin Zhiqiu, 'The Criminal Justice System, the Party and Economic Reform", in his unpublished MA thesis, 'Politics and the "Autonomy" of the Chinese Criminal Justice System, 1978–88', University of Calgary, March 1989, pp. 86–115.

75 Gao Xijing, '*Guanyu xiugai xingfa zhidao sixiang fangmiandi jige wenti*'(On problems concerning the guiding thoughts of the revision of criminal law') *Faxue pinglun*, no. 1, 1989, pp. 1–3.

76 Luo Hua, '*Guanyu xiugai he wanshan woguo xingfadi ruogan shexiang*' (Tentative ideas about revising and improving China's Criminal Law) *Faxue pinglun*, no. 1, 1988, pp. 4–10.

77 See Sun Qian and He Yong, '*Faren fanzui zhiyi*' (Some doubt on crime by legal persons) *Xibei zhengfa xuebao* (Journal of the Northwestern University of Politics and Law) no. 3, 1987.

78 *Guangdongsheng gaoji renmin fayuan yanjiushi* (Research office of the Guangdong Higher People's Court), '*Guanyu xiugai xingfadi jidian jianyi*' (Recommendations on revision to the criminal law) *Guangdong faxue* (Guangdong Study of Law) no. 2, 1989, pp. 32–5.
79 Li Li and Li Shaoping agreed with Luo on this. See their article, '*Shenhua gaige yu xingfa xiugai*', (Deepen the reform and revision of the criminal law) *Xiandai faxue*, no. 5, October 1989, pp. 9–14.
80 Luo Hua, '*Guanyu xiugai he wanshan woguo xingfadi ruogan shexiang*' (Tentative ideas about revising and improving China's Criminal Law) *Faxue pinglun*, no. 1, 1988, pp. 4–10.
81 Gao Mingxuan, '*Luetan xingfa xiugaidi zhidao sixiang*' (Brief summary of the guiding thought on criminal law revision) *Faxue* (Law science, Shanghai) no. 3, pp. 14–15.
82 Gao Mingxuan, Zhao Bingzhi, '*1988 nian xingfaxue yanjiu jinzhan gailan*' (A brief sketch of the development of criminal law research) *Zhengfa luntan*, no. 3, 1989, in *Faxue*, no. 8, 1989, pp. 69–76.
83 Ibid., p. 70.
84 Huang Taiyun, '*Lun wanshan xingshi lifadi xingshi wenti*' (On problems in improving the forms of Chinese criminal legislation) *Falu xuexi yu yanjiu* (Legal Studies and Research) no. 2, 1989, pp. 21–5.
85 Zhao Guoqiang et al., '*Shilun jingjifa yu xingfadi xietiao* (Preliminary discussion of the coordination between economic and criminal law) *Faxue pinglun*, vol. 30, no. 4, Oct. 1986, pp. 13–17.
86 Gao Mingxuan, Zhao Bingzhi, '*1988 nian xingfaxue yanjiu jinzhan gailan*' (A brief sketch of the the development of criminal law research) op. cit., p. 76.
87 *CD*, 25 December 1987, p. 3.
88 'Foreigners Blamed', *Hong Kong AFP*, 26 June 1991, FBIS-CHI-91-124, 27 June 1991, p. 28.
89 Ibid., p. 29.
90 Cao Zidan, Bai Shanyun, '*Wanshan jin dulifa yunyong falu wuqi chengzhi*' (Perfecting the legislation on the banning of drugs as a legal weapon against narcotics crimes) *Zhengfa luntan*, no. 6, 1990, pp. 25–6.
91 Gao Mingxuan, Zhao Bingzhi and Li Xihui, '*Lun dupin fanzuidi zuiming yu xingfa shiyong*' (On the charge of narcotics crime and its penalty applications) *Zhongguo faxue*, no. 3, 1992, pp. 72–9.
92 '*Quanguo renmin daibiao dahui changwu weiyuanhui guanyu jindudi jueding*' (NPCSC Decision on the banning of drugs) in NPC Interior and Justice Committee, *Funu he weichengnianren falu baohu quanshu* (Compendium of laws protecting women and minors) (Zhongguo jincha chubanfaxing, 1991) pp. 18–19. English text in 'NPC Issues Decision on Banning Narcotics, FBIS-CHI-90-251, 31 December 1990, pp. 27–31.
93 'Song Rufen on Draft Law Revisions', *Xin Hua*, 27 December 1990, FBIS-CHI-90-250, 28 December 1990, p. 18.
94 'Fake Medicines', *CD*, 12 July 1985, p. 4.
95 'Medicine Controls Introduced in New Law', *CD*, 13 June 1985, p. 1.
96 See, for example, 'Causes of corruption analyzed', *CD*, 22 June 1988, p. 2.
97 'Cadres Get Life in Jail for Bribery', *CD*, 21 December 1985, p. 3.

98 Again this was a question of the relative weight given to *de*, virtue, and its external manifestation of *li* in relation to human nature. For example, see Xiao Bofu's discussion of Confucian theory on the origins of, and solution to criminal behaviour, '*Luelun Kongzi guanyu yufang fanzuidi falu sixiang*' (Brief introduction to Confucian legal thought on the prevention of crime) *Faxue pinglun*, no. 2, 1986, pp. 22–4.

99 For example, see Luo Hua, '*Guanyu xiugai de wanshan woguo xingfadi ruogan sixiang* (Tentative ideas about revising and improving China's criminal law) *Faxue pinglun*, no. 1, 1988, p. 8; Huang Taiyun, '*Lun wanshan xingshi lifadi xingshi wenti*' (On problems in improving the forms of Chinese criminal legislation) *Falu xuexi yu yanjiu* (Legal Studies and Research) no. 2, 1989, p. 88.

7 Hong Kong and the Rule of Law across 'Two Systems'

1 Philip W. Baker and Berry Fong-Chung Hsu, 'Common Law under Socialist Legal System: The Future of Hong Kong', *China Law Reporter*, vol. vii,, no. 1, 1991, p. 2.

2 Ibid., pp. 6–7.

3 Raymond Wacks, 'The Judicial Function', in Wacks (ed.), *The Future of Law in Hong Kong*. Hong Kong: Oxford University Press, 1989, p. 144.

4 Li Lingyan, while noting precedent was not a major source of law as in the British-American experience, in ancient China, precedent, nonetheless, had a special role in that it not only helped clarify the laws but also 'supplemented, revised and [even] replaced laws'. Li Liangyan, '*Xifangdi liangda faxi guojia he gudai Zhongguo zai panli wenti shangdi bijiao yanjiu*' (Comparative study of precedent in the countries of the two Western legal systems and in ancient China) *Shehui kexue*, no. 5, 1987, pp. 46–8.

5 The question of a newly emerging practical regime of provincial as distinct from central legislative power is explored in Lin Sen's unpublished PhD thesis, 'China's Decentralization and Provincial Economic Legislation, 1980–1989', University of Calgary, March 1993, pp. 129–39.

6 For example see Lu Deshan, '"*Yiguo liangzhi" dui zhuantong lilun faxuedi fazhan*'('One country, two systems' in relation to the development of classical theoretical legal studies) *Xibei zhengfa xueyuan xuebao* (Journal of the Northwest Academy of Politics and Law) No. 4, 1987, pp. 15–19.

7 Li Jiaquan, Yao Yiping, '*Shi lun "yige guojia, liangzhong zhidu"*' (Preliminary remarks on 'one country, two systems') *Makesizhuyi yanjiu* (Marxist Studies) no. 3, 1985, p. 54.

8 Liu Shiguo, '*Lun "yiguo liangzhi" qingkuangxia fadi jiejixing*' (On the class nature of law under 'one country, two systems') *Faxue* (Shanghai) no. 10, 1987, pp. 37–40.

9 Zhang Guangbo, '"*Yiguo liangzhi" tichudi yige falu wenti*' ('One country, two systems' poses a question in legal theory) *Faxue pinglun*, no. 4, 1988, p. 5.

10 For example see Weng Qiyin, '*Lun "yiguo liangfa" yu quji falu chongtu*' (On 'one country, two laws' and inter-regional legal conflict) *Faxue*

(Shanghai) no. 12, 1990, pp. 11–14. Yi Jun also refers to *fayu*, 'legal territories' in '*"Yiguo liangzhi" yu Zhongguo quji sifa*' ('One Country, Two Systems' and China's inter-regional private law) *Anhui daxue xuebao* (Journal of Anhui University) no. 1, 1989, pp. 45–50.

11 China, Consultative Committee for the Basic Law of the Hong Kong Special Administrative Region of the People's Republic of China, *The Draft Basic Law of the Hong Kong Special Administrative Region of the People's Republic of China (For Solicitation of Opinions): Consultation Report*, vol. 2, October 1988, pp. 38–43. Hereinafter cited as *Consultation Report* 2.

12 For a more detailed account of these differences see Special Group on the Relationship between the Central Government and the HKSAR, Executive Committee of the Consultative Committee of the Basic Law, *Final Report on Powers of Interpretation and Amendment of the Basic Law*, 14 March, 1987, pp. 2–7.

13 Hong Kong. *Official Proceedings of the Legislative Council* (hereinafter cited as *OPLC*) 4 April 1990, p. 1210.

14 International Commission of Jurists, *Countdown to 1997* (Geneva, 1992) p. 84.

15 Ji Pengfei, '*Zai jinian "Zhonghua renmin gongheguo Xianggang tebie xingzhengchu jibenfa" banbu liangnian zuo tanhuishangdi jianghua*' (Speech commemorating the second anniversary of the promulgation of the Basic Law of the Hong Kong Special Administrative Region) (Hong Kong: Sanlian shudian, 1992) p. 2.

16 See Sun She, '*"Zhonghua renmin gongheguo Xianggang tebie xingzhengqu jibenfa" zai woguo falu tixizhongdi diwei*' (Preliminary discussion of the status of the 'PRC's Basic Law of the Hong Kong Special Administrative Region' within China's legal system) *Jiangsu shehui kexue* (Jiangsu Social Sciences) no. 4, 1991, pp. 46–50, and Xie Huaibin, '*Lun zai Xianggang tebie xingzhengqu shixingdi falu*'(On the law to put into effect the Hong Kong Special Administrative Region), *Faxue pinglun*, vol. 27, no. 1, 1988, pp. 20–7.

17 Liu Nanping, '*Jiejian Meiguozhou xianfa jiejue Xianggang jibenfadi liangda nantizhi tantao*' (Exploring the solution to two major problems of the Hong Kong basic Law by drawing on the experience of the American constitution) *Faxue pinglun*, no. 4, 1987, p. 2.

18 'Judicial Officials Attend Basic Law Forum', *Liaowang*, Overseas Edition, Hong Kong, no. 40, 2 Oct. 89, pp. 6–7, FBIS-CHI–89-198, 16 Oct. 89, p. 71. The same argument had already been cited in the Hong Kong consultative process. See 3.5.2, *Consultation Report 2*, p. 10.

19 Ibid., p. 9.

20 'China Rejects Rights Report "Interference"', *SCMP*, May 21, 1992, p. 2.

21 *Consultation Report 2*, pp. 7–8.

22 Xiao Weiyun, '*Lun yiguo liangzhixia zhongyang yu Xianggang tebie xingzhengqudi falu guanxi*' (On the legal relationship between the Centre and the HKSAR under one country, two systems) *Beijing daxue xuebao* (Journal of Beijing University) no. 4, 1991, pp. 18–26, in *Faxue*, no. 10, 1991, p. 38.

23 Albert Chen, 'The Relationship Between the Central Government and the SAR' in Peter Wesley-Smith and Albert Chen (eds.) *The Basic Law and Hong Kong's Future* (Hong Kong: Butterworths, 1988) p. 115.

24 Ibid., p. 111.
25 Ibid., p. 112.
26 *Consultation Report* 2, Oct.1988, p. 26.
27 Xiao Weiyun, '*Lun yiguo liangzhixia zhongyang yu Xianggang tebei xingzhengqudi falu guanxi*' (On legal relations between the Centre and Hong Kong SAR under 'one country, two systems') *Beijing daxue xuebao*, no. 4, 1991, pp. 18–26, in *Faxue*, no. 10, 1991, p. 38.
28 China, *Zhonghua renmin gongheguo Xianggang tebie xingzhengqu jibenfa* (The Basic Law of the Hong Kong Special Administrative Region of the People's Republic of China) (Beijing: Falu chubanshe, 1990) p. 87, in English and Chinese. Hereinafter cited as *BL*.
29 *Consultation Report* 2, p. 11.
30 *BL*, p. 93.
31 *BL*, p. 125.
32 *OPLC*, 4 December 1991, p. 1010.
33 *BL*, p. 125.
34 *OPLC*, 4 December, 1991, pp. 930, 991–2.
35 Ibid., p. 951.
36 Ibid., p. 993.
37 *BL*, p. 94.
38 *Countdown to 1997*, p. 81. Author's italics.
39 *Consultation Report* 2, p. 42.
40 *OPLC*, 4 April 1990, pp. 1198–99.
41 This article clearly states that the Chief Executive 'represents' the SAR, but it is not inclusive of explanation as to the notion of dual accountability. *BL*, pp. 104–5.
42 *BL*, p. 156.
43 Guo Zu, 'Why Those Who Study Law Act Against the Law...', *Renmin ribao*, 23 Oct. 1989, p. 4, FBIS-CHI-89-219, 15 Nov. 1989, p. 26. For Articles 35 and 51 see *The Constitution of the People's Republic of China*, 4 December 1982 (Beijing: Foreign Languages Press, 1983) pp. 32, 39.
44 *SCMP*, 28 Sep. 89, p. 1, FBIS-CHI-89-187, 28 Sep. 89, p. 89.
45 *OPLC*, 5 June 1991, p. 2327.
46 *OPLC*, 4 April 1990, pp. 1197–8.
47 'Non-interference Stressed', *SCMP*, 12 Oct. 89, p. 5, FBIS-CHI-198, 16 Oct. 1989, p. 72; 'Legislators Criticize Warning', *SCMP*, 16 Oct. 89, p. 1, FBIS-CHI-89-200, 18 Oct. 1989, p. 58.
48 'Legislators Criticize Warning', *SCMP*, 16 Oct.1989, p. 1.
49 'Basic Law Draft to Include Subversion Clause', *Hong Kong Standard*, 12 Dec. 89, pp. 1, 4, FBIS-CHI-89-237, 12 Dec. 89, p. 55.
50 China, *The Criminal Law and the Criminal Law of Procedure Law of the People's Republic of China* (Beijing: Foreign Languages Press, 1984) pp. 35, 39.
51 'Exile Chinese Dissident Group Opens Office', *Hong Kong AFP*, 18 Sept. 91, FBIS,-CHI-91-181, 18 Sept. 1991, p. 72.
52 Stanley Leung and Ma Miu-wah in Guangzhou, *Hong Kong Standard*, 13 Dec. 89, pp. 1, 3, in FBIS-CHI-98-241, 18 Dec. 1989.
53 *BL*, p. 93.
54 *Countdown to 1997*, pp. 93–4.

55 Mr. Tam as a participating drafter of Chapter Three stated this point in the Legislative Council's debate on the draft Bill of Rights Ordinance. He favoured an emphasis on the monitoring of and carrying out of Chapter Three, and he voted against the proposed ordinance as 'legally unnecessary and untimely'. *OPLC*, 27 June 1990, pp. 1798, 1800.

56 'Law Drafters Question Rights Bill's Supremacy', *SCMP*, 12 Dec. 89, pp. 1, 5 in FBIS-CHI-89-248, 28 Dec. 1989, pp. 59–60. While this suggests considerable reservation as to the question of entrenchment, Mr. Justice Li indicated to the author in an interview of 5 May 1992 that he could see considerable agreement between the human rights content of the Basic Law and that of Hong Kong's new Bill of Rights Ordinance.

57 *OPLC*, 27 June 1990, p. 1768.

58 *OPLC*, 27 June 1990, p. 1802.

59 *Countdown to 1997*, p. 101.

60 *OPLC*, 27 June 1990, p. 1789.

61 China, Special Group on Inhabitants' and Other Persons' Rights, Freedom, Welfare and Duties, Consultative Committee for the Basic Law, *Final report on Fundamental Rights and Duties of Hong Kong Inhabitants* (Part I) 12 June 1987, p. 5.

62 *OPLC*, 5 June 1991, p. 2338.

63 See Legal Supplement No. 2 to the *Hong Kong Government Gazette*, No. 23, 7 June 1991, B872–73.

64 *The Constitution of the People's Republic of China*, op. cit., p. 39.

65 Gong Xiangrui, 'Constitutional Protection of Human Rights: the Chinese View Under the Notion of "One Country, Two Systems"', Hong Kong's Bill of Rights Conference, 20–22 June 1991, Faculty of Law, University of Hong Kong, pp. 5–6.

66 Ibid., p. 9.

67 *Countdown to 1997*, p. 96.

68 Lau Siu-kai, *Society and Politics in Hong Kong* (Hong Kong: The Chinese University Press, 1984) p. 35.

69 OMELCO Standing Panel on Constitutional Affairs, *First Report, The 1987 Review of the Further Development of Representative Government*, p. 19.

70 See, for example, Joseph Cheng's comments on this attitude in his edited volume, *Hong Kong in Transition* (Hong Kong: Oxford University Press, 1986) pp. 10–11.

71 *Countdown to 1997*, p. 37.

72 *OPLC*, 4 December 1991, p. 960.

73 *OPLC*, 4 December 1991, p. 1002.

74 There is a tendency to describe only the government in terms of allegedly specious quiet diplomacy which makes concessions to China or 'mutes confrontations with China' whereas there is support for a 'sinological approach' within the Legislative Council and within the community. See, for example, the entry on Hong Kong in *Human Rights Watch: World Report* (New York, Dec., 1991) p. 402. This approach is assumed in *Countdown to 1997*. In fact, the Chairman of the ICJ Executive Committee, Mr Justice Michael Kirby, described the British record in decolonisation of Hong Kong Kong as 'shabby in the extreme' and he regarded the UK's position as 'pusillanimous'. 'UN Focus on Rights Criticism' SCMP, 13 May, 1992.

75 At least this was how the issue was represented by the Secretary of Constitutional Affairs, Michael Sze, whose critics accused him of having gotten 'the wrong end of the stick'. *OPLC*, 4 December 1991, p. 965.

76 For his description of this attitude see *OPLC*, 28 February 1990, p. 879.

77 See Lau Siu-kai, *Society and Politics in Hong Kong* (Hong Kong; Chinese University Press) p. 72. Albert Yee relates this to the 'Chinese stepping stone syndrome', in *A People Misruled* (Hong Kong: API Press, 1989) p. 155.

78 Lau Siu-kai and Kuan Hsin-chi, *The Ethos of the Hong Kong Chinese* (Hong Kong: Chinese University Press, 1988) p. 143.

79 Lau Siu-kai, 'Public Attitude toward Political Parties in Hong Kong', Occasional Paper No. 11, Hong Kong Institute of Asia-Pacific Studies, Chinese University of Hong Kong, March 1992, passim.

80 See Liang Yu-ying, 'Controversy over Hong Kong's Democratic Reform', *Issues and and Studies*, December, 1992, pp. 112–15. Patten's proposals are in his policy address of 7 October 1992. See 'Text of Governor's Televised Policy Address', FBIS-CHI-92-106, 8 October 1992, pp. 27–42.

81 *OPLC*, 27 June 1990, p. 1826. See the Mainland historiographical debate on this concept as discussed in Chapter 2, fn. 14.

82 *OPLC*, 27 June 1990, p. 1783.

83 *OPLC*, 27 June 1990, p. 1803.

84 *OPLC*, 27 June 1990, p. 1823.

85 See Ann Wan Wynen Thomas and A.J. Thomas, Jr., for a gloss on Jennings in *A World Rule of Law* (Dallas: SMU Press, 1975) p. 4.

8 Conclusion: Before and After Tiananmen Square

1 The Declaration was cited in Hong Kong political debate over the propriety of functional representation in Hong Kong's future political process. See 'No Misunderstanding on Bicameral Model', *SCMP*, 23 October 1989, p. 8.

2 Arthur Rosenbaum (ed.), *State and Society in China: The Consequences of Reform* (Boulder: Westview Press, 1992) p. 3.

3 US Senate Committee on Foreign Relations & US House of Representatives Committee on Foreign Affairs, *Country Reports on Human Practices for 1990* (Washington, DC: GPO, 1991) p. 849.

4 Carlos Lo, 'Deng Xiaoping's Ideas on Law', *Asian Survey*, vol. XXXII, no. 7, July 1992, p. 662.

5 For example, in Charles Humana's 1991 rating of 104 states the PRC was given the fourth worst rating. Only Burma, Iraq and Sudan had worse ratings. See Charles Humana (ed.), *World Human Rights Guide* (New York & Oxford: Oxford University Press 1992) pp. 72–5. Also, the PRC received the worst possible rating from the Freedom House Survey Team in *Freedom in the World, Political Rights and Civil Liberties 1989–1990* (New York: Freedom House, 1990) pp. 71–4.

6 Baum's critique notes the failure of this thesis to anticipate the attenuation of Leninist centralised political control, internal challenge to the social relevance of Marxism–Leninism and the spread of free markets within socialist economies. See Richard Baum, 'Communism, Convergence, and

China's Political Convulsion', in Richard Baum (ed.), *Reform and Reaction in Post-Mao China* (New York & London: Routledge, 1991) pp. 184–5.

7 An extract of the July 26th editorial as translated in 'Lessons Learned, Future Prospects', *CD*, 29 July 1989, p. 4.

8 Peng Zhen, 'Report on the Draft of the Revised Constitution of the People's Republic of China', in *Fifth Session of the Fifth National People's Congress* (Beijing: Foreign Languages Press, 1983) p. 80.

9 Guo Zu, 'Why those who Study Law Act against the Law – Meditation by Teachers and Students of the China Politics and Law University', *Renmin ribao*, 23 October 1989, p. 4 in FBIS-CHI-89-219, 15 November 1989, pp. 26–31.

10 Fang Li, 'How Should We Ensure that Democracy and the Building of the Legal System Develop Healthily along the Orientation and Track of Socialism', *Jiefangjun bao*, 9 November 1989, FBIS-CHI-89-233, 6 December 1989, p. 2.

11 'Jiang Urges More Legal Learning', *CD*, 8 January 1990, p. 1.

12 'Disseminating the Law among Citizens', *BR*, no. 31, 30 July–August 5 1990, p. 20.

13 'Deng Liqun Pessimistic on "Peaceful Evolution"', *SCMP*, 14 December 1991, p. 13 in FBIS-CHI-91-241, 16 December 1991, p. 33.

14 Chen Chunlong, '*Fazhi yu guojia wending*', (Rule of law and stability of country) *Faxue yanjiu*, no. 2, 1992, pp. 6–10.

15 '*"Jiaqiang fazhi cujin shehui jingji fazhan" – fazhi yu shehui jingji fazhan guoji xueshu taolunhui zongshu*' ('Strengthen legality, promote social and economic development' – summary of the international symposium on the rule of law and social and economic development) *Faxue yanjiu*, no. 1992, pp. 85–6.

16 Gorbachev made these remarks in a speech at Stanford University. '"Anarchy" in Russia Explained', *SCMP*, 14 May 1992, p. 14.

17 Li Long, '*Fazhi moshi lun*' (On models of the rule of law) *Zhongguo faxue*, no. 6, 1991, pp. 29–35.

18 In 1990, the reported incidence of crime, *fa'an lu*, stood at 2 per 1000, whereas the 'crime rate', *fanzui lu*, stood at 0.6 per 1000. State Council, *Human Rights in China* (Beijing: Information Office, State Council, Nov. 1991) p. 42.

19 Lawrence Friedman and Stewart Macaulay, *Law and the Behaviour Sciences* (New York: Bobbs-Merrill 1969, pp. 1003–4. On Jennings see Chapter 7, n. 85.

20 'Dictator Pinochet's future dominant issue in Chile', *Calgary Herald*, 17 October 1989, p. A9.

21 Weber, Max (ed. with introduction by Max Rheinstein), *On Law in Society and Economy* (Cambridge, Mass: Harvard University Press, 1966) pp. 67, 198. For brief comment see Lin Zhiqiu, 'Politics and the "Autonomy" of the Chinese Criminal Justice System, 1978–88', unpublished MA thesis, University of Calgary, April 1989.

22 'Deng Xiaoping unhurt in minor traffic accident', *SCMP*, 6 April 1991, p. 1.

23 Cai Ximei, "Lee Kuan Yew Talks about China's Economic Reform and Assimilation of Eastern and Western Cultures', *Liaowang* (Overseas) no. 36, 7 September 1992, pp. 3–5, in FBIS-CHI-191-, 1 October 1992, p. 19.

24 See Chapter 1, note 44.

25 Extracted from the '*Lunyu*' (Analects) in *Sishu* (Four Books) (Macao: Juwendang, 1962), Book III, p. 168.

26 Liang Qichao, *History of Chinese Political Thought during the early Tsin Period* (New York: AMS Press, 1969, reprint of 1930 edition) p. 137.

Select Glossary of Chinese Political/Legal Terms

accordance with time; accordance with place	*yinshi zhiyi; yindi zhiyi* 因时制宜 因地制宜
act according to law	*yifa banshi* 依法办事
administrative legal person	*xingzheng faren* 行政法人
analogy	*leitui* 类推
citizen's fundamental rights	*gongmin jiben quanli* 公民基本权利
collective economic organisation	*jiti jingji zuzhi* 集体经济组织
collective of the entire peasantry; collective of the working masses	*quanti nongmin jiti; laodong qunzhong jiti* 全体农民集体 劳动群众集体
collective owned enterprise	*jiti suoyouzhi qiye* 集体所有制企业
collective rights	*jiti quanli* 集体权利
combining all types of law into one	*zhufa heti* 诸法合体
combining rights as fundamental with society as fundamental	*quanli benwei yu shehui benweidi jiehe* 权利本位与 社会本位的结合
combining ritual and law	*lifa jiehe* 礼法结合

combining severe punishment with leniency	*chengban he kuanda xiang jiehe*	惩办和宽大相结合
compensation for the use of land as a commodity principle	*youchang zhuanrangdi yuanze*	有偿转让的原则
comprehensive management of public order	*shehui zhi an zonghe zhili*	社会治安综合治理
conflict principle	*chongtu yuanze*	冲突原则
counterrevolutionary crime	*fangeming zui*	反革命罪
credits turned into crimes; crimes turned into credits	*yougong bian youzui; youzui bian yougong*	有功变有罪 有罪变有功
crime endangering state security	*guoshizui; weihai guojia anquan zui*	国事罪 危害国家安全罪
cultivating oneself in order to obey heaven	*xiuji shuntian*	修己顺天
democratisation	*minzhuzhiduhua*	民主制度化
deterrent force	*weishe li*	威慑力
direct intention; indirect intention	*zhijie guyi; jianjie guyi*	直接故意 间接故意
dividing and breaking up criminals [strategy]	*fenhua wajie fangzui fenzi*	分化瓦解犯罪分子
division of labour with individual responsibilities and mutual interaction	*fen gong fuze huxiang zhiyue*	分工负责 相互制约

dual unity [of clan and state law] — *eryuan*
二元

economic rule of law system engineering — *jingji fazhi xitong gongcheng*
经济法制系统工程

elite politics — *jing ying zhengzhi*
精英政治

embezzlement — *tanwuzui*
贪污罪

equality before the law — *falu mianqian renren pingdeng*
法律面前人人平等

ethics are primary, criminal punishment secondary — *dezhu, xingfu*
德主刑辅

even an upright official finds it hard to settle a family quarrel — *qing guan nanduan jia wushi*
清官难断家务事

execute one to warn one hundred — *sha yi jing bai*
杀一儆百

feudal autocratic rule of man — *fengjian zhuanzhizhuyidi renzhi*
封建专治主义的人治

flexibility — *linghuoxing*
灵活性

follow heaven's course — *shun tian zeshi*
顺天择时

four [legal] territories, one country — *siyu, yiguo*
四域一国

functions of law; functions of man — *fadi zuoyong; rendi zuoyong*
法的作用 人的作用

general enemies: immediate enemies — *pubian yuantou: zhijie yuantou*
普遍冤头 直接冤头

good people do not bring suits and those who bring suits are not good — *haoren bu da guansi, da guansi bushi haoren*
好人不打官司
打官司不是好人

good person politics	*xianren zhengzhi* 贤人政治
group rights	*qunti quanli* 群体权利
growing original narcotics plants	*zhongzhi dupin yuan zhiwu* 种植毒品源植物
interest groups	*liyi qunti* 利益群体
handle all the affairs of state according to law	*yi ben yu fa* 一本于法
human entitlements; actual rights; legal rights	*yingyou quanli; shiyou quanli; fading quanli* 应有权利 实有权利 法定权利
human rights; natural rights	*renquanli; tianfu renquan* 人权利 天赋人权
human rights are without state boundaries	*renquan wu guo jie* 人权无国界
human rights diplomacy	*renquan waijiao* 人权外交
interest structure	*liyi jiegou* 利益结构
judicial independence (Montesquieu) judicial independence (PRC)	*sifaduli* *shenpan duli* 司法独立 审判独立
judiciary and administration are inseparable	*sifa yu xingzheng bufen* 司法与行政不分
law comes from the sovereign	*fa zi jun chu* 法自君出
law is better than no law, faster [law-making] is better than slower	*you bi meiyou hao, gao kuai bi gao man hao* 有比没有好 搞快 比搞慢好

law respects rank and status	*fa you dengcha*	法有等差
legal consciousness	*falu yishi*	法律意识
legal culture	*fa wenhua*	法文化
legal illiteracy	*famang*	法盲
legal nihilism	*falu xuwuzhuyi*	法律虚无主义
legal person	*faren*	法人
legal psychology	*falu sixiang*	法律思想
legal regulations	*fagui*	法规
legal system; rule of law	*fazhi; fazhi*	法制 法治
legalisation	*faluhua*	法律化
less killing policy	*shaosha zhengce*	少杀政策
little compassion opposes great compassion	*xiaorenzhe daren zhi zei*	小仁者大仁之贼
mass society; citizen society	*qunzhong shehui; gongmin shehui*	群众社会 公民社会
meritorious service	*ligong biaoxian*	立功表现
mild criminal law	*huanhedi xingfa*	缓和的刑法

mini-constitution	*xiao xianfa*	小宪法
mutual cooperation and restriction	*xianghu hezuo xianghu zhiyue*	相互合作 相互制约
natural persons	*ziran ren*	自然人
no crime without a law	*fa wumingwen buwei zui*	法无明文不为罪
object	*keti*	客体
obligation fundamentalism	*yiwubenweizhuyi*	义务本位主义
officials bartering position for leniency	*guandang*	官档
one centre, two basic points	*yige zhongxin, liangge jiben dian*	一个中心 两个基本点
one country, two systems, three laws	*yi guo, liangzhi, san fa*	一国 两制 三法
open door policy	*kaifang zhengce*	开放政策
ordinance	*fa'an*	法案
organic naturalism	*you ji ziranzhuyi*	有机自然主义
organising and leading counter-revolutionary groups	*zuzhi lingdao fangeming jituan*	组织领导反革命集团
organising others for prostitution; assisting in organising others for prostitution	*zuzhi taren maiyin;* *xiezhu zuzhi taren maiyin*	组织他人卖淫 协助组织他人卖淫
other's right to ownership of things	*tawuquan*	它物权

ownership of the enterprise legal person	*qiye faren suoyouquan* 企业法人所有权
peaceful evolution	*heping yanbian* 和平演变
plan is law	*jihua jiushi falu* 计划就是法律
policy is the soul of law	*zhengce shi faludi linghun* 政策是法律的灵魂
political re-structuring	*zhengzhi tizhi gaige* 政治体制改革
positive theory; negative theory	*kendingshuo; foudingshuo* 肯定说 否定说
preceding legislation; overdue legislation	*chaojian lifa;* *lifa zhihou* 超前立法 立法滞后
presumption of innocence; presumption of guilt	*wuzui tuiding;* *youzui tuiding* 无罪推定 有罪推定
public corporation	*gongfa ren* 公法人
public surveillance	*guanzhi* 管制
punishment fits the crime	*zuixing yizhi* 罪刑一致
purpose [of counterrevolution]	*mudi* 目的
red hat [phenomenon]	*hong maozi* 红帽子
relative ownership	*xiangdui suoyouquan* 相对所有权
respect for law	*zunzhong fa* 尊重法

rights and interests	*quanyi* 权益
right of subsistence	*shengcun quan* 生存权
right over things	*wuquan* 物权
right to contract out operations	*chengbao jingyingquan* 承包经营权
right to independent control over state property; state's right of sole possession	*zhipeiquan; duzhanquan* 支配权 独占权
ringleaders	*shouyao fenzi* 首要分子
ritual does not apply to the commoner, and law does not apply to the noble	*li buxia shuren, xing bushang daifu* 礼不下庶人 刑不上大夫
rule-by-law state	*yifa zhi guo* 以法治国
rule of law; legal system	*fazhi; fazhi* 法治 法制
rule of law-ism	*fazhi zhuyi* 法治主义
rule of man; rule-of-man-ism	*renzhi; renzhizhuyi* 人治 人治主义
rule of virtue	*dezhi* 德治
ruling the country by criminal punishment	*yixing zhi guo* 以刑治国
sedition	*shandong panluan* 煽动叛乱
separate criminal laws	*danxing xingshi falu* 单行刑事法律

separation of functions and mutual restriction	*fenquan yu zhiyue* 分权与制约
separation of powers	*sanquan fenli* 三权分立
separation of state administration and enterprise	*zhengqi fenkai* 政企分开
similar crime	*xiangsizui* 相似罪
socialist market economy	*shehuizhuyi shichang jingji* 社会主义市场经济
socialist spiritual civilisation	*shehuizhuyi jingshen wenming* 社会主义精神文明
speaking out freely, airing views fully, holding great debates and writing big-character posters	*sida* 四大
strongly emphasising criminal law, lightly emphasising civil law	*zhongxing, qingmin* 重刑轻民
substituting party discipline for the laws of the state	*yi dangji daiti guo fa* 以党纪代替国法
substituting [the leader's words] for the law	*yiyan daifa* 以言代法
subversion	*dianfu* 颠覆
system of legal relations	*falu guanxi tixi* 法律关系体系
take the clan as the basis	*jiazu benwei* 家族本位
taking law as education	*yifa wei jiao* 以法为教
taking policy as substitute for law	*yi zhengce daiti falu* 以政策代替法律

theory of combining rule of law and rule of man
fazhi renzhi jiehe lun
法治人治结合论

theory of ownership by legal person
faren suoyouquan shuo
法人所有权说

theory of product economy
chanpin jingji lun
产品经济论

transforming function
gaizao gongneng
改造功能

unity of law
falu tongyi
法律统一

unity of delegation of responsibility [public] supervision and review
shouquan weituo yu jiandushencha tongyi
授权委托与
监督审查统一

unity of rights and obligations
quanli yiwu yizhixing; quanli yiwu xiang tongyi
权利义务一致性
权利义务相统一

use virtue and law together
dexing bing yong
德刑并用

value virtue, devalue law
gui de, jian xing
贵德贱刑

whole people grasping the law
quan min zhi fa
全民执法

will subordination relations
yizhifucong guanxi
意志服从关系

workstyle
gongzuo zuofeng
工作作风

Select English–Chinese Bibliography

CHINESE REFERENCE BOOKS

Dong Yunhu and Liu Wuping (eds), *Shijie renquan yuefa zonglan* (World documents of human rights) (Chengdu: Sichuan renmin chubanshe, 1991).

Faxue cidian bianji weiyuanhui (ed.), *Faxue cidian* (Law dictionary) (Shanghai cishu chubanshe, 1984).

Faxue jiaocai bianjianbu (ed.), *Zhonghua renmin gongheguo changyong falu daquan* (The complete compendium of PRC law in common use) (Beijing: Falu chubanshe, 1988).

Gao Mingxuan et al. (eds), *Zhongguo xingfa cidian* (Chinese criminal law dictionary). (Xuelin chubanshe, Shanghai, 1989).

Gonganbu faguiju, *Gongan fagui huibian* (Collection of public security regulations) (Beijing: Qunzhong chubanshe, 1988).

Guowuyuan fazhiju (ed.), *Zhonghua renmin gongheguo xin fagui huibian 1991* (New laws and regulations of the PRC, 1991) vol. 3 (Beijing: Zhongguo fazhi chubanshe, 1991).

Jiang Ping et al. (eds), *Xiandai shiyong minfa cidian* (Contemporary dictionary of practical civil law) (Beijing: Beijing chubanshe, 1988).

Qiao Wei et al. (eds), *Xinbian faxue xidian* (Newly compiled legal studies dictionary) (Jinan: Shangdong renmin chubanshe, 1985).

Quanguo rendanei sifa weiyuanhui (ed.), *Funu he mochengnianren baohu quanshu* (The complete volume on the legal protection of women and minors) (Beijing: Zhongguo jiancha chubanshe, 1991).

Sun Guanghua (ed.), *Shiyong falu cidian* (Practical legal dictionary) (Taiyuan: Shuhai chubanshe, 1989).

Xianfa cidian bianjizu, *Xianfa cidian* (Constitutional law dictionary) (Changchun: Jilin renmin chubanshe, 1988).

Zhongguo falu nianjian she, *Zhongguo falu nianjian 1990* (Law Yearbook of China, 1990) (Chengdu, Nov. 1990).

Zou Yu and Gu Ming (general eds), *Faxue da cidian* (Great dictionary of legal learning) (Beijing: Zhongguo chengfa daxue chubanshe, 1991).

CHINESE LAW AND POLITICS JOURNAL

Note: Only the titles of journals are cited herein. Detail regarding specifically cited articles are given in full in the chapter notes. This listing is representative of the new generation of law journals, but it is not exhaustive. Please note the invaluable compendiums of extracted materials, provided by the Materials Centre of People's University under the general title, *Fuyin baokan ziliao*, (Duplicated materials from newspapers and journals). The following three compendiums are particularly useful to the study of contemporary law and politics: *Faxue* (Legal studies, to be distinguished from the Shanghai journal of the same name) *Jingjifa*, (Economic law) and *Zhongguo zhengzhi* (Chinese politics). These compendiums can be supplemented with reference to the compendium of national and provincial newspaper items in *Xin Hua yuebao* (New China monthly).

Beijing daxue xuebao (Journal of Beijing University)
Falu xuexi he yanjiu (Legal studies and research) Beijing
Falu yu shenghuo (Law and life) Beijing
Faxue jikan (Legal studies quarterly) Zhongjing
Faxue pinglun (Law review) Wuhan
Faxue yanjiu (Studies in law) Beijing
Faxue zazhi (Law magazine) Beijing
Fazhi jianshe (Law and order) Ministry of Justice, Beijing
Fazhi ribao (Law daily) Beijing
Hebei faxue (Hebei legal studies) Shijiazhuiang
Jingjixue zhoubao (Economic studies weekly) Beijing
Neimenggu daxue xuebao (Journal of the University of Inner Mongolia)
Qiushi (Seeking the truth) (formerly Hongqi, Red Flag) Beijing
Qunyan (Masses speak) Beijing
Shanxi daxuebao (Journal of Shanxi University)
Shehui kexue (Social sciences) Shanghai
Xinanshifan daxue xuebao (Journal of the Southwest Normal School)
Xibei zhengfa xueyuan xuebao (Journal of the Northwestern Academy of Politics and Law) Sian
Zhengfa luntan (Tribune of political science and law) (formerly *Zhongguo zhengfa daxue xuebao* (Journal of the China University of Politics and Law), Beijing
Zhongguo faxue (Chinese legal science) Beijing
Zhongguo shehui kexue (Chinese social sciences) Beijing

CHINESE BOOKS

Beijing daxue faluxuexi (ed.), *Gaige he fazhi jianshe – Beijing daxue jiushi zhounian xiaoning* (Reform and establishing the legal system – in celebration of the 90th school anniversary of Beijing University) (Beijing: Guangming ribao chubanshe, 1989).

Chen, Albert, *Xianggang fazhi yu jibenfa* (Hong Kong legal system and the Basic Law) (Hong Kong: Wide Angle Press, 1986).

Chen, Albert H.Y. and Johannes M.M. Chan, *Renquan yu fazhi* (Human rights and the rule of law) (Hong Kong: Wide Angle Press, 1987).

Chen Yuyuan, *Zhongguo fazhi shi* (A history of the Chinese legal system) (Beijing: Zhongguo shudian reprint of 1934 edition, 1988).

Faxuejiaocai bianjianbu (ed.), *Xianfa xue* (Constitutional studies) (Beijing: Qunzhong chubanshe, 1983).

Fazhan shehuizhuyi minzhu jian quan shehuizhuyi fazhi (Develop socialist democracy and establish socialist legality) (Beijing: falu chubanshe, 1988)

Gao Mingxuan (senior ed.), *Xingfaxue* (Criminal law science) (Beijing: falu chubanshe, 1981).

Gao Mingxuan, *Zhonghua renmin gongheguo xingfadi yunyu he dansheng* (The conception and birth of the criminal law of the People's Republic of China (Beijing: falu chubanshe, 1980).

Gong Xiangrui (ed.), *Xingzhengfa yu xingzheng gaosufa* (Administrative law and administrative procedural law) (Beijing: Falu chubanshe, 1989).

Gu Ming, *Jingjifa wenji* (Collected works on economic law) (Beijing: Qunzhong chubanshe, 1988).

Li Buyun, *Fazhi, minzhu, ziyou* (Legal system, democracy and freedom) (Chengdu: Sichuan renmin chubanshe, 1985).

Ma Jie, *Zhongguo shehui zhi'an zonghe zhili yanjiu* (The study of China's comprehensive management of public order) (Beijing: Falce chubanshe, 1990).

Mao Zedong, *Mao Zedong xuanji* (Selected works of Mao Zedong) vol. 2. (Beijing: Renmin chubanshe, 1969).

Peng Zhen, *Peng Zhen wenxuan, 1941–1990* (Selected works of Peng Zhen 1941–1990) (Beijing: Renmin chubanshe, 1991).

Quanguo dachangweihui bangongting yanjiushi (ed.), *Fazhan shehuizhuyi jian quan shehuizhuyi fazhi* (Developing socialist democracy and invigorating the socialist legal system) (Beijing: Falu chubanshe, 1988).

Shen Zongling, *Bijiaofa zonglun* (Outlines of comparative law) (Beijing: Beijing daxue chubanshe, 1987).

Wang Liming and Guo Mingrui, *Minfa xinlun* (New civil law theory) 2 vols (Beijing: Zhongguo zhengfa daxue chubanshe, 1988).

Wang Shuwen (general ed.), *Xianggang tebie xingzhengqu jibenfa daolun* (An overview of the Basic Law of the Hong Kong Special Administrative Region) (Beijing: Zhonggong zhongyang dangjiao chubanshe, 1990).

Wang Zhongfang, *Zhongguo shehui zh'an zonghe zhilidi lilun yu shijian* (Theory and practice of comprehensive management of public order in China) (Beijing: Qunzhong chubanshe, 1989).

Xiao Weiyun (general ed.), *Yiguo liangzhi yu Xianggang tebie xingzhengqu jibenfa* (One country, two systems and the Basic Law of the Hong Kong Special Administrative Region) (Hong Kong: Wenhua jaioyu chubanshe, 1990).

Xiao Weiyun and Wei Dingren, *Xianfaxue gailun* (Introduction to constitutional studies) (Beijing: Beijing daxue chubanshe, 1985).

Xu Chongde, *Zhongguo xianfaxue* (Studies in Chinese constitutional law) (Tianjin: Tianjin renmin chubanshe, 1986).

Yue Zong and Xing Zhi (eds), *Dui Deng Xiaoping yu lilun yanjiu huibian* (Collection on Deng Xiaoping and theoretical research) (Beijing: Zhonggong danshi ziliao chubanshe, 1988).

Zhang Guohua et al. (eds), *Zhongguo falu sixiangshi* (History of Chinese legal thought) (Beijing: Falu chubanshe, 1988).

Zhang Guohua (general ed.), *Zhongguo shehuizhuyi fazhi jianshedi lilun yu shijian* (Theory and practice in the establishment of China's socialist legal system) (Xiamin: Lujiang chubanshe, 1986).

Zhang Lansun and Liu Peng (eds), *Deng Xiaoping di sixiang lilun yanjiu* (Theoretical research of Deng Xiaoping thought) (Beijing: Zhongguo shuji chubanshe, 1988).

Zhang Xipo and Han Yanyu, *Zhongguo geming fazhi shi (1921–1949)* (China's revolutionary legal history) vol. 1 (Beijing: Zhongguo shehui kexue chubanshe, 1987).

Zhang Xin, *Zhongguo fazhizhi xianguang ji gaige* (Conditions and reform of China's legal system) (Singapore: Mingbao chubanshe, 1989).

Zhang Youyu, *Guanyu shehuizhuyi fazhidi ruogan wenti* (On the problems of the socialist legal system) (Beijing: falu chubanshe, 1982).

Zhongguo renmin gongheguo, *Zhonghua renmin gongheguo Xianggang tebie xingzhengqu jibenfa* (The basic law of the Hong Kong Administrative Region of the PRC) (Beijing: Falu chubanshe, 1990).

Zhonghua zhengfa daxue minfa jiao yanshi (ed.), *Zhonghua renmin gongheguo minfa tongze jianghua* (Lectures on the general principles of civil law of the PRC) (Beijing: Zhongguo zhengfa daxue chubanshe, 1986).

ENGLISH ARTICLES, BOOKS AND DOCUMENTATION

Amnesty International, *China: Punishment without Crime: Administrative Detention* (New York: Amnesty International Publications, 1991).

____, *China: Violations of Human Rights* (London: Amnesty International Publications, 1984).

____, *Political Imprisonment in the People's Republic of China* (London: Amnesty International Publications, 1978).

Baker, Philip W. and Barry Fong-Chung Hsue, 'Common Law under Socialist Legal System: The Future of Hong Kong', *China Law Reporter*, vol. vii, no. 1, 1991.

Baum, Richard, 'Modernization and Legal Reform in Post-Mao China: The Rebirth of Socialist Legality', *Studies in Comparative Communism,* vol. xix, no. 2, Summer, 1986, pp. 69–104.

____, (ed.), *Reform and Reaction in Post-Mao China* (New York & London: Routledge, 1991).

Beehler, Roger, 'Waiting for the Rule of Law', *University of Toronto Law Journal,* vol. xxxviii, 1988, pp. 298–332.

Bilancia, Philip R., *Dictionary of Chinese Law and Government: Chinese English.* (Stanford: Stanford University Press, 1981).

Bodde, Derk & Clarence Morris, *Law in Imperial China* (Cambridge: Harvard University Press, 1967).

Bogdanor, Vernon (ed.), *The Blackwell Encyclopaedia of Political Science* (Oxford: Basil Blackwell Publishers, 1991).

Brady, James P., *Justice and Politics in People's China: Legal Order of Continuing Revolution?* (London & New York: Academic Press, 1982).

Burton, Charles, *Political and Social Change in China Since 1978* (New York: Greenwood Press, 1990).

Chan, Ming K. and David J. Clark (eds), *The Hong Kong Basic* Law (Hong Kong: Hong Kong University Press, 1991).

Cheng, Joseph (ed.), *Hong Kong: In Search of a Future* (Hong Kong, Oxford, New York: Oxford University Press, 1984).

____, (ed.), *Hong Kong in Transition* (Hong Kong: Oxford University Press, 1986).

China, *The Constitution of the People's Republic of China* (Beijing: Foreign Languages Press, 1983).

China, *The Criminal Law and the Criminal Procedure Law of China* (Beijing: Foreign Languages Press, 1984), English and Chinese.

China, Consultative Committee for the Basic Law of the HKSAR, 'The Draft Basic Law of the HKSAR of the PRC: Consultation Report', vol. 2, October 1988.

China, Special Group on the Relationship Between the Central Government and the SAR, Consultative Committee for the Basic Law of the HKSAR, 'Final report on Coordination between the Central Government the SAR in Foreign and Defence Affairs...', passed by Hong Kong Executive Committee, 4 April 1987.

____, 'Final Report on Powers of Interpretation and Amendment of the Basic Law', passed by Hong Kong Executive Committee, 14 March 1987.

China, State Council, *Human Rights in China* (Beijing: Information Office, State Council, November 1991).

Chinese Communist Party, *Resolution on CCP History* (1949–1981) (Beijing: Foreign Languages Press, 1981).

Cohen, Jerome, 'The Criminal Process in the People's Republic of China: An Introduction', *Harvard Law Review*, vol. 79, No. 3, Jan. 1966, pp. 469–522.

Cooper, John F., Franz Michael and Yuan-li Wu, *Human Rights in Post-Mao China* (Boulder & London: Westview Press, 1985).

Creel, Herrlee G., *Chinese Thought from Confucius to Mao Zedong* (Chicago: University of Chicago Press, 1975).

Davis, Michael, *Constitutional Confrontation in Hong Kong* (London: Macmillan, 1989).

Davis, Stephen, 'The Death Penalty and Legal Reform in the PRC', *Journal of Chinese Law*, vol. 1, no. 2, Fall, 1987, pp. 303–13.

Deng Xiaoping, *Fundamental Issues in China Today* (Beijing: Foreign Languages Press, 1987).

____, *Selected Works of Deng Xiaoping (1975–1982)* (Beijing: Foreign Languages Press, 1984).

Dicks, Anthony, 'The Chinese Legal System: Reforms in the Balance', CQ, no. 119, September 1989, pp. 540–76.

Edwards, R. Randle, Louis Henkin and Andrew Nathan, *Human Rights in Contemporary China* (New York: Columbia University Press, 1986).

Fairbank, John K., *China: A New History* (Cambridge: Belknap Press of Harvard University Press, 1992).

Fei Xiaotong, *A Great Trial in Chinese History* (Beijing: New World Press, 1981).

Feng Yu-lan (trans. by Derk Bodde), *A History of Chinese Philosophy,* vol. 1 (Princeton: Princeton University Press, 1983).

Freedom House Survey Team, *Freedom in the World, Political Rights and Civil Liberties, 1989–1990* (New York: Freedom House, 1990).

Friedman, Lawrence, and Stewart Macaulay, *Law and Behaviour Science* (New York: Bobbs-Merrill, 1969).

Gellhorn, Walter, 'China's Quest for Legal Modernity', *Journal of Chinese Law*, vol. 1, no. 1, Spring 1987, pp. 1–22.

Ghai, Yash, Robin Luckham, Francis Synyder (eds), *The Political Economy of Law: A Third World Reader* (Delhi: Oxford University Press, 1987).

Gold, Thomas B., 'The Resurgence of Civil Society in China', *Journal of Democracy,* Winter 1990, pp. 18–31.

Gong Xiangrui, 'Constitutional Protection of Human rights: the Chinese View under the Notion of 'One Country, Two Systems', Hong Kong Bill of Rights Conference, Faculty of Law, University of Hong Kong, June 1991.

Greer, Charles (ed.), *China, Facts and Figures Annual, 1992*, vol. 16 (Gulf Breeze, Florida: Academic International Press, 1992).

Griffin, Patricia, *The Chinese Communist Treatment of Counterrevolutionaries: 1924–1949* (Princeton: Princeton University Press, 1979).

Hannon, Hurst, *Guide to International Human Rights Practice*, 2nd ed. (Philadelphia: University of Pennsylvania Press, 1992).

Hershatter, Gail, 'Making a Friend: Changing Patterns of Courtship in Urban China', *Pacific Affairs*, vol. 57, no. 2, Summer, 1984).

Hong Kong, China, *Official Proceedings of the Legislative Council.*

Hong Kong, China, OMELCO Standing Panel on Consitutional Affairs, 'First Report: The 1987 Review of the Further Development of Representative Government'.

Hong Kong, China, OMELCO Standing Panel on Constitutional Development, 'Report on Draft Basic Law', August 1988.

Hsia, Tao-tai, and Constance Johnson, 'Lawmaking in China–Part 1', *East Asian-Executive Reports*, January 1987, pp. 6-11.

Hsia, Tao-tai, and Wendy Zeldin, 'Recent Legal Developments in the People's Republic of China', *Harvard International Law Journal*, vol. 28, no. 2, Spring 1989, pp. 249–87.

Human Rights Watch, *Human Rights Watch World Report 1992* (New York & Washington, DC, 1991).

Humana, Charles (ed.), *World Human Rights Guide* (New York & Oxford: Oxford University Press, 1992).

Hung, William S.H. (ed., Joseph Wang), *Outlines of Modern Chinese Law* (Arlington, Va: University Publications of America 1976, reprint of 1934 edition).

Hutchinson, Allan and Patrick Monahan (eds), *The Rule of Law: Ideal or Ideology* (Toronto: Carswell Press, 1987).

International Commission of Jurists, *Countdown to 1997* (Geneva, 1992).

Jones, William, *Basic Principles of Civil Law in China* (Amronck, NY: M.E. Sharpe, 1989).

Jones, William, 'Civil Law in China', *Chinese Law and Government*, vol. xviii, no. 3–4, Fall–Winter, 1985-6.

Keith, Ronald C., 'Chinese Politics and the New Theory of the "Rule of Law"', *CQ*, no. 125, March 1991, pp. 109–118.

____, '"Egalitarianism" and "Seeking the Truth from the Facts" in the People's Republic of China', *Dalhousie Review*, vol. 63, no. 2, Summer, 1983, pp. 322–40.

____, 'Law and Society in Confucian Thought', in Anthony Parel & Ronald C. Keith (eds), *Comparative Political Philosophy: Studies Under the Upas Tree* (New Delhi, Newbury Park & London: Sage Publications, 1992) pp. 71–86.

____, 'Socialist Legality and Proletarian Democracy in the People's Republic of China', *Canadian Journal of Political Science*, vol. xiii, no. 3, September 1980, pp. 565–82.

____, 'Transcript of Discussions with Wu Daying and Zhang Zhonglin Concerning Legal Change and Civil Rights', *CQ*, no. 81, March 1980, pp. 111–21.

____, & Lin Zhiqiu, 'To Revise or not to Revise China's Law on Counter-revolution', *China Information* , vol. 5, no. 4, Spring 1991, pp. 24–41.

Kim, Chim (trans.), *The Criminal Procedure Code of the People's Republic of China and Related Documents* (London: Sweet & Maxwell, 1989).

Kim, Hyung I., *Fundamental Legal Concepts of China and the West: A Comparative Study*. (Port Washington, NY: Kennikat Press, 1981).

Kim, Samuel, 'The Development of International Law in Post-Mao China: Change and Continuity', *Journal of Chinese Law*, vol. 1, no. 2, Fall 1987, pp. 117–60.

Kleinberg, Robert, *China's 'Opening' to the Outside World* (Boulder, San Francisco & Oxford: Westview Press, 1990).

Lau Siu-kai, 'Public Attitude towards Political Parties in Hong Kong', Occasional Paper, No. 11, Hong Kong Institute of Asia-Pacific Studies, Chinese University of Hong Kong, March 1992.

____, *Society and Politics in Hong Kong* (Hong Kong: Chinese University Press, 1984).

____ & Kuan Hsin-chi, *The Ethos of the Hong Kong Chinese* (Hong Kong: Chinese University Press, 1988).

Lawson, Edward, *Encyclopedia of Human Rights* (Washington, DC: Taylor & Francis, 1991).

Leng Shao-chuan & Hungdah Chiu, *Criminal Justice in Post-Mao China* (Albany: State University of New York Press, 1985).

Liang Ch'i-ch'ao (Liang Qichao) (trans. by L.T. Chen), *History of Chinese Political Thought During the Early Tsin Period* (New York: AMS Press, 1969 reprint of 1930 edition).

Lin Sen, 'China's Decentralization and Provincial Economic Legislation, 1980–1989', unpublished PhD dissertation, Political Science, University of Calgary, March 1993.

Lin Sen, 'A New Pattern of Decentralization in China: The Increase of Provincial Powers in Economic Legislation', *China Information*, vol. vii, no. 34, Winter 1992–93, pp. 27–38.

Lin Zhiqiu, 'Politics and the "Autonomy" of the Chinese Criminal Justice System, 1978–1988' unpublished MA. thesis, Political Science, University of Calgary, April 1989.

Lo, Carlos Wing-Hung, 'Deng Xiaoping's Ideas on Law', *Asian Survey,* vol. xxxii, no. 7, July 1992, pp. 649–65.

____, 'Trials of Dissidents of the 1989 Democracy Movement: The Limits of Criminal Justice under Tend Hsiao-p'ing', *Issues and Studies,* vol. 28, no. 12, December 1992, pp. 23–46.

MacFarquhar, Roderick, Timothy Cheek and Eugene Wu (eds), *The Secret Speeches of Chairman Mao* (Cambridge: Harvard University Press, 1989).

Mao Zedong, *Selected Works of Mao Zedong,* vol. v. (Beijing: Foreign Languages Press, 1977).

McCormick, Barrett, Su Shaozhi and Xiao Xiaoming, 'The Democracy Movement: A Review of the Prospects for Civil Society in China', *Pacific Affairs*, vol. 65, no. 2, Summer, 1992, pp. 182–202.

McKenzie, Paul D., 'China and the Women's Convention: Prospects for the Implementation of an International Norm', *China Law Reporter*, vol. vii, no. 1, 1991, pp. 23–59.

Nathan, Andrew, *China's Crisis* (New York: Columbia University Press, 1990).

Needham, Joseph, *The Shorter Science and Civilisation in China*, vol. 1. (London: Cambridge University Press, 1978).

Ogden, Suzanne, *China's Unresolved Issues* (Englewood Cliffs, NJ: Prentice Hall, 1989).

Pearson, Margaret, *Joint Ventures in the People's Republic of China* (Princeton: Princeton University Press, 1991).

Pinard, Jeanette, 'The People's Republic of China: A Bibliography of Selected English-Language Legal Materials', Law Library, Library of Congress, 1985.

James Seymour (guest editor), 'Cadre Accountability to the Law', *Chinese Law and Government,* vol. 21, no. 3, Fall 1988, pp. 1–28.

Schwartz, Benjamin, *The World of Thought in Ancient China* (Cambridge: Harvard University Press, 1985).

'Symposium on the Hong Kong Basic Law', *Journal of Chinese Law*, vol. 2, no. 1, Spring, 1988.

Thomas, Ann and A.J. Thomas, Jr., *A World Rule of Law* (Dallas: SMU Press, 1975).

Thornburgh, Richard, 'The Soviet Union and the Rule of Law', *Foreign Affairs,* vol. 69, no. 2, 1990, pp. 13–27.

United States Department of State (Reports to Senate and House Committees on Foreign Relations and Foreign Affairs), *Country Reports on Human Rights Practices for 1990* (Washington, DC: GPO, 1991).

____, *Country Reports on Human Rights Practices for 1991* (Washington, DC:, GPO, 1992).

Vyshinsky, Andrei Y. (ed.), *The Law of the Soviet State* (London: Macmillan: 1948).

Wacks, Raymond (ed.), *The Future of Law in Hong Kong* (Hong Kong: Oxford University Press, 1989).

Watson, Ruby, & Patricia Ebrey (eds), *Marriage and Inequality in Chinese Society* (Berkeley: University of California Press, 1991).

Weber, Max (Guenther Roth and Claus Wittich, eds), *Economy and Society,* 2 vols. (Berkeley: University of California Press, 1978).

Weber, Max (ed., with introduction, by Max Rheinstein), *On Law in Society and Economy* (Cambridge: Harvard University Press, 1966).

Wesley-Smith, Peter and Albert Chen (eds), *The Basic Law and Hong Kong's Future* (Hong Kong: Butterworths, 1988).

Whyte, Martin, 'Urban China: A Civil Society in the Making', in Arthur Rosenbaum (ed.), *State and Society in China* (Boulder: Westview Press, 1992).

Wu, Yuan-li, Ta-ling Lee, Franz Michael et al., *Human Rights in the Republic of China* (Boulder & London: Westview Press, 1988).

Index